T0054622

"We give deep thanks to the Lord for Paul Tripp's unique ability to apply the gospel of grace to the ins and outs of everyday life. For many years, Tripp has shaped our own lives, family, and ministry through his biblical wisdom, generous friendship, and wonderful way with words. Now, as the parents of four daughters, we are thrilled for our girls to receive the same blessing of biblical truth, beautifully distilled in devotional form, that speaks to the joys and fears, delights and concerns, questions and hopes of their growing hearts. We pray that they, and all other young people who engage the daily rhythms of this book, will find ever-increasing joy and peace as they encounter the glory of the Savior."

Keith and Kristyn Getty, hymn writers and recording artists, "In Christ Alone"; authors, *Sing! How Worship Transforms Your Life, Family, and Church*

"Paul Tripp's writing has been a great source of life to me. *New Morning Mercies for Teens* encourages those who have grown weary of the struggle, living under the weight of the world."

TobyMac, hip-hop recording artist; music producer; songwriter

"In an age when teens are more distracted and anxious than ever, Paul Tripp's book is a clarion call to remember the one thing that is necessary. He urges young readers to examine the depth of their personal beliefs and consider how they will live out their faith in tangible ways as they move into adulthood. What a great resource to get teens thinking about and talking with God every day!"

Jim Daly, President, Focus on the Family

"What a valuable application of Paul Tripp's classic devotional for teenagers. *New Morning Mercies for Teens* retains the timeless and life-giving gospel message while adding reflection questions to help young Christians meditate on the truths. This book is a welcomed gospel resource for young people."

Cameron Cole, Founding Chairman, Rooted Ministry; coeditor, *Gospel-Centered Youth Ministry*; author, *Therefore I Have Hope*

"Solid countercultural truth! That's what you can count on in this treasure trove for teens who are serious about nurturing their faith in God. Paul David Tripp does not serve up spiritual milk to teens but the meaty truth they need. Each day he provides a daily truth statement at the top of each day's devotional. That single daily sentence alone is worth the price of this book."

Dannah Gresh, bestselling author, *Lies Young Women Believe and the Truth That Sets Them Free*

"Paul Tripp is one of the most skilled at connecting the gospel to all of life. In *New Morning Mercies for Teens*, he connects the everyday struggles and joys of teenagers to the hope found in the finished work of Jesus. I couldn't be more excited to put this in the hands of my own children, and I would encourage you to do the same."

John Perritt, Director of Resources, Reformed Youth Ministries; Host, *The Local Youth Worker* podcast; author; father of five

New Morning Mercies for Teens

NEW MORNING MERCIES FOR TEENS

A Daily Gospel Devotional

PAUL DAVID TRIPP

WHEATON, ILLINOIS

New Morning Mercies for Teens: A Daily Gospel Devotional

Published by Crossway
1300 Crescent Street
Wheaton, Illinois 60187

Cover design: Matt Lehman

First printing 2024

The text of *New Morning Mercies for Teens* has been adapted from Paul David Tripp, *New Morning Mercies: A Daily Gospel Devotional* (Wheaton, IL: Crossway, 2014).

Printed in the United States of America

All emphases in Scripture quotations have been added by the author.

Hardcover ISBN: 978-1-4335-9236-2
ePub ISBN: 978-1-4335-9238-6
PDF ISBN: 978-1-4335-9237-9

Library of Congress Cataloging-in-Publication Data

Names: Tripp, Paul David, 1950- author.
Title: New morning mercies for teens : a daily gospel devotional / Paul David Tripp.
Description: Wheaton, Illinois : Crossway, [2024] | Includes index.
Identifiers: LCCN 2023029891 (print) | LCCN 2023029892 (ebook) | ISBN 9781433592362 (hardcover) | ISBN 9781433592379 (pdf) | ISBN 9781433592386 (epub)
Subjects: LCSH: Teenagers—Prayers and devotions. | Devotional calendars. | Christian teenagers—Religious life.
Classification: LCC BV4850 .T76 2024 (print) | LCC BV4850 (ebook) | DDC 242/.63—dc23/eng/20231020
LC record available at https://lccn.loc.gov/2023029891
LC ebook record available at https://lccn.loc.gov/2023029892

Crossway is a publishing ministry of Good News Publishers.

LB 33 32 31 30 29 28 27 26 25 24
15 14 13 12 11 10 9 8 7 6 5 4 3 2 1

To the members of my ever-expanding team, you are faithful, godly, and smart, and I am beyond grateful for each of you.

INTRODUCTION

You are a teenager: that means you are in one of the most exciting and most important times of your life! As you begin to read through this special edition of *New Morning Mercies for Teens*, I want to alert you to seven issues you will face that will influence the shape and direction of the rest of your life.

1. *During these years you will begin to decide the meaning and purpose of your life.* So far, your values—the things you think are worth living for—have been shaped by your parents. You begin to make that critical decision for yourself during your teen years. What will be the thing that will capture your heart and shape the direction of your life?

2. *Will you internalize the faith you have been taught?* There is probably no more significant decision in life than this one. Everyone believes something. Every home has religious convictions, whether or not they consider themselves religious. Every home seeks to instill their "faith" in their children. In the teen years, you will decide what you will believe about God, about yourself, about right and wrong, about what is true and what is false, about the gospel of Jesus Christ, and about how you will live out your beliefs in everyday life.

3. *You will make significant decisions that shape your future.* Wow, there are huge decisions ahead of you! What are your gifts, interests, and passions? What do you see as your life's work? Where will you go to college? Will the church be an essential part of your life? If you could have your dream future, what would it be?

4. *You will begin stepping out of some daily parental protection.* During the younger years of your life, your parents made all of your decisions for you. During the teen years, you begin to make more and more of those decisions for yourself. I don't mean that you no longer need parents. However, you are moving into

a stage where rather than exercising total control over your life, your parents will offer you wise counsel, while you will bear more and more of the burden of making the decisions that will shape how you live.

5. *What kind of community will you surround yourself with?* This is a big one. Until now, your mom, dad, grandparent, or guardian have chosen the community they felt comfortable having you in. They were the gatekeepers, vetting the friends that came into your life. But now, you will increasingly have that responsibility. Who will you allow into your life? Whose advice and counsel will you listen to? Who will you entrust with the important things in your life? Who will you allow to influence the way you think and the way that you live? You will surround yourself with others, and those people will significantly impact who you become.

6. *How seriously will you pursue your relationship with God?* Most teens were first exposed to God, his will, and his way in their homes and by their parents. My mom and dad thought a relationship with God was the most important thing for me, but I had to decide that for myself at some point (which I did during my teen years). No one can make you love God. No one can make you willing to surrender your heart and life to him. No one has the power to produce faith in you. Will you make God the center of your life? Will you pursue him every day?

7. *What kind of success will you value most?* Every human being runs after some type of success. Everybody defines what a successful life is. Will you live for material success? Will you live for career success? Will you define success in money terms? Will success be determined by how many people love and respect you? Will success be defined as living a life pleasing to your Creator? You will define success somehow, and how you define it will determine how you live.

Since you will be asked to grapple with life-shaping issues in your teen years, you will need reliable, true, and trustworthy guidance. What will be your life GPS? Whose plan for life will you follow? I love what the Bible says in Psalm 119:105, "Your word is a lamp to my feet and a light to my path." God gave you his word to be a guide to you. As you walk through the forest of life, often dark with roots that will trip you up, the Bible has been given to you to light the way so you can be sure of where to go and how to get there. The central theme of the word of God is the story of the transforming grace that is ours because of the life, death, and resurrection of Jesus.

I am excited that you are about to embark on a journey through this special edition of *New Morning Mercies*, designed specifically for teens. Each daily reading includes a brief devotional, a passage from Scripture to meditate on, and a reflection question that applies to what you're facing in life. We've also added a new Q&A bonus chapter, with questions about topics that every teen will experience and how the Bible provides answers. So be sure to visit and revisit the back of this book when these issues arise in your life.

My prayer is that in your daily devotional time with the Lord and this book, you will be reminded of the truths of God's word day after day. May it cause you to admit how much you need the forgiving, reconciling, and transforming grace of Jesus. And may it give you wisdom from God's word to live by. There is no better way to prepare for all the significant issues that will shape your future than to spend time every day meditating on God's truth, remembering his grace, and recommitting yourself to a life shaped by following him.

May God use these devotions to light the exciting path before you.

PAUL DAVID TRIPP
May 26, 2023

JANUARY 1

Here's the bottom line. The Christian life, the church, and our faith are not about us, they're about him—his plan, his kingdom, his glory.

It really is the struggle of struggles. It is the thing that makes our lives messy. It is what sidetracks our thoughts and kidnaps our desires. It is the one battle that one never escapes. It is the one place where ten out of ten of us need rescue. It is the fight that God wages on our behalf to help us to remember this: life is simply not about us.

This is precisely why the first four words of the Bible may be its most important words: "In the beginning, God . . ." (Gen. 1:1). Everything that was created was made by God and for God. All the glories of the created world were designed to point to his glory. That includes you and me. We were not meant to live independently for our own moments of glory. No, we were created to live for him.

Where is this godward living meant to find expression? I love how Paul captures this in 1 Corinthians 10:31: "So, whether you eat or drink, or whatever you do, do all to the glory of God." When Paul thinks of the call to live for the glory of God, he doesn't first think of the big, life-changing, spiritual moments of life. No, he thinks of something mundane and repetitive, like eating and drinking. Even the most regular, seemingly unimportant tasks of my life must be shaped and directed by a heartfelt desire for the glory of God.

Let's start the new year by admitting that there is nothing less natural for us than to live for the glory of another. This admission is not the doorway to despair but to hope. God knew that in your sin you would never live this way, so he sent his Son. Jesus lived the life you couldn't, died on your behalf, and rose again, conquering sin and death. He did this so that you would be forgiven for your allegiance to your own glory. When you admit your need for help, you connect yourself to the rescue he has already provided in his Son, Jesus.

> Not to us, O Lord, not to us, but to your name give glory,
> for the sake of your steadfast love and your faithfulness! (Ps. 115:1)

Reflect: Where do you feel hopeless this week? How does reaching out for God's rescue actually give you hope to live for God's glory?

JANUARY 2

Your rest is not to be found in figuring your life out but in trusting the one who has it all figured out for your good and his glory.

We were on our way to the local mall with our two young boys when the three-year-old asked out of the blue, “Daddy, if God made everything, did he make light poles?” When he asked, I had the same thought that all parents have: “Why does he have to ask me ‘why’ questions all the time?”

Human beings have a deep desire to know and understand. Each day we spend a lot of mental time trying to figure things out. We don’t live by instinct. We are all archaeologists who dig into the mounds of our lives to try to make sense of the civilization that is our story. We are all theologians.

God gave us this drive to know, and he also gave wonderful abilities to analyze. This motivation and ability set us apart from the rest of creation. They are created by God to draw us to him, so that we can know him and understand ourselves in light of his existence and will.

But sin makes this drive and these gifts dangerous. They tempt us to think that we can find our hearts by figuring it all out. We think: “If only I could understand this or that, then I’d be secure.” But it never works.

In your most brilliant moment, you will still be left with mystery in your life; sometimes even painful mystery. We all face things that appear to make little sense. So we never find rest in our quest to understand it all. No, rest is found in trusting the one who understands it all and rules it all for his glory and our good.

In moments when you wish you knew what you can’t know, there is one who knows. He loves you and rules what you don’t understand with your good in mind. Few passages capture this kind of rest better than Psalm 62:

> For God alone, O my soul, wait in silence,
> for my hope is from him.
> He only is my rock and my salvation,
> my fortress; I shall not be shaken.
> On God rests my salvation and my glory;
> my mighty rock, my refuge is God. (Ps. 62:5–7)

Reflect: Do you ever struggle with doubt? How does God’s love give better rest to your soul than God’s answers?

JANUARY 3

If eternity is the plan, then it makes no sense to shrink your living down to the needs and wants of this little moment.

There is no doubt about it—the Bible is a big-picture book that calls us to big-picture living. Often we shrink our focus to whatever spontaneous thought, emotion, or need grips us at any given time. Yet the Bible simply does not permit you to live for the moment. God's word calls you to think about things that happened before the world began and thousands of years into eternity in the future.

But it's hard to live with eternity in view. Again and again, life shrinks our focus down to the moment in front of us. There are moments when it seems that the most important thing in life is getting through this day of classes, winning this game, or getting more food. There are moments when who we are, who God is, and where this whole thing is going shrink into the background of the thoughts, emotions, and needs of the moment. There are moments when we get lost, even though we're in the middle of God's story. We lose our minds, we lose our sense of direction, and we lose our remembrance of him.

God reminds us that this is not all there is, that we were created and re-created in Christ Jesus for eternity. He reminds us not to live for the treasures of the moment: "Do not lay up for yourselves treasures on earth, where moth and rust destroy and where thieves break in and steal, but lay up for yourselves treasures in heaven" (Matt. 6:19–20).

Think about this: if God has already granted you a place in eternity, then he has also granted you all the grace you need along the way, or you'd never get there. There is grace for our easily distracted hearts. There is rescue for our self-absorption and lack of focus. The God of eternity grants you his eternal grace so that you can live with eternity in view.

> But God said to him, "Fool! This night your soul is required of you, and the things you have prepared, whose will they be?" So is the one who lays up treasure for himself and is not rich toward God. (Luke 12:20–21)

Reflect: At the beginning and ending of your day, how can you set your mind on eternity?

JANUARY 4

The best theology will not remove mystery from your life, so rest is found in trusting the one who rules, is all, and knows no mystery.

In 2006, a drunk and unlicensed driver swerved up on the sidewalk and crushed our daughter Nicole against a wall. She had devastating injuries. The injury shattered her pelvis and triggered massive internal bleeding. I rushed to the hospital. When I entered Nicole's intensive-care room, I wasn't sure if she could hear me. I crawled up on Nicole's bed and whispered, "It's Dad, you're not alone. God is with you too."

That day, I felt like the whole world went dark. My heart cried, "Why, why, why?"

If I could choose, I wouldn't have any of my children go through such a thing. And if I had had to choose one of my children, I wouldn't have chosen Nicole at that moment in her life. She seemed so vulnerable. But in an instant, we had been cast into life-changing mystery. And all our belief in God didn't take that mystery away. Nicole did recover well, but we lived through four years of hardship.

During that time, here was my comfort: when it came to Nicole's accident, God was neither surprised nor afraid. You see, there is no mystery with God. He is never caught off guard. I love the words of Daniel 2:22: "He knows what is in the darkness, and light dwells with him."

God is with you in your moments of darkness because he will never leave you. But your darkness isn't dark to him. He understands all the things that confuse you the most. Your mysteries aren't mysterious to him. More than that: he is in complete charge of all that is mysterious to you and me.

Remember this: what you see as dark, God sees as light. He holds both you and your mysteries in his gracious hands. And that means you can find rest even when the darkness of mystery has entered your life.

> Can you find out the deep things of God?
>   Can you find out the limit of the Almighty?
> It is higher than heaven—what can you do?
>   Deeper than Sheol—what can you know?
> Its measure is longer than the earth
>   and broader than the sea. (Job 11:7–9)

Reflect: What confuses you about life right now? Ask God to give you his light about that area. And ask him for strength to trust him in the dark, while you wait for his light.

JANUARY 5

If you obey for a thousand years, you're no more accepted than when you first believed; your acceptance is based on Christ's righteousness and not yours.

Sin is a bigger disaster than we think, and grace is more amazing than we seem able to grasp. Because if you know what the Bible says about sin, you know it's impossible for someone to rise to God's standard of perfection. No one can perform his or her way into acceptance with God. What an insane delusion! Yet we all tend to think that we are more righteous than we are. And when we think this, we've taken the first step to embracing our own delusion: maybe we're not so bad in God's eyes after all.

This is why the reality check of Romans 3:20 is so important. Paul writes, "For by works of the law no human being will be justified in his sight." If you prayed every moment of your life, you could not pray enough prayers to earn acceptance with God. If you gave every penny of every dollar that you ever earned in every job you ever had, you could not give enough to deserve acceptance with God. If every word you ever spoke was uttered with the purest motives, you would never be able to speak your way into reconciliation with God. Sin is too big. God's bar is too high. It is beyond the reach of every human being who has ever taken his or her first breath.

This is why God, in love, sent his Son (Rom. 5:8). You see, there was and is no other way. There is only one portal to acceptance with God—the righteousness of Christ. His righteousness is given over to our account; sinners are welcomed into the presence of a holy God based on the perfect obedience of another.

Christ is our hope, Christ is our rest, Christ is our peace. He perfectly fulfilled God's requirement so that in our sin, weakness, and failure we would never again have to fear God's anger. This is what grace does! So as the children of grace, we obey as a service of worship, not in a desperate attempt to do what is impossible—independently earn God's favor.

> God shows his love for us in that while we were still sinners, Christ died for us. (Rom. 5:8)

Reflect: What's been the biggest hardship of your week? Take a few minutes to compare this hardship with the disaster of sin. How is Christ your hope over all of it?

JANUARY 6

Contentment celebrates grace. The contented heart is satisfied with the giver and is therefore freed from craving the next gift.

Sin does two very significant things to us all. First, it causes us to focus on ourselves, to make life all about us. We are too motivated by our wants, our needs, and our feelings. We tend to be more aware of what we don't have than of the many wonderful blessings we've been given. And this self-focus tends to make us scorekeepers; we constantly compare our piles of stuff to the piles of others. It's a life of discontentment and envy. Envy is always selfish.

There is a second significant thing that sin does to us. It causes us to look horizontally for what can only ever be found vertically. So we look to creation to give us life, hope, peace, rest, contentment, identity, meaning and purpose, inner peace, and motivation to continue. The problem is that nothing in creation can give you these things. Creation was never designed to satisfy your heart.

Creation was made to point you to the one who alone has the ability to satisfy your heart. Many people go through life asking creation to be their savior, that is, to give them what only God is able to give.

> Whom have I in heaven but you?
>   And there is nothing on earth that I desire besides you.
> My flesh and my heart may fail,
>   but God is the strength of my heart and my portion forever.
>   (Ps. 73:25–26)

These are the words of a man who learned the secret to contentment.

When you are satisfied with the giver, you are free. You are free from the discouraging existence that consumes so many people. Your heart will rest only ever when it has found its rest in him.

Here is one of the most beautiful fruits of grace—a heart that is content. It is grace and grace alone that can make this kind of peaceful living possible for each of us. Won't you reach out today for that grace?

> But godliness with contentment is great gain, for we brought nothing into the world, and we cannot take anything out of the world. (1 Tim. 6:6–7)

Reflect: Is your heart more given to worshiping God or demanding from God? Are you more given to the joy of gratitude or the anxiety of want?

JANUARY 7

Every day you need it. You and I simply can't live without it. What is it? The indwelling presence of the Holy Spirit.

For years, I had a terrible gap in my understanding of the gospel. I can't tell you why it was missing, but it made my Christian life pretty miserable. I knew that by grace I had been granted God's forgiveness. I knew that I had been graced with an all-inclusive pass into eternity. In the meantime, I thought it was my job to just gut it out. It was my responsibility to identify sin, to cut it out of my life, and to give myself to living in better, more biblical ways.

I tried this, trust me. I tried it and found it didn't work. It seemed that I failed more times than I succeeded. I became more and more frustrated and discouraged. I can remember the moment in college when it all came to a head. It was six o'clock in the morning. I was having the devotions that I really didn't want to have, when I finally put my head down on my desk and cried, "I can't do what you're asking me to do!" Then I read the next chapter in my daily Bible reading, and by God's grace it was Romans 8.

I read that chapter over and over, including these words: "For if you live according to the flesh you will die, but if by the Spirit you put to death the deeds of the body, you will live" (8:13). They were like fireworks going off in my head. God knew my need as a sinner was so great that he had to come and live inside me. If he didn't, I would not be or do what I had been re-created to be or do.

I need the presence and power of the Holy Spirit living inside me because sin kidnaps the desires of my heart, blinds my eyes, and weakens my knees. My problem is not just the *guilt* of sin; it's the *inability* of sin as well. So God graces his children with the convicting, sight-giving, desire-producing, and strength-affording presence of the Spirit. It can't be said any better than Paul says it at the end of his discussion of the gift of the Spirit:

> [He gives] life to your mortal bodies. (Rom. 8:11)

Reflect: What temptations trip you up most often? How is putting "to death the deeds of the body" different than doing the same thing "by the Spirit" (cf. Rom. 8:13)?

JANUARY 8

God calls you to believe and then works with zeal to craft you into a person who really does live by faith.

I don't know how much you've thought about this, but faith isn't natural for you and me.

Doubt is natural. Fear is natural. Living based on your brain's thoughts and your body's senses is natural. Pushing the current catalog of personal "what-ifs" through your mind before you go to sleep is natural. Envying the life of someone else is natural. Looking horizontally for the peace that you will only ever find vertically is natural. Anxiously wishing for change in things that you have no ability to change is natural. Giving way to despondency, discouragement, depression, or despair is natural. Numbing yourself with busyness, material things, media, food, or some other substance is natural. Lowering your standards to deal with your disappointment is natural. But faith simply isn't natural to us.

As Paul says in Ephesians 2:8, faith really is "the gift of God." To the average, sin-damaged human being, there is nothing more counterintuitive than faith in God. So God gives us the power to first believe. Yet he doesn't stop there. By grace he works in the situations, locations, and relationships of our everyday lives to change us. He's crafting us into people who hold the radical belief that he really does exist and he really does reward those who seek him (Heb. 11:6).

Next time you face a difficult or unexpected moment, remember: your situation actually reflects a God who is near to you and doing in you a very good thing. He is rescuing you from relying on the inadequate resources of your wisdom, experience, righteousness, and strength. He is transforming you into a person who is shaped by radical God-centered faith. He is the ultimate craftsman, and we are his clay. He will not take us off his wheel until his fingers have molded us into those who really do believe.

> But when they saw him walking on the sea they thought it was a ghost, and cried out, for they all saw him and were terrified. But immediately he spoke to them and said, "Take heart; it is I. Do not be afraid." (Mark 6:49–50)

Reflect: What difficult situation in life might God be using to build greater reliance on him? How are you tempted to respond to this situation naturally?

JANUARY 9

For the believer, fear is always God-forgetful. If God is sovereign and his rule is complete, wise, righteous, and good, why would you fear?

The words of King Hezekiah (below) ring as true today as they did in the scary moment centuries ago when they were first spoken. Judah had been invaded by the powerful king of Assyria, Sennacherib. King Hezekiah prepared and armed Judah for battle, but that is not all he did. He addressed the people with a more significant issue. He knew that in these moments God's people were often given to fear. And he knew where that fear came from.

Often in moments of challenge the people of God would panic because they were *identity amnesiacs*. They would forget who they were as the children of the all-powerful God. So at this moment, Hezekiah knew he couldn't just be a good king and a skilled general. He must also be a wise pastor to his people.

As they were preparing for the Assyrian onslaught, Hezekiah didn't want the people of Judah to think that they were left on their own. He wanted them to know they had more than just their battle courage, war experience, and skill with weapons. He wanted them to realize they had been amazingly blessed with another ingredient, one that they could not and must not forget. So Hezekiah said: "Be strong and courageous. Do not be afraid or dismayed before the king of Assyria and all the horde that is with him. . . . With him is an arm of flesh, but with us is the Lord our God, to help us and to fight our battles" (2 Chron. 32:7–8).

There will be a moment when you will ask, "Where can I find courage to face what I am facing?" Hezekiah gives you your answer: "Look up and remember your God." As God's child, you are never left to battle on your own.

I, I am he who comforts you;
    who are you that you are afraid of man who dies,
    of the son of man who is made like grass,
and have forgotten the Lord, your Maker,
    who stretched out the heavens
    and laid the foundations of the earth. (Isa. 51:12–13)

Reflect: In what situations around friends is it easy for you to become an "identity amnesiac," forgetting who you really are? Why do you think that you forget in these kind of situations?

JANUARY 10

The DNA of joy is thankfulness. Have you noticed that entitled, complaining people don't happen to be very joyful?

I imagine that you are like me; that is, that you tend to think that a good life is a comfortable life. We get irritated, impatient, and angry at even minor difficulties. Long lines make us mad. Having to listen to an overtalkative person makes us impatient. A day when we don't feel great causes us to grumble and complain. We complain when it's cold, when it's hot, when it rains, when the sun is too bright, or when it gets dark too early for our liking. We grumble if our food is too hot, too cold, too salty, or not seasoned enough; we complain if the portions are too big, if we're still hungry, or if it's not the kind of food we like.

Sadly, we spend many of our days being dissatisfied with our lives because we are not getting our comfortable way.[1]

I wish I always
carried it with me.
I wished it always
shaped the way
I look at life.
I wish it directed
my desires.
I wish it was
the natural inclination of
my heart.
I wish remembering
your boundless grace
would silence
my grumbling.
I wish
my worship of you,
my trust of you,
my rest in you
would drive away
all complaint.
If my heart is ever
going to be freed of
grumbling
and ruled by
gratitude,
I need your grace:
grace to remember,
grace to see,
grace that produces
a heart of humble joy.

Oh give thanks to the Lord, for he is good,
  for his steadfast love endures forever!
Let the redeemed of the Lord say so,
  whom he has redeemed from trouble
and gathered in from the lands,
  from the east and from the west,
  from the north and from the south. (Ps. 107:1–3)

Reflect: When you're tempted to grumble, try to answer this question: At this moment, what do I feel like I deserve? How does God's grace affect what you deserve?

JANUARY 11

If you have been freed from needing success and acclaim to feel good about yourself, you know grace has visited you.

It is an intensely human endeavor. Here's the quest we all pursue: We all want to feel good about ourselves. We all want to think that we are okay. And this is a fearful and anxious quest from which only grace can free you.

Here's how it happens to all of us. We seek horizontally for the personal rest that we are supposed to find vertically. And it never works.

Looking to others for your inner sense of well-being is pointless. First, you will never be good enough consistently enough to get the regular praise of others that you are seeking. You're going to mess up. You're bound to disappoint. You will have a bad day. You'll lose your way. At some point, you'll say or do things that you shouldn't.

Add to this the fact that the people around you probably don't want the burden of being your personal messiah. They don't want to live with the responsibility of having your identity in their hands. Looking to people for your inner self-worth never works.

Second, the peace that success gives is unreliable as well. Since you are less than perfect, whatever success you are able to achieve will soon be followed by failure of some kind. Then there is the fact that the buzz of success is short-lived. It isn't long before you're searching for the next success to keep you going.

That's why the reality that Jesus has become your righteousness is so precious. His grace has forever freed us from needing to prove our righteousness and our worth. So we remind ourselves every day not to search horizontally for what we've already been given vertically. Our righteousness is found in Christ alone.

> And the effect of righteousness will be peace,
> and the result of righteousness, quietness and trust forever. (Isa. 32:17)

Reflect: What makes you feel good about yourself? What makes you feel bad?

JANUARY 12

God calls you to persevere by faith, and then, with powerful grace, he protects and keeps you.

In Romans 15:5, Paul calls our Lord "the God of endurance." This title really gets at the center of where hope is to be found. Let me state it plainly: your hope is not to be found in your willingness and ability to endure. Your hope lies in God's unshakable, enduring commitment to never turn from his work of grace. Your hope is that you have been welcomed into communion with one who will endure no matter what.

Why is this so important to understand? Because your endurance will be spotty at best. There will be moments when you will forget who you are and what God has done for you in his grace. There will be times when you will get discouraged and for a while quit doing the good things God calls you to do. There will be moments, big and small, when you will willingly rebel. You may be thinking, "Not me." But think with me—when you, as a Christian, say something nasty to another person, you don't do it because you're ignorant that it is wrong. You talked that way because in that moment you don't give a rip about what is wrong.

You see, perfect endurance demands just that, perfection. And since none of us is there yet, we must look outside ourselves for hope. Your hope of enduring is not to be found in your character or strength, but in your Lord's. Because he will ever be faithful, you can bank on the fact that he will give you what you need to be faithful too.

When difficulty exposes the weakness of your resolve and the limits of your strength, you do not have to panic. Here's why: Even in those moments when you don't feel able to do so yourself, God will endure.

> But as for you, O man of God, flee these things. Pursue righteousness, godliness, faith, love, steadfastness, gentleness. Fight the good fight of the faith. Take hold of the eternal life to which you were called and about which you made the good confession in the presence of many witnesses. (1 Tim. 6:11–12)

Reflect: How has God shown his enduring patience with you this past week? This past year?

JANUARY 13

Yes, it is true—God will remain faithful even when you're not because his faithfulness rests on who he is, not on what you're doing.

"If we are faithless, he remains faithful—for he cannot deny himself" (2 Tim. 2:13). This verse pictures a radically different way of living, one that's not natural to most of us. Most human beings buy into a view of life that says you are the master of your fate. In this view, you'll hear phrases like, "life is on your shoulders," "you make or break your life," "pay your money and take your choice," or "you have no one to look to or blame but yourself." You have little to rely on other than your instincts, your strength, the wisdom that you've collected over the years, your ability to anticipate what is around the corner, your character and maturity, and the natural gifts that you have been given. It is a scary "you against the world" way of living.

But your welcome into God's family turns all of this upside down. God not only forgives your sins and guarantees you a seat in eternity, but welcomes you to a radically new way of living. This new way of living is not just about submitting to God's moral code. No, it is about God committing himself to be faithful to you forever, unleashing his wisdom, power, and grace for your eternal good.

Think about this. You can take your life off your shoulders because God has placed it on his. This doesn't mean that it doesn't matter how you live. Instead, it does mean that your security is not found in your faithfulness but in his. He can be trusted even when you cannot. He will be faithful and good even when you're not. He will do what is right and best even when you don't. And he is faithful to forgive you when convicting grace reveals how unfaithful you have been.

God's grace calls you to invest in the one thing that will never come up short, and that one thing is the faithfulness of your Lord.

> God is faithful, by whom you were called into the fellowship of his Son, Jesus Christ our Lord. (1 Cor. 1:9)

Reflect: Does God's faithfulness to you make you want to obey him more or less? Why?

JANUARY 14

Don't be discouraged today. You can leave your "what-ifs" and "if-onlys" in the hands of the one who loves you and rules all things.

Even though you're a person of faith who knows something about the Bible, there's one thing you can be sure of—God will confuse you. The theology, commands, and principles of Scripture will take you only so far in your quest to figure out your life. There will be moments when you simply don't understand what is going on. In fact, you will face moments when what God brings into your life won't seem good. It may even seem bad, very bad.

Now, if your faith is based on your ability to fully understand your life, then your moments of confusion will become moments of weakening faith. But you are not left with only two options—understand everything and rest in peace *or* understand little and be tormented by anxiety. There is a third way.

The Bible tells you that real peace is found in resting in the wisdom of the one who holds all of your "what-ifs" and "if-onlys" in his loving hands. Isaiah captures this well with these comforting words: "You keep him in perfect peace whose mind is stayed on you, because he trusts in you" (Isa. 26:3).

Real, sturdy, lasting peace isn't to be found in picking apart your life until you have understood all its components. You will never understand it all because God, for your good and his glory, keeps some of it covered in mystery. So peace is found only in trusting the one who is in careful control of all the things that tend to rob you of your peace. He is never out of control or surprised. He is never confused, and he never worries.

You need to remind yourself again and again of his wise and loving control. This won't immediately make your life make sense. Yet it will give you rest and peace in those moments when life doesn't seem to make any sense.

> And do not seek what you are to eat and what you are to drink, nor be worried. For all the nations of the world seek after these things, and your Father knows that you need them. Instead, seek his kingdom, and these things will be added to you. (Luke 12:29–31)

Reflect: What about the future triggers your anxiety? What would you love to know that God hasn't shown you? How can you give this to God in trust?

JANUARY 15

Unlike human love, which is often fickle and temporary, God's love never fails, no matter what.

I love all of the psalms, but Psalm 136 blows me away every time I read it. I love the fact that Psalm 136 is a history psalm that, because of its repeated refrain, gets turned into a love poem. I love that it affirms again and again what we desperately need to hear again and again—not once or twice, but twenty-six times! Now, I think that we should pay careful attention to those places where God chooses to repeat himself, and even more so when he repeats himself so many times!

Why does God repeat, over and over through the pen of the psalmist, "For his steadfast love endures forever" (Psalm 136)? There are two answers to this question.

First, there is no reality more radical and foundational to a biblical worldview and a personal sense of identity than this. What is the biblical story? It's the story of a God of love invading the world in the person of his Son of love. Why? To establish his kingdom of love by a radical sacrifice of love, to forgive us in love and draw us into his family of love, and to send us out as ambassadors of the very same love. Without this redeeming love, the Bible is a book of interesting stories and helpful principles, but it is devoid of any power to fix what sin has broken.

The second reason God repeats this refrain is that, in our lives, we don't experience this kind of love. All the human love we've experienced has been flawed in some way. But not God's. His love is perfect and perfectly steadfast forever. It is the single most stunning reality in the life of a believer. God has placed his love on us and he will never again remove it. There's a reason to continue, no matter how hard life seems and how weak you feel.

> Give thanks to the Lord, for he is good,
> for his steadfast love endures forever.
> Give thanks to the God of gods,
> for his steadfast love endures forever.
> Give thanks to the Lord of lords,
> for his steadfast love endures forever. (Ps. 136:1–3)

Reflect: Which best describes the default setting of your heart? (a) God loves me; (b) God likes me; (c) I'm not sure God loves or likes me. Which of these is actually true?

JANUARY 16

There's not a day without sin rearing its ugly head and not a day in which God's abundant mercies are not new.

They really are the two foundation stones of a God-honoring life: (1) you still have sin living inside you, and (2) God is abundant in mercy. Because I am a sinner, I need mercy, and because God is merciful, I can face the reality of my sin.

The words in Nehemiah 9 describe us all: "They . . . did not obey your commandments, but sinned against your rules" (9:29). Maybe it's a thoughtless word, a selfish act, a proud thought, a moment of envy, a flash of lust, a willing act of disobedience, a minor moment of thievery, or giving into an addiction. None of us is sin free yet. It is humbling to admit—and important. Because only when you admit how deep and comprehensive your problem is, can you get excited about the rescue that only God's mercy can supply.

We aren't just left in our sins. Nehemiah 9 continues, "Nevertheless, in your great mercies you did not make an end of them or forsake them, for you are a gracious and merciful God" (9:31). You can be courageous in admitting your sin precisely because God is abundant in his mercy.

He comes to you in mercy, not because you are good, but because you are a sinner. He knows that you are a bigger danger to you than anything else in your life. And that it's impossible for you to run from you. Therefore, there is only one hope for you. It is that someone with power, wisdom, and mercy will invade your life, forgive your sins, and progressively deliver you from the hold that sin has had on you. That mercy comes to you in a person, the Lord Jesus Christ, and his mercy is always fresh, uniquely fashioned for the sin struggles of this new day.

> But God, being rich in mercy, because of the great love with which he loved us, even when we were dead in our trespasses, made us alive together with Christ—by grace you have been saved—and raised us up with him and seated us with him in the heavenly places in Christ Jesus, so that in the coming ages he might show the immeasurable riches of his grace in kindness toward us in Christ Jesus. (Eph. 2:4–7)

Reflect: During a typical day, which of the two foundation stones (above) are you most easily tempted to neglect?

JANUARY 17

To think today, when your life doesn't work as planned, that it's out of control is to forget that Jesus reigns for your sake and his glory.

What are you facing today that you wouldn't be facing if you were in control? What do you really wish you could avoid? Where have your plans dripped like sand through your fingers? Where would you like to take back choices and redo decisions? Where do you tend to look over the fence and wish you had someone else's life? Where do you feel troubled, inadequate, weak, defeated, overwhelmed, alienated, or alone? Where do thoughts of the past tend to flood you with regret, or visions of the future make you a bit afraid? What causes you to wish life was easier or at least a bit more predictable? Where does it feel to you as if you're on an amusement park ride that you never intended to be on?

Life in this fallen world is often very hard. This world and everything in it are not functioning the way God intended. In those moments, it is tempting to conclude that you don't have much power and that life is all about surviving the chaos.

But this is not where God's word leaves us. Yes, it does confront us with our smallness, weakness, and lack of control, but it doesn't leave us there. The Bible declares something to us that is the opposite of the way we tend to think. It tells us that the chaotic difficulties that we face every day are not the result of the world being out of control, but the result of one who reigns in complete control.

So no matter how it looks to you at street level, your world is not out of control. No, it is under careful rule. As radical as that thought is, it's not radical enough because it does not do justice to all that Paul says in the verse below. Paul wants you to know something else. That rule has you in view! Right now, Jesus rules over all things for the sake of his children. This is where peace is to be found.

> And he [God] put all things under his [Christ's] feet and gave him as head over all things to the church. (Eph. 1:22)

Reflect: When juggling all the activities in your life is crazy and chaotic, what untruths do you tend to tell yourself? Why?

JANUARY 18

If you're God's child, you will never again have just you to depend on. No, you've been blessed, right here, right now, with grace.

It's a bigger problem than most of us think. It's something I have encountered again and again—in the lives of singles and the married, the old and the young, men and women, and leaders and followers. It's subtle, but has the power to leave you feeling frustrated and unable or overwhelmed and discouraged. It has the power to put your Bible on the lower shelves of your life. It changes the way you think about yourself and the way you make decisions.

What's the problem that I'm fretting about? It's the fact that so many of us have a huge dark hole in the middle of our gospel.

Sure, we have a pretty good understanding of the gospel past: the forgiveness we've received through the sacrifice of Jesus. We also have a fairly clear understanding of salvation future: the eternity that we will spend with Jesus. Yet have we really understood the benefits of the work of Christ in the here and now?

The Bible powerfully declares that Jesus didn't just die for your past or your future, but for all the things that you face right here, right now. Listen to the present tense, the *now-ism* of the gospel in Galatians 2:20:

> I have been crucified with Christ [a statement of historical redemptive fact]. It is no longer I who live, but Christ who lives in me [a statement of present redemptive reality]. And the life I now live in the flesh I live by faith in the Son of God, who loved me and gave himself for me [living in light of the gospel right here, right now].

What does the gospel say you have been given right here, right now, so that you can be what you've been called to be and do what you've been called to do? The answer is Christ! He is in you. He is with you. He is for you. In him, you really do have everything you need. You simply have not been left to yourself.

> For you did not receive the spirit of slavery to fall back into fear, but you have received the Spirit of adoption as sons, by whom we cry, "Abba! Father!" (Rom. 8:15)

Reflect: Where even in your family relationships do you feel that you're on your own? How does the gospel correct that feeling?

JANUARY 19

If you look into the mirror of God's word and see someone in need of grace, why would you be impatient with others who share that need?

It is so easy to forget the amazing grace that's been freely showered upon us. I wish I could say that this is not my problem, but it is. And when you forget the grace that you've been given, it's easy to respond to the people around you with non-grace.

When you try to be gracious—because it's your duty, it isn't pretty. Pretend with me that I plop down on the couch next to my dear wife, Luella, and say these words: "You know, Luella, I have come to the realization that it's my duty to be gracious to you. So I'll tell you what I'm going to do. I'm going to give you grace, not because I really want to, but because I guess it's what I have to do." Do you think that Luella would be encouraged by that statement for a moment? I think not.

A joyful life of grace toward others grows best in the soil of gratitude. When I take time to remember that that grace has been lavished on me at the cost of the life of another, then I am joyfully motivated to give that grace to others.

For the believer, impatient, and irritated responses are always connected to forgetting who we are and what we have been given in Jesus. No one gives grace better than a person who's deeply convinced of his own need of it. And no one gives grace more graciously than someone who is aware of the grace he has been, and is being, given.

Because we forget so quickly, we all need to be given grace right at the very moment when we are called to be a tool of grace in the life of another. First John 4:19 really is true: "We love because he first loved us." Now, that's worth remembering.

> So that Christ may dwell in your hearts through faith—that you, being rooted and grounded in love, may have strength to comprehend with all the saints what is the breadth and length and height and depth, and to know the love of Christ that surpasses knowledge, that you may be filled with all the fullness of God. (Eph. 3:17–19)

Reflect: When are you most impatient and grumpy? What helps you become most aware of the grace that God has given you in Christ?

JANUARY 20

Where is hope to be found? In five life-altering words: "I am with you always."

You and I are on a constant quest for hope. We all want a reason to get up in the morning. Here are some things you have to know about hope:

- *God hardwired human beings for hope.* We don't live by instinct; we all find our identity, meaning, purpose, and inner sense of well-being in something.
- *What you place your hope in will set the direction of your life.* Whether it's hope in a person, a dream, or whatever, your life will be shaped by what you place your hope in.
- *Hope always includes an expectation and an object.* I am hoping for something and hoping that someone or something will deliver it.
- *Hope, to be hope, has to fix what is broken.* Hope that does not address your needs isn't very hopeful. You place your hope in your mechanic only if he has the ability to fix what's broken in your car.
- *You always preach to yourself a gospel of some kind of hope.* You're always reaching for hope and preaching to yourself the validity of what you reach for.

In life, you have something profoundly deeper to hold on to than the hope that people will be nice to you, that your job will work out, that you will make good choices when tempted, that you'll be smart enough to make good decisions, that you'll be able to avoid poverty or sickness, or that you'll have a good place to live and enough to eat.

So here is the radical truth of the gospel. Hope is not a situation. Hope is not a location. Hope is not a possession. Hope is not an experience. Hope is more than an insight or a principle. Hope is a person, and his name is Jesus! He comes to you and makes a commitment of hope: "And behold, I am with you always, to the end of the age" (Matt. 28:20). If nothing you envisioned ever works out and all the bad things that you've dreaded come your way, you still have hope because he is with you in power and grace.

> Then Haggai, the messenger of the Lord, spoke to the people with the Lord's message, "I am with you, declares the Lord." (Hag. 1:13)

Reflect: Do you struggle with being discouraged or cynical? How does Jesus's being with you provide hope? If he weren't with you, how would that take away hope?

JANUARY 21

When we ask the present to give us what only eternity can give, we end up driven, frustrated, discouraged, and ultimately hopeless.

We all have a functional contradiction between what we believe and how we live. This division—between belief system and daily life—causes us so much confusion, frustration, and discouragement. It leads us to expect far too much from the people and situations around us. It even results in some of us beginning to doubt the goodness of God. More specifically, here's the problem. We declare that we *believe* in forever, yet we *live* as if this is all there is. Trying to hold these together cannot work. Here's why.

First, you cannot make any sense out of the Christian life without eternity (see 1 Corinthians 15). If the one you've given your life to doesn't ultimately fix all that sin has broken, so that you can live with him forever without its effects, what is your faith worth? Second, you and I have been hardwired for eternity. God has placed eternity in every person's heart (Eccles. 3:11). That means everyone hungers for paradise. No one is satisfied with things the way they are.

So although you're sad that things are as broken as they are, you can work to be an agent of change in God's gracious and powerful hands. But you're not anxious or driven. You know that this world is not stuck and that it hasn't been abandoned by God. You can't see it every day, but you know that God is working his eternal plan. In the middle of your sadness there is celebration because you've read the final chapter and you know how God's grand story is going to end. So you get up every morning and give yourself to doing the things that God says are good because you know that if grace has put eternity in your future, there's nothing that you could ever do in God's name that is in vain.

> Therefore, my beloved brothers, be steadfast, immovable, always abounding in the work of the Lord, knowing that in the Lord your labor is not in vain. (1 Cor. 15:58)

Reflect: Identify two areas where you're dissatisfied. How might God use those to point your heart to eternity?

JANUARY 22

You and I don't need to be rescued only from the idols around us. No, we need to be rescued from our idolatrous hearts.

I was in northern India, in one of the high, holy cities of Hinduism. It was my first time ministering there, so I was on a four-day introduction tour of Hinduism. We had entered a temple that held the most horrific idol I had ever seen. I had no idea that things like this existed. It was a huge, sexually offensive statue. The Hindu pilgrims around me seemed joyous, grateful that they were there. Many of them laid down flat on their stomachs before it. They kissed its base. It was one of the darkest spiritual scenes I had ever seen. The scene was so spiritually oppressive that all I wanted to do was get out of the building.

I found myself trying to get through the busy streets to our vehicle, and as I did I kept saying to myself, "I thank God I'm not like these people. I thank God I'm not like these people." Then it hit me—I am! No, my idols aren't the dark idols of formal religion; they're the subtle idols of my everyday world. They're things that claim the place in my heart that only God should have. And they are just as vomitous to my Lord as that idol was to me. At that moment, I confessed to the worship war that takes place in my heart every day. I cried out for the rescue that only the grace of the Lord Jesus Christ could provide. And I longed for the day when that war would finally be over.

Worship is not something we do only in formal religious settings once a week. God designed us to be worshipers. We are always giving our hearts to something. That's why John counsels us in 1 John 5:21 to keep ourselves from idols. There is no greater argument for our need for grace than the ease with which our hearts fall under the rule of things other than God. And that grace is yours for the taking.

> And I said to them, "Cast away the detestable things your eyes feast on, every one of you, and do not defile yourselves with the idols of Egypt; I am the Lord your God." (Ezek. 20:7)

Reflect: Won't you live in God's rescuing grace today? How will you resist and run from the idols that challenge God's place in your heart?

JANUARY 23

Hope is not a thing, not a location, not a situation, not an experience. Hope is a person, and his name is Jesus.

If you pay attention and listen carefully to what you and the people around you are saying, you will realize that we are hope obsessed. Day after day, the things we do are fueled by hope. Little third-grader Sally says to her mom as she gets ready for school, "I sure hope the girls at school like me." Teenager Tim says to his buddy, "I got a new job after school; I hope it's decent." From hoping that a certain meal will be good to hoping that we will have the moral strength to do the things we should do, our lives are fueled and directed by hope.

What we're all searching for is hope that won't disappoint us, that won't leave us hopeless in the end. What are you asking of something when you place your hope in it? You're asking it to give you peace of heart. You're asking it to give your life meaning. You're asking it to give you purpose and direction. You're asking it to help you get through difficulty and disappointment. You're asking it to free you from envy or anxiety. You're asking it to give you joy in the morning and rest at night. Now, that's a lot to ask of anything. That fact confronts you with this reality—if your hope disappoints you, it's because it's the wrong hope.

Romans 5:1–5 talks about a hope that won't disappoint you even in times of suffering. Maybe you're thinking, "Where can I find that hope?" Whether you have realized it or not, what you've really been searching for is life, real heart-changing, heart-satisfying life. People can love and respect you, but they can't give you life. Situations can make your life easier, but they can't give you life. Locations can bring some changes to your life, but they can't give you life. Achievements can be temporarily satisfying, but they can't give you life. True lasting hope is never found horizontally. It's only ever found vertically, at the feet of Jesus. He's the Messiah, the one who *is* hope. Place your hopeful heart in his hands today.

Waiting for our blessed hope, the appearing of the glory of our great God and Savior Jesus Christ. (Titus 2:13)

Reflect: Think about your past week. What has given you hope to continue on?

JANUARY 24

Your little kingdom cannot compete with the glory of the kingdom of God, which is yours by grace and grace alone.

One of the sweetest, most encouraging things that Jesus said to his followers is recorded in Luke 12:32: "Fear not, little flock, for it is your Father's good pleasure to give you the kingdom." You and I are always in pursuit of and in service to some kind of kingdom. We are either living in allegiance to the King of kings, celebrating our welcome into his kingdom of glory and grace, or we are anointing ourselves as kings and working to set up our own little kingdoms.

Here is what is important for us to understand. God didn't give us his grace in order to make our little claustrophobic kingdoms work. Instead, he invited us to a much, much better kingdom. We think we know what is best for us, but we don't. We set our hearts on things that we think will make us happy, but they won't. We think we are able to rule our own lives, but we aren't. Every human being is in need of a king. All human beings need the rescue, forgiveness, justice, mercy, refuge, and protection that they are unable to give themselves.

The beauty of the work of Christ is more than his life, death, and resurrection we are offered forgiveness forever. We're also welcomed into the kingdom of the universe's most powerful and only perfect king. He blesses us with what no human kingdom can ever give. He showers us with forgiveness, reconciliation, peace, and hope. He rules over all the moments that seem to us to be out of control. He sets up his kingdom in our hearts, rescuing us from all the other things that would rule us. And he patiently teaches us that we weren't created to live as kings, anxiously working to set up our own little kingdoms. He teaches us what it means to rest in his kingship and to live for his glory. And he encourages us with the truth that his kingdom will never, ever end.

> But the saints of the Most High shall receive the kingdom and possess the kingdom forever, forever and ever. (Dan. 7:18)

Reflect: Are you loading kingly burdens onto your shoulders today, trying to build what you cannot and forgetting what God has already built for you? Or are you resting in this peace: that it's the Lord's good pleasure to give you his kingdom?

JANUARY 25

Theology without love is simply very bad theology.

It was one of those amazing moments teachers are given—moments that you can't plan for. I was teaching a course about pastoral care and counseling. My class was filled with prospective pastors who thought that if they preached theologically correct sermons, no one who heard them would need counseling. Since I knew that many students in my class weren't really hungry for what I had to offer, I began each semester by telling stories of the messes that some people had made of their lives and how they had looked to me to help them through difficulty and disaster. I would tell these stories until someone in the class would say, "Okay, we get it, we really *will* need what this class has to offer."

In the middle of one of these stories, a student raised his hand and said, "All right, *Professor* Tripp, we know we're going to have these projects in our churches; tell us what to do with them so we can get back to the work of ministry." I was both stunned by what he said and thankful for what it allowed me to say. Here was a man heading for ministry who clearly loved ideas more than he loved people! My poor student was far from what the Bible expected: "[Speak] the truth in love" (Eph. 4:15).

I cannot forsake truth for relationships, and I cannot forsake relationships for truth. They need to be held together. Why? Because the goal is that we progressively become like the one who is the ultimate definition of love. In his grace, God provides everything we need to be both a loving community and theologically pure, at the same time. To forsake either is not only a failure to love; it's bad theology as well. It is in a community of humble love that we are best positioned to understand all that God has said to us in his word.

> Rather, speaking the truth in love, we are to grow up in every way into him who is the head, into Christ, from whom the whole body, joined and held together by every joint with which it is equipped, when each part is working properly, makes the body grow so that it builds itself up in love. (Eph. 4:15–16)

Reflect: Think about your friendships. What happens if you love without truth? Or speak truth without love?

JANUARY 26

Mercy for others will reveal your ongoing need for mercy, driving you to the end of yourself and into the arms of your merciful Savior.

It's natural to make sure all your needs are met. It's natural to carry around with you a long catalog of things you want for yourself. It's natural to be more in tune with your feelings than with the feelings of others. It's natural to want mercy for yourself but justice for others. It's natural to be very aware of the sin of others yet blind to your own. Yet if we are ever going to be people of mercy, we need bountiful mercy ourselves!

It's impossible for me to think about God's call for us to be his instruments of mercy and not reflect on Jesus's powerful parable in Matthew 18:21–35. Please stop and read it right now. Christ had two reasons for telling this story. The first was to reveal the heart behind Peter's question: "All right, Lord, how many times do I have to forgive?" This question evidenced a heart that lacked mercy.

Christ's second reason for telling this story was to reveal *our* hearts. You see, like the unjust servant in Jesus's parable, we celebrate God's mercy but forsake a friendship because someone has been momentarily disloyal. We are thankful that we've been forgiven but when a person suffers the result of his decisions, we say he's getting what he deserves. We're simply not that good at mercy because we tend to see ourselves as more deserving than the poor and needy.

But when God's call of mercy collides with your lack of mercy, you begin to see yourself with accuracy. You begin to confess that you don't have inside you what God requires. You begin to admit to yourself and others that you cannot live up to God's standard. And you begin to cry out for the very thing that you have refused to give to others. Then as you meditate on the grandeur of the mercy you've received but don't deserve, you begin to want to help others experience that same mercy. You see, we daily need God's work of mercy in order to do his work of mercy.

> The Lord is merciful and gracious,
> slow to anger and abounding in steadfast love. (Ps. 103:8)

Reflect: When was the last time you admitted to yourself or another that you didn't live up to God's standard? When was the last time you knew you needed mercy?

JANUARY 27

God's call to obey is itself a grace. In this call, he is actively rescuing you from you.

We're all slaves; the question is, to whom or to what? Everyone is willing to make sacrifices; the question is, to whom or for what? We all follow sets of rules; the question is, whose and for what? We all give our hearts to something; the question is, to whom or to what? We were never hardwired to be free, if by "freedom" we mean an independent, self-sufficient life. We were created by God to be connected to something vastly bigger than ourselves, bigger than our personal desires and goals. We were carefully built by God to have every aspect of our personhood connected to him and his plans for us. When we reject him, we're not free and on our own. We always replace him with something or someone.

So God in his grace doesn't set you free because he knows you wouldn't be free. You and I would quickly enslave ourselves once again. And the sad reality is that it doesn't take much to enslave us again to a person or a thing that begins to function as our replacement messiah.

So what does grace offer you? The answer is the world's most wonderful, heart-satisfying, life-changing, and hope-producing slavery. The one who is the final definition of love, wisdom, mercy, and power makes us his slaves. He is freeing us from our slavery to what is not true and cannot deliver. He is rescuing us from serving what will never give us life. He is protecting us from seeking hope where hope will never be found.

He really does know how short-lived our resolve tends to be. He really understands our wandering eyes and our oft-disloyal hearts. That's why he commands our allegiance: so that we will not serve other masters. God's call to obey doesn't end your life; it is meant to protect the life that only he can give you.

> Likewise, my brothers, you also have died to the law through the body of Christ, so that you may belong to another, to him who has been raised from the dead, in order that we may bear fruit for God. (Rom. 7:4)

Reflect: What comes to your mind when you read or hear God's call to obey? What are some reasons why you might not think of it as a tool of his rescuing grace?

JANUARY 28

Prayer calls me to abandon the present as my only lens on life and commit to look at life from the perspective of reality.

What is the most needed, yet the most dangerous, prayer you could ever pray? It is the one prayer that takes you beyond the small-picture hopes and dreams that kidnap so much of your prayers. Sure, it's all right to pray about your job, family, finances, friends, school, church, health, government, and the weather, but these are not enough. These kinds of prayers follow the "right now-me" model of prayer. Yes, God cares about your present life. But he calls you to view yourself and your life from a perspective that goes far beyond this moment.

The one prayer Christ calls us all to pray requires us to let go of our momentary agendas and take up his eternal one. It requires us to surrender our distorted sense of need to his perfect sense of what is best. Instead of the "right now-me" model of prayer, it's the "forever-you" model of prayer. It is captured by a few dangerous words.

Why "dangerous"? Because the words of this prayer have the power to turn your life upside down, to make you a very different you than you have been. Here is what we have been called to pray: "Your kingdom come, your will be done, right here, right now in my life as it is in heaven" (see Matt. 6:10). It is only in the context of the surrender of these words that Jesus welcomes you to pray about your right-here, right-now needs.

Here is grace. I don't have to carry the burdens of a king because I have been gifted with a King. In his kingdom, I am blessed with every good thing I will ever need. So pray that prayer because it's dangerous grace is really what you (and I) need. Don't hesitate. Do it now. Why live for what will pass away? Why give your searching heart to what can never satisfy? Why tell yourself that you know what you need, when the one who created you knows better and has promised to deliver?

> And he withdrew from them about a stone's throw, and knelt down and prayed, saying, "Father, if you are willing, remove this cup from me. Nevertheless, not my will, but yours, be done." (Luke 22:41–42)

Reflect: What's been discouraging you right now? How do "right now-me" prayers paint "small-picture hopes and dreams"?

JANUARY 29

Today your heart will search for satisfaction. Will you look for it in the creation or in relationship with the Creator?

It was obvious what was happening but not to him. What he was trying to do would never work. I was his gardener, and I was at the base of his property, near the entrance, when he drove in with yet another new car. I had seen him do this same thing again and again. In fact, he was quickly running out of room. As he hopped out of his expensive new toy, he asked me what I thought. I said, "I don't think it's working." He said, "I don't know what you're talking about, it's a brand-new car." I said, "I think what you're trying to do will never work." He said, "I have no idea what you're trying to say to me." I asked, "How many cars is it going to take before you realize that an automobile has no capacity whatsoever to satisfy your heart?" Disappointed, he said, "Boy, you're raining on my parade." I was, and it was a big gospel moment.

The sight-sound-smell-touch-taste created world is amazing and beautiful. There seems to be an endless display of glories for us to discover around each corner. The song of a bird, the smell of a grilling steak, the grandeur of a mountain, the power of the wind, the grace of a deer, the lapping waves of the sea, the beauty of the sunset, and the tenderness of a kiss are all amazing in their own way. But there's one thing you must always remember. Creation does not have the ability to satisfy your heart. Earth simply will never be your savior. When you ask the created thing to do what it was not designed to do, you get short-term fulfillment, so you have to go back again and again. And that can leave you fat, addicted, and in debt.

All the glories of the created world together are meant to point you to the God of glory. He made each one of them, and he alone is able to give you life.

> But the Lord is the true God;
> he is the living God and the everlasting King.
> At his wrath the earth quakes,
> and the nations cannot endure his indignation. (Jer. 10:10)

Reflect: Today, will you give your life to the Creator, whose grace alone can satisfy and transform your heart? Or will you give it to the creation, which was designed to do neither?

JANUARY 30

Face it, your most brilliant act of righteousness wouldn't measure up to God's standard; that's why you've been given the grace of Jesus.

The more you understand the magnitude of God's grace, the more accurate will be your view of the depth of your sin. And the more you understand the depth of your unrighteousness, the more you will appreciate the magnitude of God's gift of grace. So let's talk about the essentiality of God's grace and the significance of sin.

Sin isn't primarily about acts of rebellion. Sin is, first of all, a condition of the heart that results in acts of rebellion. You and I commit sins because we are sinners. Because we're sinners, each of us is unable to live up to God's standard. Sin leaves us without the desire, will, or ability to do perfectly what God declares is right. Whether it's a situation in which we try and fail or a moment when we rebel and don't care, the playing field is level. We all fall short of God's standard (see Romans 3). It is a devastating analysis that shows us all to be in a dire and unalterable spiritual condition. We are all unable, we are all guilty, and there is not a thing we can do to help ourselves. None of us is good in God's eyes. None of us can satisfy his requirement. It is an inescapable, humbling, and sad reality.

But God didn't leave us in this sorry, helpless, and hopeless state. He sent his Son to do what we could not do, to die as we should have died, and to rise again, defeating sin and death. He did all this so that we could rest in a righteousness that is not our own, but a righteousness that fully satisfies God's requirement. So we can stand before a perfectly holy God, broken, weak, and failing, and be completely unafraid. That's because we stand before him in the righteousness of Jesus Christ. You no longer have to hope and pray that someday you will measure up because Jesus has measured up on your behalf. How could you hear better news than that?

> But the Scripture imprisoned everything under sin, so that the promise by faith in Jesus Christ might be given to those who believe. (Gal. 3:22)

Reflect: When you engage in self-talk, do you tend to think that you're good enough or that you're never good enough? How is the righteousness from Jesus the answer to both?

JANUARY 31

If you're God's child, it's no more you against the world than it was David, by himself, against the great warrior Goliath.

I love the story of the Israelite army as they faced the Philistine army (1 Samuel 17). On the first day of the face-off, that giant warrior, Goliath, called for Israel to send out its best man to do battle with him. Remember, these Israelite soldiers were the army of the Most High God. He had promised that he would deliver these enemies into their hands. Yet how did the soldiers respond? They were immediately filled with fear and withdrew to their tents. This was their response for forty days.

Why didn't these soldiers stand up to Goliath's challenge and fight for the Lord? The answer is clear and unavoidable—they were an army of *identity amnesiacs*. Because they had forgotten who they were, they were filled with fear and drew a false spiritual conclusion. They compared their puny selves to this massive warrior and concluded there was no path to victory.

Then David showed up, and he wondered why this Philistine was permitted to taunt God's army. He shockingly said that he would answer this man's challenge. Was he arrogant or delusional? No, he knew who he was. He understood what it means to be a child of the living God. David drew the right spiritual conclusion. It was not little him against this huge warrior. No, it was this puny Philistine warrior against almighty God. David walked into that valley because he had his identity clear, and he won a victory because he knew what he had been given.

Today, will you deal with life based on what you think you bring to the table? Or will you approach life based on who you now are as a child of the King of kings—the Savior who is always with you in power and grace? Will you live in timidity and fear? Or will you move toward those difficulties, resting not in your own ability but in the presence, power, and grace of your Father, who rules all? In those challenging moments may God give you grace to remember your identity as his child.

> There is no fear in love, but perfect love casts out fear. For fear has to do with punishment, and whoever fears has not been perfected in love. (1 John 4:18)

Reflect: Your friends will make you feel various ways about yourself today. What true, God-designed identity will you believe about yourself today?

FEBRUARY 1

Sure, you'll face difficulty. God is prying open your fingers so you'll let go of your dreams, rest in his comforts, and take up his call.

Think about the words penned by Peter near the beginning of his New Testament letter: "Now for a little while, if necessary, you have been grieved by various trials, so that the tested genuineness of your faith—more precious than gold that perishes though it is tested by fire—may be found to result in praise and glory and honor at the revelation of Jesus Christ" (1 Pet. 1:6–7).

Of all of the words that he could use to describe what God is doing now, he selects these three: *grieved*, *trials*, and *tested*. These are three words that most of us hope would never describe our lives. None of us gets up in the morning and prays, "Lord, if you love me, you will send more suffering my way today." Rather, when we are living in the middle of difficulty, we are tempted to view it as a sign of God's unfaithfulness or inattention.

Peter, however, doesn't see moments of difficulty this way. No, for him they are an important part of God's plan. Rather than being signs of his inattention, they are sure signs of his redemptive love. In grace, God leads you where you didn't plan to go in order to produce in you what you couldn't achieve on your own. In these moments, he works to alter the values of your heart so that you let go of your own little kingdom and give yourself to his kingdom of glory and grace.

God is working right now, but not so much to give us predictable, comfortable, and pleasurable lives. He isn't so much working to transform our circumstances as he is working through hard circumstances to transform you and me. In those moments, we are being blessed—not with grace like a soft pillow, but with the heart-transforming grace of difficulty. That's because the God who loves us knows that this is exactly the grace we need.

> Count it all joy, my brothers, when you meet trials of various kinds, for you know that the testing of your faith produces steadfastness. And let steadfastness have its full effect, that you may be perfect and complete, lacking in nothing. (James 1:2–4)

Reflect: What has caused you repeated frustration recently? Do you think that going through trials means God is not giving you his grace? Why?

FEBRUARY 2

Today you are not alone against temptation because the one who is your Savior is also your fortress, your hiding place, and your defense.

The Bible calls you, as a believer, to live with three realities in view. The first is the reality that you live in a world that has been dramatically broken by sin and doesn't function the way God intended (Rom. 8:22–24). Because the world you live in isn't operating as per God's original design, it presents you with temptations everywhere you live. Every day these temptations play to the sin and weakness that still live inside you. You and I must live temptation-aware; to fail to do so is to fail to recognize the fallenness of the world we live in every day.

The second reality is that even though we are God's children, we lack the power on our own to fight the spiritual battles of temptation. So as we face our vulnerability and weakness, we should regularly pray for purity of desire, for wisdom to recognize the enemy's tricks, and for strength to fight the battles we can't avoid. All of this comes out of a humble recognition that wrong doesn't always look wrong to us. What God says is dangerous doesn't always seem dangerous. So we need protection, not just from external temptation but also from our own blind eyes and wandering hearts.

Finally, as God's children, you and I can rest in the reality that in this fallen world of daily temptations, we are never, ever alone. God is with us. He provides the safety we could never provide for ourselves. He fights on our behalf even when we don't have the sense to resist. He gives us wisdom and strength at those moments when that's exactly what we need. You and I can face the harsh realities of life in this broken world with courage and hope because we do not face them all by ourselves. The words of Zephaniah 3:17 ring with as much hope today as they did generations ago when they were penned: "The Lord your God is in your midst, a mighty one who will save."

> No temptation has overtaken you that is not common to man. God is faithful, and he will not let you be tempted beyond your ability, but with the temptation he will also provide the way of escape, that you may be able to endure it. (1 Cor. 10:13)

Reflect: Which of today's three realities (above) is easiest for you to forget? Why?

FEBRUARY 3

God's grace not only provides you with what you need, but also transforms you into what God in his wisdom created you to be.

What is it that you need most? No, it's not that romantic relationship or that new car that you've had your eyes on. No, it's not a closer circle of friends, recovery from physical sickness, or restoration to your estranged family. It's not freedom from addiction, fear, depression, or worry. All of these things are very important in their own ways, but they don't represent your biggest need. There is one thing that every human being desperately needs, whether he knows it or not. This need gets to the heart of who you are and what God designed you to be and do.

Your biggest need (and mine) is a fully restored relationship with God. We were created to live in worshipful community with him. Our lives were meant to be shaped by love for him. If you are still living in a broken relationship to him, you are missing the primary purpose for your existence. So God in grace made a way for that essential relationship to be fully restored. Through the life, death, and resurrection of his Son, we are once again given access to the Father and are restored to his family.

But God does even more than this. Sin not only left us separated from God, it left us damaged too. The damage of sin extends to every aspect of our personhood. So God not only meets our deepest need; he commits himself to the long-term process of personal heart- and life-transformation. He is not satisfied that we have been restored to him; he now works so that we will become like him. Paul says it this way: "For those whom he foreknew he also predestined to be conformed to the image of his Son" (Rom. 8:29).

So God has welcomed you into his arms, but he's not satisfied. He will not leave his work of redemption until every heart of every one of his children has been fully transformed by his powerful grace. Now that we are *with* him by grace, he works by the very same grace so that we will be *like* him.

> For those whom he foreknew he also predestined to be conformed to the image of his Son, in order that he might be the firstborn among many brothers. (Rom. 8:29)

Reflect: Take a moment to review your calendar and to-do list from last week. What do they say about what you think you really need?

FEBRUARY 4

Every day you preach to yourself some kind of gospel—a false "I can't do this" gospel or the true "I have all I need in Christ" gospel.

No one is more influential in your life than you are because no one talks to you more than you do. Most of us have learned that it's best not to move our lips because people will think we're crazy, but we never stop talking to ourselves. In this endless inner discussion, we're always talking about God, life, others, and ourselves. These conversations are important because they shape what we desire, choose, say, and do. What have you been saying to you about yourself? Or about God? Or about life, meaning and purpose, right and wrong, true and false, and good and bad?

In Psalm 42, we are invited to eavesdrop on a man's private preaching. Yes, you read that right; like us, the psalmist was always preaching some kind of gospel to himself. You are either preaching to yourself a gospel that produces fear and timidity or one that propels you with courage and hope. You are preaching to yourself of a God who is distant, passive, and uncaring or of a God who is near, caring, and active.

Today, when it feels as if no one understands, what gospel will you preach to yourself? As you face physical sickness, the loss of a spot in a group, or the disloyalty of a friend, what message will you bring to you? When you are tempted to give way to despondency or fear, what will you say to you? When life seems hard and unfair, what gospel will you preach to you? When your dreams elude your grasp, what will you say to you? When you face a disease that you thought you'd never face, what gospel will you preach to you?

It really is true—no one talks to you more than you do. So God in his grace has given you his word so that you may preach to yourself what is true in those moments when the only one talking to you is you.

> Why are you cast down, O my soul,
>   and why are you in turmoil within me?
> Hope in God; for I shall again praise him,
>   my salvation and my God. (Ps. 42:11)

Reflect: What have you been saying to you recently? Is the message that you are preaching to yourself rooted in God's truth?

FEBRUARY 5

God will not rest from his redemptive work until he has once and for all presided over the funeral of sin and death.

If someone asked you, "What is God doing right now?" what would you answer? I am afraid that many of us are confused about the present activity of Jesus. We get that we have been forgiven and we understand that we have eternity with him in our future. Yet we're not sure what the agenda is in the here and now. Because we don't understand what God has committed himself to in the present, we are tempted to question his wisdom, doubt his love, and quit running to him for help.

So what is God up to right here, right now? Redemption! He is actively working out the spoils of the victory that Christ accomplished on the cross of Calvary. Listen to the encouraging words of 1 Corinthians 15:25–26: "For he must reign until he has put all his enemies under his feet. The last enemy to be destroyed is death."

Now, you and I need to understand two things in these words that answer our question. What is God doing? First, he's reigning! No, your world is not out of control. No, the bad guys are not going to win. No, sin will not have the final victory. This means that you can have hope even when it looks to you as if darkness is winning the day.

What else is God doing? This passage gives a second answer. He is putting the enemies of his redemptive purpose under his feet. He will not sit down, he will not rest, he will not relent until sin and death are completely defeated and we are finally and forever delivered. Right here and right now, hope doesn't depend on your understanding or strength. It rests in the sin- and death-defeating rule of the King of kings and Lord of lords. His reign is your present protection and your future hope.

> Behold! I tell you a mystery. We shall not all sleep, but we shall all be changed, in a moment, in the twinkling of an eye, at the last trumpet. For the trumpet will sound, and the dead will be raised imperishable, and we shall be changed. For this perishable body must put on the imperishable, and this mortal body must put on immortality. (1 Cor. 15:51–53)

Reflect: What feels out of control in your life or relationships or schedule right now? How does Jesus's present work help you?

FEBRUARY 6

You don't have to be anxious about the future. A God of grace has invaded your life, and he always completes what he starts.

All of us wonder about what is to come. Some of us think about the future and hope our dreams will come true. Some of us dread the future and pray that we will not have to face the things that we fear. For all of us, it's hard to look into the future and be secure because the future is simply out of our hands. We think and plan for what is to come, but things never turn out the way we envisioned. It doesn't take long for us to realize that we don't ever quite know what is around the next corner.

But we don't have to live plagued by the anxiety of the unknown. We don't have to go to sleep wondering what the next day will bring or wake up working our way through all the "what-ifs" we can think of.

No, we can have rest when we are confused. We can feel an inner well-being in the face of the unknown. Why? Because our peace of heart does not rest on how much we know, how much we have figured out, or how accurately we can predict the future. No, our rest is in the person who holds our individual futures in his wise and gracious hands. We have peace because we know that he will complete the good things that he in grace has started in our lives. He is faithful, so he never leaves the work of his hands. He is gracious, so he gives us what we need, not what we deserve. He is wise, so what he does is always best. He is sovereign, so he rules all the situations and locations where we live. He is powerful, so he can do what he pleases, when he pleases. There's no reason to be anxious.

Are you experiencing anxiety because you've forgotten who you are and what you've been given? Are you experiencing the fear that results from trying to know what you'll never know? He knows, he cares, and he will complete the job he's begun.

> When I thought, "My foot slips,"
>   your steadfast love, O Lord, held me up.
> When the cares of my heart are many,
>   your consolations cheer my soul. (Ps. 94:18–19)

Reflect: What is something that more than anything else you wish you knew? Is that unknown something driving you to self and anxiety or to Christ and his grace?

FEBRUARY 7

Corporate worship is designed to humble you by pointing out the depth of your need and enthrall you by pointing to the glory of God's provision.

We all do it in our own way. Seldom does a day go by without our doing it again. We even do it in the middle of worship services. But it's dangerous and doesn't lead us anywhere good. We all work to convince ourselves that we are better off than we are. We rewrite our history to make ourselves look better than we really are. We evaluate ourselves by looking into mirrors other than the one truly accurate mirror: the mirror of the word of God. We list our good deeds to ourselves. We argue to ourselves and to others that what looked like sin was not sin at all. It is all a function of the delusional self-righteousness of sin. It involves daily acts of self-atonement. It is us working to convince ourselves that we really don't need the amazing grace of a faithful, loving Savior.

God knew that this would be our tendency. He is fully aware of the self-righteousness that still lives inside all of us. God knew that we would convince ourselves that we are okay when we're not okay. So he designed a way for us to be confronted again and again with the depth of our sin and the expansive glory of the Savior, Jesus Christ. His design is that we gather again and again in services of corporate worship to be confronted with our true identity as both sinners and children of grace.

You see, corporate worship really does confront us with the fact that we are worse off than we thought and that God's grace is more amazing than we ever could have imagined. We will continue to need that reminder until our sin is no more and we are with him and are like him forever. Corporate worship is not a thankless duty for the religiously committed. No, it's another gift of mercy from a God of glorious grace (see Heb. 10:23–25).

> Now we know that whatever the law says it speaks to those who are under the law, so that every mouth may be stopped, and the whole world may be held accountable to God. For by works of the law no human being will be justified in his sight, since through the law comes knowledge of sin. (Rom. 3:19–20)

Reflect: When you attend church, do you think about your sin? Why? How are you letting those thoughts direct you to Christ?

FEBRUARY 8

Quit being paralyzed by your past. Grace offers you life in the present and the guarantee of a future.

It is a simple fact of nature that once the leaves are off the tree, you cannot put them back again. Once you have uttered words, you cannot rip them out of another's hearing. Once you have behaved in a certain way at a certain time, you cannot ask for a redo. You and I just don't have the option of reliving our past to try to do better any more than we have the power to glue the leaves back on the tree and make them live once again. What's done is done and cannot be redone.

But we all *wish* we could live certain moments and certain decisions over again. All of us experience regret. None of us has always desired or said the right thing. None of us has always made the best decision. None of us has always been humble, kind, and loving. None of us. So all of us have reason for remorse and regret. All of us are left with the sadness of what has been done and can't be undone.

That's why all of us should daily celebrate the grace that frees us from the regret of the past. This freedom is not the freedom of retraction or denial. It's not the freedom of rewriting our history. No, it's the freedom of forgiving and transforming grace. This grace welcomes me to live with hope in the present because it frees me to leave my past behind. Everything I'd like to redo has been fully covered by the blood of Jesus. I no longer need to carry the burden of the past. So now I am free to fully give myself to what God has called me to in the present.

Are you paralyzed by your past? Are you living under the dark shroud of the "if-onlys"? Does your past influence your present more than God's past, present, and future grace? Have you received and are you living out of the forgiveness that is yours because of the life, death, and resurrection of Jesus?

> But one thing I do: forgetting what lies behind and straining forward to what lies ahead, I press on toward the goal for the prize of the upward call of God in Christ Jesus. (Phil. 3:13–14)

Reflect: What is more real to you—what you've done in the past or what Christ has done in the past for you?

FEBRUARY 9

Today you will celebrate that grace has made you part of God's great plan or mourn the places where you aren't getting your own way.

He may have been the hardest person I ever counseled. He was self-assured and controlling. He argued for the rightfulness of everything he had ever done. He acted like the victim when in fact he was the victimizer. He had crushed his marriage and alienated his children. He loved himself and had a wonderful plan for his life. He made everyone a slave to his plan or he drove them out of his life. He made incredible sacrifices to get what he wanted but resisted the sacrifices God called him to make. But in a moment of grace I will never forget, he quit fighting, controlling, and defending. He said: "Paul, I get it. I have been so busy being God that I have had little time or interest in serving God." It was one of the most accurate moments of self-diagnosis I had ever experienced. No sooner had the words come out of his mouth than he began to weep like I had never seen a man weep.

But my friend was not unique. Think about children: from a young age, all kids really want their own way. A young child doesn't want to be told what to eat, what to wear, when to go to bed, how to steward his possessions, or how to treat others. He wants to be in the center of his own little world and to write his own set of rules. And he is surprised that you have the nerve to tell him what to do. But it isn't just children.

Sin causes this self-sovereignty to live in all of us. We want people to follow our way and stay out of our way. But when we wish for these things, we are forgetting who we are, who God is, and what grace has blessed us with. We are always either mourning the fact that we aren't getting our way or celebrating that grace welcomes us to a new and better way. I think there is probably a mix of mourning and celebration in all of us.

> Whom have I in heaven but you?
> And there is nothing on earth that I desire besides you. (Ps. 73:25)

Reflect: Today, will you give way to the frustration that you are not getting your way? Or will you celebrate the grace that has included you in the most wonderful plan that was ever conceived?

FEBRUARY 10

There's not a day that you won't need it; there's not a situation that won't demand it. What is it? The power of Jesus.

I knew there was only one way to help him—because he didn't want my help. He was only four years old. He desperately wanted to be independently strong and wise, but he wasn't. He wanted to believe that he didn't need the wise words and strong arms of a parent, but he did. So one day at home, he fought my parenting care once again. Then it hit me—he needed to experience his weakness so that he would run for my care.

So I walked away. No, not because I was mad at him or thought that this was the best way to punish him. I walked away because I loved him, and it was the best way to get him to seek and esteem that love. I knew that at some point he would give up, admit his weakness to himself, and seek my help.

About a half hour later, I heard the pitter-patter of his little feet on the hallway floor. He peeked around the corner and said, "I can't do it." I said, "What do you want Daddy to do?" And he said words that were good for his heart to say: "I need your help."

You and I were created to be dependent on God. Add to this the fact that sin leaves us broken and weak. This means we all need strength beyond our own. We need power that we'll never independently possess. So God, in grace, gives us power in the person of the Holy Spirit inside us.

To remind us of all this, God will "walk down the hallway" and let us experience our weakness once again so that we will seek and celebrate the strength that is only ever found in him. This is not an act of divine anger but a response of tender parental grace. This is the kind of grace you and I will continue to need until grace has finished its work.

> Now to him who is able to do far more abundantly than all that we ask or think, according to the power at work within us, to him be glory in the church and in Christ Jesus throughout all generations, forever and ever. Amen. (Eph. 3:20–21)

Reflect: How do your friends perceive you? Would you rather be weak and need God's strength, or be strong on your own? Why?

FEBRUARY 11

Grace works to free you from your eternity amnesia so that you will be willing and able to live with the purifying hope of what is to come.

You and I don't always live what we say we believe. There is often a disconnect between, on the one hand, the doctrines we say we have embraced and, on the other hand, the choices we make and the anxieties that we feel. One of the places where this disconnect exists for many of us is the biblical teaching about eternity.

We say we believe in the hereafter. We say that this moment in time is not all there is. We say that we are hardwired for forever. But often we live with the compulsion, anxiety, and drivenness of *people who have amnesia about eternity*. We get so focused on the opportunities, responsibilities, needs, and desires of the here and now that we lose sight of what is to come.

You cannot make sense out of life unless you look at it from the vantage point of eternity. When you forget eternity, you tend to lose sight of what's important. When you lose sight of what's truly important, you live for what is temporary, and your heart seeks for satisfaction where it cannot be found.

Looking for satisfaction where it cannot be found leaves you spiritually empty and potentially hopeless. Meanwhile, you are dealing with all the difficulties of this fallen world with little hope that things will ever be different. Living as an eternity amnesiac just doesn't work. It leaves you either hoping that now will be the paradise it will never be or you're hopeless that what's broken will ever be fixed.

So it's important to fix your eyes on what God has promised will surely come. Let the values of eternity be the values that shape your living today. Keep telling yourself that the difficulties of today will someday completely pass away. Belief in eternity can clarify your values and renew your hope. Pray that God, by his grace, will help you remember forever right here, right now.

> If in Christ we have hope in this life only, we are of all people most to be pitied. (1 Cor. 15:19)

Reflect: If God's grace only gave you a little better here and now, what would be the benefit of believing and resting in that grace? How would you describe the advantage of an eternity of grace?

FEBRUARY 12

Faith isn't natural for us. Doubt is, fear is, and pride is, but faith in the words and works of another isn't, and for that there's grace.

God hasn't just forgiven you—praise him that he has—but he has also called you to live by faith. Now, here's the rub. Faith is not normal for us. Yet doubt is quite natural for us. Wondering what God is doing is natural. It's normal to think your life is harder than that of others. Envying the life of someone else is natural. Wishing life were easier and that you had more control is natural. It's typical for you and me to try to figure out the future. Worry is natural. Wanting to give up is natural. And sometimes it's normal to wonder whether what you have staked your life on is really true. But faith isn't natural.

This means that faith isn't something you can work up inside yourself. Faith comes to you as God's gift of grace (Eph. 2:8). Not only is your salvation a gift of God, but the faith to embrace it is his gift as well. But here is what you need to understand: God not only gives you the grace to believe for your salvation, but he also works to enable you to live by faith. If you are living by faith, you know that you have been visited by powerful transforming grace. That's because that way of living just isn't normal for you and me.

Could it be that the things that confuse you and that you never would've chosen for yourself are God's tools to build your faith? By progressive transforming grace, he is enabling you to live the brand-new life he calls all of his children to live. You don't have to hide in guilt when weak faith gets you off the path because your hope in life isn't your faithfulness but his. You can run in weakness and once again seek his strength. And you can know that in zealous grace he will not stop until faith fully rules your heart. He always freely gives what we need so we may do what he has called us to do.

> For by grace you have been saved through faith. And this is not your own doing; it is the gift of God. (Eph. 2:8)

Reflect: What hardship in your life should you start thinking about as one of God's transforming tools to build your faith? Why would God strengthen your faith this way?

FEBRUARY 13

Tear up your list and throw it away—what God has planned for you is better than anything you've dreamed of for yourself.

As long as sin is still an issue for us, pride will be as well. At the root of every sin is pride. Pride is not only wanting your way, but convincing yourself that your way is better than God's way. It is thinking, if even for a moment, that you're smarter than God.

The proud person craves to be recognized, to be seen, to be given credit, and to get attention. Pride is taking credit for what you could never achieve or produce on your own. Pride is putting your pleasure before the pleasures of God. The sad brokenness and disharmony of the human community is the dark harvest of proud hearts.[2]

It is the big delusion,
the height of arrogance,
the seductive trap,
the big, dark danger.
It leads nowhere
good.
It's destiny is
death.
It sat at the center of the
disaster in the garden.
It propelled the sad
rebellion of Adam and Eve.
It tempts us all
again and again in
situation after situation,
location after location,
relationship after relationship.
We fall into thinking
what multitudes of our
lost forefathers thought.
We buy into this one fateful
thought,
that perhaps we're smarter than
God,
that maybe our way is better than
his way.
Only grace can deliver
the deluded from the
danger that they are
to themselves.

Oh, that salvation for Israel would come out of Zion!
When the Lord restores the fortunes of his people,
let Jacob rejoice, let Israel be glad. (Ps. 14:7)

Reflect: If you could change one thing that God has said, what would you desire to change? Why? What does that desire actually say about you?

FEBRUARY 14

God's grace will expose what you want to hide, not to shame you but to forgive and deliver you.

"It's a sad way to live," I thought as I listened to him recount the events of the night before. He worked next to me on the long packing table that kept our hands busy eight hours a day. But our mouths were free to talk. He was being unfaithful to his wife. He thought he was in charge, he thought he was free, but he wasn't. He talked about taking his girlfriend to a certain restaurant in the small community where he lived, only to see his wife's car parked outside. He went to another place but had to make sure the coast was clear before they left so they wouldn't get caught. I said to him: "You think you're free, but you're not free. You have to hide. You have to worry about being caught. You have to lurk around in the darkness." I then said: "You think I'm bound, but I'm the one who's free. When I go out with my wife, I never have to worry about where we're going. I never have to fear being caught. I can boldly live in the light."

Sin causes all of us to be committed to low-light living. We hide, we deny, we cover, we lie, we excuse, we shift the blame, we rationalize, we defend, and we explain away. These are all acts of darkness by people who fear exposure.

What does grace do? It shines light on what once lived in darkness (John 3:19–20). The grace of Jesus illumines our dank hallways and our dark corners. This isn't an act of vengeance or punishment. Instead, it's a move of forgiving, transforming, and delivering grace. He dispels our self-inflicted darkness because he knows that we cannot grieve and confess what we do not see.

The light has come. Run to the light; it is not to be feared. Yes, it is the light of exposure, but what will be exposed has already been covered by the blood of the one who exposes it.

> And this is the judgment: the light has come into the world, and people loved the darkness rather than the light because their works were evil. For everyone who does wicked things hates the light and does not come to the light, lest his works should be exposed. (John 3:19–20)

Reflect: What would you fear being exposed before other people? How can you take that darkness into the light of Jesus and his grace?

FEBRUARY 15

We will never get the freedom and long-term satisfaction we thought self-rule would bring. Ignoring God is never a pathway to blessing.

There are two lies that tempt each of us in some way. They are the lies that fueled the disastrous choice of Adam and Eve in that moment of temptation in the garden. Yes, it is true, these lies have as much power today as they did then. The first is the lie of *independence*. This lie says that you are a self-governing human being with the right to live as you wish. Now all parents know that children fall into embracing that lie. From day one, all children want to believe that their lives belong to them and that they are the only authority that they need. But we *don't* belong to ourselves. If God created us—and he did—then we belong to him.

The second lie is the lie of *self-sufficiency*, which tells me that I have everything I need within myself to be what I was created to be and to do what I was designed to do. The fact is that God is the only self-sufficient being in the universe. We were created for dependency, first on God and then on one another in loving community. We need to be taught, encouraged, warned, strengthened, forgiven, healed, restored, counseled, loved, rebuked, and delivered—all things we cannot provide for ourselves. Human self-sufficiency is a lie.

So Jesus calls us to reject these lies and come to him. Under his yoke is the only place where true freedom can be found (Matt. 11:28–30). There is freedom to be found, but not in empty promises of independence and self-sufficiency. True freedom is only ever found when grace ties your heart to Christ. If you are freed from trying to be what you can't be and from trying to do what you were not designed to do, you are now free to carry the light burdens of forgiveness-giving and life-restoring grace.

> Come to me, all who labor and are heavy laden, and I will give you rest. Take my yoke upon you, and learn from me, for I am gentle and lowly in heart, and you will find rest for your souls. For my yoke is easy, and my burden is light. (Matt. 11:28–30)

Reflect: Which of the two lies (independence or self-sufficiency) are you most tempted to believe? When you're tempted to believe that lie, what truth will you need to remind yourself about instead?

FEBRUARY 16

In Christ, you have everything you need to live in peace with God and the people he has placed in your life.

Jesus really is the Prince of Peace! Sin makes us the enemies of God and casts us into constant conflict with other people. Sin cuts us off from the two communities of love that we were created to live in—loving and worshipful community with God and loving community with others. We desperately need peace, but it often seems as if there is no peace to be found. This is why Isaiah's Old Testament prophecy of a Prince of Peace who was to come was so important, so exciting, and so encouraging (Isa. 9:6). The world was groaning, burdened and broken by vertical and horizontal conflict. The world and the people in it could not fix themselves. Peace seemed to be a distant and delusional hope.

Yet God had a solution for peace. It would not be a negotiation. It would not be a call to action. It would not be a strategy for peace. No, God's solution would come in the gift of his Son. He would live the life we could not live, fulfilling God's requirement. He would bear our punishment, satisfying God's anger. He would rise from the grave, defeating sin and death. He would do it all so that we could experience what we could never have achieved, earned, or deserved—peace with God. And peace with God is the only road to lasting peace with one another. It is only when the peace of God rules my heart that I can know real peace with you.

This is the good news of the gospel. Peace came. Peace lived. Peace died. Peace rose again. Peace reigns on your behalf. Peace indwells you by the Spirit. Peace convicts, forgives, and delivers you. Peace will welcome you into glory. Peace isn't a faded dream. No, Peace is real. Peace is a person, and his name is Jesus.

> But now in Christ Jesus you who once were far off have been brought near by the blood of Christ. For he himself is our peace, who has made us both one and has broken down in his flesh the dividing wall of hostility by abolishing the law of commandments expressed in ordinances, that he might create in himself one new man in place of the two, so making peace. (Eph. 2:13–15)

Reflect: How could the peace of Jesus bring harmony to the relational drama in your life?

FEBRUARY 17

Don't fear your weaknesses—God supplies all the strength you need. Be afraid of those moments when you think you're independently strong.

Admit it, you don't like being weak. It's not fun being the last one chosen to play on the team. It's embarrassing to be asked a question you can't answer. It's humbling to fail at a task, to drop the ball, or to make a promise and not be able to keep it. We don't like being confused or not knowing. We covet the muscles and the brains of others. We all hate being afraid and wish we had more courage. We don't like facing the truth that we're all weak in our own ways. It is the universal condition of humanity.

In a world where you are on your own, where you have to find your own way, weakness is a thing to be feared. In a world where all you have in the end is your performance, weakness is a thing to be regretted. In a world where you have no one to turn to for strength and few who accept you when you don't have it, weakness is a thing to be avoided. But here is what you need to understand. Weakness is not the big danger to be avoided. What you need to avoid is your *delusions* of strength. Your ideas about having independent strength are much more dangerous.

Are you confused? The fact is that we are all weak. We're weak in wisdom, weak in strength, and weak in righteousness. Sin has left us weak of heart and hands. But God's grace makes weakness a thing to be feared no longer. The God of grace, who calls you to himself and calls you to live for him, blesses you with all the strength you need to do what he's called you to do. The way to enter into that strength is to admit how little strength you actually have. Grace frees me from being devastated that I can no longer trust me. Here's why: because grace connects me to one who is worthy of my trust and who will always deliver what I need.

> Some trust in chariots and some in horses,
>   but we trust in the name of the LORD our God.
> They collapse and fall,
>   but we rise and stand upright. (Ps. 20:7–8)

Reflect: Can you list three ways you are weak? Think about each one. How can you use each of these three weaknesses to rely on the Lord today?

FEBRUARY 18

Today you'll look to find rest by trying to understand your life, or you'll rest in the one who understands everything, including your life.

Yes, it's true, we're all created by God to be meaning makers. Like archaeologists, we pick through our lives all the time, trying to make sense out of them. We investigate our past, we leaf through the layers of our present, and we try our best to figure out the future. Made in the image of God, we live our lives based not on the facts of our experiences, but on our unique interpretations of those facts. That's why the little girl asks that seemingly endless list of "why" questions; she has an inner drive to know. That's why the teenager sometimes seems a bit lost; he is trying to figure his life out.

It's not a sin to want to understand life. God created you with the ability to think and the desire for life to make sense. These traits were given to you so that you could come to know God and understand what he's communicated to you.

But it is important to remember that rest is never to be found in trying to figure it all out because you never will. God will always surprise you with what he brings your way. You will always be confronted with the unplanned and the unexpected. All this is because you don't rule your own life and you don't write your own story. And the one who does rule and write doesn't tell you everything about your life and his plan. No, he tells you the things you need to know to live, and then he graces you with his presence and his power.

Because he controls the details of your life, he is always near. At any moment, you can reach out and touch him (see Acts 17:26–27). Rest is only ever found in trusting the one who has everything figured out for your good and his glory. Because he is wise, gracious, faithful, and powerful, he is worthy of your trust and is alone able to give your heart rest.

> You hem me in, behind and before,
>   and lay your hand upon me.
> Such knowledge is too wonderful for me;
>   it is high; I cannot attain it. (Ps. 139:5–6)

Reflect: What's one thing you wish you could know about your life? How can you take that longing to God and then rest in the fact that he knows?

FEBRUARY 19

When hardship comes your way, will you tell yourself it's a tool of God's grace and a sign of his love, or will you give in to doubting his goodness?

One of the most important questions you could ask is: "What is God doing in the here and now?" The follow-up question is also important: "How should I respond to it?" It is nearly impossible to respond properly, if you are fundamentally confused about what God is doing. If someone were to ask you the first of those two questions, how would you respond? Are you after what God's after? Do you struggle with questions of God's love, faithfulness, wisdom, and goodness? Do you ever envy the life of another? Do you fall into thinking that no one understands what you're going through? Are you ever plagued by doubts as to whether Christianity is true after all? If you aren't struggling with these things, are you near someone who is?

Here's the bottom line. Right here, right now, God isn't so much working to deliver your personal definition of happiness. He's not committed to give you happy relationships, comfortable surroundings, or a predictable schedule. He hasn't promised you a successful career, a nice place to live, and a community of people who appreciate you. What he has promised you is *himself*, and what he brings to you is his transforming grace.

No, he's not first working on your happiness; he's committed to your holiness. That doesn't mean he is offering you less than you've hoped for, but much, much more. In grace, he is intent on delivering you from your greatest, deepest, and most long-term problem: sin. He has not unleashed his power in your life only to give you things that quickly pass away and that can't satisfy your heart. The hardships that you are facing aren't in your life because God is distant and uncaring, but rather because he loves you so fully. These hard moments are the tool of his exposing, forgiving, liberating, and transforming grace. These moments become moments of faith and not doubt when by grace you begin to value what God says is truly valuable.

> Blessed is the man who remains steadfast under trial, for when he has stood the test he will receive the crown of life, which God has promised to those who love him. (James 1:12)

Reflect: Think about all your free-time activities over the past few weeks. Do they show that you value what God values? What do your responses to hardship reveal about what you value?

FEBRUARY 20

Today you'll face things bigger than you, but you needn't be afraid because none is bigger than the one who rules them all for your sake.

You might not know it, you might not be aware as you're doing it, but you are always measuring your potential. The toddler who is just beginning to walk stands with wobbling legs and holds on to his mommy's knee as he measures his potential to walk across the room to daddy without falling on his face. The teenager walks up to his first job with clammy hands and a rapidly beating heart as he measures his potential to get through the day without being fired. The senior citizen sits nervously in her doctor's office as she measures her potential to deal with the physical hardships of old age. We are all constantly measuring our potential to do what is before us.

Now, the typical way to measure your potential is to compare the size of the problem to your natural gifts and your track record so far. No, it's not irrational to measure your potential this way. Yet for the believer in Christ Jesus, it simply isn't enough. By grace, God doesn't leave you with the tool box of your own strength, righteousness, and wisdom. No, he invades you with his own presence, power, wisdom, and grace. Paul captures this reality with these life-altering words: "It is no longer I who live, but Christ who lives in me" (Gal. 2:20). He's obviously not saying that he's dead because if he was, he wouldn't be writing those words. No, he's reminding you and me that if you are God's child, the life force that energizes your thoughts, desires, words, and actions is no longer you. It's Christ! God didn't just forgive you. No, he has come to live inside of you so you will have the power to desire and do what he calls you to do. He also rules all the situations, locations, and relationships that are out of your control. And he does all of this with your redemptive good in mind.

Oh come, let us worship and bow down;
    let us kneel before the LORD, our Maker!
For he is our God,
    and we are the people of his pasture,
    and the sheep of his hand. (Ps. 95:6–7)

Reflect: Do you struggle with regular attacks of fear that are focused on what other people think of you? If Christ is your indwelling Savior and reigning King, how can he help you not give way to fear?

FEBRUARY 21

Today you will fight temptation but not alone because a warrior Spirit lives inside of you and fights on your behalf.

I did it for my children again and again. I did it in moments when they didn't have the sense to do it for themselves. I did it with commitment and joy because I knew what the world that surrounded them was like. I knew the vulnerability of their hearts. What is this thing that I was committed to as a father? I did everything I could do to protect my children from evil.

I knew that they would minimize or forget two very important realities. First, they didn't understand or would soon forget that they had been born into a very broken world that doesn't function as God intended. They would forget that every day they woke up to a fallen world where real evil still exists. They often didn't seem to understand that this meant they would face temptation of various kinds every single day of their lives. Their eyes would see, or ears would hear, things that God, in his original plan, never intended them to see or hear. The alluring, deceitful, and seductive pleasures of sin would be held before them again and again.

Second, they also tended to minimize or forget the sin *inside* of them. They didn't seem to understand that the biggest danger to them was not the evil outside of them but the sin that still lurked with power in their hearts. And when you forget how vulnerable and temptable you are, you don't take precautions for your protection. So I knew that I had to work not only to protect my children from the evil in their environment, but also and more importantly to protect them from themselves.

God knows that we too minimize the fallenness of our world and the power of remaining sin. When we do, we do not guard ourselves from temptation as we should. Isn't it good to know that God in grace has placed his warrior Spirit inside of us? He battles on our behalf even in those moments when we don't have the sense to battle for ourselves (see Gal. 5:16–26).

> But I say, walk by the Spirit, and you will not gratify the desires of the flesh. (Gal. 5:16)

Reflect: Which do you most easily forget—the sin around you or the sin inside you? Why? Facing this reality, how can you remind yourself about God's grace?

FEBRUARY 22

Envy denies grace. The assumption of envy is that we deserve what another has been given, when, in fact, you and I deserve nothing.

Envy is self-focused. It inserts you into the center of your world. It makes it all about you. It tells you that you deserve what you don't deserve. Envy is expectant and demanding. Envy tells you that you are someone you aren't and you are entitled to what is not rightfully yours. The world of envy no more mixes with the world of grace than oil does with water. Envy forgets who you are, forgets who God is, and is confused about what life is all about.

Yet the fact is that all of us struggle with envy in some ways. We're jealous that the person next to us has achieved the financial success that we have never enjoyed. We wish our relationships were as happy as others seem to be. We're envious of the other person's group, which seems to be such a loving community. We wish that we could eat as much as that person does and still stay as slim as she is. The tall guy wishes he wasn't so tall and the short guy would love to look down on people for a change. The nerd envies the athlete and the athlete wishes he could get better grades. Envy is universal because sin is.

Envy has its roots in the selfishness of sin (see 2 Cor. 5:14–15). Envy is self-focused; because it's self-focused, it's entitled; because it's entitled, it's demanding; because it's demanding, it tends to judge the goodness of God by whether he has delivered what you feel entitled to; because it judges God on that basis, it leads you to question his goodness. Because you question God's goodness, you won't run to him for help. Envy is a spiritual disaster.

Grace, in contrast, reminds you that you deserve nothing, but it does not stop there—it confronts you with the truth that God is gloriously loving, gracious, and kind, that he lavishes on us things we could have never earned. Grace also reminds us that God is wise and he never gets a wrong address—he gives each of us exactly what he knows we need.

> For where jealousy and selfish ambition exist, there will be disorder and every vile practice. (James 3:16)

Reflect: What do you find yourself wishing you could have or change? How does this envy affect how much you enjoy your relationship with God?

FEBRUARY 23

Why do we say we place our hope in the cross of the Lord Jesus Christ and yet practically ask the law to do what only grace can accomplish?

It's done every day in Christian homes around the world. Maybe you've experienced it personally. Well-meaning parents want to see their children doing what is right. So they think that if they have the right set of rules, the right threat of punishment, and consistent enforcement, their children will be okay. Sadly, they've reduced parenting to being a law-giver, a lawyer, a jury, and a jailer. They think that their job is to do anything they can to shape, control, and regulate the behavior of their children. And in their zeal to control behavior, they look to the tools of threat ("I'll make you afraid enough that you'll never do this again"), manipulation ("I'll find something you really want and tell you that I'll give it to you if you obey"), and guilt ("I'll make you feel so bad, so ashamed, that you'll decide to not do this again"), not grace.

This way of thinking denies two significant things that the Bible tells us. The first is that before sin is a matter of behavior, it is always a matter of the heart. We sin because we are sinners. For example, anger is always an issue of the heart before it is an act of physical aggression. This is important to recognize because no human being has the power to change the heart of another human being. The second is that if threats, manipulation, and guilt could create lasting change in the life of another person, Jesus would not have had to come. So this way of thinking denies the gospel that we say we hold dear. It really does ask the law to do what only God in amazing grace is able to accomplish.

Thankfully, even when we face "law," God meets us with transforming grace and calls us to be tools of that grace in his redemptive hands. He lifts the burden of change off our shoulders and never calls us to do what only he can do.

> Now the law came in to increase the trespass, but where sin increased, grace abounded all the more, so that, as sin reigned in death, grace also might reign through righteousness leading to eternal life through Jesus Christ our Lord. (Rom. 5:20–21)

Reflect: If you've experienced this "law" approach, how has it made you feel? How can you respond in grace?

FEBRUARY 24

Admit it: we're all still a bit of a mess; that's why we need God's grace today as much as we needed it the first day we believed.

When we look in the mirror each morning, here's something we all need to say: "I am not a grace graduate." We never grow out of our need for grace.

Instead, it's so easy to think we're okay. Have you ever thought this way?

- "That really wasn't lust. I just enjoy beauty."
- "That really wasn't gossip. It was just a very detailed prayer request."
- "I'm not coldhearted and stingy. I'm just trying to protect and take care of what God has given me."
- "I wasn't being proud. Someone needed to take control of the conversation."
- "It wasn't really a lie. It was just a different way of recounting the facts."

Don't we all want to think we're better than we actually are? Who likes to think about how much we need God's rescuing grace? And we surely don't want to face the fact that what we need to be rescued from is us!

When you think you're okay, when you work hard to deny the evidence of your sin, then you're actually failing to seek God's grace. You're failing to seek your only hope. That's because grace is only ever attractive to sinners.

You only seek God's riches if you know you are poor. You only seek the spiritual healing of the Great Physician if you still suffer from the spiritual disease of sin.

So look in the mirror and face this fact today: you'll never outgrow your need for grace. No matter how much you learn and how much you mature, you'll need God's grace every day (see Phil. 3:12–16). Wonderfully, God gives daily grace and it's absolutely free! The way to begin to celebrate that grace is by admitting how much you need it.

> For when I kept silent, my bones wasted away
>   through my groaning all day long.
> For day and night your hand was heavy upon me;
>   my strength was dried up as by the heat of summer.
>
> I acknowledged my sin to you,
>   and I did not cover my iniquity;
> I said, "I will confess my transgressions to the LORD,"
>   and you forgave the iniquity of my sin. (Ps. 32:3–5)

Reflect: When was the last time you truly felt you needed God's grace? Why did you feel that way? Think of three ways you need his grace today.

FEBRUARY 25

You're going to hunger for some success in life. May you hunger for the complete success of the gospel in your heart.

You and I don't live by instinct. We are value-oriented, goal-oriented, purpose-oriented human beings. We all have things that are important to us and things that are not. We willingly make sacrifices for one thing and refuse to sacrifice for another. We love what another person hates, and we see as a treasure something that another person thinks is trash. Some things are so important to us that they shape the decisions that we make and the actions that we take.

In the center of this value system is our definition of success. No one wants to think that he has wasted his life. Everyone wants to think that his or her life is or will be successful. But what is success? Is it judged by the size of your house, the fame of your friends, the success of your career, the power of your position, the size of the pile of your possessions, the perfection of your physical beauty, the breadth of your knowledge, or the list of your achievements? The problem with all of these things is that they quickly pass away. And because they do, if you have lived for these things, you will eventually come up empty.

Contrast that view of success with God's view. God offers you things of supreme value (his forgiveness, his presence, welcome into his kingdom, a clean conscience, and a pure heart). These things will never pass away. They are the eternally valuable gifts of divine grace. This leaves you with this question: "What do I really want in life: the success of God's agenda of grace or the fulfillment of my catalog of desires?" Be honest. What kind of success are you hooking your heart to? And how is it shaping the decisions you make and the actions you take?

> Therefore do not be anxious, saying, "What shall we eat?" or "What shall we drink?" or "What shall we wear?" For the Gentiles seek after all these things, and your heavenly Father knows that you need them all. But seek first the kingdom of God and his righteousness, and all these things will be added to you. (Matt. 6:31–33)

Reflect: At the end of the day, what do you really long for: for God's grace to do its work? Or for more of the stuff and experiences that this physical created world has to offer?

FEBRUARY 26

Your life is not good because it is easy or predictable, but because the "I AM" has invaded your existence by his grace.

In Mark 6:45–52 Jesus had sent his disciples across the Sea of Galilee. They've encountered impossible headwinds and angry seas and had been rowing for about eight hours. They're in a situation that seems impossible, exhausting, frustrating, potentially dangerous, and far beyond their strength and ability. Why would Jesus ever want his disciples in this kind of difficulty? They're not in this mess because they've been foolish, but because they've obeyed Jesus.

Jesus sees all this and sets out to walk across the sea. Now, the moment he begins to take this walk, you are confronted with two things. The first is the fact that Jesus of Nazareth is the Lord God almighty because no other human being could do what he is doing. But secondly, if all Jesus wants to do is relieve the difficulty, he wouldn't have to take the walk. He could've prayed from the shore and the wind would cease. He takes the walk because he is not after the difficulty. He is after the men in the middle of the difficulty. Standing next to the boat as the wind still blows and the waves still crash, he says: "It is I. Do not be afraid" (6:50). He is actually taking one of the names of God. He is saying the "I AM" is with them—the God of Abraham, Isaac, and Jacob, the one on whom all the covenant promises rest.

Why did Jesus send his disciples into that storm? He did it for the same reason he sometimes sends you into storms—because he knows that sometimes you need the storm in order to be able to see the glory. For the believer, peace is not to be found in an easy life. Real peace is only ever found in the presence, power, and grace of the "I AM." That peace is yours even when the storms of life take you beyond your natural ability, wisdom, and strength. You can live with hope and courage in the middle of what once would have produced discouragement and fear because you know you are never alone.

> Fear not, for I am with you;
>   be not dismayed, for I am your God;
> I will strengthen you, I will help you,
>   I will uphold you with my righteous right hand. (Isa. 41:10)

Reflect: How do you usually react to difficult storms in life? How does the "I AM," who is present with you, change your perspective?

FEBRUARY 27

You've been born into a world of authority, and it is not you. Disobedience dethrones God and enthrones you in your heart.

You could argue that the most important words in all of the Bible are the first four words, "In the beginning, God . . ." (Gen.1:1). Those words are meant to change the way you think about yourself, life, God, and everything else. God was on site before you were. Because he is the Creator of all things, all things belong to him. God created you. That means you belong to him. We are not the result of impersonal forces. We are the direct product of God's creative power and will.

Now, think about this. When I make something, it belongs to me precisely because I made it. The Bible says, "The earth is the LORD's and the fullness thereof, the world and those who dwell therein" (Ps. 24:1). This means there is no such thing as human independence. To deny this is to tell myself that my life belongs to me for my use for the purpose of my happiness. This is not only about denying God's existence and authority, but it also is about denying my own humanity. All human beings were created to live with a life-shaping God consciousness and a willing submission to God's authority.

To deny this is like denying the existence of the sun. If you did that, the people around you would think you were crazy. Sin makes us just that crazy. We tell ourselves that we are the only authority that we need. We tell ourselves that we know what is best for us. We willingly step over God's wise and protective boundaries. We deny him as King and set ourselves up as the kings of our little worlds.

This is why grace is essential. It takes grace for me to acknowledge that there is a King and that he is not me. It takes God's rescuing hand for me to forsake the purpose of my kingdom and take up the purpose of his. Jesus submitted himself to the Father's will even to death so that you and I would have the grace we need to do the same.

> Let the words of my mouth and the meditation of my heart
> be acceptable in your sight,
> O LORD, my rock and my redeemer. (Ps. 19:14)

Reflect: Do you go through most days living for God's glory or for your own pleasure, power, comfort, and ease?

FEBRUARY 28

Love that calls wrong right and right wrong simply isn't love. Real love rebukes and forgives.

There are an awful lot of things that we call love that don't really rise to the level of what true love is and does. Maintaining peace at any cost isn't love. Remaining silent when I should speak up isn't love. Asking you to tolerate whatever I do or say because you say you love me is a fundamental misunderstanding of love. Much of what we think love is simply isn't love after all.

Real, biblical, self-sacrificing, God-honoring love never compromises what God says is right and true. Truth and love are inextricably bound together. Love that compromises truth simply isn't love. Truth without love ceases to be truth because it gets bent and twisted by other human agendas. If love works for what is best for you, then love is committed to what God says is best in your life.

I think often we opt for silence, willingly avoiding issues, and letting wrong things go on unchecked, not because we love the other person, but because we love ourselves. We are unwilling to make the hard personal sacrifices that are the call of real love. Now, I'm not talking about being self-righteous, judgmental, critical, and condemning. No, I'm talking about choosing not to ignore wrong, but dealing with wrong with the same grace that you have been given by God. Grace never calls wrong right. If wrong were right, Jesus would never have had to come.

The cross of Jesus Christ is the only model you need of what love does in the face of wrong. Love doesn't call wrong right. Love doesn't ignore wrong and hope it goes away. Love moves toward you *because* you are wrong and need to be rescued from you. Love is willing to make sacrifices and endure hardships so that you may be made right again and be reconciled to God and others. God graces us with this kind of love so that we may be tools of this love in the lives of others.

> [Love] does not rejoice at wrongdoing, but rejoices with the truth. Love bears all things, believes all things, hopes all things, endures all things. (1 Cor. 13:6–7)

Reflect: When no one is watching, do you tend to move toward people and problems or away from them? Why?

FEBRUARY 29

Do you need anything more than the cruel cross of Jesus Christ to convince you of how deep your need for grace is?

Think about it—God was so sure of the depth and breadth of your sin, and of your complete inability to free yourself from it, that he was willing to go to extraordinary lengths to rescue you. He was willing to harness the forces of nature and to carefully control the events of human history so that at a certain point Jesus would come to live the life you could not live, die the death that you should have died, and rise again, conquering death. Why did God go to this elaborate and sacrificial extent? There is only one answer to the question. God the Father planned it, God the Son was willing to do it, and God the Holy Spirit applied this work to your heart and mine because there just was no other way.

Sin is every human being's core disease (Gen. 6:5–6). It is completely beyond the power of any human being to escape it. It separates you from God, for whom you were created. It damages every aspect of your personhood. It robs you of inner contentment and peace, and it puts you at war with other human beings. It renders you blind, weak, self-oriented, and rebellious. It reduces all of us to fools, and ultimately it leads to death. Sin is an utter, almost incalculable disaster. You can run from a certain situation, you can get yourself out of a relationship, and you can move to another location and choose not to go back again. But you and I have no ability whatsoever to escape from the hold that sin has on us.

But in grace God was not satisfied leaving us in the disaster of sin. The words of Genesis 6:8—"But Noah found favor in the eyes of the Lord"—tell you that Genesis 6 is not the end of the story. God would not just punish sin; he would raise up a nation out of which his Son would come to live and die to deliver us from it. The cross of his Son stands as a lasting reminder of just how desperate our need is for the grace that the cross represents.

> For the wages of sin is death, but the free gift of God is eternal life in Christ Jesus our Lord. (Rom. 6:23)

Reflect: When you think about your sin, how can you propel your thoughts and heart toward the cross?

MARCH 1

Mercy means I am so deeply grateful for the forgiveness I have received that I cannot help offering you the same.

We all do it, probably every day. We have no idea that we're doing it, yet it has a huge impact on the way we view ourselves and the way we respond to others. It is one of the reasons there is so much relational trouble even in the house of God. What is it that causes so much harm? We all forget. In the busyness and self-centeredness of our lives, we sadly forget how much our lives have been blessed by and radically redirected by mercy. As we begin the day, the fact that God has blessed us with his favor when we deserved his wrath fades from our memories like a song whose lyrics we once knew but now cannot recall. When we lay our exhausted heads down at the end of the day, we often fail to look back on the many mercies that dripped from God's hands onto our little lives. Sadly, we all tend to be way too mercy-forgetful.

Mercy-forgetfulness is dangerous because it shapes the way you think about yourself and others. When you remember mercy, you also remember that you simply did nothing to earn that mercy. When you remember mercy, you are humble, thankful, and tender. When you remember mercy, complaining gives way to gratitude. But when you forget mercy, you proudly tell yourself that what you have is what you've achieved. When you forget mercy, you take credit for what only mercy could produce. When you forget mercy, you name yourself as righteous and deserving and you live an entitled and demanding life.

When you forget mercy and think you're deserving, you find it all too easy not to extend mercy to others. Your proud heart is not tender, so it is not easily moved by the sorry plight of others. You forget that you are more like than unlike your needy brother. You fail to acknowledge that neither of you stands before God as deserving. Humility is the soil in which mercy for others grows. When you're grateful to have received mercy, you'll be motivated to extend mercy to others.

> Be kind to one another, tenderhearted, forgiving one another, as God in Christ forgave you. (Eph. 4:32)

Reflect: Pause and recall two ways you've received mercy recently. How can you extend mercy to others today, whether you think they deserve it or not?

MARCH 2

Waiting on God doesn't mean sitting around and hoping. Waiting means believing he will do what he's promised and then acting with confidence.

Waiting on God is not at all like the meaningless waiting that you do at the dentist's office. You know, he's overbooked, so you're still sitting there more than an hour past your scheduled appointment. Frustrating! And there's nothing you can do, except wonder how much longer you'll be sitting there.

But waiting on God is not like that. Waiting on God is an active life based on confidence in his presence and promises. It's not a passive existence haunted by occasional doubt. Waiting on God isn't internal torment that results in paralysis. No, waiting on God is internal rest that results in courageous action.

Every one of God's children has been chosen to wait because every one of God's children lives between the "already" and the "not yet." Already this world has been broken by sin, but not yet has it been made new again. Already your sin has been forgiven, but not yet have you been fully delivered from it. Already Jesus reigns, but not yet has his final kingdom come. Already you have been given grace, but not yet has that grace finished its work. You see, we're all called to wait because we all live right smack dab in the middle of God's grand redemptive story. We all wait for the final end of the work that God has begun in and for us.

We don't just wait—we wait in hope. And what does hope in God look like? It is a confident expectation of a guaranteed result. We wait believing that what God has begun he will complete. So we get up every morning and act upon what is sure to come. We wait and act. We wait and fight. We wait and conquer. We wait and proclaim. We wait and sacrifice. We wait and give. We wait and worship. Waiting on God is an action based on confident assurance of grace to come.

> No unbelief made him waver concerning the promise of God, but he grew strong in his faith as he gave glory to God, fully convinced that God was able to do what he had promised. (Rom. 4:20–21)

Reflect: As you wait to finally one day become an adult, what aspect of your life do you wish you could hurry up? Until then, what might God be teaching you about waiting?

MARCH 3

Prayer is abandoning my reliance on me and running toward the rest that can be found only when I rely on the power of God.

Prayer abandons independence. Prayer forsakes any thought that you can make it on your own. Prayer acknowledges weakness. Prayer embraces the reality of failure. Prayer tells you that you are not at the center. Prayer calls you to abandon your plans for the wiser plans of another. Prayer flows from a deep personal sense of need and runs toward God's abundant grace.

Because of what prayer really is, prayer is not natural for us. It's not natural for us to embrace our sin, weakness, and failure. It's not natural for us to be comfortable depending on the mercy of another. It's not natural for us to surrender our hopes and dreams, our wisdom and control to someone greater than us. It's not natural for us to think that we need grace.

On the other hand, it is natural for us to think that our righteousness, wisdom, strength, and work are enough. As a result, many of our prayers are the religious pronouncements of self-righteous people. Our prayers become either the long wish lists of entitled people or the impatient demands of people who are wondering what in the world God is doing. So many of our prayers aren't prayers at all (see Luke 18:9–14).

Here is the bottom line. It is only by grace that we will ever acknowledge our need for grace. Prayer is fundamentally counterintuitive. And that means we need grace to rescue us from our self-oriented religious ideas so that, with humble hearts, we may cast ourselves on God's gracious care and kingship. Prayer always forsakes the kingdom of self for the kingdom of God. And for that we all need forgiving, rescuing, and transforming grace. This is just the kind of grace for which true prayer leads us to cry out.

> And at the evening sacrifice I rose from my fasting, with my garment and my cloak torn, and fell upon my knees and spread out my hands to the LORD my God, saying: "O my God, I am ashamed and blush to lift my face to you, my God, for our iniquities have risen higher than our heads, and our guilt has mounted up to the heavens." (Ezra 9:5–6)

Reflect: Do you misuse prayer? How might you be using prayer merely to get rid of anxiety or get hold of what you want?

MARCH 4

If you don't acknowledge sin, you won't value grace. If you don't value grace, you won't seek the forgiveness and rescue it provides.

Our problem, whether we know it or not, is that sin doesn't always seem sinful to us. Our ability to minimize or deny the seriousness of our iniquity before God is a personal moral disaster. Our willingness to be blind never leads us anywhere good. Holiness begins with the desire to see ourselves with heart-convicting clarity and accuracy. This clarity comes only when we stand before the throne of our holy God. Remember, you cannot confess what you do not grieve, you cannot grieve what you have not seen, and you cannot repent of what you have not confessed. Cry out for eyes to see and a heart to weep. And in weeping, may you find the joy of discovering mercies that are new once again.[3]

I will make this confession,
although it hurts to do so:
I am a very skilled
self-swindler.
I am very good at playing
monkey games with my
morality.
All too often, I argue for
righteousness that simply
is not there.
It's too easy for me
to convince myself that
the wrong
that I have done is not
so wrong after all.
And as I work to minimize
the gravity of my condition,
I in turn devalue
the grace
that is my only hope of
rescue,
transformation,
deliverance.
Lord,
please crush my heart with
the guilt of my sin
so that you may fill it once again
with the glory of your
redeeming grace.

There is no soundness in my flesh
    because of your indignation;
there is no health in my bones
    because of my sin.
For my iniquities have gone over my head;
    like a heavy burden, they are too heavy for me. (Ps. 38:3–4)

Reflect: What aspects of your online interactions and explorations have you been hiding from God or others? How can you bring these actions into the light of confession, repentance, and grace?

MARCH 5

If you're God's child, you can rest assured today that both your standing before God and his rule on your behalf are sure and secure.

Every day, you and I carry some important life concerns. It's right to be concerned about your school work and grades. It's good to focus much concern on the welfare and development of your mind and body. It's vital to take your church and your relationship to the body of Christ seriously. And it'd be silly not to see your friends as an important concern. It is responsible and wise to carry these concerns.

But you do not have to plague yourself with concern about the two most important things. You can wake up morning after morning with a smile on your face. Here's why: because you know that the most important things in your life are simply never, ever at risk.

You can lose your house, your job, your family, your friendships, your health, and your church, but you will not lose these things. You can face disappointment and loss, but these things will remain. You can suffer the pain of defeat, but these things will still be yours.

Here they are, and there aren't two things in all of life more important than these. First, that grace has purchased for you a place in God's family. And second, that, because you are in his family, God rules over all things for your good. You could never have earned these two unshakable realities. They are only ever yours by grace.

It is because of grace that you have a forever place in God's family. It is because of grace that, on your darkest day, you are still loved and accepted. It is because of grace that when nothing in life makes sense, your life is still under the control of his kingship. There is much for you to be concerned about, but not these two things. His love will never fail, and his rule on your behalf is eternal.

> My sheep hear my voice, and I know them, and they follow me. I give them eternal life, and they will never perish, and no one will snatch them out of my hand. My Father, who has given them to me, is greater than all, and no one is able to snatch them out of the Father's hand. (John 10:27–29)

Reflect: What two things do you find yourself anxious about most regularly? When you're tempted to worry about them today, meditate on the two unchangeable things above.

MARCH 6

Since your standing with God is based not on your righteousness but on Christ's, in moments of failure, you can run to him and not from him.

It's what we all are. We're all failures. Own it; it will be good for you. There is not a day in any of our lives when we don't fail at something. Maybe it's in an unkind word, an ugly thought, or an ungodly desire. Maybe it's in a moment of selfish envy or unbridled greed. Maybe it's in a moment of pride, when we want to be the center of attention or steal some of God's glory. Somehow, some way, we all do it every day—we fall short of God's righteous standard. We all fail to be what he has created and called us to be.

Now, when confronted with your failure—and you will be if you're at all humble and honest—you have only three choices. (1) You can commit to be an evidence denier. You can try to convince yourself that you're okay when you're really not okay. Or (2) in the face of your failure, you can wallow in guilt and shame. You can beat yourself up because you did not do better and can work hard to hide your failure from God and others. Or (3) in the brokenness and grief of conviction, you can run not away from God but to him. You can run into the light of his holy presence utterly unafraid, filled with the confidence that although he is righteous and you are not, he will not turn you away. You can do this because your standing with him has never been based on your righteous performance, but on the perfect obedience of your Savior.

Yes, you are called to live a holy life, but your way of living has not been and never will be the basis of your standing with God. You can bow at his feet and confess your sins, knowing that you will receive grace and not punishment. Why? Because righteous Jesus took the full brunt of your penalty so that you would never, ever bear it.

> He himself bore our sins in his body on the tree, that we might die to sin and live to righteousness. By his wounds you have been healed. (1 Pet. 2:24)

Reflect: So when you fail again today in your pride or lust, where will you run?

MARCH 7

It's the heart that's the problem. People, locations, and situations don't cause me to sin; they're where the sin of my heart gets revealed.

If you ask the little boy why he hit his sister, he won't tell you it was because of the sin that's in his heart. No, he'll say, "She was bothering me." When we do something wrong, we all tend to point outside ourselves for the cause: "This traffic makes me so angry"; "She gets me so upset"; or "My teacher pulls the worst out of me."

It feels good to think that your biggest problems exist outside of you and not inside you. But the problem is that it's simply not true. Jesus devastated this excuse-making perspective on human behavior. In the Sermon on the Mount, Jesus said:

> You have heard that it was said to those of old, "You shall not murder. . . ." But I say to you that everyone who is angry with his brother will be liable to judgment. . . . You have heard that it was said, "You shall not commit adultery." But I say to you that everyone who looks at a woman with lustful intent has already committed adultery with her in his heart. (Matt. 5:21–22, 27–28)

Sin is a matter of the heart before it's ever an issue of our behavior. This means that our biggest problem exists inside us and not outside us. It's the evil inside me that connects me to the evil outside me. So I must confess that I am my greatest problem. And if I confess this, I am saying that I don't so much need to be rescued from people, locations, and situations. I desperately need the grace that is alone able to rescue me from me. I can escape situations and relationships, but I have no power to escape me. That's why David prayed that God would create a clean heart in him (Psalm 51). God's grace is grace for the heart, and that is very good news.

> Draw near to God, and he will draw near to you. Cleanse your hands, you sinners, and purify your hearts, you double-minded. Be wretched and mourn and weep. Let your laughter be turned to mourning and your joy to gloom. Humble yourselves before the Lord, and he will exalt you. (James 4:8–10)

Reflect: When people have tried to correct you recently, have you made excuses for yourself? What does this reveal about your heart, God's grace, and what you should do next?

MARCH 8

Yes, your life is messy and hard, but that's not a failure of the plan; it is the plan. It's God working to complete what he's begun in you.

You are tempted to think that because you're God's child, your life should be easier, more predictable, and definitely more comfortable. But that's not what the Bible teaches. And it's not how we normally think either.

Instead, struggles are part of God's plan for you. This means that if you're God's child, you must never allow yourself to think that the hard things you are now going through are failures of God's character, promises, power, or plan. You must not allow yourself to think that God has turned his back on you. You must not let yourself do any of these things. Here's why: Because when you begin to doubt God's goodness, you quit going to him for help. You see, you don't run for help to those you have come to doubt.

God plans to employ the difficulties of a fallen world to continue and complete his work in you. This means that those moments of difficulty are not an interruption of his plan or the failure of his plan. Instead, they're rather an important part of his plan. I think there are times when many of us cry out for God's grace and we get it—but it's not the grace that we're looking for. We want the grace of relief. We get those in little pieces, but largely they are yet to come.

We all need to teach and encourage one another that God's grace often comes to us in uncomfortable forms. It may not be what you and I want, but it is precisely what we need. God is faithful. He will use the brokenness of the world you live in to complete the loving work of personal transformation that he has begun. Now, that's grace!

> Bless our God, O peoples;
>   let the sound of his praise be heard,
> who has kept our soul among the living
>   and has not let our feet slip.
> For you, O God, have tested us;
>   you have tried us as silver is tried. (Ps. 66:8–10)

Reflect: When you compare your life and its difficulties with what you see of other people on social media, how do you feel? If it's God's plan to use brokenness, how does that plan change the way you view other people's posts?

MARCH 9

God questions us, "Why spend money on what's not bread and labor for what doesn't satisfy?" Sadly, many of us do that day after day.

We all tend to look for life in all the wrong places. We all tend to look for life horizontally when the reality is that we will only ever find life vertically. Somehow, some way, we all tend to look to the created world to give us life. We all carry around with us our personal catalog of "if-onlys." "If only I was dating, then I'd be happy." "If only I could have those friends, then I'd be satisfied." "If only we could buy that car, I don't think I'd want another thing." "If only my family life was better, then I'd be okay."

Whatever sits on the other side of your "if-only" is where you are looking for life—for peace, joy, hope, and lasting contentment of heart. The problem is that you continue to spend time and money on what won't fill you. It'll be a big, disastrous spiritual mess that leaves you fat, addicted, in debt, and with a still unsatisfied heart. Why? Because this world will never be your savior.

This physical, created world, with all of its sights, sounds, locations, experiences, and relationships, has no capacity to make your heart content. This physical world was designed by God to point you to the only place where your heart will find satisfaction and rest. Your heart will rest only when it finds its rest in God alone.

Where will you look for peace and rest of heart? What will you reach for to give you hope, courage, and a reason to continue? Why would you frantically look to creation to give you what you already have been given in Christ? Why would you ask this broken world to be your savior when Jesus has come as your Savior to supply in his grace everything that you need?

> Why do you spend your money for that which is not bread,
> and your labor for that which does not satisfy?
> Listen diligently to me, and eat what is good,
> and delight yourselves in rich food.
> Incline your ear, and come to me;
> hear, that your soul may live. (Isa. 55:2–3)

Reflect: What will you hook your heart to today in the hope that it will give you life?

MARCH 10

The stuff outside you, no matter how troubling, is not as dangerous as the mess inside you—and for that you have the grace of Jesus.

Listen to the words of Jesus:

> "Do you not see that whatever goes into a person from outside cannot defile him, since it enters not his heart but his stomach, and is expelled?" (Thus he declared all foods clean.) And he said, "What comes out of a person is what defiles him. For from within, out of the heart of man, come evil thoughts, sexual immorality, theft, murder, adultery, coveting, wickedness, deceit, sensuality, envy, slander, pride, foolishness. All these evil things come from within, and they defile a person." (Mark 7:18–23)

Jesus is making a very powerful point. You don't defeat the disaster of sin by separating yourself from sinful people, places, or experiences. Now, that may be a very good thing to do, but it will never fix your sin problem. If you could defeat sin by separating yourself from its external issues, Jesus would never have needed to come. The history of the church is filled with people who thought they could defeat sin by running away from the sinful world and hiding behind big walls. You know what the big mistake was? When people walked inside the walls, they brought their sinful hearts with them. As a result, they re-created all the things they were seeking to escape.

In his words, Jesus calls us to humbly admit that the biggest danger to each of us is not the evil that lurks outside us, but the sin that still resides in our hearts. Once you admit this, you begin to get excited about God's grace in Jesus Christ. If your biggest problem lives outside of you, you don't really need grace. You just need changes to your situation or relationships. But once you admit that you are your biggest problem, then you will celebrate the grace that rescues you from you.

> Then what becomes of our boasting? It is excluded. By what kind of law? By a law of works? No, but by the law of faith. For we hold that one is justified by faith apart from works of the law. (Rom. 3:27–28)

Reflect: What failures do you despise in other people who are part of groups or teams alongside you? What does this say about your own heart?

MARCH 11

Of course you haven't been fulfilled in this world. It's a sign that you have been designed for a world to come.

We say we really do believe that there is life after this one ends. But we tend to live with the anxiety and drivenness that come from believing that all we have is this moment.

Here's the real-life, street-level issue: if you don't keep the eyes of your heart focused on the paradise that is to come, you will try to turn this poor, fallen world into the paradise it will never be. In the heart of every living person is the longing for paradise. The tears of the school-age child who has been rejected on the playground are tears of someone reaching out for paradise. The pain of aloneness that a person without friends or family feels is the pain of one longing for paradise. We all have this longing, even when we are not aware of it because he has placed eternity in each one of our hearts (Eccles. 3:11). Our cries are more than cries of pain; they are also cries of longing for more and better than we will ever experience in this fallen world.

When you forget this, you work very hard to try to turn this moment into the paradise it will never be. Your friendships will not be the paradise your heart craves. Your parents will not deliver paradise to you. Even your church will not live up to the standard of paradise. If you're God's child, paradise has been guaranteed for you, but it will not be right here, right now. And all the things that disappoint you now will help cause you to long for the paradise that is to come. Live in hope because paradise is surely coming, and stop asking this fallen world to be the paradise it will never be.

> These all died in faith, not having received the things promised, but having seen them and greeted them from afar, and having acknowledged that they were strangers and exiles on the earth. For people who speak thus make it clear that they are seeking a homeland. If they had been thinking of that land from which they had gone out, they would have had opportunity to return. But as it is, they desire a better country, that is, a heavenly one. (Heb. 11:13–16)

Reflect: Take a moment and try to connect your anxiety with wanting something in your life to give you paradise.

MARCH 12

If you mourn the fallenness of your world rather than curse its difficulties, you know that grace has visited you.

Life in this terribly broken world *is* hard. It's like living in a disheveled, crumbling house that doesn't function as it was meant to. The doors constantly get stuck shut. The plumbing only occasionally works properly. You are never sure what's going to happen when you plug an appliance in, and it seems that the roof leaks even when it's not raining. So it is with the world that you and I live in. It really is a broken-down house.

Now, there are really only two responses we can have to the brokenness that complicates all of our lives: *cursing* or *mourning*. Let's be honest. Cursing is the more natural response. We curse the fact that we have to deal with flawed people and broken things. We curse the fact that we have to deal with pollution and disease. We curse the fact that promises get broken, relationships shatter, and dreams die. Yes, it's natural to find these things frustrating. That's because, as Paul says in Romans 8, the whole world groans as it waits for redemption. But cursing is the wrong response. We curse what we have to deal with because it makes our lives harder than we want them to be. Cursing is all about our comfort, our pleasure, our ease. Cursing is fundamentally self-centered.

Mourning is the much better response. Mourning embraces the tragedy of the fall. Mourning acknowledges that the world is not the way God meant it to be. Mourning cries out for God's redeeming, restoring hand. Mourning acknowledges the suffering of others. Mourning is about something bigger than the fact that life is hard. Mourning grieves what sin has done to the cosmos. Mourning longs for the Redeemer to come and make his broken world new again. Mourning, then, is a response that is prompted by grace.

This side of eternity in this broken world, cursing is the default language of the kingdom of self, but mourning is the default language of the kingdom of God.

> For we know that the whole creation has been groaning together in the pains of childbirth until now. And not only the creation, but we ourselves, who have the firstfruits of the Spirit, groan inwardly as we wait eagerly for adoption as sons, the redemption of our bodies. (Rom. 8:22–23)

Reflect: When you face disappointment today, which language will you speak—cursing or mourning?

MARCH 13

You don't have to worry about whether your world is under control. God rules. You just have to learn to trust him when his rule isn't evident.

I looked everywhere. I looked high and low. There wasn't a drawer, a cabinet, or a dark closet I didn't tear apart in my search. I even went out to the car twice to make sure I hadn't left it there. The file contained important papers, and I had lost it somewhere. It was so frustrating. And after all my searching, it was just as lost as when I had begun. That night it hit me that my lost file was a picture of how little control I have over my own life. It's scary, but you and I have very little power and control over the most significant things in our lives. We don't have a clue what will happen to us next week or next month. We have little control over the people in our lives, little power over the situations in which we live, and almost no control over the locations of our lives.

Honestly facing your lack of sovereignty over your own life produces either anxiety or relief. Anxiety is God-forgetting. It is the result of thinking that life is on your shoulders. You act like it's your job to figure it all out and keep things in order. If this is the way you think, your life will be burdened with worry and your heart will be filled with dread.

But there is a much better way. It is God-remembering. It rests in the relief that, although it may not look like it, your life is under the careful, loving, and powerful control of God. In all of those moments when life is out of *your* control, it is not out of *his* control.

You see, rest is not to be found in your control but in God's absolute rule over everything. You will never be in a situation, location, or relationship that is not under his control.

> For his dominion is an everlasting dominion,
>   and his kingdom endures from generation to generation; . . .
>   and he does according to his will among the host of heaven
>   and among the inhabitants of the earth;
> and none can stay his hand
>   or say to him, "What have you done?" (Dan. 4:34–35)

Reflect: Where do you feel like life is out of control? How have you been trying to regain a sense of control? Have your efforts been with or without God in mind?

MARCH 14

Corporate worship is designed to once again clear up our confusion as to what is truly important in life.

This side of eternity, it's easy for things to rise to levels of importance far beyond their true importance. Then they begin to command the thoughts, motives, desires, choices, and allegiance of our hearts. As human beings made in the likeness of God, we are value-oriented, goal-oriented, purpose-oriented, and importance-oriented beings. We are always in pursuit of some vision, some desire, or some dream. Every day we all name things as important, and when we do, we work to have those things in our lives.

What I am describing is a huge spiritual battle that is fought on the turf of your heart. You see, whatever important thing rules your heart also shapes your words and behavior. The fact is that we all lose sight of what is truly important. Winning an argument becomes too important for us. Getting approval on social media becomes more important to us than the favor of God. Physical beauty and pleasure take on too much value in our hearts. A cool car, the latest clothes, or the last bowl of cereal from the box rises in value far beyond its true significance. We all need to be reminded again and again of what God has declared are the most important things in life.

So in grace, God has designed us to regularly gather together in corporate worship and remember his power, glory, and grace. It reminds us of the depth of our spiritual needs. It reminds us of the eternity that is to come. It reminds us of salvation past, present, and future. And as it reminds us of these things, it clears up our values confusion once again. It rescues us from our wandering hearts and points us to the one who rightly commands our allegiance. He is the one who, in his grace, gives us every important thing that we would ever need.

> For I received from the Lord what I also delivered to you, that the Lord Jesus on the night when he was betrayed took bread, and when he had given thanks, he broke it, and said, "This is my body, which is for you. Do this in remembrance of me." (1 Cor. 11:23–24)

Reflect: How do you react when people don't like your personality, clothes, or social media posts and comments? Do your reactions tell you anything about what you consider important?

MARCH 15

Any time you question God's wisdom or step over his boundaries, you are telling yourself that you are smarter than God.

It is one of those "put-you-in-your-place responses." God is speaking to Job. And he is drawing a bold line of distinction between the creation and the Creator. It's a stunning description of God's majesty and Job's smallness. These are words we should read again and again:

Then the Lord answered Job out of the whirlwind and said:

> "Who is this that darkens counsel by words without knowledge?
> Dress for action like a man;
> I will question you, and you make it known to me.
>
> Where were you when I laid the foundation of the earth?
> Tell me, if you have understanding.
> Who determined its measurements—surely you know!
> Or who stretched the line upon it?
> On what were its bases sunk,
> or who laid its cornerstone,
> when the morning stars sang together
> and all the sons of God shouted for joy?" (Job 38:1–7)

Now turn to your Bible and continue reading through Job 40. Let your heart take in the grandeur of God's wisdom and power. Let your soul rest in jaw-dropping awe of his majesty. Then remember your own smallness and frailty. Let yourself be humbled by how little you know and how few things you are able to do. In any situation, location, or relationship, would it ever be possible for you to be smarter than God? That'd be utterly and laughably irrational. So laugh at the delusion of your own grandeur. Mock the illusion of your own glory. And in humble gratitude for grace that humbles, bow down and worship.

After you have bowed down and worshiped, get up and serve this God of awesome glory. Refuse to question his will. Refuse to let yourself think that his boundaries are misplaced. Be thankful his majesty is your protection, his glory is your motivation, his grace is your help, and his wisdom is your direction. He is infinitely smarter than you and me in our most brilliant moments.

Then Job answered the Lord and said:

> "Behold, I am of small account; what shall I answer you?
> I lay my hand on my mouth.
> I have spoken once, and I will not answer;
> twice, but I will proceed no further." (Job 40:3–5)

Reflect: Where do you find God's boundaries for your life annoying? What does that say about how smart you think God really is?

MARCH 16

Discontent is good if it makes you long for home, but bad if it makes you doubt the one who prepares a place for you in his home.

Answer me when I call, O God of my righteousness!
    You have given me relief when I was in distress.
Be gracious to me and hear my prayer!

O men, how long shall my honor be turned into shame?
    How long will you love vain words and seek after lies?
But know that the Lord has set apart the godly for himself;
    the Lord hears when I call to him.

Be angry, and do not sin;
    ponder in your own hearts on your beds, and be silent.
Offer right sacrifices,
    and put your trust in the Lord.

There are many who say, "Who will show us some good?
    Lift up the light of your face upon us, O Lord!"
You have put more joy in my heart
    than they have when their grain and wine abound.

In peace I will both lie down and sleep;
    for you alone, O Lord, make me dwell in safety. (Psalm 4)

These words were penned by David in one of the most heartbreaking moments of his life. He's hiding out in a cave because his son is out to take his throne. In this kind of kingdom, the only way to securely take a throne is by ending the life of the person who is on the throne. Imagine where your thoughts and emotions would go in a situation like this?

Is David content? Of course not. It appears that little good can come out of this moment in his life. Yet in his grief and discontent, he knows remarkable peace and even abundant joy! Why? Because at the deepest of levels, neither his peace nor his joy is based on the circumstances, but on the God who rules the circumstances. If David's security is in God and God alone, then he has as much security in that cave as he does in the palace. Why? Because it is the Lord alone who makes him dwell in safety. Only grace that can deliver us from fear and give our hearts rest even when we're in the cave once again.

But as for me, I will look to the Lord;
    I will wait for the God of my salvation;
    my God will hear me. (Mic. 7:7)

Reflect: What will it be for you today—the discontent of doubt and fear? Or the contentment of peace and rest?

MARCH 17

If you put too many things in your need category, you will end up frustrated with life, hurt by others, and doubting God's goodness.

"Need" is one of the sloppiest words used in human culture. If *need* means "essential for life," then most things we say we need, we don't actually need. Perhaps you've seen a kid at the mall, who stops at a shoe store and says, "Mom, I neeeeeeeed those sneakers." You look down at the kid's feet, which are encased in perfectly good shoes. Then you hear the mother say: "No, we're not getting those. You already have perfectly good shoes." Now, when the kid hears this, he does not think: "What a wise mother I have. She's seen through my distorted sense of need. And she's lovingly rescued me from my selfishness." No, this kid lashes out against the mom: "You always say no to me. I don't know why I have to have the one mom who hates sneakers." Then the kid refuses to talk for the rest of the time at the mall.

When you tell yourself that something is a need, three things follow. First, you feel entitled to the thing because, after all, it is a need. Second, because it is a need, you feel it's your right to demand it. And third, you then judge the love of another person by his or her willingness to deliver the thing. This happens in our relationships with one another and in our relationship with God. When you name something as a need and God doesn't deliver it, you begin to doubt his goodness. What's deadly about this is that you don't run for help to someone whose character you've come to doubt.

In Matthew 7:11, Jesus reminds us that we have a heavenly Father who knows exactly what we need, even though we don't really understand. We constantly get needs and wants confused. And Jesus also comforts us because, by grace, we have been made children of the wisest, most loving Father in the universe. We can rest in the grace that has made us his children, knowing that our place in his family guarantees that we will have what we need.

> If you then, who are evil, know how to give good gifts to your children, how much more will your Father who is in heaven give good things to those who ask him! (Matt. 7:11)

Reflect: What "need" do you see your friends enjoying that you do not have?

MARCH 18

Facing disappointment and failure? Don't be surprised—you're still flawed and your world is still fallen. For this, there's grace.

If you fail to take seriously what the Bible says about who we are and the world we live in, you will live with unrealistic expectations and disappointment. You'll also be naive when it comes to temptation. Let's examine what the Bible says about us and our world.

Although God's work of redemption has begun, you and I still live in a world that is terribly broken. It simply does not function in the beautiful way that God intended when he put it together. No passage captures the current brokenness of our world better than Romans 8. Paul employs three provocative phrases to capture this brokenness: "subjected to futility" (8:20), "bondage to decay" (8:21 NIV), and "in the pains of childbirth" (8:22). There is a constant futility to life in a fallen world. No matter how hard you try, you can't escape the frustration of a world that's not operating properly. There is decay all around. People die. Things die. Dreams die. Relationships die. Then there are times when the suffering is severe, just like the acute pain of childbirth. Under the weight of all this brokenness, Paul says that this world is "groaning together" (8:22).

The Bible also has clear and humbling things to say about you and me (1 John 1:8). Yes, the power of sin has been broken and God is progressively changing you by grace, but the presence of sin still remains inside us. So every day we all still carry around inside us the darkness of iniquity, transgression, and sin. We have not yet fully escaped the dire danger that is us.

Now, if you fail to take all this seriously, you won't seek your only hope: the forgiving, rescuing, protecting, transforming, and delivering grace of God. His grace alone has the power to protect you from the evil outside you and to deliver you from the evil that lives inside you.

In a real way, things are worse than you ever thought they could be. Yet God's grace is greater than you could ever have imagined it would be. Biblical faith lives at the intersection of shocking honesty and glorious hope.

> If we say we have no sin, we deceive ourselves, and the truth is not in us. (1 John 1:8)

Reflect: Why do you think it's so hard to be real about the brokenness inside us?

MARCH 19

Faith is about measuring your potential, not on the basis of your natural gifts and experience, but in the surety of God's presence and promises.

It is almost a humorous story. It's found in Judges 6:

> Now the angel of the LORD came and sat under the terebinth at Ophrah, which belonged to Joash the Abiezrite, while his son Gideon was beating out wheat in the winepress to hide it from the Midianites. And the angel of the LORD appeared to him and said to him, "The LORD is with you, O mighty man of valor. . . ." And the LORD turned to him and said, "Go in this might of yours and save Israel from the hand of Midian; do not I send you?" And he said to him, "Please, Lord, how can I save Israel? Behold, my clan is the weakest in Manasseh, and I am the least in my father's house." And the LORD said to him, "But I will be with you, and you shall strike the Midianites as one man." (Judg. 6:11–12, 14–16)

God calls Gideon to lead Israel in battle and calls him a "mighty man of valor." Where does he find this "mighty man"? He finds him threshing wheat (something you normally do outdoors) in a winepress (indoors). Why? Because Gideon is afraid of the very people whom God is going to call him to attack! God calls him a mighty man not because of Gideon's natural strength and courage, but because of what God will give him. We know this is true because God next says: "The LORD is with you" (6:12).

Then Gideon essentially says: "God, you must have the wrong address. I'm in the most inconsequential tribe in all of Israel. How could I save Israel?" Gideon both misunderstands who he is and who God is. If you fail to remember who God is in his power, glory, and grace, and if you forget who you are as a child in his family, you will always mismeasure your potential and your challenges. Thankfully, since God is with you, you have been blessed with wisdom and power beyond your own.

> God chose what is low and despised in the world, even things that are not, to bring to nothing things that are, so that no human being might boast in the presence of God. (1 Cor. 1:28–29)

Reflect: How is today's devotional saying something different than the common expression: "You've got this!"?

MARCH 20

Christ's sacrifice satisfied the Father's anger so that, as his child, you will receive his discipline but need not fear his wrath.

Here's the bottom line of your acceptance with God. *Jesus fully and completely satisfied the Father's anger so that you and I will never, ever again face the penalty for our sin.* You do not have to live in fear of God's anger. On your very worst, most rebellious, and most faithless day, you can run into the holy presence of your heavenly Father and he will not turn you away. Your acceptance has not been, nor will it ever be, based on your performance. You have not been welcomed into an eternal relationship with God because you have kept the law but because Jesus did. If you obey God for a thousand years, you will not have earned more of his acceptance than you were granted the very first moment you believed.

Since you are God's child and he loves you dearly, he disciplines you. But his discipline is not punishment for your sin because all of your punishment has been borne by your Savior, Jesus. By grace, his fatherly discipline aims to transform you, not penalize you. His careful, loving discipline doesn't earn your place in his family. Instead, it actually proves that you *are* one of his children.

So God's discipline is an instrument of his grace. It is a continuation of his work of personal heart-and-life transformation. God's discipline is not him turning his angry back on us. It is God turning his face of grace toward us once again, and he will continue to do this until his grace has finished its work.

> It is for discipline that you have to endure. God is treating you as sons. For what son is there whom his father does not discipline? If you are left without discipline, in which all have participated, then you are illegitimate children and not sons. Besides this, we have had earthly fathers who disciplined us and we respected them. Shall we not much more be subject to the Father of spirits and live? For they disciplined us for a short time as it seemed best to them, but he disciplines us for our good, that we may share his holiness. (Heb. 12:7–10)

Reflect: How do you feel when you perform better than you had hoped? Or how about when it's worse than you had hoped? How might the Father's unchanging love for you affect how you feel on your best and worst days?

MARCH 21

There is no need to be paralyzed by regret because your slate has been wiped clean by God's amazing, forgiving grace.

Let yourself bask today in the comfort of these passages:

> And you, who once were alienated and hostile in mind, doing evil deeds, he has now reconciled in his body of flesh by his death, in order to present you holy and blameless and above reproach before him. (Col. 1:21–22)
>
> For by grace you have been saved through faith. And this is not your own doing; it is the gift of God, not a result of works, so that no one may boast. (Eph. 2:8–9)
>
> And you, who were dead in your trespasses and the uncircumcision of your flesh, God made alive together with him, having forgiven us all our trespasses, by canceling the record of debt that stood against us with its legal demands. This he set aside, nailing it to the cross. (Col. 2:13–14)
>
> There is therefore now no condemnation for those who are in Christ Jesus. For the law of the Spirit of life has set you free in Christ Jesus from the law of sin and death. (Rom. 8:1–2)
>
> In this is love, not that we have loved God but that he loved us and sent his Son to be the propitiation for our sins. (1 John 4:10)

The message is clear! It is most clearly stated by that comfort-stimulating passage from Colossians 2, quoted above. Let your mind embrace the comfort of these words, comfort that is nowhere else to be found: God has canceled "the record of debt that stood against us with its legal demands. This he set aside, nailing it to the cross" (2:14).

If God has willingly canceled whatever regret causes you to hold on to, you are free to let it go as well. You are free to quit punishing yourself for debts that God has already canceled. Now, that's freedom!

> For if while we were enemies we were reconciled to God by the death of his Son, much more, now that we are reconciled, shall we be saved by his life. (Rom. 5:10)

Reflect: Do you struggle with regret? Because Jesus has freed you completely, how are you—your identity and self-image—so much more than your shame?

MARCH 22

Obedience is freedom. Better to follow the Master's plan than to do what you weren't wired to do—master yourself.

The greatest danger that we face is the danger that we are to ourselves, and we don't even realize it. If you have a younger brother or sister, you've likely seen this in them. They act like little kings or queens, who think they need no authority in their lives but themselves. Even if they cannot yet walk or speak, they reject your parent's wisdom and rebel against their authority. They have no idea what is good or bad to eat, but they fight your parent's every effort to put into their mouth something that they don't want. As they grow, your brothers or sisters have little ability to comprehend the danger of the electric wall outlet, but they try to stick their fingers in it precisely because they've been instructed not to. They want to exercise complete control over their sleep, diet, and activities. So they fight your parent's attempts to help them obey their loving authority.

Not only this, but they try to exercise authority over your parents as well. The little one is quick to tell them what to do. He lets them know when they have done something that he does not like. He celebrates when your parents submit to his desires and finds ways to punish them when they fail to submit to his demands.

Now, here's what you have to understand: you are more like your brother or sister than unlike them. We all want to rule our worlds. Each of us wants God to sign the bottom of our personal wish list. If he does, we celebrate his goodness. But if he doesn't, we begin to wonder if it's worth following him at all. Like little children, each of us is on a quest to be and to do what our Creator did not design us to be or do.

So grace comes to demolish our delusions of self-sufficiency. Grace works to destroy our dangerous hope to live as our own authority. Grace helps to make us reach out for what we really need and submit to the wisdom of the giver. Yes, it's true, grace rescues us from us.

> You are good and do good;
>   teach me your statutes. (Ps. 119:68)

Reflect: Do you resent an authority figure in your life? What might that say about your submission to God's authority?

MARCH 23

Because God rules all the places where you live, he is able to deliver his promises to you in the very circumstances where they are needed.

God's promises are only as good as the extent of his sovereignty. If his reign is not firm and unchanging, his promises are not either. I think that many of us fail to make this connection. When we do, we allow ourselves to celebrate his promises while subtly resisting his rule. He is your sovereign Savior.

Think for a moment about the many generations of people that existed between the fall of Adam and Eve and the birth of Jesus Christ. Think of the millions of situations, locations, and decisions that people made in that span of time. Think of the constant life-and-death cycle of the physical creation. Now consider this—in order for Jesus to be born as was promised (and live and die and rise on our behalf as he said he would), God had to exercise absolute rule. He would sovereignly rule over the forces of nature and over the events of human history so that, at just the right moment, Jesus would be born, live, die, and rise again for our redemption.

Without the rule of the Almighty, there would've been no prophets predicting the birth of the Messiah, no angels announcing it to the shepherds, and no Mary wondering about the babe in the manger. There would've been no miracles in Israel. There would've been no perfectly obedient Son of Man. There would've been no unjust trial and cruel cross. No gospel, no Scripture, no church, and no hope of eternal life.

If you are going to reach for the life-giving promises of the gospel, you must also celebrate the absolute rule of the sovereign Savior. Because of his reign, he is able to deliver those promises to you. Hope is not found in just the beauty of those promises, but in the infinite power and authority of the one who has made them. You can have hope because your Lord has complete rule over all the places where you will need his promises to become your reality.

> Ah, Lord God! It is you who have made the heavens and the earth by your great power and by your outstretched arm! Nothing is too hard for you. (Jer. 32:17)

Reflect: When have you been disappointed by people not keeping their promises? How has this affected the way you think about God's power and promises?

MARCH 24

Only the gargantuan glory of God can rescue you from all the miniglories of creation that regularly seduce and kidnap your heart.

Imagine that I decided to take my family to Walt Disney World in about a year's time. Imagine further that through the year, as the children lost sight of what was to come and complained about the sacrifices we were having to make, I sat down at the computer with my children and showed them the multifaceted sight-and-sound glories of Disney. Imagine now that finally we've loaded ourselves into the car and begun the long trip to this glorious place. And imagine that after many long hours of travel, we are coursing our way down the highway in Florida and we see a sign that says, "Walt Disney World 120 miles." Now, imagine that I park beside this sign, and we have our vacation there. You would think that I have lost my mind. Yet millions of people do that every day. Confused? Permit me to explain.

There is one thing that you know for sure—the sign is not the thing. The sign was created to only point you to where the thing can be found. The sign pointing to Walt Disney World will not ever give you what Walt Disney World can. So it is with the physical glories of creation.

Here's what you need to understand: only two types of glory exist—*sign* glory and *ultimate* glory. Sign glory is all the wondrous display of sights, sounds, colors, textures, tastes, smells, and experiences of the physical world that God created. These glories were not made to give you contentment, peace, meaning, and purpose. Rather, all of creation was designed to be one big sign that points you to the one of ultimate glory who alone has the power to give you life and to satisfy your heart. God alone is able to give rest to your searching heart. He designed his world to point to him, not to replace him (see Psalm 19). Your heart will only ever be satisfied when it finds its satisfaction in him.

> You shall eat in plenty and be satisfied,
>   and praise the name of the LORD your God,
>   who has dealt wondrously with you.
> And my people shall never again be put to shame. (Joel 2:26)

Reflect: Where will you look for life today? Will you live like the father having his vacation next to the sign along the highway? Or will you run to where the sign points?

MARCH 26

Today you'll encounter things that will confuse you, but rest assured the one who rules all those things is not confused.

When our children were very young and I would refuse to let them do something, they didn't understand why, so they would begin to protest. I would then get down on my knees so we could be face to face, and then I would talk with them. The conversation would go like this:

"Do you know that your daddy loves you?"

"Yes, I know my daddy loves me."

"Is your daddy mean and bad to you?"

"No, you don't like to be mean."

"Is your daddy a horrible, bad daddy?"

"No."

"Then listen to what daddy is going to say. I would like to tell you why I had to say no to what you wanted to do, but I can't. If I explained it to you, you wouldn't understand anyway, so here's what you need to do. You need to walk down the hallway and say to yourself, 'I don't know why daddy said no to me, but I know my daddy loves me and I'm going to trust my daddy.' I really do love you."

"I love you too."

There is so much that we don't understand. There is so much that we are incapable of understanding. So rest is found in trusting the Father. He is not confused, and he surely does have your best interest in mind. Yes, he will ask you to do hard things, and he will bring difficult things your way. Yet he is worthy of your trust and he loves you dearly. Today your heavenly Father reaches down to you and says: "I know you don't understand all that you face, but remember, I love you. Trust me and you will find peace that can be found no other way."

> Have you not known? Have you not heard?
> The LORD is the everlasting God,
> the Creator of the ends of the earth.
> He does not faint or grow weary;
> his understanding is unsearchable.
> He gives power to the faint,
> and to him who has no might he increases strength. (Isa. 40:28–29)

Reflect: Where do you wrestle with doubt? How can you turn that feeling of doubt into a childlike prayer of trust instead?

MARCH 25

We are often quick to anger and slow to love, but God is not like us. He's slow to anger and abounding in love.

You know the scene. Your family has rushed to the grocery store to get a important items. You hope to get in and out as quickly as is humanly poss You sprint down the aisles and grab your stuff, then run to the checkout l only to discover that the self-serve lanes are closed for repair and only one c is working. Just as you reach her lane, a woman pulls in front of you with a of 150 items. You can feel your chest tighten. It's not enough that she slo reexamines every item as she puts it on the belt, but after emptying her cart pulls out 120 coupons that have to be cross-checked with the correspond grocery items. You're beginning to get angry. Finally, her quest to save eve last penny is over, but then she discovers that she has to pay. It's as if it's a fre concept to her. Until this point, she has made no move toward her purse, whi is about the size of a camping tent for six. As she begins to pull makeup, coo ies, and small children out of her purse, you bellow, "Come on, are you kiddin me?" As everyone at the front of the store turns to look at you, you realize yo said it louder than you planned.

Examine the moment with me. You are livid at this woman, but she didn' purposefully delay you. You are seething, but you have lost only ten minutes ou of your day. You have not loved the woman in front of you because you wer too focused on yourself.

Isn't it comforting to know that God is the opposite of this? He has the righ and power to be angry with us. Yet he is in fact slow to anger. The Bible reassure us that he is abounding in love. Be thankful that God is not like us, that he i incredibly patient, that he does not treat you as your sins deserve. Be thankfu that because of the work of Jesus, he will respond to you with loving-kindnes even on your worst day.

> The LORD is slow to anger and abounding in steadfast love, forgiving iniquity and transgression. (Num. 14:18)

Reflect: Where are you most overwhelmed with anger—online, in-person, o just deep inside? The next time you feel irritation rise, what can you rememb about the Lord's patience with you?

MARCH 27

Get up and face life with courage because, as God's child, you have not been left to the limits of your own strength and wisdom.

Galatians 2:20 beautifully captures who you are as a child of God and what you have been given:

- **A statement of redemptive-historical fact.** "*I have been crucified with Christ*" (2:20). On the cross of Calvary, Jesus didn't die to make salvation possible. No, Jesus took names to the cross. His death was just as specifically effective for us as if we had died ourselves. Because he died as our representative, his death satisfied God's anger against us, so that we face it no more.
- **A statement of present redemptive reality.** "*It is no longer I who live, but Christ who lives in me*" (2:20). Paul's not talking about physical life here but spiritual. The power that now animates, motivates, and propels your spiritual life is not you but Christ! By grace, he makes you the place where he dwells. This means you are never in a situation, location, or relationship by yourself. He is always with you, and you are never left to the limited resources of your own wisdom, strength, and righteousness (see Eph. 3:20–21).
- **The life-shaping result.** "*The life I now live in the flesh I live by faith in the Son of God, who loved me and gave himself for me*" (Gal. 2:20). I place my faith in the fact of his death for me and his life within me. I live on that basis. I live with peace, hope, and courage, but not because I understand all that is going on inside me or around me. Yet I am sure that he is with me, he is in me, and he is for me. Here's the bottom line—I am comfortable with not knowing because he knows and he is with me forever.

Though the fig tree should not blossom,
    nor fruit be on the vines,
the produce of the olive fail
    and the fields yield no food,
the flock be cut off from the fold
    and there be no herd in the stalls,
yet I will rejoice in the Lord;
    I will take joy in the God of my salvation. (Hab. 3:17–18)

Reflect: What do you feel is most central to your identity? How does your being crucified with Christ challenge your view of who you are?

MARCH 28

You were hardwired for love, so everything you decide, desire, think, say, and do is an expression of love for someone or something.

You are a lover; we all are. We love. It's what human beings do every moment of every day, in every location, and in every situation. You are never not loving. It's in the very fiber of your being. It's the way God carefully constructed you. Why did he hardwire you to love? God created you with this capacity so that you would have what you need to live in a deeply loving, heart-controlling, motivation-producing, worship-initiating, joy-stimulating relationship with him. Your capacity to love was meant to draw you to him. So that your heart would find its final and complete fulfillment in him.

Here is the tragedy. Sin causes us all, in some way, to turn our backs on the love of God. Instead, we give the principal love of our hearts to someone or something else. We seek to have our hearts fulfilled by love for something other than God. We love the creation more than the Creator. We love ourselves so much that we have little energy left to love the one who is love. We run from thing to thing, hoping our hearts will be content in love. The Bible is the story of a love drama that looked as if it would end in tragedy—but then Jesus came.

You see, God, who is love, sent the Son of his love to make the ultimate sacrifice of love so that we would become people who love him as we have never loved him before. In love, he showers us with love that does not quit even on our most unloving day. And by grace, he transforms our hearts so that increasingly we are able to keep the ultimate love of our hearts for him and him alone. Now celebrate the gift of that rescuing love!

> Do not love the world or the things in the world. If anyone loves the world, the love of the Father is not in him. For all that is in the world—the desires of the flesh and the desires of the eyes and pride of life—is not from the Father but is from the world. And the world is passing away along with its desires, but whoever does the will of God abides forever. (1 John 2:15–17)

Reflect: What do your online habits and social media "likes" say about what you love?

MARCH 29

Living in this present broken world is designed by God to produce longing, readiness, and hope in me.

This fallen world isn't your home because God didn't think through his redemptive plan very well. You are living where you're living and facing what you're facing because that's exactly how God wanted it to be. The hardships that we all face are not a sign that God's redeeming work is failing, but rather a very important tool of it. God is daily employing the brokenness of this present world to clarify your values.

You need this because you struggle in this life to remember what is truly important, that is, what God says is important. You and I place much more importance on things than they truly possess. And when we do so, these things begin to claim our heart allegiance. So God planned for us to experience that physical things get old and break. The people in our lives fail us. Relationships sour and become painful. Our physical bodies weaken. Flowers die and food spoils. All of this is meant to teach us that these things are beautiful and enjoyable. Yet they cannot give us what we all long for—life.

And God is doing more with brokenness. In this world that is groaning, God is protecting our hearts . . . from us. We can worship God one day, only to turn and give the worship of our hearts to something else the next. So, in love, God lets pieces of the creation die in our hands. Why? So that increasingly we are freed from asking earth to give us what only he can give. He works through loss to protect us from giving our allegiance to things that will never deliver what our hearts seek. This is all designed to deepen our love and worship of him.

So in tender, patient grace, the Lord keeps you in a world that teaches you that he alone is worthy of the deepest, most worshipful allegiance of your heart.

> In this you rejoice, though now for a little while, if necessary, you have been grieved by various trials, so that the tested genuineness of your faith—more precious than gold that perishes though it is tested by fire—may be found to result in praise and glory and honor at the revelation of Jesus Christ. (1 Pet. 1:6–7)

Reflect: How are your sexual desires broken and difficult or confusing? How might God be using this brokenness by his grace to change and help you?

MARCH 30

If you are God's child, you're either giving in to sin or giving way to the operation of rescuing grace, but your heart's never neutral.

Here's a beautiful result of God's redeeming grace in your life and mine: that the hearts of stone have been taken out of us and replaced with hearts of flesh. Think of the word picture here. If I had a stone in my hands and I pressed it with all of my might, what do you think would happen? Well, if you could see the size of my arms, you would immediately know the answer to the question. I could press that stone with all of the strength that I have and nothing whatsoever would happen. Before your conversion, you had that kind of heart. It resisted change. But that is not true any longer. Grace has given you a fleshy heart, one that is moldable by transforming grace.

Now, this means that when you sin—when you desire, think, say, or do what is wrong in God's eyes, your conscience bothers you. What we're talking about here is the convicting ministry of the Holy Spirit. When your conscience bothers you, you have only two choices. You can gladly confess that what you've done is sin and place yourself once again under the justifying mercies of Christ. Or you can create some system of self-justification that takes what God says is wrong and makes it acceptable to your conscience.

Here's what's deadly about this. When you convince yourself that you are righteous, you quit seeking the grace that's your only hope in life or death. The fact of the matter is that not one of us are grace graduates, including the man who is writing this devotion. We are all in daily, desperate need of forgiving, rescuing, transforming, and delivering grace. When you resist humbly acknowledging your sin, you resist the ever-present Redeemer who is making that sin known to you. He's not humiliating or punishing you. Instead, it's because he loves you so much that he will not turn from his work of grace in your heart until that work has accomplished all that Jesus died to give you. Today you will resist grace or you will humbly run to grace. May the latter be your choice.

> If we confess our sins, he is faithful and just to forgive us our sins and to cleanse us from all unrighteousness. (1 John 1:9)

Reflect: Are there hidden sins in your life that you've been trying to hide from God as well? Take time to bring those sins to God's grace today.

MARCH 31

The cross is evidence that in the hands of the Redeemer, moments of apparent defeat become wonderful moments of grace and victory.

At the center of a biblical worldview is this radical recognition—the most horrible thing that ever happened was the most wonderful thing that ever happened. Consider the cross of Jesus Christ. Could it be possible for something more terrible to happen? Could any suffering or injustice be greater? The only man who ever lived a life that was perfect in every way possible, who gave his life for the sake of many, and who willingly obeyed and suffered from birth to death was cruelly and publicly murdered in the most vicious of ways. If something this horrible could happen, is there any hope for the world?

Well, the answer is yes. There is hope! The cross was not the end of the story! In God's righteous and wise plan, this dark and disastrous moment was ordained to fix all the dark and disastrous things that sin had done to the world. This moment of death was at the same time a moment of life. This hopeless moment was the moment when eternal hope was given. This terrible moment of injustice was at the very same time a moment of amazing grace. This moment of sadness welcomed us to eternal joy of heart and life. The capture and death of Christ purchased for us life and freedom. The very worst thing that could happen was, at the very same time, the very best thing that could happen. Only God is able to do such a thing.

The same God who planned that the worst thing would be the best thing is your Father. He takes the disasters in your life and makes them tools of redemption. He takes your failure and employs it as a tool of grace.

So be careful how you make sense of your life. What looks like a disaster may in fact be grace. What looks like the end may be the beginning. What looks hopeless may be God's instrument to give you real and lasting hope. Your Father is committed to taking what seems so bad and turning it into something that is very, very good.

> Let all the house of Israel therefore know for certain that God has made him both Lord and Christ, this Jesus whom you crucified. (Acts 2:36)

Reflect: What loss and pain have seemed hopeless and perhaps made you feel depressed? How does Jesus's death give you hope instead?

APRIL 1

Worshiping with other believers helps you view all of life from the vantage point of the resurrection of the Lord Jesus Christ.

The resurrection of Jesus is not just the most important miracle ever. It's not just the most astounding event in the life of the Messiah. It's not just an essential truth you believe. And it's not just your hope for the future. In addition to these, the resurrection is also meant to be the window through which you view all of life. But how do you look at life through the window of the resurrection? Let me suggest five things about the resurrection you must remember.

1. *The resurrection of Jesus guarantees your resurrection too.* Life is not a constantly repeating cycle of the same old same old. No, under God's rule this world is marching toward a conclusion. There will be a moment when God will raise you out of this broken world, and sin and suffering will be no more.
2. *The resurrection tells you what Jesus is now doing.* Jesus now reigns. Paul says that Jesus will continue to reign until the final enemy is under his feet (1 Cor. 15:25). You see, your world is not out of control. Instead, it's always under the careful control of one who is still doing his sin-defeating work.
3. *The resurrection promises you all the grace you need between Jesus's resurrection and yours.* If your destiny has already been guaranteed, then all the grace you need along the way has been guaranteed as well.
4. *The resurrection of Jesus motivates you to do what is right, no matter what you are facing.* The resurrection tells you that God will win. His truth will reign. Every part of his plan will be accomplished; nothing will be in vain.
5. *The resurrection tells you that you always have reason for thanks.* Quite apart from anything you have earned, you have been welcomed into the most exciting story ever. You have been granted a future of joy and peace forever.

No matter what happens today, look at life through this window.

> [We know] that he who raised the Lord Jesus will raise us also with Jesus and bring us with you into his presence. For it is all for your sake, so that as grace extends to more and more people it may increase thanksgiving, to the glory of God. (2 Cor. 4:14–15)

Reflect: It's easy to doubt in a broken world. How can Jesus's resurrection bring confidence even when some doubt still remains?

APRIL 2

Prayer is abandoning my addiction to other glories and delighting in the one glory that is truly glorious—the glory of God.

Sadly, for many of us, prayer is shrunk to basically asking God to sign our personal wish lists. If God comes through for us, we celebrate his faithfulness and love. But if he doesn't, we not only wonder if he cares, we are also tempted to wonder if he's even there. In this way, prayer often amounts to shopping at the divine department store for things that you have told yourself you need, and you just hope that they will be free.

But consider the Lord's Prayer for a moment. It doesn't look anything like what I've just described.

How does this prayer begin? It begins by reminding you of the most astounding reality of your life. It begins with a celebration of grace: "Our Father in heaven . . ." (Matt. 6:9). You and I must never stop celebrating this reality. God, the Creator, Savior, and King exercised his power and grace so that people like us would become his children. What's next? "Hallowed be your name" (6:9). Here I surrender myself to the agenda of agendas. It is why you and I, and the world, were created: so that God would get the glory that he is due. Here I let go of all the other glories that may lay claim to my wandering heart. Here I cry out for rescuing grace for my disloyal heart.

Then this model prayer hits its bottom line. The next words contain a comfort and a call: "Your kingdom come, your will be done, on earth as it is in heaven" (6:10). The comfort is that the Father has graciously blessed us with his rule, which is always wise, loving, faithful, true, and good, and in so doing, rescues us from our little kingdoms of one. The call is to let go of our Vise-Grip hold on our tiny kingdoms and give ourselves to his kingdom of glory and grace. It is only when our hearts have been protected by the worship and celebration of these requests that we are able to properly pray what comes next.

> But when you pray, go into your room and shut the door and pray to your Father who is in secret. And your Father who sees in secret will reward you. (Matt. 6:6)

Reflect: What scares you most about asking God for his will to be done? Why?

APRIL 3

Obedience never ends freedom; it is the evidence that true freedom has entered your life and liberated your heart.

Human beings need boundaries. Even Adam and Eve needed boundaries, although they were living as perfect people in a perfect world and in a perfect relationship with God. No human being has enough knowledge or wisdom to be able to set his or her own boundaries. Only the Creator—who knows his creatures, this world he's made, and how life works best—can lay down the right set of boundaries. God's boundaries, that is, his laws, are an expression of his love for us. They protect us from danger and draw us toward a deeper dependency and communion with him. God the Father, in his word, does not do that to rob us of our freedom and joy. Instead, he wants to free us from the bondage and sadness that always result when sinners choose their own way.[4]

I have been liberated,
set free,
and given new life,
new hope,
new motivation,
and new peace
of heart and mind.
No, I have not been freed
from the authority of
another.
I have not been freed
to walk my own way,
to write my own rules,
or to do what I choose.
No, I have been given
the best of freedoms.
I have been freed,
not from God's rule,
but from my bondage
to me.
Following,
obeying,
serving,
submitting to God
is the thing I was created to do,
so it is the place where
true freedom is to be found.
Rebellion never gives life.
Self-rule never brings freedom.
So grace has worked to rescue
me from me,
so that I can know the true
freedom
of serving him.

Now the Lord is the Spirit, and where the Spirit of the Lord is, there is freedom. (2 Cor. 3:17)

Reflect: Where do you still feel in bondage to yourself and your own desires? Confess that to the Lord and ask him to help you submit to his authority. Ask him to give you true freedom in serving him.

APRIL 4

Human beings, who were created to live in awe of God, are in grave danger when familiarity causes them to be bored with God.

Familiarity is a beautiful thing. For example, it's wonderful to be familiar with a beautiful song. It means you've been blessed to hear it over and over again. But the blessing of blessings is to be familiar with the ways, the character, the presence, and the promises of God. That means that grace has bridged the separation between you and God, and has drawn you into close communion with him. It also means that the Spirit of God has opened your heart to the things of God. Now the things that were once foolishness to you, instead bring you hope, comfort, and joy.

However, familiarity can also be a very dangerous thing. What happens when you are near something so it becomes more familiar? You actually see and appreciate that thing less than you once did. Remember how excited you were last Christmas? But something has happened to those amazing gifts. You don't really see them as fun as you used to. Familiarity can be a dangerous thing.

Now, here's the vertical connection. Every human being was designed by God to have his hopes, dreams, choices, words, actions, desires, and motivations shaped by a jaw-dropping, life-shaping awe of God. But something happens to us as we are drawn into a close relationship with God and are blessed to live close to his secret things. Familiarity causes us to lose our awe of God. What once stunned us doesn't anymore. What produced worship in our hearts doesn't anymore. What caused us to act with hope and courage and obedience doesn't anymore. I am afraid that many of us have lost our awe of God, and we don't even know it.

> And one called to another and said:
>
> "Holy, holy, holy is the Lord of hosts;
> the whole earth is full of his glory!"
>
> And the foundations of the thresholds shook at the voice of him who called, and the house was filled with smoke. And I said: "Woe is me! For I am lost; for I am a man of unclean lips, and I dwell in the midst of a people of unclean lips; for my eyes have seen the King, the Lord of hosts!" (Isa. 6:3–5)

Reflect: Is there evidence in your life that you are awe deficient? Cry out for eyes to see once again, for a heart gripped by awe once again.

APRIL 5

Rejoice; the Lord who has redeemed you is worthy of your love and worship.

You should enjoy food because it is God's gift. However, if you *love* it, you'll end up fat and unhealthy. You should be thankful for the money that God provides, but if you *love* it, you will find yourself a workaholic or in debt. Surely you should celebrate the pleasures and comforts that God puts in your life, but if you love them, you will soon be addicted.

Here is the spiritual reality you need to understand—*if you love the gifts and not the giver, your heart will never be satisfied. However, if you love the giver, your heart will be content and you will be able to enjoy his gifts while keeping them in their proper place.* Beneath this reality are even deeper spiritual realities. Every human being's life is designed to be a quest to be loved and to find something to love. This means that whatever commands the love of your heart also shapes the direction of your life. But there is more to be said. You were also created to worship. You don't just occasionally worship in moments at church services; you are a worshiper. You are always looking for something to which you can attach your identity, your hopes and dreams, and your inner peace. Whatever controls the worship of your heart controls your choices, words, emotions, and actions.

Now, because you are a sinner, it is very tempting to give the love and worship, that you were meant to give to God alone, to something in the creation (see Rom. 1:22–25). We all do this in some way. So the desire for good possessions or comfort is not wrong, but it must not rule your heart. The desire for the love of another person is not wrong, but it must not rule your heart. *A desire for even a good thing becomes a bad thing when that desire becomes a ruling thing.*

Grace works to rescue you from you by gradually breaking your bondage to the created world and turning the deepest affection of your heart toward God. Yes, grace is at work, yet our hearts and our loyalties are still confused. But we need not fret because grace will win and bring final rest to our worship and our love.

We love because he first loved us. (1 John 4:19)

Reflect: What do your addictive patterns and habits say about your heart?

APRIL 6

Don't be discouraged at the spiritual war you're called to fight every day. The Lord almighty is with you and wars on your behalf.

Life is war. It can be exhausting, frustrating, and discouraging. We all go through moments when we wish life could just be easier. We wonder why relating to parents seems to be such a continual battle. We all wish our friendships could be free of war. We all would love it if there were no conflicts at church or school. This world has been broken by sin and is constantly under the attack of the enemy. At the end of Ephesians, Paul concludes by talking about spiritual warfare (see the passage below).

Yet as you read, it's tempting to think that he has entirely changed the subject. No longer, it seems, is he talking about everyday Christianity. But that's exactly what he's talking about. He is saying to the Ephesian believers, "You know all that I've said about marriage, parenting, communication, anger, the church, and so on—it's all one big spiritual war." Paul is reminding you that daily Christianity is war. There really is an enemy. There really is temptation. You really are spiritually vulnerable. But he says more. He reminds you that by grace you have been properly armed for the battle.

> Finally, be strong in the Lord and in the strength of his might. Put on the whole armor of God, that you may be able to stand against the schemes of the devil. For we do not wrestle against flesh and blood, but against the rulers, against the authorities, against the cosmic powers over this present darkness, against the spiritual forces of evil in the heavenly places. Therefore take up the whole armor of God, that you may be able to withstand in the evil day, and having done all, to stand firm. Stand therefore, having fastened on the belt of truth, and having put on the breastplate of righteousness, and, as shoes for your feet, having put on the readiness given by the gospel of peace. In all circumstances take up the shield of faith, with which you can extinguish all the flaming darts of the evil one; and take the helmet of salvation, and the sword of the Spirit, which is the word of God, praying at all times in the Spirit, with all prayer and supplication. (Eph. 6:10–18)

Reflect: Today how will you use the implements of battle that the cross of Jesus Christ has provided for you?

APRIL 7

Corporate worship is designed to confront you with a view of life that has at its center a dead man's cross and a living man's empty tomb.

There are two themes that I have repeated in writing and speaking again and again. I will repeat them here:

1. Human beings made in the image of God do not live life based on the facts of their experience but based on their interpretation of the facts. Whether you know it or not, you have been designed by God to be a meaning maker. You have a constant desire for life to make sense. You don't actually respond to what is going on around you. You respond to your understanding of what is going on around you. This means that you always carry around some kind of interpretive grid or wisdom that helps you to make sense out of your life.

2. No one is more influential in your life than you are because no one talks to you more than you do. We never stop talking to ourselves—about God, others, ourselves, meaning and purpose, identity, and such. The things you say to you about you, God, and life are profoundly important because they form and shape the way you then respond to the things that God has put on your plate. You see, you are always preaching to yourself some kind of worldview, some kind of "gospel," if you will. The question is, in your private moment-by-moment conversation, what are you saying to you?

Paul argues very powerfully that the "cross and empty tomb" gospel of the Lord Jesus Christ, which the world sees as utter foolishness, is in fact the wisest of wisdom. It is the only way to make sense out of life. It is the only kind of wisdom that really does give a final and reliable answer to the fundamental questions of life. And at the center of this message of wisdom is not a set of ideas but a person. And this person, in his life and death, offers you not only answers, but every grace you need: to be what you were created to be and to do what you have been called to do.

> For the word of the cross is folly to those who are perishing, but to us who are being saved it is the power of God. (1 Cor. 1:18)

Reflect: How does the fact that Jesus left heaven and gave up his life affect the way you view your life and personal identity?

APRIL 8

God uses the picture of physical food to point to universal spiritual hunger. Life is all about what we look to to fill us.

Come, everyone who thirsts,
come to the waters;
and he who has no money,
come, buy and eat!
Come, buy wine and milk
without money and without price.
Why do you spend your money for that which is not bread,
and your labor for that which does not satisfy?
Listen diligently to me, and eat what is good,
and delight yourselves in rich food. (Isa. 55:1–2)

These words from Isaiah are beautiful! They invite you to feast on God's grace. And they are spoken in a language that we can all understand.

When was the last time you were hungry, even after a meal? You know what it's like—to consume a meal and find it just doesn't satisfy. The Bible uses this powerful food metaphor because there's an even deeper hunger within you!

Yes, your body hungers to be filled with food, but your soul hungers even more. This is true for all of us. Every person who has ever lived has worked to satisfy the hunger of his soul in some way.

When you want this food for your soul, you've got only two options—two feast tables. You can try to fill your soul at the costly, unsatisfying table of the physical world. Or you can accept the Lord's invitation to the soul-satisfying table of his abundant mercy and grace.

So God's question for you today is this: "Why do you spend your money for that which is not bread, and your labor for that which does not satisfy?" It is a question worth considering.

> Truly, truly, I say to you, whoever believes has eternal life. I am the bread of life. Your fathers ate the manna in the wilderness, and they died. This is the bread that comes down from heaven, so that one may eat of it and not die. I am the living bread that came down from heaven. If anyone eats of this bread, he will live forever. (John 6:47–51)

Reflect: What do you hunger for in your soul? How will you seek to satisfy that hunger?

APRIL 9

Don't be discouraged today. Yes, you're aware of your weaknesses and failures, but for each of them there's forgiving, transforming grace.

When you read the passage below, it doesn't seem right. It seems that you've entered some topsy-turvy, inside-out universe. But Paul is both serious and dead right in what he says in 2 Corinthians 12:7–10.

Fasten your seat belts; here we go. God chooses for you to be weak in order to protect you from you. And he wants you to value the strength that only he can give. In this way, your weaknesses are not signs of his lack of care. They are not indications that the Bible contradicts itself when it says that God will meet all of your needs. No, these weaknesses are tools of his amazing grace. They protect you from the arrogance of self-reliance that tempts us all. They remind you that you are needy and were created to be dependent on one greater than you. They cause you to do what all of us in some way resist doing—humbly running to God for the help that only he can give.

So your weaknesses are not the big danger that you should fear. What you should really fear are your delusions of strength. When you tell yourself that you are strong, you quit being excited about God's rescuing, transforming, and empowering grace. Paul actually celebrated his weaknesses. Why? Because as he did, the power of God rested upon him. He didn't live a fearful, discouraged, and envious life; he was content because he knew weakness is the doorway to real power, power that only God can and willingly supplies.

> So to keep me from becoming conceited because of the surpassing greatness of the revelations, a thorn was given me in the flesh, a messenger of Satan to harass me, to keep me from becoming conceited. Three times I pleaded with the Lord about this, that it should leave me. But he said to me, "My grace is sufficient for you, for my power is made perfect in weakness." Therefore I will boast all the more gladly of my weaknesses, so that the power of Christ may rest upon me. For the sake of Christ, then, I am content with weaknesses, insults, hardships, persecutions, and calamities. For when I am weak, then I am strong. (2 Cor. 12:7–10)

Reflect: Where do you feel weak in comparison to your friends? How might God want to use this weakness in your life?

APRIL 10

Faith in Christ is not just about knowing the truths of the gospel, but about living them as well.

It is vital to know that faith is not just an action of your brain. It's also an investment of your life. Faith is not just something you think; it's something you live. Hear these words from Hebrews 11:

> Now faith is the assurance of things hoped for, the conviction of things not seen. For by it the people of old received their commendation. By faith we understand that the universe was created by the word of God, so that what is seen was not made out of things that are visible.
>
> By faith Abel offered to God a more acceptable sacrifice than Cain, through which he was commended as righteous, God commending him by accepting his gifts. And through his faith, though he died, he still speaks. By faith Enoch was taken up so that he should not see death, and he was not found, because God had taken him. Now before he was taken he was commended as having pleased God. And without faith it is impossible to please him, for whoever would draw near to God must believe that he exists and that he rewards those who seek him. (11:1–6)

What is faith? Biblical faith has this foundation—you must believe that God exists (11:6). This is the watershed, the great divide. There are only two types of people in this world: (1) those who believe that the most important fact that a human being could ever consider and consider to be true is the existence of God, and (2) those who either casually or philosophically deny his existence. But intellectual commitment to God's existence is not all that faith is about. Faith means you live as though you believe in God's existence, or as though you believe, as the writer says, "He rewards those who seek him" (11:6).

Faith is a deep-seated belief in the existence of God that also radically alters the way you live your life. Now, here's the rub. Biblical faith isn't natural for us. So we even need God's grace to believe in the one whose grace we so desperately need. And that grace is yours for the asking again today.

> For as the body apart from the spirit is dead, so also faith apart from works is dead. (James 2:26)

Reflect: Is your faith in God visible in your regular responsibilities and interests or hobbies?

APRIL 11

God will not rest from his redemptive work until every aspect of his creation has been made new again.

It was written in 1719 by the great hymn writer Isaac Watts. He wrote it as a part of his *Psalm of David Imitated* and never intended it to be a Christmas carol. But "Joy to the World" has become one of the most beloved carols ever written. With all of its powerful lyrics, the third verse of this hymn is particularly profound and encouraging:

> No more let sins and sorrows grow,
> Nor thorns infest the ground;
> He comes to make his blessings flow
> Far as the curse is found,
> Far as the curse is found,
> Far as, far as the curse is found.[5]

What was the mission of Jesus? What is the promise of the bloody cross and the empty tomb? What is the scope of the work of redemption? What does the final chapter of the grand redemptive story look like? The words of this great old hymn capture it with accuracy and power. Jesus really did come "to make his blessings flow." That is true to say, but it's not enough. You must add, "far as the curse is found." You see, Jesus didn't simply come to rescue only souls. Yes, thank God he saves our souls from eternal damnation. But he also came to unleash his powerful restoring grace as far as the furthest effect of sin. He came to restore every single thing that sin has broken. He came to fix it all! His redemptive mission is as complete as sin's destruction is comprehensive.

Are you tired of the futility and frustration of this broken world? Are you exhausted by sin, suffering, and death? At times, do you wonder if anyone knows, if anyone understands, or if anyone cares? Then the words of this great hymn and this encouraging passage from the final book of the Bible (below) are for you. Your Redeemer knows. Your Redeemer understands. Your Redeemer cares. His grace has been unleashed, and its work will not be done until every last sin-broken thing has been fully and completely made new again. Be encouraged, your Redeemer is at work!

> Behold, I am making all things new. (Rev. 21:5)

Reflect: What aspect of your emotions do you feel most needs Jesus's restoring work? Will you call out to him today to make even that broken feeling new?

APRIL 12

If God is your Father, the Son is your Savior, and the Spirit is your indwelling Helper, you have hope no matter what you're facing.

Who in the world do you think you are? I'm serious. Who do you think you are? You and I are always assigning to ourselves some kind of identity. And that identity shapes our actions and lives. So it's important to acknowledge that God has not just forgiven you (and that is a wonderful thing), but he has also given you a brand-new identity. If you're God's child, you are now a son or daughter of the King of kings and the Lord of lords. You are in the family of the Savior, who is your friend and brother. You are the temple where the Spirit of God now lives. Yes, it really is true—you've been given a radically new identity.

The problem, sadly, is that many of us live in a constant, or at least a rather regular, state of *identity amnesia*. We forget who we are, and when we do, we begin to give way to doubt, fear, and timidity. It makes you feel alone when in fact, since the Spirit lives inside of you, it is impossible for you to be alone. You feel unloved when in fact, as a child of the heavenly Father, you have been graced with eternal love. You feel like you don't measure up when in fact the Savior measured up on your behalf. Identity amnesia sucks the life out of your Christianity.

If you've forgotten who you are in Christ, what are you left with? You're left with *Christless Christianity*, which is little more than a system of theology and rules. And you know that if all you needed was theology and rules, Jesus wouldn't have had to come. All God would have needed to do was drop the Bible down on you and walk away. But he didn't walk away; he invaded your life as Father, Savior, and Helper. By grace, he made you a part of his family. By grace, he made you the place where he lives. And he did all this so that you not only would receive his forgiveness, but so that you would have everything you need for life and godliness.

> See what kind of love the Father has given to us, that we should be called children of God; and so we are. (1 John 3:1)

Reflect: What does your anxiety say about how you view yourself and your identity?

APRIL 13

God's story has a beginning and an end that never ends, and if you're God's child, his story is now your biography. Wow!

Whether it's a TV drama, a box-office hit movie, or a million-seller novel, we tend to line up for the good story. Or maybe someone tells you a fantastic story, and you can't wait to tell it to someone else. We all love a good story.

Now, most great stories are great because, through myriad characters, relationships, situations, and locations, they march you to an incredible ending. When someone is talking to you about a great movie or book, he'll often say, "And you will just not believe the ending!" But the best story ever conceived, written, and acted out in real life is the best story precisely because it has no ending. The one story you need to know and understand is hopeful, encouraging, and life-transforming because it offers you the two wonderful things that no other story can. First, it offers you a place in the story, a place that was planned for you long before the story was written. But it also offers you something that is hard for the human brain to grasp and the human imagination to envision. It offers you life that never, ever ends.

We are all so used to death that we sadly think of it as a normal part of life. Things die, people die, end of story. But that's not the end of this story. God's amazing story of redemption, which is written for you on the pages of your Bible, is radically different because in this story, death dies. Yes, you read it right. The main character of God's story (which is your story if you're his child) comes to earth and defeats sin and death. And because he does, he offers us the one thing that no other character in no other story can offer us—real life now and eternal life to come.

Quite apart from anything you have ever achieved, earned, or deserved as God's child, you have been welcomed into the best story ever by grace and grace alone. And thankfully, this story that is your story has an end that never ends.

> Truly, truly, I say to you, whoever hears my word and believes him who sent me has eternal life. He does not come into judgment, but has passed from death to life. (John 5:24)

Reflect: Compare and contrast the plot of your favorite movie with the story described above.

APRIL 14

You can rest in God's care. If he freely offered up his Son for you, will he forget you now?

Pay attention to the comforting logic of redemption, so powerfully captured by Paul in Romans 8:31–39 (below). Now, it simply defies redemptive logic to allow yourself to think that God would go to the extent to provide you with salvation and then lose you along the way. If he controlled nature and history so that at the right time Jesus came to live, die, and rise again on your behalf; if he worked by grace to expose you to the truth and gave you the heart to believe; and if he now works to bring the events of the universe to a final glorious conclusion, does it make any sense to think that he would fail to provide you with everything you truly need?

Paul is arguing that God's gift of and sacrifice of his Son is your guarantee that he will grace you with every good thing you need. You do not have to fear that he will leave you on your own. You do not have to wonder if he will be there for you in your moment of need. If he gave you Jesus, he will give you along with him everything you need.

> What then shall we say to these things? If God is for us, who can be against us? He who did not spare his own Son but gave him up for us all, how will he not also with him graciously give us all things? Who shall bring any charge against God's elect? It is God who justifies. Who is to condemn? Christ Jesus is the one who died—more than that, who was raised—who is at the right hand of God, who indeed is interceding for us. Who shall separate us from the love of Christ? Shall tribulation, or distress, or persecution, or famine, or nakedness, or danger, or sword? As it is written,
>
> "For your sake we are being killed all the day long;
> we are regarded as sheep to be slaughtered."
>
> No, in all these things we are more than conquerors through him who loved us. For I am sure that neither death nor life, nor angels nor rulers, nor things present nor things to come, nor powers, nor height nor depth, nor anything else in all creation, will be able to separate us from the love of God in Christ Jesus our Lord. (Rom. 8:31–39)

Reflect: In what areas do you struggle most with doubt? How does the rational logic of Romans 8:31–39 help you doubt your doubt?

APRIL 15

Since my need for spiritual help is so great, the Bible teaches that I need the daily intervention of the body of Christ.

It really is true—your walk with God is a community project. The isolated, separated, Jesus-and-me religion often marks modern church culture. Yet it's not the religion that is described in the New Testament. Many of us live in endless networks of constantly casual relationships. Our conversations seldom go deeper than the weather, food, politics, the coolest movie that's out, or the latest cute thing on your favorite social media platform. Most of what we call "fellowship" never really rises to the level of the humble self-disclosure and mutual ministry that make fellowship actually worthwhile according to the Bible.

Hebrews 3:12–13 describes the essence of community, and relates it to the work that God has done and is continuing to do in you and me: "Take care, brothers, lest there be in any of you an evil, unbelieving heart, leading you to fall away from the living God. But exhort one another every day, as long as it is called 'today,' that none of you may be hardened by the deceitfulness of sin."

I need the daily intervention of the body of Christ because I am a blind man spiritually. And as long as there is still sin inside me there will be pockets of blindness in how I view myself. It's actually more serious than what I have just described. Here's why. Every physically blind person knows that he is blind, but spiritually blind people are blind to their blindness. They actually think that they see, when in fact they don't.

What about you? Have you embraced your daily need for the help of the body of Christ? When someone who knows you points out a sin, a weakness, or a failure, are you thankful? Or do you feel your chest tighten and your ears get red as you silently prepare yourself to rise to your own defense? Are you skilled at giving non-answers to personal questions? Or, instead, do you run toward the daily help that God has provided? That help is not something to be afraid of or shy away from because it is a tool of God's forgiving, rescuing, transforming, and delivering grace.

Now you are the body of Christ and individually members of it. (1 Cor. 12:27)

Reflect: Who really knows you? Whom have you invited to intrude into your private space to help you see more clearly?

APRIL 16

What could comfort you more than these words: "I came that they may have life and have it abundantly" (John 10:10)?

Everybody searches for life somewhere. God has placed this quest in each of our hearts. It is there to drive us to the one we were made for. But sadly, in their life-long quest for life, most people ignore God. In their God amnesia, they look for life where it cannot be found. And because they do, they always come up empty.

It's important to realize that you can search for life in only two places. Either you have found life to the fullest vertically or you are shopping for it horizontally. This is a major piece of Romans 1:25: "They exchanged the truth about God for a lie and worshiped and served the creature rather than the Creator, who is blessed forever! Amen." What is that lie? It is the cruel lie first told in the garden of Eden—that heart-satisfying life could be found somewhere outside the Creator. If you believe it, it will not only leave you empty and discouraged, but it will set your life on a course of destruction.

The physical, created world is full of engaging and entertaining delights. However, the delights of the physical world were carefully crafted to point to the one who alone is able to bring the deepest joy and contentment to your heart. He alone is able to give you a reason for getting up in the morning and a purpose for living. So in amazing grace, he welcomes you to surrender all your hopes and dreams to him.

And again today, he promises you life. It's what he came to live, die, and rise again to give you. That empty tomb not only means he has conquered death, but it also tells you he has life in his hands. You can't find or earn that life on your own. It is yours only by means of the work of another.

> Jesus said to her, "Everyone who drinks of this water will be thirsty again, but whoever drinks of the water that I will give him will never be thirsty again. The water that I will give him will become in him a spring of water welling up to eternal life." (John 4:13–14)

Reflect: Could it be today that you will fretfully search horizontally for what you have already been given in Christ? Will you try to drink from an empty well when you have already been given thirst-quenching living water?

APRIL 17

Faith means you take God at his word, you never let yourself think that you're smarter than him, and you live inside his boundaries.

Faith is a response of your heart to God that completely changes the way you live your life. Faith so completely takes God at his word that you're willing to do what he says and stay inside his boundaries. You don't just think by faith; you live by faith.

Now, this kind of real, living faith means two things. First, faith is simply never natural for us. We tend to live by sight, personal experience, collective research, or good old intuition, but faith isn't natural. It's natural to wonder about mysteries in your life you'll never solve. It's natural to imagine where you'll be in ten or twenty years. It's natural to wonder why someone else's life has turned out so very differently from yours. But putting your entire existence in the hands of one whom you cannot see, touch, or hear is far from natural. This is why faith is only ever a gift of divine grace. So if you are living by faith, don't proudly pat yourself on the back as if you did something great. No, raise your eyes and your hands toward heaven and thank God for gifting you with the desire and ability to believe.

Second, participating in activities of Christianity is a part of a life of faith, but it doesn't mean you're a person of faith. You can praise God for his wisdom in that service on Sunday but be breaking his law on Tuesday. You can sing in thanks for his grace on Sunday and resist the work of that grace the rest of the week. It's so easy to swindle yourself into believing that you're living by faith when you're really not. So look into the mirror of Hebrews 11 and examine your faith. You don't need to do that fearfully, anxious at what you'll see. You don't need to deny the reality of your spiritual struggle. You don't have to fear exposure because your struggle of faith has been more than adequately addressed by the grace of the cross of the Lord Jesus. Run to him and confess the off-and-on-again faith of your heart. He will not turn you away.

> Immediately the father of the child cried out and said, "I believe; help my unbelief!" (Mark 9:24)

Reflect: Are you afraid to get real about your faith—or lack of faith? Why?

APRIL 18

You have no reason for fear when you answer God's call; you have every reason to be afraid when you put your life in your own hands.

The Bible is dotted with story after story of people who were scared to death to answer God's call. Moses did everything he could to get out of going back to Egypt, confronting Pharaoh, and leading the children of Israel out (Exodus 3–4). Gideon also argued with God, sure that it had to be a divine mistake for him to be called as the one who would lead Israel against the Midianites (Judges 6). God had to assure Joshua that he need not be afraid to lead Israel into the land of promise (Joshua 1). The people of Israel rebelled against the Lord and refused to go into Canaan because they were afraid of being destroyed by the Amorites (Deuteronomy 1). Peter was afraid to identify himself as a disciple of Jesus and with anxious curses denied his Lord (Matt. 26:69–75).

Each moment of fear, each act of refusal, was an act of spiritual irrationality. Each fearful person had been invited to be part of the massive work of the kingdom of God. The one who called them created the world and holds it together by his will. He powerfully rules every situation, location, and relationship in which his call is to be followed. He is saving, forgiving, transforming, and delivering. What he says is always best and what he requires is always good. When he calls, he goes with you. What he calls you to do, he empowers by his grace. When he guides, he protects. He stands with power and faithfulness behind every one of his promises. He has never failed to deliver anything that he has promised. There is simply no risk in answering the call of the King of kings.

Only grace can work to remind us that faith in God is a resting place and trust in self is a minefield. It is grace and grace alone that empowers us to follow and to rest.

> Woe to those who go down to Egypt for help
>   and rely on horses,
> who trust in chariots because they are many
>   and in horsemen because they are very strong,
> but do not look to the Holy One of Israel
>   or consult the LORD! (Isa. 31:1)

Reflect: What call of God are you afraid of answering? Which truth (above) could you hold on to as you face your fear and answer God's call?

APRIL 19

It is grace to not be paralyzed by regret. The cross teaches that you are not stuck, not cursed to pay forever for your past.

He sat before me with his head in his hands and kept saying over and over again: "I just wish I could have it all back. I just wish I could press a button and do it all over again. I wish I knew then what I know now. I wish I could try again, but I can't." He was incredibly distraught and regretful. I really did feel his pain, and I was very happy that he felt it too because I knew that what he was experiencing was the pain of grace.

He was a hard, driven, and demanding man who kept moving forward no matter what and never looked back. He didn't care what trail of destruction he left behind him. He had loved his work more than his family, and in the process, he had lost it all—family, job, and wealth. But now his eyes were open, and the scene broke his heart. Bankrupt and alone, he looked back with grief at every arrogant moment. It was painful, but it was grace. God was making his eyes see, so that he would never go back there again.

It's a grace to regret. Grace allows you to face your sin, to own it and not shift the blame. Grace forces you to feel the pain of your regrets, not be paralyzed by them. Grace never asks you to pay for them because the price has already been paid by Jesus.

This means you don't have to rewrite your past, making yourself look more righteous than you ever really were. You can stare the truth in the face because of what Jesus has done for you. You can own what needs to be owned and confess what needs to be confessed, and then move on to live in a new and better way. The same grace that forgives your past empowers you to live in a new way in the future.

> And you, who were dead in your trespasses and the uncircumcision of your flesh, God made alive together with him, having forgiven us all our trespasses, by canceling the record of debt that stood against us with its legal demands. This he set aside, nailing it to the cross. (Col. 2:13–14)

Reflect: If you could, what would you go back and tell yourself five years ago? What do you think you might come back in five years and tell yourself now?

APRIL 20

Grace doesn't make it okay for you to live for you. No, grace frees you to experience the joy of living for one greater than you.

It is universally true that what seems to us to be freedom isn't really freedom after all. When Adam and Eve stepped outside of God's boundaries, they didn't step into freedom. They stepped into toil, temptation, suffering, sin, and bondage.

You and I weren't designed to live independently either. We weren't meant to live in our own strength. We weren't given the ability to write our own moral codes. We weren't put together with the independent knowledge of how to live, how to steward the physical world, or how to properly relate to one another. We were not created to live *by* ourselves or *for* ourselves, and to attempt to do so never leads anywhere good.

So as God blesses us and changes us with his grace, the result isn't a greater ability to live an independent life. The opposite is true. The purpose of God's grace is to free you from your slavery to yourself so that you can live for a much, much better kingdom. True freedom is never found in putting yourself at the center. Real freedom is only ever found when God's grace liberates you to live for one infinitely greater than you.

It contradicts our normal thinking, but the doorway to freedom is submission. When I acknowledge that I am a danger to myself and submit to the authority, wisdom, and grace of God, I am not killing my hopes for freedom. The opposite is true. Humble admission of need and humble submission to God open me up to the freest of lives. I was created to live in worshipful and obedient dependency on God. And when grace restores me to that place, it also gives me back my freedom. It may seem constricting that the train always has to ride on those tracks, but try driving it in a meadow and all motion stops. So grace puts you back on the tracks again and gives you the freedom of forward motion, which you can have no other way.

> And he died for all, that those who live might no longer live for themselves but for him who for their sake died and was raised. (2 Cor. 5:15)

Reflect: Where do you feel restricted by God's rules? How do these restrictions actually show grace and give you life?

APRIL 21

You obey not to get God's attention, but because you have been the object of his attention since before the world began.

Your obedience is never to be done in the hope that you will get something, but rather in recognition of what you have already been given. Carefully read the following words from Ephesians 1:

> Blessed be the God and Father of our Lord Jesus Christ, who has blessed us in Christ with every spiritual blessing in the heavenly places, even as he chose us in him before the foundation of the world, that we should be holy and blameless before him. In love he predestined us for adoption to himself as sons through Jesus Christ, according to the purpose of his will, to the praise of his glorious grace, with which he has blessed us in the Beloved. In him we have redemption through his blood, the forgiveness of our trespasses, according to the riches of his grace, which he lavished upon us, in all wisdom and insight making known to us the mystery of his will, according to his purpose, which he set forth in Christ as a plan for the fullness of time, to unite all things in him, things in heaven and things on earth. (1:3–10)

So here's the humbling and comforting truth of the gospel. Your obedience doesn't initiate anything. Instead, God initiated a redemptive process that resulted in our forgiveness and transformation. We don't obey to get his favor. We obey because his favor has fallen on us and transformed our hearts. God's work of rescue and forgiveness didn't begin just before you first believed. It didn't begin just before you were born. It began before the world was born. He placed his grace on you and wrote your story in such a way that, at a certain point in time, you would hear the truths of the gospel of Jesus Christ and believe. His love for you is never a result of your character; it is a clear demonstration of his. He granted you and me what we never could have deserved; our new life is his choice, his gift.

> So then it depends not on human will or exertion, but on God, who has mercy. (Rom. 9:16)

Reflect: Finish this sentence: Since God planned to save me before I did anything, then . . .

APRIL 22

If God intended for all the days of your life to be easy, they would be. No, in grace, he intends for your days to be his tools of refinement.

I am deeply persuaded that many of us struggle with questions of God's goodness, faithfulness, and love. Why? Not because God has been unfaithful to any promise in any way, but because we simply do not share his agenda. Our agenda, our definition of what a good God should give us, is a life that is comfortable, pleasurable, and predictable. We want a life where there's lots of human affirmation and an absence of suffering. But consider God's agenda, as it's revealed in the following passages:

> Count it all joy, my brothers, when you meet trials of various kinds, for you know that the testing of your faith produces steadfastness. And let steadfastness have its full effect, that you may be perfect and complete, lacking in nothing. (James 1:2–4)

> But whatever gain I had, I counted as loss for the sake of Christ. Indeed, I count everything as loss because of the surpassing worth of knowing Christ Jesus my Lord. For his sake I have suffered the loss of all things and count them as rubbish, in order that I may gain Christ. (Phil. 3:7–8)

The message is consistent through all of these passages. God is not working to deliver your personal definition of happiness. If you have that agenda, you are going to be disappointed with God and you are going to wonder if he loves you. God is after something better—your holiness, that is, the final completion of his redemptive work in you. The difficulties you face are not in the way of God's plan, they do not show the failure of God's plan, and they are not signs he has turned his back on you. No, those tough moments are a sure sign of the zeal of his redemptive love.

> Beloved, do not be surprised at the fiery trial when it comes upon you to test you, as though something strange were happening to you. But rejoice insofar as you share Christ's sufferings, that you may also rejoice and be glad when his glory is revealed. (1 Pet. 4:12–13)

Reflect: When life gets difficult, what do you turn to for relief? Have you found that impulse leads toward addiction and not toward God's redemptive plan for you?

APRIL 23

As God's child, there's never a moment when you're not under God's care, never a time when you're not the object of his love.

The big question is not, Does God care for me? Over and over again, the Bible declares that he does. It tells us that God's eyes are on the righteous and his ears are open to their prayers (Ps. 34:15). It says that he is with us wherever we go (Gen. 28:15). The Bible welcomes us to bring our cares to God because he cares for us (1 Pet. 5:7). It tells us that he will never leave us or forsake us (Heb. 13:5). The message is clear and consistent—if you are God's child, you are never outside the scope of his constant care. The Bible is also clear—his love is eternal and unshakable. From the verse-by-verse refrain of Psalm 136, "for his steadfast love endures forever," to Paul's declaration in Romans 8 that nothing can separate us from the "love of God in Christ Jesus our Lord" (8:39), the message is undebatable—God will never turn from the love he has lavished on us.

So if you're God's child, you're wasting your spiritual time and energy worrying about God's love. If you try to unpack little moments in your life to see if they indicate whether God loves you, you're not spending your time well. Questioning God's love never goes anywhere good. When life is hard and you're tempted to do so, you need to run to his word. You'll never establish personal peace by picking apart little moments and mysteries of life. The Bible gives you peace even when it's hard to figure out what in the world God is doing.

More than that, if the big question isn't whether God cares, then maybe the real question is, Will I recognize God's care when it comes? Perhaps our problem is our definition and expectation of God's care. You see, God's care is not always relief from circumstances, release from trouble. There are many moments in our lives when the very thing that causes us to wonder about God's care *is* his care. Often trouble is a tool of care in the hands of the one who knows best what we need. He cares; therefore, make sure your definition of his care is not too narrow.

Give thanks to the God of heaven,
    for his steadfast love endures forever. (Ps. 136:26)

Reflect: What kind of stress or hardship most often causes you to doubt God's care for you? Why?

APRIL 24

Since God writes your story, he knows what you're facing and exactly what grace you'll need to live his way.

Admit it: your life hasn't worked out according to your plan. Last month didn't work out according to your plan. Today won't work out according to your plan. That's because you aren't the author of your story. Yet even though there is very little that we know for sure about our lives, we need not give way to panic. Yes, our lives are out of our control, but that doesn't mean they are out of control.

Instead, God is the author of every detail of your story. And since he writes into your story every situation, location, and relationship, then he knows exactly what you're facing and precisely what grace you need to face it. You could say it this way: his sovereign control is the guarantee that you will have everything that he has promised you. His sovereign control means he knows what you need because he has planned for you everything that you're now facing. But his sovereignty is also your security because he can guarantee the delivery of his promises—only in the location where he rules. Because he rules over all things at all times in all stories, he can guarantee that you and I will have what he has promised us exactly when and where they are needed.

Paul says it this way: "And he made from one man every nation of mankind to live on all the face of the earth, having determined allotted periods and the boundaries of their dwelling place, that they should seek God, and perhaps feel their way toward him and find him. Yet he is actually not far from each one of us" (Acts 17:26–27). Paul doesn't think of God as an "out-there and distant sovereign." He reminds us that God is involved with every detail of our lives. He is so near that every grace that you and I will ever need is near and available to us as well. So reach out today. The author is near, and he has grace in his hands.

> Your eyes saw my unformed substance;
> in your book were written, every one of them,
> the days that were formed for me,
> when as yet there was none of them.
>
> How precious to me are your thoughts, O God!
> How vast is the sum of them! (Ps. 139:16–17)

Reflect: What do you tend to do when life feels out of control? What does this reveal about what you think of God?

APRIL 25

Today you will spend solitary moments of conversation with yourself, either listing your complaints or counting your blessings.

Do you live a life of blessing or complaint? It is so easy to grumble. It is so easy to be discontent. It is so easy to be irritated and impatient. It is so easy to groan and moan about the difficulties of life. Why are these things so easy? Well, they're easy because sin really is selfishness at its core. We then tend to judge the good of our lives by how much of what we want we are able to actually have. If you put yourself in the center of your world, you will find plenty of things to complain about.

It is also true that you live in a fallen world where people and things are not functioning the way God intended. In this broken world, you face all kinds of difficulties, big and small, every day. Friends, teachers, coaches, and parents disappoint you. Combine the hardships of life in this fallen world with the self-centeredness of sin, and you have a recipe for disaster or at least a miserable life of discontentment.

The Bible does not see grumbling and complaining as little things. In Deuteronomy 1, Moses recounts how the people of Israel "murmured" (grumbled) about their lives (1:27). And this murmuring is basically questioning the goodness and wisdom of God. So God's assessment was that by their grumbling the people had rebelled against him. The joy or complaint of your heart always shapes your willingness to trust God and to do his will.

Complaining forgets God's grace. It fails to see the beauty of his promises. It questions his goodness, faithfulness, and love. It wonders if he is there and if he cares. If you believe in God and his control over everything that exists, then you have to accept that all of your grumbling is ultimately grumbling against him. Yes, it is so easy to complain. It is so easy to forget the daily blessings that fall down on each of us. Our readiness to complain is another reason to trust the forgiving and rescuing grace that Jesus, without complaint, willingly died to give us.

> Then they despised the pleasant land,
> having no faith in his promise.
> They murmured in their tents,
> and did not obey the voice of the LORD. (Ps. 106:24–25)

Reflect: When are you most tempted to complain during the course of a week? What does that reveal about what you think? And how might today's truth about God change the way you think?

APRIL 26

If you have quit being defensive and are now willingly and humbly approachable, you know that transforming grace has visited you.

We all point the finger of blame, and we all work to convince ourselves that the party to blame is not us. It started in the garden of Eden. Adam pointed his finger at Eve, and Eve pointed her finger at the serpent; neither one of them accepted blame. And there have been generations and generations of finger pointers ever since.

You see, when you've done something wrong, it's not natural to look inside yourself for the cause. Sin makes us all shockingly self-righteous. It makes us all natural self-excusers. Somehow, some way, we all buy into the delusion that our biggest problems live outside us, not inside us. We all have very active inner lawyers, who rise to our defense in the face of any accusation of wrong. When our consciences bother us because of the faithful convicting ministry of the Holy Spirit, we are all tempted to dodge blame by locating the cause elsewhere. We all tend to be much more concerned about the sin of others than we are about our own.

Because accepting blame is not natural, it takes rescuing, transforming grace to produce a humble, willing, broken, self-examining, help-seeking heart. Only divine grace can soften a person's heart. Only grace can help your eyes to see what you need to see. Only grace can destroy your defenses and lead you to confess. Only grace can cause you to quit pointing your finger and to run to your Redeemer for his forgiveness and delivering power. Only grace can enable you to forsake your own righteousness and find your hope and rest in the righteousness of another. Only grace can make you more grieved over your sin than about the sins of others. Only grace can make you accept your need for grace. Only grace can cause you and me to abandon our confidence in our own performance and place our confidence in the perfectly acceptable righteousness of Jesus Christ. Only grace can cause us to put our hope in the only place where hope can be found—in God and God alone. Every moment of our defensiveness argues how much grace we still need.

> Whoever conceals his transgressions will not prosper,
> but he who confesses and forsakes them will obtain mercy. (Prov. 28:13)

Reflect: How does hiding increase your stress? And how might confessing your faults and failures help you deal with your anxiety?

APRIL 27

Your hope is not in your ability to love God, but in his unrelenting and unshakable love for you.

There is nothing that argues more for our desperate need for grace than the two greatest commandments: that we love God and love other people (Matt. 22:34–40). The call to love exposes how dark and depraved our hearts really are. Let's be honest here. It doesn't take much for us to be irritated with other people. Little interruptions, disagreements, and obstacles can cause us to well up with impatience and anger. In a variety of ways, we look down on others, failing to see them with eyes of compassion and hearts of mercy. It's so easy for us to judge others as foolish, lazy, or otherwise incompetent. I know I'm not the only one who struggles with these things.

But if horizontal love is hard for us, vertical love is even harder. The connection between the two is cogently made in 1 John 4:20: "If anyone says, 'I love God,' and hates his brother, he is a liar; for he who does not love his brother whom he has seen cannot love God whom he has not seen." Wow! There it is. If I have such a struggle loving the people around me, how great and deep must be my struggle to love God?

Yes, the power of sin has been broken by the work of Jesus, but the presence of sin still remains and is being progressively eradicated. That means we still rebel and want our own way, we still forget God and his glory, we still write our own rules, we still love our kingdoms more than we love his, we still demand what we don't deserve, and we still question God's goodness when we don't get our own way. We all fall into doing these things because we tend to love ourselves and we tend to love the world. We just do not love God as we should.

So your hope is never to be found in the degree of your love for God. It is only ever found in the magnitude of his love for you. This love is yours as a gift of his grace even on those days where your heart has run after other lovers.

> Beloved, if God so loved us, we also ought to love one another. (1 John 4:11)

Reflect: What do your shopping habits reveal about your love for God? How might his love for you change those habits?

APRIL 28

Today the true love of your heart will be revealed by what you grieve and what you celebrate.

Our lives are shaped by grief and celebration. This isn't true only for the big moments of our lives. Even in our everyday lives, we are sad, mad, upset, or disappointed by something, and every day we are excited, happy, joyful, pumped, or thankful for something. It's at the intersection between sadness and celebration that the true love of our hearts is exposed.

Be honest as you read this—when you look back on a good week, what are the things that excited you, satisfied you, or otherwise made you so happy that you name it as a good week? Or look at the other side. When you're really disappointed with life, what is it that discourages you? Take time to let these questions function as a window to your heart.

Here's the bottom-line question: How much of your joy, celebration, grief, or anger in the last several weeks had anything whatsoever to do with the kingdom of God? Even when I type these words, I'm convicted by how much of my joy is connected to getting my own way, to people and things not being in my way, or to actually getting some physical thing I've set my heart on.

Yet, by grace, that is not always true. There are times when my heart grasps the magnitude of God's grace, and I celebrate. There are times when I am captured by the work of God's kingdom, when I do find joy in serving others. There are times when I am deeply content in the worship of God. I wish I could say that these things were always true of me, but they are not.

So take time today to examine your heart. Take time to unpack your grief and your joy. If you do, you will see that there *is* evidence of God's transforming grace at work. Yet there is also evidence of the need for that grace to do more. Yes, you have been and are being rescued. Yet your grief and celebration tell you that the war for your heart still rages on. And, like me, you need for grace to continue to do its rescuing and transforming work every day.

> We always thank God, the Father of our Lord Jesus Christ, when we pray for you. (Col. 1:3)

Reflect: When you are happy with a relationship in your life, how can you turn that joy into praise to God?

APRIL 29

Today you will be tempted to buy into the delusion that you're smarter than God, that your way is better than his.

It's crazy. Even though sin reduces us all to fools, at the very same time it also convinces us that we are smarter than God. How many people have said, "How could you ever worship a God who would ______?" How many people have wondered, "If God really loved me, why would he ______?" How many people have said, "I don't see what's so wrong with a little ______"? I am convinced that most of us do this far more often than we think. We basically convince ourselves that we know what's best and that we really don't need wisdom greater than our own. Every day in some situation or boundary or relationship, we are tempted to think that we are smarter than God.

Without the rescue of God's grace, we are all wise fools heading for danger we simply don't see. We eat more than we should, while denying the physical evidence of our foolishness. We spend ourselves into hopeless debt, and are surprised when we can no longer pay our bills. We live selfishly and judgmentally in relationships, and then wonder why so much tension and distance exist. That's why Paul says, "For the foolishness of God is wiser than men, and the weakness of God is stronger than men" (1 Cor. 1:25). Paul is saying that if it were possible for God to be foolish, his most foolish moment would be infinitely wiser than our wisest moment. How humbling!

So where are you tempted to tell yourself that you're wiser than God? Where do you argue that your plan for you is better than his? Where do you take life into your own hands so that you can have it your way? Confess the utter foolishness of ever thinking that you're smarter than God, and run to the one who is wisdom. Ask him to make you, by his grace, into a person who loves God's wisdom more than you love your own.

Then the Lord answered Job out of the whirlwind and said:

> "Dress for action like a man;
> I will question you, and you make it known to me.
> Will you even put me in the wrong?
> Will you condemn me that you may be in the right?" (Job 40:6–8)

Reflect: Where are you tempted to name sin as something less than sin? Where do you tell yourself that you don't really need grace?

APRIL 30

Prayer is abandoning hope of independent capability and believing that in Christ you're given everything you need for life and godliness.

Prayer is an act of worship. Prayer is an act of obedience. But prayer is also an act of admission. Every instance of prayer is a confession in which I own my condition and embrace my need. Prayer that doesn't do this may be some sort of religious ritual, but it ceases to be prayer. Real prayer destroys my independent self-confidence. It puts my need and utter dependency before my eyes. No passage gets at this more clearly than Christ's parable of the Pharisee and the tax collector in Luke 18:9–14:

> He also told this parable to some who trusted in themselves that they were righteous, and treated others with contempt: "Two men went up into the temple to pray, one a Pharisee and the other a tax collector. The Pharisee, standing by himself, prayed thus: 'God, I thank you that I am not like other men, extortioners, unjust, adulterers, or even like this tax collector. I fast twice a week; I give tithes of all that I get.' But the tax collector, standing far off, would not even lift up his eyes to heaven, but beat his breast, saying, 'God, be merciful to me, a sinner!' I tell you, this man went down to his house justified, rather than the other. For everyone who exalts himself will be humbled, but the one who humbles himself will be exalted."

We should pray the tax collector's prayer for mercy all the time. To reduce prayer to a grocery list of things that you want demeans prayer and God. The heart of true prayer is vertical confession not horizontal desire. In contrast, the Pharisee's prayer was not a prayer at all. He basically said: "Here I am, God. I'm as righteous as I need to be, so I don't really need your help at the moment." Self-righteousness crushes prayer, reducing it to an empty religious ritual spoken by one who sees himself as a grace graduate. Run to Jesus in your poverty and weakness, and know that he is never revolted when you do. Instead, he always greets you with arms of grace.

> Therefore, confess your sins to one another and pray for one another, that you may be healed. The prayer of a righteous person has great power as it is working. (James 5:16)

Reflect: How are your prayers different from, or similar to, what you post on social media?

MAY 1

Jesus commands you to take up your cross and follow him, and then he gives you the strength to carry the load.

Pay careful attention to 2 Thessalonians 2:16–17 because it offers you a very pointed and practical summary of how the gospel works on your life: "Now may our Lord Jesus Christ himself, and God our Father, who loved us and gave us eternal comfort and good hope through grace, comfort your hearts and establish them in every good work and word." If someone asked you what in the world God is doing in your life, what would you answer? I am persuaded that one of the primary reasons many of us struggle with moments of disappointment with God is that we misunderstand what God is doing. Paul really summarizes the work of God into two essential aspects of his agenda.

First, God has been and is exercising his grace to bring real comfort to our hearts. What is that comfort? It's not that he will make sure that our hopes and dreams are realized, that the people around us like us, or that we escape suffering. His comfort is more foundational and redemptive. Here it is: despite our sin, we have been welcomed into an eternal relationship with the Lord almighty. Why? Because Jesus fully met all the requirements of God that we failed to meet. So we no longer have to fear God's wrath. We no longer have to measure up in order to achieve his acceptance. He will never withdraw his presence and his promises, no matter how messed up we continue to be because our standing with him is not based on our performance but on the perfect record of his Son.

Second, in addition to this reconciliation, there's also *transformation* ("establish them in every good work and word"). There are no more powerful promises of transformation than those found in the grace of that cross. By gracious love, God is actively transforming our hearts. The result of this grace is that our works and our words will progressively become more like he chose us to live.

We are his by grace, and we are being changed by grace—all because of his reconciling and transforming zeal.

> Finally, brothers, rejoice. Aim for restoration, comfort one another, agree with one another, live in peace; and the God of love and peace will be with you. (2 Cor. 13:11)

Reflect: Today, if you're struggling with disappointment, bask in the comfort God gives. Take a few minutes to respond to his gracious love in prayer.

MAY 2

True, humble, joyful, and perseverant love is not born out of raw duty but out of worshipful gratitude. We love because he first loved us.

Think with me about the character qualities of real love (that I just wrote above). *True* here means consistent and reliable. Sadly, there is still inconsistency in my love. When someone disagrees with me, when someone gets in the way of my plan, when I am forced into an unexpected wait, or when someone gets what I think I deserve, it's very tempting to respond in a less-than-loving way.

The second word, *humble*, explains why I respond as I do. I still lack humility. I still tend to make life about my plans, my feelings, my desires, and my expectations. I am still tempted to assess the "good" of a day by whether it pleased me versus whether I pleased God and was loving toward others. I still am tempted to live as if I own my life.

And all of this causes love to be burdensome rather than *joyful*, the third descriptive word. When you're living for you, the call to love others is always a burden for you.

The final word points us to the highest and hardest standard of love: *perseverant*. Love that isn't faithful is love that has little value. Love that changes with the wind is not really love at all and does more damage than good. That is why God's faithful, eternal love is such a huge and motivating comfort.

The question then is, "Where in the world am I going to get this kind of love?" Well, it never comes from picking yourself up and telling yourself that you're going to do better. If you had the power to change yourself, the cross of Jesus Christ would not have been necessary. The only way I can escape the bondage of self-focused love and actually begin to love others is for forgiving, liberating, empowering, and eternal love to be placed in me. The more I am thankful for that love, the more I find joy in giving it to others. God's love, willingly given, provides the only hope that I can have love in my heart that I joyfully give as well.

> By this we know love, that he laid down his life for us, and we ought to lay down our lives for the brothers. (1 John 3:16)

Reflect: How is the advice to "love yourself more" not really helpful? Why?

MAY 3

God's care for you is secure because it does not depend on your faithfulness but on his.

You and I live between the "already" and the "not yet." Already God has set his plan of grace in motion. Already Jesus has come. Already he has suffered and died. Already he has risen in victory from the tomb. Already the Spirit has come. But not yet is God's work in the world finished. Not yet is his work in our hearts done. Not yet is the last enemy under his feet. Not yet is he ready to say: "Beloved, all things are now ready. Enter into my final kingdom."

We are right smack dab in the middle of the world's most important incomplete process—sanctification. The war for what will functionally rule our hearts still rages. We are not yet even near being blameless in and of ourselves. No, the reality is that between the already and the not yet of God's transforming process, we are all a bit of a mess. We still fall into temptation. We still give way to wrong thoughts and desires. We still say things that we should never say. So there is simply no way our personal security can be found in ourselves, even on our best days. Our well-being rests in the utterly unshakable promise of grace that he has made to us.

God never regrets that promise. He never grows bored or weary. He doesn't debate with himself as to whether he should walk away. He never withdraws his commitment to us because he has his eye on another. He never makes a promise he doesn't intend to keep. He never keeps a record of wrongs against us so that he can use it to get something from us that he wants. He is completely faithful in the fullest sense of what that means. And most importantly, his faithfulness is not a demonstration of how well you're doing. Instead, it's a revelation of how completely holy, righteous, kind, and good he is. He remains faithful even on your most unfaithful day.

> Now may the God of peace himself sanctify you completely, and may your whole spirit and soul and body be kept blameless at the coming of our Lord Jesus Christ. He who calls you is faithful; he will surely do it. (1 Thess. 5:23–24)

Reflect: What makes you doubt God and his faithfulness? How does today's truth—about God's unshakable faithfulness—help with that doubt?

MAY 4

"Our Father in heaven . . ." (Matt. 6:9). There is no situation or location where I am ever alone because my heavenly Father is always with me.

These words—"our Father in heaven"—communicate one of the most astounding, life-altering gifts of the grace of the Lord Jesus Christ. They are a deeply personal, heart-satisfying recognition that we must carry with us wherever we go. This opening line of Jesus's model prayer for his disciples (Matt. 6:9–13) teaches this unspeakably marvelous truth: *if you're God's child, you have a Father in heaven!*

Stop for a moment and let that sink in. What a glorious and encouraging way Christ instructs us to begin our prayers. We are to start with the most shocking and encouraging thing that our minds could ever consider. Here it is: the being who has such incomparable wisdom and power that he was able to design and create everything—that being is our Father. The deity who has by supreme authority controlled every event of history—that deity is our Father. The one who in magnificent love put the plan of redemption in motion, so that at the right moment his Son came to live, die, and rise again so that we would have new and eternal life—that one is our Father. The God who never needed a teacher or a counselor, who knows the stars by name, and who can hold the waters of the universe in the palm of his hand—that God is our Father.

What's more important than to wake up every morning and remind yourself that the one who created and controls everything is, by grace, your Father? He thinks of you with pure and faithful fatherly love. He acts toward you with the giving, providing, instructing, patient, and forgiving love of a perfect father. He is always with you. His heart is always for you. He is always at work accomplishing his plans for you and through you. He lifts your burdens and lightens your load. He is your God, your Savior, your friend—your Father. Nothing can ever be the same again because you now live in the Father's house, where glorious grace decorates every room.

> As a father shows compassion to his children,
> so the LORD shows compassion to those who fear him. (Ps. 103:13)

Reflect: What are some reasons why it might be hard for you to think of God as your Father? Are you willing to take those concerns to him in prayer?

MAY 5

"Hallowed be your name . . ." (Matt. 6:9). In the little moments of daily life, I must live for a greater honor and glory than my own.

I remember the lecture well. At the end of my junior year of high school, my dad called me into the room and said, "Sit down; I want to talk to you for a moment." I hadn't done anything wrong; my dad was preparing me for the next phase of my life. He told me that my job was to get up every day and look for a job until I had found one. Then he said: "Remember, as you're out there, you carry the name of this family with you. What you do that is good will reflect on this family, and the bad things that you do will reflect on this family as well." This was a crushing burden. I thought, "I'm only sixteen years old, and I have to carry the burden of the reputation of this family on my shoulders?"

In case you are wondering, this is not what the second statement in our Lord's model prayer is about. It is not about you and me carrying on our shoulders the crushing burden of the reputation of God. No fallen human being could carry such a burden. No, this statement frames everything that prayer is about.

Prayer recognizes that something exists in the world that is greater and more glorious than you. Prayer is meant to remind you that your little world, filled with your little plans, is not ultimate.

Instead, this prayer reminds me that the grandeur of God is meant to shape and direct everything in my life. I was made for his glory, not my own. This reality exposes what's in my heart: I don't really want to live for a greater glory. What I really want is for the people, places, and things in my life to serve the glory of my comfort and satisfaction. So this reminds me that I need to pray for something else—grace. Without rescuing grace, I will continue to live as a glory thief, and so will you. Thankfully, that grace is ours in Jesus our Lord.

> For my own sake, for my own sake, I do it,
> for how should my name be profaned?
> My glory I will not give to another. (Isa. 48:11)

Reflect: What in life automatically fills you with awe? How do you respond? Ask God to help you feel the same way about what is most awe-inspiring—him.

MAY 6

"Your kingdom come . . ." (Matt. 6:10). I must remember that God didn't give me grace for my kingdom to work but to capture me for a better kingdom.

Jesus's disciples were already really focused on "the kingdom." Not that they were concerned about the honor of the King or the success of his kingdom. No, what obsessed them was their place in that kingdom. For them, the kingdom was about personal power, prominence, and position. Take a moment to read the incident recorded in Mark 9:30–35. As that story concludes, here's what it says about the disciples:

> But they kept silent, for on the way they had argued with one another about who was the greatest. And he sat down and called the twelve. And he said to them, "If anyone would be first, he must be last of all and servant of all." (9:34–35)

Right after Jesus told them that he was going to be captured and killed, they didn't say: "Lord, no, no, you can't let this happen. What will we do without you?" They weren't filled with remorse. No, they began fighting with one another about which one of them was the greatest. This is what sin does to all of us. What we really want is for *our* kingdoms to come and our will to be done right here, right now in our jobs and families. We love being in control. We love getting our own way. We have a wonderful plan for the people in our lives. It is humbling to admit, but we are more like the disciples than unlike them.

So it was a moment of beautiful grace when Jesus looked at these self-oriented disciples and said, "Fear not, little flock, for it is your Father's good pleasure to give you the kingdom" (Luke 12:32). He was saying: "Don't you understand? I didn't come to exercise my power to make your little kingdoms work. Instead, I came to welcome you, by grace, to a much better kingdom than you could ever quest for on your own." Real life is found only when his kingdom comes and his will is done, and that is exactly what grace welcomes you to.

> Your kingdom come,
> your will be done,
> on earth as it is in heaven. (Matt. 6:10)

Reflect: How does this prayer affect your understanding of God's will for your life? How can it guide you with decisions you have to make?

MAY 7

"Your will be done . . ." (Matt. 6:10). The good life is not found in the success of my will but in the submission of all things to God's will.

Father Knows Best was a 1950s television program unlike anything that would be broadcast today. Even its title is politically incorrect in today's culture. Maybe today the program would be called *Everyone but Father Knows Best.*

Yet perhaps *Father Knows Best* is not such a bad title for this section of the Lord's Prayer. Here's what we all need to keep in mind at all times: the one who rules over this world is the ultimate definition of what is good, wise, right, loving, faithful, and true. He really does know what is best for you and for everything he created. And that means hope is found in only one place—in the wise and faithful rule of your Father in heaven.

Now, here's the problem—we all go through times in our lives when we slide into thinking that we're smarter than God. We think that what we want for ourselves is better than what he wants for us. We chafe against what he has put on our plates. We wonder why breaking one of God's little laws to make things better is such a bad thing.

The temptation to think that you know better still has the power to capture you. So cry out for grace. The war between God's will and your will has not yet ended. The desire for God to exercise his power to deliver your personal dreams is not yet gone. So reach out for the help your Savior died to give you. Ask him again to rescue you from you. Pray that you'll take refuge in no safer place than in submission to the will of your Father in heaven. And have the courage this morning to look toward heaven and say, "Your kingdom come, your will be done right here, right now in my life as it is in heaven." When you're joyfully willing to submit to the will of the Father, you know grace has taken residence in your heart.

The Lord is good to those who wait for him,
  to the soul who seeks him.
It is good that one should wait quietly
  for the salvation of the Lord. (Lam. 3:25–26)

Reflect: Have human authorities in your life made it hard to trust the Father and his goodness? How is God the Father different and better than even the best human authorities?

MAY 8

"Give us this day our daily bread . . ." (Matt. 6:11). I am not independent or self-sufficient but dependent on the goodness of God for my needs.

In Deuteronomy 8, Israel was entering the promised land, where they would now face the temptation of wealth. So God gave them a very important warning:

> And you shall remember the whole way that the LORD your God has led you these forty years in the wilderness, that he might humble you, testing you to know what was in your heart, whether you would keep his commandments or not. And he humbled you and let you hunger and fed you with manna, . . . that he might make you know that man does not live by bread alone, but man lives by every word that comes from the mouth of the LORD. . . . So you shall keep the commandments of the LORD your God by walking in his ways and by fearing him. For the LORD your God is bringing you into a good land, a land of brooks of water, of fountains and springs, . . . a land of wheat and barley, of vines and fig trees and pomegranates, a land of olive trees and honey, a land in which you will eat bread without scarcity,. . . . And you shall eat and be full, and you shall bless the LORD your God for the good land he has given you.
>
> Take care lest you forget the LORD your God by not keeping his commandments . . . which I command you today. (Deut. 8:2–11)

This is also the temptation we all face. When things are going well and supplies are many, we're tempted to forget our utter dependence on God for everything in life. The prayer for daily bread reminds me that I am dependent on God for even the most basic needs of my life. Only he has the power to control everything so that I have the things that I need to live my life. Even an atheist is dependent on God for his life and breath. No one lives a self-sufficient life. No one can say, "Look how successfully I have been able to care for myself without any outside assistance." No one! So look up and give thanks. There really is a great and loving supplier.

> Every good gift and every perfect gift is from above. (James 1:17)

Reflect: What makes you, you? Take time to thank God who made you just the way you are.

MAY 9

"Forgive us . . . as we also have forgiven . . ." (Matt. 6:12).

I must always remember the grace I am given daily and extend that grace to the people in my life.

One of the greatest sins in our relationships is the sin of forgetfulness. Consider the following parable of Jesus:

> Therefore the kingdom of heaven may be compared to a king who wished to settle accounts with his servants. When he began to settle, one was brought to him who owed him ten thousand talents. And since he could not pay, his master ordered him to be sold, with his wife and children and all that he had, and payment to be made. So the servant fell on his knees, imploring him, "Have patience with me, and I will pay you everything." And out of pity for him, the master of that servant released him and forgave him the debt. But when that same servant went out, he found one of his fellow servants who owed him a hundred denarii, and seizing him, he began to choke him, saying, "Pay what you owe." So his fellow servant fell down and pleaded with him, "Have patience with me, and I will pay you." He refused and went and put him in prison until he should pay the debt. . . . Then his master summoned him and said to him, "You wicked servant! I forgave you all that debt because you pleaded with me. And should not you have had mercy on your fellow servant, as I had mercy on you?" (Matt. 18:23–33)

All of us can fail to remember the magnificence of the mercy that has been showered on us. We can all forget that we never could have earned or deserved the best things in our lives. They're only ours by means of grace. Here's the problem: to the degree that you forget the grace that you've been given, to that same degree it's easier to not extend grace to others.

If God gives what we never could have earned; why, then, do we turn and refuse to give grace to others until they've measured up? May God give us the grace to remember and the willingness to give to others what we have been given.

> Be kind to one another, tenderhearted, forgiving one another, as God in Christ forgave you. Therefore be imitators of God, as beloved children. (Eph. 4:32–5:1)

Reflect: Are you more eager to remember someone's faults or God's grace? Why?

MAY 10

"Lead us not into temptation . . ." (Matt. 6:13). I rest assured that I am loved by a holy God. His will for me is always right, good, and true.

"But why, Dad, why can't I? All the other kids are doing it. I don't get why this is such a big deal. Can't I do it just this one time?" I can't tell you how many times we had this conversation. Sometimes it was a quick plea, thankfully followed by submission. At other times it disintegrated into a major debate. But each time it was an instructive reminder: sinners don't like boundaries. Sinners don't like to be told what to do. Sinners tend to want to author their own moral codes. So you can't even pray this prayer, "Lead us not into temptation," unless grace has visited you. Only powerful, rescuing grace can take you from saying, "Let me do what I want to do" to "Guard me against the temptation to do what you know is not best for me."

When you pray, "Lead us not into temptation," you're acknowledging three things that only grace can produce. First, there is one of ultimate authority who rules over this world and knows what is best. This means that even if I am the most powerful human being on earth, I am still a person under authority. Second, this one who is the ultimate authority has clearly communicated how I should live. There is a set of God-given boundaries that I have been designed to live within. Real life is found inside these boundaries, not in discovering and experiencing what's outside of them. Third, this prayer means that I live in a world of moment-by-moment temptation. The world whispers seductive lies into my ears every day. It works to deceive me into thinking that what is ugly in God's eyes is really beautiful and that what God has said is wrong is really all right after all. So ask God to help you remember his authority, to love his law, and to have the strength and desire to resist temptation. There is ample grace for all of these things!

Your decrees are very trustworthy;
holiness befits your house,
O Lord, forevermore. (Ps. 93:5)

Reflect: Where are you tempted to think that goodness lies outside of the boundaries that God has put around your life? Why?

MAY 11

"But deliver us from evil . . ." (Matt. 6:13). I admit that it's the evil inside me that hooks me to the evil outside me, and I seek grace's rescue.

If little Billy pushes Suzy, causing her to fall and hit her head, and you come into the room and ask Billy why he did it, he won't talk about himself. He'll talk about what Suzy did or how he tripped over the toys in the room. Yet he won't say: "I've got sin in my heart that makes me selfish. So I push others when they get in my way. Please pray for me, Mom." You won't hear that because, even though Billy is only five years old, he has already believed the lie that his biggest problems in life exist outside him not inside him.

Like Billy, we are all very skilled at explaining away our wrong behavior by pointing to the situations, locations, events, and people in our lives. We work very hard to convince ourselves that the problem cannot be us by saying:

- "She misunderstood me."
- "I just ran out of time; I was so busy."
- "I really didn't mean it that way."
- "I wasn't feeling well."
- "It's just my personality."
- "Sorry, I just forgot."
- "I must not have heard you."
- "He talked me into it."

We are all very good at deceiving ourselves. We resist the truth that it is only ever the evil inside us that magnetizes us to the evil outside us. When grace has made you able to pray, "Deliver us from evil," you are admitting that the evil that is the greatest danger to you is the evil inside you. You are admitting that you can escape the evil in a certain location, you can avoid an evil situation, and you can run from an evil person, but you cannot run from yourself. Only grace can deliver you from the most threatening evil of all—the evil that still resides in your heart. Cry out for that grace.

> The LORD looks down from heaven on the children of man,
> to see if there are any who understand,
> who seek after God.
>
> They have all turned aside; together they have become corrupt;
> there is none who does good,
> not even one. (Ps. 14:2–3)

Reflect: Ask some close friends or family members today, "Where do you hear me making excuses for my sin or my weaknesses?" Then listen carefully to what they say.

MAY 12

You were hardwired to live for God, so even though you may not be aware of it, every good thing or bad thing you do today has verticality to it.

In the physical realm, you were hardwired to breathe. Without thinking, you are always inhaling oxygen and exhaling carbon dioxide. You don't have the option of saying, "I'm tired of breathing, I think I'll just stop." You don't have the option of denying it. Breathing is an inescapable part of your physicality.

In the same way, you were made for relationship with God. This means that everything you do and say, every choice you make is somehow done in reference to God. You may ignore or deny his existence, but you cannot escape that he crafted you in his image. This means that all your life is spiritual and vertical. Religion is not just an aspect of your being. You and I are by nature religious beings. We all come from God, we all exist through God, and all that we do is meant to be done for him.

In his grace God has purposefully created the physical world in a way that points to his existence. I like to think of it this way: you can't get up in the morning without bumping into God (see Ps. 19:1–3).

The radical truth of God's existence isn't just preached to us on Sundays. It's preached every day—through the beauty of the sunset, the power of the storm, the inexhaustible wings of the hummingbird, the hugeness of the mountain, the whisper of the breeze, the smell of the sizzling steak, the beauty of the petal of a rose, and so on. You have to work to deny God's existence because it is so readily visible everywhere you look. God did this because he is a God of grace. He did this so that we would run to him and not from him. He did this so that we would recognize our position as his creatures and bow to his glory. He did this so that we would live in recognition of him.

I will say to the north, Give up,
    and to the south, Do not withhold;
bring my sons from afar
    and my daughters from the end of the earth,
everyone who is called by my name,
    whom I created for my glory,
    whom I formed and made. (Isa. 43:6–7)

Reflect: Today how will you connect the goodness of conversations with friends to the glory of your relationship with God?

MAY 13

You have not been left to secure your own future because God in grace has secured an end to your story more glorious than you can grasp.

One of the most common human fears is the fear of the future. We all ask, "What will happen if . . . ?" or "What will happen next?" It's not a sin to be concerned about what is to come. It is not wrong to plan for the future. In fact, you and I should live with the future in view every day of our lives. But there is a huge difference between worrying about things you have no power over and resting in what God has revealed about his future plans for you.

You'll never find peace and hope by trying to figure out the future. God's "secret will" is called his secret will precisely because it is secret! Instead, real hope is found in living inside the future God says he has for you. God holds your future in his wise, powerful, and gracious hands. In 1 Peter 1:3–5, Peter essentially says, "Don't ever let yourself forget that Jesus has purchased a future for you that is better than anything you could have dreamed of or planned for yourself." If you remember that you have this wonderful future ahead of you, you won't live as if this moment is all you have. You can be free of the anxiety of fearing that somehow this moment will pass you by. I love the qualifying words that Peter uses to describe our inheritance as the children of God: "Imperishable, undefiled, and unfading" (1:4). That means that this inheritance is protected and untouchable. Nothing will be allowed to happen that would damage it in any way. But Peter says more: God is also protecting you. So no matter how hard your story is right here, right now, it is guaranteed for you as God's child that it will end better than anything you can now imagine, and that glory will never end!

> Blessed be the God and Father of our Lord Jesus Christ! According to his great mercy, he has caused us to be born again to a living hope through the resurrection of Jesus Christ from the dead, to an inheritance that is imperishable, undefiled, and unfading, kept in heaven for you, who by God's power are being guarded through faith for a salvation ready to be revealed in the last time. (1 Pet. 1:3–5)

Reflect: How does social media stoke your fears of missing out? How is this fear, according to 1 Peter 1:3–5, actually a lie or myth?

MAY 14

Never forget that what God required, you couldn't do. Christ did it for you. His grace is your hope.

At times we all want to swindle ourselves into thinking that we are righteous enough to be accepted in the eyes of God. Maybe for you it is:

- "Look at how much I volunteer for good causes."
- "Look at how welcoming I am."
- "Look at the level of my Bible knowledge."
- "Look at how often I share the gospel with others."
- "Look at how I've resisted pornography."
- "Look at how I never curse or swear."
- "Look at how many short-term mission trips I've been on."
- "Look at how consistent my personal devotions are."
- "Look at my willingness to serve at church."

You and I tend to point to anything we can to prove that we are not lawbreakers. Yet the whole argument of the Bible is that if we were able to keep the law perfectly, Jesus would not have had to come. The sad reality is that alone, none of us is righteous. None of us measures up. So it was essential that Jesus would come and live in a way that none of us could ever live, to die the death that we all deserve to die, and to rise, defeating sin and death. You can never find hope in your performance, no matter how good or great your actions. Sin is your infection, and without the grace of the Lord Jesus Christ, it will also lead to your destruction.

So abandon the delusion that somehow you can measure up. Run to the place where hope can be found and throw yourself again today on the grace of Jesus. Because of Jesus, you can be fully accepted even though, in reality, you are anything but righteous. Yet how can God accept you and not compromise his own righteousness? He can do this because Christ's righteousness has been credited to your moral account. Now, that's amazing grace!

> If anyone else thinks he has reason for confidence in the flesh, I have more: circumcised on the eighth day, of the people of Israel, of the tribe of Benjamin, a Hebrew of Hebrews; as to the law, a Pharisee; as to zeal, a persecutor of the church; as to righteousness under the law, blameless. But whatever gain I had, I counted as loss for the sake of Christ. (Phil. 3:4–7)

Reflect: How does today's devotional affect how you view your performance in various areas of life?

MAY 15

Corporate worship is designed to alert you to the war for control of your heart and to the help that is found only in Jesus.

One of the reasons God has called us to gather together regularly is that we are so forgetful. We forget who God is and endeavor to live based on our own merit and strength. We forget how magnificent and complete our resources are in Christ. We forget how wise, encouraging, protective, and freeing God's word is. We forget our need for the body of Christ. We forget that we have been created to live for a glory that is bigger than our own and for a kingdom that is greater than what we would construct on our own. Yes, we need to gather again and again—through worship, preaching, and mutual fellowship—to remember what we would otherwise forget.

One of the things we forget is that the major, big-deal war in our lives is not a war with things outside us. It's the war that still rages inside us. In every situation, location, and relationship in our lives, there is a war for control of our hearts. And what rules our hearts, shapes our words and actions.

So will we live for ourselves, reducing life down to the small confines of our wants, feelings, needs, demands, expectations, or will we live for God? Every day you attach the hopes and dreams of your heart, your satisfaction, and your joy to something. Every day you attach your identity to something, and there are only two places to look. You are either looking for life in the creation and are on your way to crushing disappointment. Or you are looking to the Creator and are on your way to lasting peace of heart. Corporate worship is designed to remind you again and again where life can be found so that you can quit searching horizontally for what you have already been given in Jesus.

> For none of us lives to himself, and none of us dies to himself. For if we live, we live to the Lord, and if we die, we die to the Lord. So then, whether we live or whether we die, we are the Lord's. For to this end Christ died and lived again, that he might be Lord both of the dead and of the living. (Rom. 14:7–9)

Reflect: Where is the war raging in your life right now—self-image, reputation, relationships? Are you looking for these to give you what only God can provide?

MAY 16

We are guilty. The cross purchased our forgiveness. We are unable. The Spirit gives us power. We are foolish. God's word provides wisdom.

We look up to confident people. We love the stories of strong people who walk confidently into tough places and accomplish amazing things. Because we all want to be confident, we all love a hero story. And we like it even better if it's the story of an unlikely hero. We all like to think that in tough and important moments, we would rise to the challenge with confidence too.

But the Bible teaches us that independent self-confidence is a delusion. None of us is strong enough to never be defeated. None of us has that power. None of us has that control. We all know in our heart of hearts that we're pretty small. When it comes to the most significant dilemmas of life, even the strongest of people are weak.[6]

What did I bring
to your salvation table?
I had
no righteousness to offer,
no strength to give,
no wisdom to present.
There was
nothing
that I could deliver
that would commend me
to you.
I crawled broken
to your table,
weighed down and crippled by
my sin,
my guilt,
my weakness,
my foolishness,
my pride,
my shame.
I had no right
to be with you,
but you picked me up
and placed me there.
You fed me
the life-giving nutrients
of grace
with your
nail-scarred hands.
And I haven't left your
table of mercy since.

> Likewise the Spirit helps us in our weakness. For we do not know what to pray for as we ought, but the Spirit himself intercedes for us with groanings too deep for words. (Rom. 8:26)

Reflect: In your struggle for purity, how are you feeling "weighed down and crippled"? Take those burdens and failures to Jesus today.

MAY 17

The grand delusion of every act of sin is that we can be disloyal to God and everything will work out in the end.

In little and not-so-little moments of disloyalty to God, we all work to excuse ourselves. And we try to convince ourselves that it will all be okay in the end. In private moments of moral self-conversation, we tell ourselves:

- "I can handle this; it will be okay."
- "I'll only do it this once."
- "I really didn't have much of a choice."
- "It's not really such a big deal."
- "Other people do it all the time."
- "God is good; he'll forgive me."
- "It's not really clearly forbidden by the Bible."
- "What else could I do?"
- "I just chose the lesser of two evils."
- "It's not like I do this all the time."
- "Doesn't God want me to be happy?"

Each statement aims to relieve the burden of conviction. Each is meant to mask the reality that we have chosen to be disloyal to God and rebellious to his authority. Each is meant to cover the true allegiance of our hearts. Each is designed to enable us to feel okay about what God clearly says is not okay. Each is meant to make sin look not so sinful after all.

There are moments when we are all tempted to give in to the same delusional logic that gripped Adam and Eve in the garden of Eden (see Genesis 3). In the mundane moments of our daily lives, we buy into the lie that we can step over God's loving and wise moral boundaries without consequences. In countless little moments, we're disloyal to the one who is our wisdom, righteousness, and hope.

And here's what is so important about that. The character of a life isn't set in three or four big moments of life, but in the ten thousand little, virtually unnoticed moments. These tiny acts of disloyalty expose the war that still rages for the rulership of our hearts. They expose the depth of our ongoing need for rescuing and forgiving grace. Isn't it good to know that this grace is ours in Christ Jesus?

> But thanks be to God, that you who were once slaves of sin have become obedient from the heart to the standard of teaching to which you were committed, and, having been set free from sin, have become slaves of righteousness. (Rom. 6:17–18)

Reflect: How might your excuses for angry or bitter thoughts actually be a lie that you're telling to yourself?

MAY 18

Change is not found in defending our righteousness, but in admitting our weakness and crying for help.

I wish I could say that I am always open and approachable. When I'm approached about a wrong I've committed, I don't tend to say to the other person: "Thank you so much for confronting me. I know that I suffer from spiritual blindness and don't see myself accurately. Please keep rebuking me; I know it's a visible sign of God's love." No, as I feel my ears redden and my chest tighten, there are two things that tend to be more natural for me. First, I activate my internal defense system. *Perhaps I was misunderstood. Perhaps what this person thought I did, I just didn't do.* Second, I build arguments for my righteousness. I list all of the good, but maybe unnoticed, things I am doing. I work to convince myself and the person confronting me that I am righteous.

Here's the sad part: in doing both of these things, I'm devaluing the grace that is my only hope in life and death. When I try to convince myself that my little wrongs do not really rise to the level of what Jesus died for, I am not really that excited about grace. Why? Because I have convinced myself that I don't really need the rescue and forgiveness that grace offers. And when I try to persuade myself into believing that I am righteous, I have less esteem for the perfect righteousness of Christ, which is the only righteousness with which I can stand before God.

So I may have a crisp and clear theology of grace, but where the rubber meets the road in everyday life, grace is not transforming my life. Instead, my own self-righteousness stands in the way. My defensiveness stands as a practical denial of what I say I believe. It keeps me supporting what I should flee from and stops me from running to the place where help is only ever found.

What about you? Have you really abandoned your own righteousness? Does that make you run toward the grace of Jesus? Or will you defend today what Jesus died to destroy? Perhaps before you start confessing your sin you should first confess your self-righteousness.

> But he gives more grace. Therefore it says, "God opposes the proud but gives grace to the humble." (James 4:6)

Reflect: How would the people closest to you score your openness to correction? Why? In grace, what next steps should you take?

MAY 19

If your heart isn't ruled by God's honor and your life by God's plan, you may seem religious, but what you're living isn't biblical faith.

I want to use friendship as a case study for the principle stated above. None of us has enjoyed a friendship that is completely free of conflict and tension. None of us has escaped all moments of irritation and impatience. We all have been disappointed by our friends in some way. Now if you were to read the average Christian book about friendship, you would be led to conclude that all of the fights and quarrels are about navigating boundaries and poor self-image. On the surface, it sounds right, but consider the following provocative passage from the Bible:

> What causes quarrels and what causes fights among you? Is it not this, that your passions are at war within you? You desire and do not have, so you murder. You covet and cannot obtain, so you fight and quarrel. You do not have, because you do not ask. You ask and do not receive, because you ask wrongly, to spend it on your passions. . . . But he gives more grace. Therefore it says, "God opposes the proud, but gives grace to the humble." (James 4:1–3, 6)

Notice how James explains why we have so many fights and quarrels. He doesn't say, "They come from those difficult friends you have" or "They are the result of the drama that you're forced to deal with." No, he says they come from the "passions" that wage war in our hearts. In this context, *passion* means a powerful, ruling desire. I fight with you because I have a heart problem. Rather than my heart being ruled by God and motivated by God's honor, my heart is ruled by my wants, my needs, and my feelings. I am always in some kind of conflict with you. Furthermore, James tells us that human conflict is rooted in spiritual adultery. When we put ourselves where God alone belongs, conflict always results. It is all just another argument for the essentiality of God's grace in Jesus.

> And the Lord said:
> "Because this people draw near with their mouth
> and honor me with their lips,
> while their hearts are far from me,
> and their fear of me is a commandment taught by men." (Isa. 29:13)

Reflect: What do your friend-problems say, not about your friends and their issues, but about your heart and its desires?

MAY 20

It's never hopeless and you're never helpless if Immanuel has invaded your life with his glory and grace.

The book of Joshua contains a remarkable story that's a window on what every believer needs and has been given by God's grace. Take a moment to read Joshua 6:1–7. In this story, the children of Israel had entered the promised land, but God didn't want them to forget who they were and what they had been given. So he put a trial in front of them that would powerfully demonstrate his glory and grace, which he was willing to exercise for their salvation. There was no way that this ragtag group of pilgrims would ever be able to defeat the fortified city of Jericho, but that was precisely the point. So God asked them to march around the city one time a day for six days, and then, on the seventh day, to parade around it seven times. Now, from a human perspective, what God was proposing was military suicide. God was teaching Israel that they must no longer look at life from the vantage point of human wisdom and strength. Why? Because they were now the children of the Lord almighty.

Their world of weakness and limits had been invaded by one of awesome grace and glory. As they walked around Jericho, God was confronting Israel with their inability, vulnerability, and dependency. He was also comforting them with the reality that he would be with them wherever they went and whatever they faced. They would face no enemies on their own. They would carry no needs by themselves. They would not have to bear the burden or carry their destiny in their own hands. Grace and glory had come to them in the presence of the Lord, and in the power of the Lord the walls would come down.

If you're God's child, you too must remember who you are and what you've been given. It is never you against the world because your life has been invaded by the grace and glory of Immanuel.

> "I will never leave you nor forsake you." So we can confidently say,
>
> "The Lord is my helper;
> I will not fear;
> what can man do to me?" (Heb. 13:5–6)

Reflect: When you feel anxiety smother your heart, say no to fear. Ask the Lord to help you live with the hope and courage that come only when you remember that he is near.

MAY 21

The gift of eternal life guarantees that I have been and will be forgiven, and that every broken thing inside me will be completely repaired.

There are two markers of the "already/not-yet" work of God that really do reveal what God is doing in your life. They also inform you as to how you should live. First, we live in the "already" of *complete forgiveness*. Forgiveness is not a "hope it will be" thing. It's an "accomplished and done" thing. You do not have to be concerned that the process of forgiveness will somehow fail. Why? Because the perfect sacrifice of the completely righteous Lamb fully satisfied the holy requirements of God and left you righteous and without penalty in his sight. So you never have to worry that you will be so bad that God will reject you. You never have to hide, rationalize, excuse, defend, or shift the blame. You never have to pretend that you are better than you are. You never have to fear being known or exposed. You never have to parade your righteousness so it can be seen by others. You never have to wonder if God's going to get exhausted with how often you mess up. All of these are acts of gospel irrationality because you have been completely forgiven.

And second, it's essential to understand the "not yet" of your *final repair*. Yes, you have been fully forgiven, but you have not yet been completely rebuilt into all that grace will make you. Sin still remains and the war for your heart still rages. You've not yet been fully re-formed into the image of the Lord Jesus Christ. Yet the cross of Jesus guarantees that all this will be fixed. But they are not fixed yet.

So, as I enjoy God's forgiveness and the freedom from being anxious that I will not measure up, I cannot live unwisely. One danger (sin) still lives inside me and another (temptation) still lurks outside me. So I am still a person in daily and desperate need of grace. Forgiveness is complete. Final restoration is yet to come. Knowing you live in between the two is the key to a restful and wise Christian life.

> Since all these things [the heavens and earth] are thus to be dissolved, what sort of people ought you to be in lives of holiness and godliness. (2 Pet. 3:11)

Reflect: Which tends to make you more full of anxiety—the sin that still lives inside you or the temptation that lurks outside you?

MAY 22

No need to wonder what you have to do to get God's acceptance. Jesus purchased your acceptance on the cross.

The cross of Jesus Christ took the "acceptance with God" issue off the table for every one of his blood-purchased children. Now, you just can't get any better news than that! On the cross, the worst thing that could ever happen became the best thing that could ever happen. Let me explain.

The cruelest aspect of the suffering of Christ was not the human mockery, the slaps and thorns, the whip, or the nails. No, the most horrible moment for Jesus on the cross is recorded in Matthew 27:45–46: "Now from the sixth hour there was darkness over all the land until the ninth hour. And about the ninth hour Jesus cried out with a loud voice, saying, 'Eli, Eli, lema sabachthani?' that is, 'My God, my God, why have you forsaken me?' " Those words of utter grief echo back to another horrible moment. It was the moment when the sinful rebellion of Adam and Eve separated them from the God who had created them to know and enjoy him forever. It was a moment of horror when God drove them out of the garden and far away from his presence. From that moment, the deepest need of all humanity was that somehow communion with God would be restored.

So Jesus willingly endured the Father's rejection so that we would know his acceptance. This unthinkably awful separation, by sovereign grace, met our deepest need. In Christ's rejection came our acceptance. In Christ's moment of horror, we were given eternal hope. Because he was willing to endure the terrible pain of the Father's rejection, you and I will never, ever again live in separation from God. As God's child, there's nothing that you can do to get more of God's acceptance. And there's nothing you can do that would cause him to take your acceptance away. Your acceptance with God is just as secure on your very worst day as it is on your very best day. Why? Because it was purchased once and for all by your suffering Savior, the Lord Jesus Christ.

> For God has done what the law, weakened by the flesh, could not do. By sending his own Son in the likeness of sinful flesh and for sin, he condemned sin in the flesh. (Rom. 8:3)

Reflect: Which feels more important—your acceptance by friends or your acceptance by God? Stop and ask yourself why? Take these thoughts to Jesus in prayer.

MAY 23

You can gaze over the fence and covet another person's life or tell yourself that God has blessed you in ways you never could have earned.

Do you ever battle with envy? Why do some people's lives seem to be easier than yours? Have you ever struggled to celebrate when someone else gets what you wanted? Have you ever wished you could just switch lives with someone? Envy haunts us all. So it's worth learning more about it. Here are five fruits that may point to a root of envy.

1. *Envy is forgetful.* When you focus on what you don't have, you forget all the blessings that God has already given you. This forgetfulness brings more comparing and complaining than praising and resting.
2. *Envy misunderstands blessing.* It's easy to think that care means that God will provide what you want or help you get out of hard situations. But sometimes God uses difficulties to give you blessings you could get no other way.
3. *Envy is short-sighted.* Envy wants everything right here, right now. It overlooks the fact that this moment is not all there is. Envy cannot see that this moment isn't meant to be a destination. Instead, today is a preparation for a final destination that will be beautiful beyond your wildest imagination.
4. *Envy questions God's wisdom.* When you envy, you tend to believe the lie that you are smarter than God. You start to believe that if your hands were on the steering wheel, you would handle things a different way.
5. *Envy is impatient.* Envy doesn't like to wait. Envy complains quickly and tires easily. Envy doesn't just cry for blessings; it cries for blessings now.

Worst of all, envy questions God's goodness, and when you do that, you quit running to him for help.

So cry out for God to rescue you from envy. Ask him to give you a thankful, humble, and patient heart. His transforming grace is your only defense against envy.

> Oh, taste and see that the Lord is good!
> Blessed is the man who takes refuge in him!
> Oh, fear the Lord, you his saints,
> for those who fear him have no lack!
> The young lions suffer want and hunger;
> but those who seek the Lord lack no good thing. (Ps. 34:8–10)

Reflect: Think of one thing you want but God has not given you. Which two fruits of envy (above) fit you most? Ask for God's forgiveness and help!

MAY 24

We don't seek satisfaction, hoping that God will deliver it.
No, we seek God, and the result is satisfaction of heart.

If you give your heart to seeking satisfaction, satisfaction will be the one thing you'll never find. Your heart will never be satisfied in things. No, your heart will be satisfied only in the giver of the things.

I have had many wives say to me in marriage counseling, "All I ever wanted was a husband who would make me happy." Think about the dynamics that this expectation introduces into a relationship. Any woman who makes this statement is loading a marriage dream onto the shoulders of her husband. Who is this man? Well, he's a flawed human being, living in a fallen world. So it is unlikely that he will ever deliver the dream for which she is looking.

Whenever you expect something in creation to satisfy you, you are asking that thing to be your personal savior. You're looking horizontally for what will only ever be yours vertically. In other words, you are asking something in creation to do for you what only God can do. Now, the physical, created world was designed to be a sight-sound-touch-taste-feel symphony of physical glories. But these glories cannot satisfy your heart. If you ask them to, your heart will be empty, and you will be frustrated and discouraged. But if you seek God, rest in his presence and grace, and put your heart in his most capable hands, he will satisfy your heart as nothing else can. You were made for him. Your heart was designed to be controlled by worship of him. Your inner security is meant to come from rest in him. Your sense of well-being is intended to come from a reliance on his wisdom, power, and love.

The reality is this—God is the satisfaction that your heart seeks. He is the rest that you crave, the joy you long for, and the comfort your heart desires. All those things that we think will bring us contentment and joy will fail to deliver. What we need in life is him, and by grace, he is with us, in us, and for us. Our hearts can rest because, by grace, we have been given everything we could ever need in him.

For he satisfies the longing soul,
    and the hungry soul he fills with good things. (Ps. 107:9)

Reflect: Are you seeking another person to fulfill your dreams? What's good about that desire? What's wrong about it?

MAY 25

What could motivate you more, as you face your weakness, than these words: "My power is made perfect in weakness"(2 Cor. 12:9)?

I don't like being weak. I want to be right, strong, able, and in control. I don't want to be confused or unready. I don't want to feel unqualified for the task at hand. I don't want to be the one who is keeping things from getting done or is holding others back. I don't want to let myself or others down. I want to have a track record that I am proud of. I don't find weakness to be very comfortable.

I guess what I'm saying is that I don't want to be who I am or face who I am. And I suspect you're a lot like me. We all dream of independent strength and ability, of knowledge and wisdom. But we are not created to be independent, and sin has also left us even weaker and more needy. Theologians call it *total depravity*. It doesn't mean that we are as bad as we could be, but that sin has done its cruel work on every aspect of our personhood. So this means that your weakness is not your great danger. Rather, the great danger is your *delusion* of strength. Because if you think you're strong, then you don't seek the help that you desperately need from God.

This is why Paul says: "But he [God] said to me, 'My grace is sufficient for you, my power is made perfect in weakness.' Therefore I will boast all the more gladly of my weaknesses, so that the power of Christ may rest upon me" (2 Cor. 12:9). You see, knowledge of personal weakness is a blessing from God. By grace, he has delivered you from the delusion of your independent ability. So now you are free to seek the real strength that you need, strength that is found only in his capable and gracious hands. The hopelessness of weakness is the only door to the hope of real strength.

> Thus says the Lord: "Let not the wise man boast in his wisdom, let not the mighty man boast in his might, let not the rich man boast in his riches, but let him who boasts boast in this, that he understands and knows me, that I am the Lord who practices steadfast love, justice, and righteousness in the earth. For in these things I delight, declares the Lord." (Jer. 9:23–24)

Reflect: How is this kind of honest weakness different from just "being real" on social media?

MAY 26

Faith is living in light of what God has said, resting in what he has done, and entrusting the future to his care.

Genesis 22 stands as a clear case study in what faith is and does. God had promised Abraham that his descendants would be like the stars in the sky and would bless all the nations of the earth. But Abraham and his wife, Sarah, didn't even have a child. They waited, decade after decade, but no son came. Abraham was an old man, and Sarah was decades beyond her childbearing years. Then, in a miracle of God's faithfulness, a son, Isaac, was born. There must have been some kind of celebration that day! God was true to his promises. It seemed like the end of a beautiful story.

Then God told Abraham to sacrifice the promised son! It made no sense whatsoever. All God's promises of faithfulness rested on this boy. If Abraham killed him, it would all be over. We don't know all the emotions that were inside Abraham, but we see Abraham immediately preparing to obey God. We know that grace had visited and transformed the heart of this man, or he would not have been able to react as he did.

It's clear that Abraham did not know why God was asking him to do what he had asked. It's clear from Hebrews 11:17–19 that he did not know what God was going to do. Abraham reasoned that maybe God would resurrect Isaac after the sacrifice. But that was not what God intended. This is where we learn what faith is about. Abraham wasn't relying on what he could see or understand. No, he was at rest because he acted on the firm platform of God's commands and his character and promises. Faith believes that God really does exist and that he rewards those who seek him (Heb. 11:6). But faith isn't natural for us; it is ours only as a gift of God's grace. Seek that grace again today.

> By faith Abraham, when he was tested, offered up Isaac, and he who had received the promises was in the act of offering up his only son, of whom it was said, "Through Isaac shall your offspring be named." He considered that God was able even to raise him from the dead, from which, figuratively speaking, he did receive him back. (Heb. 11:17–19)

Reflect: What seems confusing or unexpected in your life right now? Let that challenge direct you to trust in God's grace.

MAY 27

Don't give way to fear today. The Lord almighty is your Savior, and he is with you in whatever you're facing and wherever you go.

The apostle Paul is in Athens, waiting to make connections with fellow travelers. While there, he's so moved by what he sees and hears there that he can't resist injecting God into the conversation. Take a moment to read his comments in Acts 17:22–28. Paul concludes with these words:

> And [God] made from one man every nation of mankind to live on all the face of the earth, having determined allotted periods and the boundaries of their dwelling place, that they should seek God, and perhaps feel their way toward him and find him. Yet he is actually not far from each one of us, for
>
> "In him we live and move and have our being";
>
> as even some of your own poets have said,
>
> "For we are indeed his offspring." (Acts 17:26–28)

There are two things that should calm our fears. The first is the incredible truth that Paul speaks to the Athenians. Paul announces that the God who is in control of everything that exists, even down to the exact address where we live, has decided to rule his world so that he is near to all of us. So close that any moment we could reach out and touch him. God is always near and always reachable.

But more needs to be said. Yes, it is true that as sovereign, God is near in power and rule. But it must also be said that as Savior, he is near in presence and grace. As sovereign, he rules over all the situations, locations, and relationships. And that may cause me fear. But as Savior, he is rescuing, empowering, and transforming me by grace. Because God is my sovereign, my life is never out of control. And because he is my Savior, he blesses me with everything I need to live in the middle of things that are beyond my control. Why, then, should I fear?

> For I, the Lord your God,
> hold your right hand;
> it is I who say to you, "Fear not,
> I am the one who helps you." (Isa. 41:13)

Reflect: Over recent weeks, where do you feel most insecure? With those in mind, spend two minutes prayerfully thinking about your God as sovereign and Savior.

MAY 28

Today you'll work to deny your sin, or you'll receive the Spirit's conviction as grace and run to Christ for rescue and forgiveness.

Take a moment to read 1 John 1:5–10. The words you'll read are direct and humbling, and they are written to believers. After you read, let's examine the logic of this passage:

- *Sin is a big deal.* The darkness of our sin is what separates us from a holy God. God takes sin so seriously that he wrote the story of history so that his Son would come and, through his life and death, deal with sin. You cannot be serious about your relationship with God and not take sin seriously.
- *Because sin is a big deal, the cleansing blood of Jesus is our only hope.* Jesus came and lived and died because there was no other way to deal with sin. It is so powerful, destructive, and comprehensive that there is no way we could have ever escaped it or defeated it on our own. Sin required the radical rescue of the shed-blood grace of the Savior.
- *Denying remaining sin is the height of self-deception.* We offer huge amounts of daily evidence that we struggle with sin. So it takes deep denials for us to convince ourselves that we are, in fact, okay. Every time we excuse, minimize, rationalize, or point the finger of blame, we participate in that system of denial.
- *God is always faithful to the promises of the cross of Jesus.* Your Savior loves to forgive. He really is slow to anger and abounding in steadfast love!
- *Denying sin makes a liar out of God and denies the message of his word.* Here's the bottom line—either (a) God is true when his word says that you have a problem you can't solve, or (b) you're right that you're not so bad after all. It can't be both ways.

So why deny today what grace has so completely forgiven and covered?

> The saying is trustworthy and deserving of full acceptance, that Christ Jesus came into the world to save sinners, of whom I am the foremost. (1 Tim. 1:15)

Reflect: Have you ever asked someone to show you your blind spots?

MAY 29

Grace frees you from the dissatisfying claustrophobia of your individualism to enjoy the fulfilling freedom of loving and serving God.

Living for yourself is not liberty. It's a self-imposed prison. Doing what you want to do, when you want, and how you want, has never been the good life. In calling you to obedience, God is not robbing you of liberty but is leading you to the only place where liberty can be found.

To understand this, you must look at life from the vantage point of creation and the fall into sin. As Creator, God designed you to live a dependent life. You were built for a life of loving, worshipful dependency and obedience. You and I just don't have the power and wisdom we would need to live an independent existence. To try to live life completely independent of God is like trying to drive a beautiful boat down a superhighway. That boat is a wonderful creation, loaded with amazing design details. But it was not built to run on a hard surface. If you try to run it on land, you will destroy the boat and you will go nowhere fast.

The entrance of sin into the world and into our hearts also teaches us that we were not hardwired for independence. The fall made us all a danger to ourselves. Because of the sin in us, we think bad things, we desire bad things, we are attracted to bad things, and we choose bad things. Yet we're often blind to much of this going on inside of ourselves. So not only do we need God's presence and his wisdom to guide and protect us, but we also need his grace to rescue us.

The doctrines of creation and the fall drive us to conclude that living for ourselves—that is, working to independently rule our own little worlds—can never work. Instead, joyful submission to the grace of Jesus is the good life. Life is only ever found when we put ourselves in the hands of our Creator and cast ourselves on his amazing grace.

> So Jesus said to the Jews who had believed him, "If you abide in my word, you are truly my disciples, and you will know the truth, and the truth will set you free." (John 8:31–32)

Reflect: What promises the freedom of the good life to you right now? In what ways do you see this promise as delusional? Where are the lies?

MAY 30

There is no need to carry the burden of ownership of your life today. You've been bought with a price, so you don't belong to you anymore.

You and I have been freed from carrying the burden of all the regrets of the past, of our needs in the present, and of all the unanswered questions of the future. You and I have been freed from the stress of thinking that we have to figure it all out on our own. We have been freed from worrying about needing to control things that are actually beyond our control. You and I don't need to wring our hands wondering what might happen to us in the future. We don't have to fear that we won't be enough or that we'll come up short. As God's children, we simply do not have to carry any of these burdens. Why? Read on.

You don't have to worry about these things for one simple, transformative reason—you don't belong to you anymore! You have been bought with a price. So your life is now under new ownership and new management. The God who now owns you is committed to keep you and care for you. The God who owns you is in personal and careful control of every situation, location, and circumstance of your life. He covers your past with his grace. He protects, provides for, and empowers you in the present. And he holds every aspect of your future in his sovereign and gracious hands.

Yes, because you were purchased at the price of his blood, you don't belong to you anymore. But that is a good thing. The one who now owns you is a wiser and more powerful manager of your life than you ever would have been. He cares for you with magnificent grace, incalculable wisdom, and limitless power. It means you're no longer burdened by living for you. Being owned by him means you are in the best of hands.

So when you get up tomorrow, remind yourself of who you are and what you have become. God's grace has welcomed you to rest and peace because that grace has placed your life under new and capable management. The one who is Creator, Savior, and King has taken ownership. What could be better than that?

You were bought with a price; do not become bondservants of men. (1 Cor. 7:23)

Reflect: What situations tend to trigger your anxiety about your past, present, or future? How are those situations under the control and ownership of Christ?

MAY 31

Corporate worship rescues us again and again by reminding us that there is only one glory worth giving our lives to—the glory of God.

As human beings, we're all glory junkies. We all live for glory in some way. We love the glory of a sports trophy or of stunning tennis shoes. We love watching videos of mind-bending feats of danger or glorious artistic achievements. One bite of chocolate glory is not enough for us, and one promotion doesn't satisfy our hearts. The beautiful watch, the cool car, the best taco, and the stunning piece of music all get our attention and leave us wanting more.

But these glories were created to serve a purpose—to remind us of and point us to the glory of God. We were never meant to live for earthbound glory. We were never meant to seek peace and satisfaction of heart in what God has made. The physical world *is* wonderfully glorious. But it was never meant to be our stopping point any more than the sign that points to something is meant to be the end of the journey.

Here's what you and I need to remember about signs. The sign is not the thing. The sign points you to the thing. The same can be said of physical creation. It is not the thing that you were made to live for. It was made to point you to the thing you were made to live for: God and God alone. How sad it is when a person looks to created glory to find what cannot be found there. But many, many people do this every day.

Yet thankfully, you have corporate worship. The regular gathering of the people of God for worship is meant to remind you that we are created to live for a greater, more glorious glory—the glory of God. Worship helps you see once more that it is only when you live for God that your heart finds the peace, satisfaction, and security it seeks. And it is only God's glory that has the power to rescue you from all the earthbound glories that so easily capture your heart.

> I said in my heart, "Come now, I will test you with pleasure; enjoy yourself." But behold, this also was vanity. (Eccles. 2:1)

Reflect: Think about how some part of your favorite movie points to the greater glory of Christ.

JUNE 1

God's care comes in many forms. He cares enough to break your bones in order to capture your heart.

Our relationship with the Lord is never anything other than a relationship of grace. It is grace that brought us into his family. It is grace that keeps us in it, and it is grace that will continue us in it forever. But the grace that we have been given is not always comfortable grace. Here's why. As sinners we all become way too comfortable with our sin. So, in grace, God loves us enough to crush us, so that we would feel the pain of our sin and run to him for forgiveness and deliverance.

Like the warning signal of physical pain, the rescuing and restoring pain of convicting grace is a thing worth celebrating. God's grace isn't always comfortable because he isn't primarily working on our comfort; he's working on our character. With violent grace he will crush us because he loves us and is committed to our restoration, deliverance, and refinement. And that is something worth celebrating.[7]

I wish your care was always
easy, predictable, safe—
a cool drink
a soft pillow—
but you are too wise,
too loving,
too committed to your work of
transforming grace.
So your gracious care
comes to me
in uncomfortable forms:
the redeeming care of
disappointment,
the unexpected
trial,
suffering, loss.
These things don't tell me you're
cold-hearted,
absent,
uninvolved.
No, each is a sign of
zealous grace,
redeeming love.
I struggle to grasp how much you
care,
so I struggle to rest in that
care.
You care enough to give me
what I need,
not what I want.
You care enough to
break my bones
in order
to recapture my heart.

Let me hear joy and gladness;
let the bones that you have broken rejoice. (Ps. 51:8)

Reflect: What disappointments with the people in your life do you feel most deeply today? How might God use that disappointment to point you to himself?

JUNE 2

It never works to ask people to do for you what only God can do. It never works to wait for God to do what he has clearly called you to do.

You can't look horizontally for what you will get only vertically. And you can't wait vertically for what you have been called to do horizontally. We all get these two confused again and again. On the one hand, even your best friend is never a safe source of your happiness because that person is flawed and will inevitably fail you in some way. Only God is ever a safe keeper of the security, peace, and rest of your soul. Yet today many people say they believe in God, but they shop horizontally for what can be found only vertically.

On the other hand, there are many people who give in to the temptation to do the opposite. They wait for God to do for them what he has clearly called and empowered them to do. I've heard many people who were dealing with fractured relationships say to me, "I'm just waiting for the Lord to reconcile our relationship." It sounds spiritual, but it is simply wrong. If you have something against someone, if there is conflict between you, the Bible tells you to get up, go, and be reconciled. In the biblical book of Joshua, when it came time for Israel to enter the promised land, God was going to part the waters of the Jordan River. Yet he commanded the priests to step into it. God promises to provide, but he calls us to labor, pray, and give. God alone has the power to save, but he calls us to witness, testify, proclaim, teach, live, and preach. You see, God not only determines outcomes, but he also rules over the means by which those outcomes are realized.

So the life of faith is all about rest and work. We rest in God's presence and constant care (vertical). And we toil with our hands, busy at the work we have been commanded to do (horizontal). We rest in our work and work in our rest. It is the rhythm of the life of faith.

> Jesus said to him, "If you would be perfect, go, sell what you possess and give to the poor, and you will have treasure in heaven; and come, follow me." When the young man heard this he went away sorrowful, for he had great possessions. (Matt. 19:21–22)

Reflect: Do you find it harder to rest in God or work for God? Why?

JUNE 3

It would be amazing if a God of awesome glory recognized our existence, but for him to welcome us into his family is grace beyond amazing!

It's hard to wrap our brains around its majesty, but think about it. No human being ever kept God's law (except Jesus). No one has ever given God the honor due his name. No one has lived the life of worship that is the duty and calling of everyone who has ever taken a breath. Everyone not only has failed to worship God, but also has worshiped false gods. Every human being not only has failed to recognize the centrality of God in all things, but also has inserted himself or herself in God's position. Not only do we misuse God's creation, but we put it in God's place and give it the worship that belongs to him.

So in the face of all of this personal rebellion against God, it would be amazing if we were not exterminated. It would be an act of wondrous grace for God to recognize that we exist. But he has done so much, much more than this. Through the life, death, and resurrection of his Son, God has made a way for us to be welcomed into an intimate family relationship with him. So now, quite apart from anything we could have ever deserved, we are given the full range of rights and privileges of his children. And we're blessed with them forever and ever. Along with this, he has promised to one day finally end all the sin, sickness, sorrow, and suffering that our rebellion brought down on this world. So grace lets you have it all—everything, that is, that you need. Grace makes the King of kings your Father. It makes his Son your Savior and brother. Now, that really is beyond amazing. Pray for eyes to see it and a heart to embrace it, and then let your soul soar.

> I do not cease to give thanks for you, remembering you in my prayers, that the God of our Lord Jesus Christ, the Father of glory, may give you the Spirit of wisdom and of revelation in the knowledge of him, having the eyes of your hearts enlightened, that you may know what is the hope to which he has called you, what are the riches of his glorious inheritance in the saints. (Eph. 1:16–18)

Reflect: If you're honest, what in life blows your mind more than God's grace? Why?

JUNE 4

It's only in the mirror of God's word that you see yourself accurately, and only in his grace that you find help for what you see.

I saw it again and again in counseling. Maybe it was a husband and wife, an angry teenager, a single person who had lost her way, or a pastor who had gotten himself into trouble. They shared a common theme. All of these people thought they knew themselves, but they didn't. It didn't take long for me to realize that I was experiencing firsthand a universal human condition that the Bible talks about. It's called spiritual blindness.

Sin blinds. Sin is self-excusing and other-blaming. Sin allows me to feel all right about what God says is very wrong. The personal sight system that God wired into every human being has been terribly broken by sin. We all suffer from spiritual blindness. But that is not all.

We all also suffer from the fact that we live most of the time blind to our blindness. We don't see ourselves with clarity, but we think we do. This is why we all tend to be offended when someone points out a sin, weakness, or failure. Why? Because the other person has said something about us so fundamentally different from the way we view ourselves.

So we all need help. Empowered by the convicting ministry of the Holy Spirit, the Bible is the universe's most accurate mirror. Stand in front of it, and you will see yourself as you really are. Its diagnosis of your true condition is always accurate. So only the word of God is able to offer the real and reliable cure for your condition. And here's the good news. When you see yourself in Scripture, you don't need to be afraid of all the dark things you don't see in yourself. All of those dark things have been covered by and defeated by the powerful grace that is yours in the life, death, and resurrection of Jesus.

> For the word of God is living and active, sharper than any two-edged sword, piercing to the division of soul and of spirit, of joints and of marrow, and discerning the thoughts and intentions of the heart. And no creature is hidden from his sight, but all are naked and exposed to the eyes of him to whom we must give account. (Heb. 4:12–13)

Reflect: How did you respond to the last criticism someone gave you? As you think back on it, how do you see that criticism and your response differently now?

JUNE 5

God's grace is active, rescuing, transformative grace. You celebrate this by being as serious about your need as the God of this grace is.

Take your time, but how would you answer this good question for yourself. How serious are you about the sin that was the reason for the most costly sacrifice ever made? Consider God's seriousness, as pictured for us in the drama in the garden of Eden. Study the following words carefully:

> The LORD God said to the serpent,
>
> "Because you have done this,
> cursed are you above all livestock
> and above all beasts of the field;
> on your belly you shall go,
> and dust you shall eat
> all the days of your life.
> I will put enmity between
> you and the woman,
> and between your offspring
> and her offspring;
> he shall bruise your head,
> and you shall bruise his heel."
>
> To the woman he said,
>
> "I will surely multiply your
> pain in childbearing;
> in pain you shall bring
> forth children.
> Your desire shall be contrary
> to your husband,
> and he shall rule over you."
>
> And to Adam he said,
>
> "Because you have listened
> to the voice of your wife
> and have eaten of the tree
> of which I commanded you,
> 'You shall not eat of it,'
> cursed is the ground because of you;
> in pain you shall eat of it
> all the days of your life;
> thorns and thistles it shall
> bring forth for you;
> and you shall eat the
> plants of the field.
> By the sweat of your face
> you shall eat bread,
> till you return to the ground,
> for out of it you were taken;
> for you are dust,
> and to dust you shall
> return."
> (Gen. 3:14–19)

God took sin so seriously that he did two things when the first transgression occurred. (1) He immediately dealt out punishment, and (2) he immediately set in motion his plan of rescue and redemption. Both demonstrate God's seriousness about the sins we all too easily deny or minimize.

> The LORD passed before him and proclaimed, "The LORD, the LORD, a God merciful and gracious, slow to anger, and abounding in steadfast love and faithfulness, keeping steadfast love for thousands, forgiving iniquity and transgression and sin, but who will by no means clear the guilty." (Ex. 34:6–7)

Reflect: How do your entertainment choices affect the way you think about sin?

JUNE 6

Every human being places his hope in something, and every human being asks that hope to deliver something. Where have you placed your hope?

We've all been hardwired for hope. We all hope *in* something and we all hope *for* something. So much of how we live and look at life is connected to the things in which we place the fundamental hopes of our lives.

Hope always has three elements—an assessment, an object, and an expectation. (1) Hope looks around and assesses that something or someone could be better than it is. If things weren't broken, you wouldn't hope for something better. (2) Hope always has an object. It's the thing that you bank your hope on. You ask the object of your hope to fix what is broken or to deliver what you desire or need. (3) Hope has an expectation. This is the outcome you ask the object of your hope to give you. It's what you hope the object of your hope will deliver.

Now, there are really only two places to look for foundational life hope, for your basic meaning and purpose in life. On the one hand, you can search for hope horizontally in the situations, experiences, physical possessions, locations, and relationships of everyday life. Yet there are two problems with looking horizontally. First, every created thing suffers from some degree of brokenness. They're part of the problem, and are unable to deliver what you're seeking. Second, these things weren't created to be the source of your hope, but to be fingers that point you to where your hope can be found.

On the other hand, in Romans 5:5 Paul tells us where hope can be found. It is found only vertically. Only he is able to give you the life that your heart seeks. Only he is able to give your soul the rest and security that it needs. Only he, in his grace, can deliver the internal peace that is the hunger of every human being. So if your hope disappoints you, it's because it's the wrong hope! Today, what carries your hope?

> Then Job arose and tore his robe and shaved his head and fell on the ground and worshiped. And he said, "Naked I came from my mother's womb, and naked shall I return. The LORD gave, and the LORD has taken away; blessed be the name of the LORD." (Job 1:20–21)

Reflect: What are your hopes for romance? What do you hope that kind of relationship will do for you? Why?

JUNE 7

Are you experiencing the schizophrenia of having eternity hardwired into your heart but living as if this moment is all there is?

It is sad how many people constantly live in the craziness of eternity amnesia. We forget the long view: that we were created to live in a forever relationship with a forever God forever. You and I simply cannot live as if forever isn't a reality. But so many people try. They put all their hopes and dreams in right here, right now situations, locations, possessions, positions, and people. They load moment after moment with undeliverable expectations. They ask people to be what people will never be. They demand that a seriously broken world deliver what it could never deliver. They fail to recognize that now can never be paradise.

It's wonderful to have a good relationship with your friends, but they will never deliver paradise to you. That beautiful car that began decaying from the moment it was built will not be your paradise. Those still-flawed parents will not offer you paradise-like relationships. But forgetting the eternity that's to come, will make yourself and those around you crazy.

Your eternity amnesia makes you unrealistically expectant. You become vulnerable to temptation, too driven, too dependent on people and things that will only disappoint you. You, sadly, become susceptible to doubting the goodness of God. In contrast, recognizing the eternity that's to come allows you to be realistic without being hopeless. You can be hopeful when things around you don't encourage much hope.

Do you load paradise-like expectations into fallen-world moments? Does your eternity amnesia tempt you to question the goodness of God? Pray for grace to remember God and the unending end he has written into the story for all who put their trust in him. Long-view living is wise living. Long-view living is godward living. Long-view living is hopeful living. Long-view living will make you thankful for grace.

> I have seen the business that God has given to the children of man to be busy with. He has made everything beautiful in its time. Also, he has put eternity into man's heart, yet so that he cannot find out what God has done from the beginning to the end. (Eccles. 3:10–11)

Reflect: What would make heaven paradise for you? Is it something other than God?

JUNE 8

Corporate worship is designed to confront you with the glory of the grace of Jesus so you won't look for life, help, and hope elsewhere.

As I sat in the balcony with my wife, Luella, I remembered how important and wonderful corporate worship is. It was our church's Spring Choral Worship service. It featured original compositions and stunning hymn arrangements. In this music, we were reminded of the miserable condition in which sin left us and our world. We heard musical reminders of the glorious rescue of redeeming grace. Each piece was so full of the gospel that I felt as if my heart could not contain anything more. I thought we could sing and sing and sing and never exhaust the stunning redemptive themes of the gospel of the Lord Jesus Christ.

Finally, at the end of this lavish gospel feast, the crescendo anthem came. It was such a beautiful celebration of the glory of the gospel that when we came to the last two lines, I quit singing. I began to repeat over and over again: "Amen! Amen! Amen!" Corporate worship had performed its work in my heart once again.

Very honestly, I hadn't come to the service with celebration in my heart. I had grumbled my way into the room. It had been a long ministry weekend. I wouldn't have gone to that Sunday evening service if Luella hadn't begged me to. I really didn't want to be there. But in the middle of it all, something captured my heart—glory. The glory of the grace of Jesus suddenly loomed larger than the exhaustion of my body or the weariness of my mind. My cold heart was enlivened by the fire of the grace of the Lord Jesus Christ. Once again, the gathering of God's people for worship had done its job.

God ordained for us to gather for worship because he knows the weaknesses of our fickle, grumbling, and easily distracted hearts. So in grace he calls us to gather and consider glory once again, to be excited once again, and to be rescued once again. It's not only that corporate worship reminds us of God's grace. Corporate worship is itself a gift of grace. Run with celebration to its rescue any time it is available to you.

> I was glad when they said to me,
> "Let us go to the house of the LORD!" (Ps. 122:1)

Reflect: What's made you most excited in the last few days? How is that different than worship? Or is it?

JUNE 9

For sin, forgiveness; for weakness, strength; for foolishness, wisdom; for bondage, deliverance—such is the way of the grace of Jesus.

Luella, my wife, is the owner and director of a large private art gallery. At the beginning of each month, artwork is delivered to Luella's gallery for the next show. It's exciting for Luella to unpack the paintings and begin to experience the art that will give life to the gallery over the next month. Then Luella goes through the process of arranging and rearranging it until each piece is in the best location so it can be displayed most powerfully. The next day, a team of hangers comes into the gallery to help Luella actually affix the paintings to the walls. The final step is for each painting to be properly lit. Every month, it seems that the gallery actually changes shape with the new work. Once it's lit, I like to come down to the gallery in the evening and see the work in all its splendor. Often Luella and I stand across the street at night, look into the huge gallery windows, and take in the beauty. Then Luella does something that bothers me every time. She goes back to the gallery, gets her stuff, and hits the light switch, plunging the gallery into darkness. I always think, "No, no, these paintings should never be in the dark."

If you're God's child, you are a gallery of his glorious grace (read Col. 2:1–15). Yet for many believers, the artwork is there, but the lights in the gallery are out. These believers simply don't see the stunning beauty of what they have been given in the grace of the Lord Jesus Christ. And because they don't grasp that grace, they neither celebrate it nor live in light of its majesty. So they give way to weakness (when they actually have God's power). They give way to foolishness (when they're connected to Christ's wisdom). They hide in guilt (when they have been fully forgiven). They surrender to addiction (when they have been given freeing grace). How sad!—their hearts have been decorated with the artwork of grace, but the lights are out in the gallery.

> For at one time you were darkness, but now you are light in the Lord. Walk as children of light. (Eph. 5:8)

Reflect: How does all this grace apply to you? Are the lights on? And has that gospel light radically changed the way you live even when no one's watching?

JUNE 10

If you are in Christ, you've been chosen to transcend the borders of your own glory, to reach out toward a greater glory—the glory of God.

Jesus's disciples were glory thieves. So they desperately needed a life-changing glory display, and did they ever get one!

In order to rescue his disciples from their bondage to their own glory, it was necessary for Jesus to reveal a greater, more transcendent glory. So in one of the most incredible scenes in all of the biblical story (see below), Jesus pulled back the curtain and showed them his glory as the one and only Son of the Most High God. It was a jaw-slackening, heart-stopping, mind-blowing display of divine glory. If they had any sense at all, it would put holy awe—holy terror—in their hearts. Enough of the small glories they had been living for, and enough of the small-minded plans they had made for their lives—Christ's transfiguration was designed to transform their lives. They were being rescued from earthly glory by true glory. As a result, they could take this glory around the world to whomever would listen and hear.

Here is what life is all about. At its center is a God of awesome glory—glorious in power, wisdom, faithfulness, love, and grace. Here is what everyone needs—rescue by this glory. Here is what everyone was created for—to live for this glory. Here is grace—that God would choose to splash his eternal glory down on inglorious, unthankful, rebellious, and self-oriented people such as us. Without this rescue, we surrender our hearts to bondage, to a thick catalog of other glories. This moment is a moment of gorgeous grace, just the grace you and I need.

> And after six days Jesus took with him Peter and James, and John his brother, and led them up a high mountain by themselves. And he was transfigured before them, and his face shone like the sun, and his clothes became white as light. And behold, there appeared to them Moses and Elijah, talking with him. And . . . behold, a bright cloud overshadowed them, and a voice from the cloud said, "This is my beloved Son, with whom I am well pleased; listen to him." When the disciples heard this, they fell on their faces and were terrified. But Jesus came and touched them, saying, "Rise, and have no fear." And when they lifted up their eyes, they saw no one but Jesus only. (Matt. 17:1–8)

Reflect: What online glories have really captured your attention in the last few days? Are you settling for lesser glories?

JUNE 11

No amount of guilt or shame can do what grace is able to do—make us people who delight in the Father's will.

You will never understand your struggle with sin unless you grasp that sin is mainly a heart problem. It's not first a problem of bad behavior, although it always goes there. It's not first an external temptation problem, although we're tempted by it. It's not first a situation problem, although it expresses itself there. Sin is a matter of the heart.

The Bible uses many terms for the inner, spiritual, thoughtful, desiring, motivational you. Yet all those terms are summarized by one big term: *heart*. I am persuaded that you cannot understand the transforming message of the Bible unless you understand this term. Here's a definition to carry with you as you read your Bible: the heart is the *causal core of your personhood*. It's the seat of your thoughts, emotions, desires, and motivations. It is the worship center at the center of your person. The heart is the reason you do the things you do and say the things you say. You and I literally live out of our hearts.

Sadly, sin lives in our hearts. That means it corrupts our thoughts, desires, choices, and motivations. We were made to serve and worship the Creator, but sin causes us to serve and worship the creation. We were designed to live for God's glory, but sin causes us to make life all about our own glory. And unless these things change in our hearts, our behavior won't change at all (at least not for very long). No amount of work or guilt trips will change your heart. No running from certain situations, apps, websites, or relationships has the power to change your heart. You can't run from sin because you cannot run from you.

So you and I are left with only one final option. And we need to do this again and again. We need to run to the grace of Jesus. Run for forgiveness. Run for power. Run for transformation. Run for deliverance. Don't ever stop running to grace until Jesus has taken you home to a place where you need to run no more.

> And he said to them, "Well did Isaiah prophesy of you hypocrites, as it is written,
>
> 'This people honors me with their lips,
> but their heart is far from me.'" (Mark 7:6)

Reflect: How does today's reading make you think when you hear someone give the well-meaning advice: "Follow your heart"?

JUNE 12

Prayer is abandoning your place in the center of your world and daily surrendering that place to God alone as an act of heartfelt worship.

Prayer is much more than bringing to God your list of wants, desires, and needs. It is a radical act of worship that reminds you of who you are, who God is, and what life is all about. Prayer is surrender:

- *Prayer is surrender to the reality that there is someone more ultimate than you.* It's natural for each of us to shrink our field of hopes, dreams, and daily concerns down to the small turf of our personal wants, needs, and feelings. Prayer is surrender to the worldview of the first four words of the Bible, "In the beginning, God . . ." (Gen. 1:1). And this perspective puts us in our rightful place.
- *Prayer is surrender to the reality that life isn't just about you.* Prayer wouldn't be prayer if it did not acknowledge God's existence. Similarly, prayer defines us as well. We simply aren't the creators, kings, or owners of our lives. So prayer is letting go of personal independence and bowing in reverence to the God we depend on. We have been created to live inside God's boundaries.
- *Prayer is surrender to the reality that you need help.* Prayer means humbly confessing that we are not self-sufficient. Prayer reminds us that we cannot be what we were made to be or do without the personal, gracious, and continuous intervention of the one who made us.
- *Prayer is surrender to the reality that there is wisdom greater than ours.* Prayer confronts us with the fact that we are not as smart as we tend to think we are. It tells us that we don't discover life by searching our limited understanding, but in surrendering our lives to the care of the one whose understanding spans our entire lives and eternity.
- *Prayer is surrender of your hopes to God's grace.* Prayer is remembering that there is no hope in life and death that does not result from the grace of God. In prayer, I give up my hopes in me and place my hopes in him.

So close your eyes, bow your head, and surrender—and be thankful for the grace that meets you as you do.

> Answer me, O Lord, answer me, that this people may know that you, O Lord, are God. (1 Kings 18:37)

Reflect: What will you surrender to God as you pray to him today?

JUNE 13

If you hook the hope of your heart to the people around you, you will always be disappointed. No one is able to be your personal messiah.

You should be thankful for the people whom God places in your life. You should love them and treat them with honor and respect. You should be willing to give to them and serve them. You should be open to them as they speak into your life. But you cannot look to them to provide for you what only God can provide.

There are many, many Christian relationships that are hurtful, painful, and marked by conflict and disappointment. Why? Because the people in those relationships are placing a burden on those relationships that no human relationship can bear.

- No person can be the source of your identity.
- No one can be the basis of your happiness.
- No loved one can be the carrier of your hope.
- No one is able to change you from the inside out.
- No human being can alter your past.
- No person is able to atone for your wrongs.
- No one can give your heart peace and rest.

Asking another human being to do those things is like requiring him to be the fourth member of the Trinity. Then you sit back and judge him when he falls short. It simply cannot and will not work. Human love is a wonderful thing, but you will only ever find life—real, heart-changing, soul-satisfying life—in a vertical relationship.

You should enjoy human love, but you should look to God for your spiritual vitality and strength. You should commit to long-term, loving, mutually serving relationships, but you must remember that only God can save you, change you, and deliver you from you. You should be willing to make sacrifices of love for others, but you should place your hope only in the once-for-all sacrifice of the Lord Jesus Christ.

Could it be that the disappointment you experience in your relationships is the product of unrealistic and unattainable expectations? Could it be that you have unwittingly put people in God's place? There is but one Savior, and he is yours forever. You don't need to put that burden on the person next to you.

> But God, who comforts the downcast, comforted us by the coming of Titus. (2 Cor. 7:6)

Reflect: How might you be asking a person in your life to do for you what only God can do?

JUNE 14

One of sin's greatest rebellions is our repeated refusal to listen and submit to the wisdom of God revealed on every page of his word.

As I listened to them argue, blame, and graphically recount one another's wrongs, all colored with hurt and anger, a sad thought gripped me. Most of what these people needed to hear was clearly written in the Bible. They both said they believed the Bible. Yet their relationship was the sad casualty of refusing to actually listen to God's wisdom and seek the grace he offered.

Consider one passage loaded with essential relational wisdom: "[Live together] with all humility and gentleness, with patience, bearing with one another in love, eager to maintain the unity of the Spirit in the bond of peace" (Eph. 4:2–3). Think about these wise guidelines for relationships:

- "*with all humility* . . ." Pride always destroys a relationship. It causes you to feel more entitled than servant-hearted, to be more demanding than giving. Pride drives you to insist on control. You have to be right. Pride is an anti-relational way of having a relationship. Humility is the godly way.
- "*and gentleness* . . ." Treating a person with gentleness teaches another person that he or she is safe in your care. It is an essential relational bond.
- "*with patience* . . ." You cannot have a healthy communion with another flawed human being if you're not willing to wait. If you demand to have things your way and in your time, you are so busy loving yourself that you have little time left to love the other person.
- "*bearing with one another in love* . . ." Love requires that you be willing to be forbearing, that is, willing to suffer. Why? Because you are in a relationship with a less-than-perfect person, living together in a fallen world. Both you and that person often fail.
- "*eager to maintain the unity of the Spirit* . . ." Love means unity is more important to you than being right, having your way, and getting what you want. Love rejoices in the fact that God's Spirit in both of you gives you a wonderful platform for unity.
- "*in the bond of peace*." Love means committing to make peace not war.

There simply are no more-important relational commitments that you could cite.

> And above all these put on love, which binds everything together in perfect harmony. (Col. 3:14)

Reflect: The people mentioned above held God's wisdom in their hands, but they did not listen. Do you? Where do you find yourself struggling to listen to wisdom?

JUNE 15

Confession is a grace. Only grace can convince you to abandon your righteousness and run to the merciful arms of the Lord.

Confession is not natural for us. It's natural for us to think of ourselves as more righteous than we are. It's natural to blame our wrongs on others. It's natural to say our behavior was caused by some difficult circumstance we were in. It's natural to turn the tables when being confronted and tell our accusers that they are surely bigger sinners than we are. It's natural for you and me to be blind to the depth of our spiritual need.

This sturdy system of self-righteousness is natural for every sinner. So, it's unnatural for us to be clear-sighted, humble, and ready to confess. Blind eyes stand in the way of the broken heart of confession. We don't grieve our sin because we don't see it.

Here's how confession works. You cannot *confess* what you haven't *grieved*, and you can't *grieve* what you do not *see*. So one of the most important operations of God's grace is to give us eyes to see our sin and hearts that are willing to confess it. If you see yourself with accuracy, and if your heart is humbly willing to admit it, you know that something else is also true. It means that glorious, rescuing, forgiving, and transforming grace has visited you. Why? Because what you're doing is simply not natural for sinners. In the face of their sin, Adam blamed Eve, Eve blamed the serpent. Both of them hid, but neither stepped forward and made willing and heartfelt confession.

So cry out today for eyes to see, that is, for accurate personal insight and a humble heart. Ask God to defeat your fear of being exposed, of being known. Cry for the grace to be willing to stop, look, listen, receive, grieve, confess, and turn. Stand with courage and hope before the searching and exposing mirror of the word of God and be unafraid. Stand exposed and know that all of it has been fully and completely covered by the shed blood of your Savior. Because of him, you don't need to be afraid of your unrighteousness. No, it is your delusions of righteousness that are the grave danger.

> Repent therefore, and turn back, that your sins may be blotted out, that times of refreshing may come from the presence of the Lord. (Acts 3:19–20)

Reflect: What are you afraid of being exposed? How can Christ's grace make you honest and fearless?

JUNE 16

I still need to be rescued from me because as long as sin remains, I'll be drawn to desire, think, say, and do what God names as evil.

You and I don't live only in big moments. We probably make only a couple of big, life-altering decisions our whole lives. Years after we die, as our descendants gather for reunions, they will struggle to remember even these big events of our lives. We all live in little, unnoticed, unremarkable, mundane moments of life. Because we do, it's very easy to back away from the seriousness of our struggle with sin that is constantly being revealed in those little moments. It's easy to think this kind of sin isn't a big deal.

Yet these little moments of your life are profoundly important. Think about it this way. The character of any person's life is not shaped by two or three grand, big moments of life. A person's character is formed in ten thousand little, mundane moments of everyday life. It's the character that is formed in those little moments of life that determines how you think and respond in the few big moments of life that you encounter. So those "little sins" are not so little after all:

- the nasty retort
- the "me first" pride
- the flash of lust at the mall
- the anger at someone who got in your way
- those little bitter thoughts
- the addiction to little pleasures
- the impatience with a loved one

Sure, they all happen in little moments that go by so quickly you may fail to notice them. Yet these everyday moments remind you and me that we never rise above our need for rescuing grace. They tell us that what we have found in Christ we still desperately need. They call us to be aware and to be serious. Why? The war for our hearts is not over. Our need for a conquering Savior has not ended. These little moments actually point the finger at something that is huge—our struggle with sin and our need for the grace that can be found only in our Savior, the King, the Lamb, the Lord Jesus Christ.

> Not that I have already obtained this or am already perfect, but I press on to make it my own, because Christ Jesus has made me his own. (Phil. 3:12)

Reflect: Which of these "little sins" resonates most with you? Take a minute to turn this "little sin" into confession to God for his gracious forgiveness.

JUNE 17

Through difficult relationships and circumstances, God works to expose your heart so you will seek the grace that can be found only in him.

Where does your mind go, when difficulty enters your door? None of us likes to suffer or deal with the unexpected. We all like our plans and dreams to work. We all want a life that is comfortable and fun. The normal person simply doesn't see the spiritual value in hardship. Because of this, it tends to be difficult for us to stay on the same page as God's agenda.

Many Christians say they trust in Jesus and believe the Bible. Yet they live in an unspoken state of disappointment, irritation, impatience, or frustration with God. This state is often characterized by this classic question: "If God loves me, then why would he _____?" Let's unpack the question.

First, there is no "if" to the love of God. As the psalmist says, "His steadfast love endures forever!" (Ps. 118:1). His love never changes or grows weary. This means it is never up for question. Second, consider the content of the question. When you ask—"What good and wise thing could God possibly be doing when what's happening to me doesn't seem good and wise?"—the question immediately expresses doubt about the character of God. The answer to this kind of question never leads you anywhere spiritually good.

Here's the bottom line: you and I struggle with the faithfulness of God, not because he has been unfaithful but because we have. Faithfully, from day one, God has purposed to bring us into relationship with him and to mold us into the image of his Son. He has never promised us our definition of the good life. Rather, he has promised that he will use all the tools at his disposal to complete the work of redemption that he has begun in our lives. He has not been unfaithful. He has kept every one of his promises.

Our problem is that we tend to be unfaithful to his holy agenda. We get kidnapped by our plans and dreams. The trials in our lives exist not because he has forgotten us, but because he remembers us and is changing us by his grace. When you remember that, you can have joy in the middle of what is uncomfortable.

> So we do not lose heart. Though our outer self is wasting away, our inner self is being renewed day by day. (2 Cor. 4:16)

Reflect: What plans and dreams have kidnapped your heart away from God's agenda? Why?

JUNE 18

The temporary pleasures of this present world are meant to point you to the lasting pleasures of knowing God.

The story in John 6 didn't end the way the crowd thought it would (6:25–51). Jesus has just fed a large crowd of people with a little boy's lunch. The crowd is amazed at his power and excited about his ability to provide for them physically. Here's what happens next:

> When they found him on the other side of the sea, they said to him, "Rabbi, when did you come here?" Jesus answered them, "Truly, truly, I say to you, you are seeking me, not because you saw signs, but because you ate your fill of the loaves. Do not work for the food that perishes, but for the food that endures to eternal life, which the Son of Man will give to you. For on him God the Father has set his seal." . . . Jesus said to them, "I am the bread of life; whoever comes to me shall not hunger, and whoever believes in me shall never thirst." (John 6:25–27, 35)

The crowd thinks that this rabbi (teacher) is just the kind of king they want. But Jesus is having none of it. To the surprise of the crowd, he runs and hides. When the crowd finally catches up with him, they confess their confusion at his response. So Jesus essentially replies: "I came to earth not just to be your physical provider, but to meet your deepest spiritual needs. Every good physical thing I give you is meant to point you to the spiritual provision that you need and that I will make for you in my life, death, and resurrection."

This leaves us all with questions: What do we really want out of life? What do we really want from God? Do we value his forgiveness? Do we really care to be transformed? Do we value God's grace, or would we rather have comfortable lives—nice cars, tech, online following, clothes, and friends?

Could it be that you want him to be your King for all the wrong reasons? If your answer is yes, don't run and hide from him because there's grace for that too!

> For the grace of God has appeared, bringing salvation for all people, training us to renounce ungodliness and worldly passions, and to live self-controlled, upright, and godly lives in the present age. (Titus 2:11–12)

Reflect: Humbly meditate on this question today: What gift could Jesus offer you that would make you want to make him your King?

JUNE 19

Grace has the power to do what nothing else can do—rescue you from you—and in so doing, restore you to what you were created to be.

It's hard to admit that we have a problem that we cannot solve. We like to think that our impatience is more about the poor planning or character of the people we have to deal with every day. We like to think that our sin can be blamed on the temptations of the fallen world around us. But the Bible is quite clear. We all suffer from the same terminal disease. And it's not caused by the people or situations around us. David says it this way: "Behold, I was brought forth in iniquity, and in sin did my mother conceive me" (Ps. 51:5).

You and I can try to fool ourselves or blame others. Yet there is simply no denying the harsh reality of the Bible's hard-to-accept message—we are our own biggest problem. We need help, help that we cannot give ourselves. We need help that is deeper than education, socialization, politics, or changes of relationship or location. If left on our own, we are doomed, "having no hope and without God in the world" (Eph. 2:12).

But the hope-infused story of Scripture is that we have not been left on our own. God has controlled the events of the world as part of his unstoppable agenda of *rescue* and *restoration*. He sent his holy Son to enter the world and suffer because of sin's mess. He sent him to live the perfect life that we would never live, to sacrifice himself on account of our sin, and to defeat death. It is an agenda of awesome grace extended to lost, rebellious, and self-excusing people—people who need that grace even to understand how much they need that grace. This grace had to include *rescue* because we could not escape ourselves, and it had to include *restoration* because we had no power to transform ourselves into what God intended. So today, confess your need. Denying it never leads anywhere good. Thank God for the rescue and restoration that is your hope. And determine to look honestly into the mirror of God's word so you will continue to remember how much you need what he has freely given.

The heart is deceitful above all things,
  and desperately sick;
  who can understand it? (Jer. 17:9)

Reflect: Which people in your life do you tend to hide your weakness from most? Why?

JUNE 20

If you're God's, to tell yourself you can't do what you've been called to do is to preach private heresy. You've been enabled by grace.

As a being made in the image of God, you are a meaning maker. You are rational, which means you have a built-in desire to know, understand, and be free of things that don't make any sense to you. This means that you live life based not on the facts of your experience, but rather on your particular interpretation of the facts. It also means that you are the most influential person in your life because you talk to yourself more than anyone else does.

We never stop preaching
some kind of gospel to ourselves.
It's a gospel of
aloneness,
partiality,
poverty,
inability—
or it's the true gospel of
Jesus Christ,
a gospel of
hope,
mercy,
forgiveness,
rescue,
love,
transformation;
of never being alone,
of never being without help;
of One who is near,
of One who cares;
of a beautiful forever
awash in victory.
We're always listening to
what we're preaching.

So say to yourself, "There are many things I don't understand, but I know my Father is in control. He is wise and good, and I know he loves me." Ultimately, rest is not from knowing but trusting. Asking yourself why won't always give you rest, but reminding yourself who is in charge of whatever happens will.[8]

Put not your trust in princes,
  in a son of man, in whom there is no salvation.
When his breath departs, he returns to the earth;
  on that very day his plans perish.

Blessed is he whose help is the God of Jacob,
  whose hope is in the LORD his God,
who made heaven and earth,
  the sea, and all that is in them,
who keeps faith forever;
  who executes justice for the oppressed,
  who gives food to the hungry.

  The LORD sets the prisoners free. (Ps. 146:3–7)

Reflect: Today, what kind of gospel will you preach to you? And what effect will it have on how you live?

JUNE 21

No, you don't know what you'll face today, but your sovereign Savior does, and his mercies are new and formfitted for what you will face.

Hebrews 4:14–16 contain gloriously comforting words. All of God's children need these words to live fresh in our minds:

> Since then we have a great high priest who has passed through the heavens, Jesus, the Son of God, let us hold fast our confession. For we do not have a high priest who is unable to sympathize with our weaknesses, but one who in every respect has been tempted as we are, yet without sin. Let us then with confidence draw near to the throne of grace, that we may receive mercy and find grace to help in time of need.

Consider the hope that is built into these words:

- *We have a high priest.* If this was all the passage said, it would be amazing. The fact that Jesus sits now at the Father's right hand and constantly prays for us is a redemptive miracle worthy of eternal celebration!
- *Our high priest sympathizes with our weaknesses.* This high priest is also uniquely able to be touched by the weakness of our human condition. He is not cold or indifferent to our struggles in any way.
- *We run to a high priest who has been through what we've been through and more.* It is comforting to remember why this one is so easily touched by our struggles: because he walked in our shoes. He willingly faced all that we face and more. He faced higher and deeper pressures than we do. Yet he never broke, whereas we all give in somewhere along the way.
- *We can go to him with confidence.* The result of all of this is that in our struggles with weakness and temptation, we have someone we can turn to with complete confidence and sure hope. He really does hold in his hands everything that we need.
- *We can expect mercy that is formfitted for our particular needs.* Because of his grace, what can we expect? On the basis of his faithful presence and his reliable promises, we can expect mercies exactly right for what we are now facing and nothing less.

> When he saw the crowds, he had compassion for them, because they were harassed and helpless, like sheep without a shepherd. (Matt. 9:36)

Reflect: When you struggle and are confronted with your weakness, say to yourself, "For this weakness I have a reliable and understanding high priest."

JUNE 22

What you worship is not best shown on Sunday morning but demonstrated by your words and behavior the rest of the week.

The word *worship* is widely misunderstood. Most people who hear the word *worship* immediately think of some kind of public religious activity. Perhaps what comes to mind is a gathering of pilgrims to lay candles at the feet of Buddha; the singing of a hymn with a thousand fellow believers; or a gathering of a small group on a Wednesday night. In other words, for most people, *worship* is a word that summarizes the outward spiritual activity of their lives.

Yet the Bible portrays us not just as people who occasionally worship, but *as* worshipers. It's not just that we have a religious aspect to our living. No, we've been designed by God to be worshipers. He placed that worship impulse in all our hearts. This means that worship is first our identity before it ever becomes our activity. There's no such thing as a non-worshiping human being. The only thing that divides human beings is what or whom they worship.

This means that as humans we all attach our identity, our hopes and dreams, our inner sense of well-being, and our meaning and purpose to something. And Scripture says that there are only two possible objects of our worship. No matter what your theology is, you are either worshiping the Creator or you are worshiping some part of his creation. Worship of the one true and living God is the only place where life can be found. Worship of anything else is a pathway to doom. Yet sin reduces all of us to idolaters in some way. We all put ourselves, other people, or other things in God's rightful place.

So today, every word you say, every choice you make, and every action you take will be shaped by some kind of worship. Nothing depicts your need for the grace of Jesus better than the war of worship that will rage in your heart today.

> Ascribe to the LORD the glory due his name;
>   bring an offering and come before him!
> Worship the LORD in the splendor of holiness;
>   tremble before him, all the earth;
>   yes, the world is established; it shall never be moved.
> Let the heavens be glad, and let the earth rejoice,
>   and let them say among the nations, "The LORD reigns!"
>   (1 Chron. 16:29–31)

Reflect: Think about how you've used your phone in the last 24 hours. What does this reveal about what you worship?

JUNE 23

Grief is good when it mourns what God hates, but it's dangerous when it questions God's goodness and love.

Who can't relate to the struggle of Asaph, the author of Psalm 73? Admit it. You've been there:

But as for me, my feet had almost stumbled,
    my steps had nearly slipped.
For I was envious of the arrogant
    when I saw the prosperity of the wicked.

For they have no pangs until death;
    their bodies are fat and sleek.
They are not in trouble as others are;
    they are not stricken like the rest of mankind. . . .
Behold, these are the wicked;
    always at ease, they increase in riches.
All in vain have I kept my heart clean
    and washed my hands in innocence.
For all the day long I have been stricken
    and rebuked every morning. . . .

When my soul was embittered,
    when I was pricked in heart
I was brutish and ignorant;
    I was like a beast toward you. (Ps. 73:2–5, 12–14, 21–22)

Asaph is filled with grief, but it is a dangerous, angry, and accusatory grief. I've been there. I've felt Asaph's feelings. I've said similar words. In a fallen world, you have reasons to grieve. You should mourn your struggle with sin. You should mourn the sorry, broken condition of this fallen world. You should mourn corruption, injustice, poverty, pollution, and disease. It is right to mourn these things, but you had better guard your mourning. Your mourning is never neutral; you are either mourning with God, who weeps for the condition of the world he made. Or you're mourning against God, questioning his goodness, wisdom, and love.

Sometimes it seems that the good guys are being hammered and the bad guys have it easy. In the face of this reality, Asaph essentially says, "I've obeyed, and this is what I get?" It's an angry charge against the goodness of God. When you don't understand what's going on, run to God's goodness rather than questioning whether it exists. Say with Asaph, the following prayer:

My flesh and my heart may fail,
    but God is the strength of my heart and my portion forever. (Ps. 73:26)

Reflect: When you see or experience some form of injustice this week, how can Psalm 73 direct your heart?

JUNE 24

God is unwilling to be your means to what you call the "good life." Your relationship with him must be your definition of the good life.

We do tend to turn God into a delivery system. We get excited about what he can do for us and what he can give us. We fall into thinking of prayer as asking God to sign the bottom of our self-oriented wish lists. We set our hearts on things that we think will make us happy. Perhaps it's the love of another person, or it's a certain level of wealth and all the things we could enjoy as a result. Maybe it's personal success, influence, fame, health, or comfort. Now, in a way, none of these things is inherently evil, but there's something wrong about the whole system.

So many of our ideas of what the "good life" is don't actually have God in them. We envision the "good" quite apart from the grace of his presence, promises, and provisions. And because we fall into believing that life can be found outside him, God isn't central to our dreams. He's not *in* our dreams. Unless we see him as the delivery mechanism of the good life we are dreaming about. He is not life to us; he's just the deliverer of life.

It's all a spiritual world turned upside down. In our fantasies of the good life, we decide what is right, good, important, and valuable. We define what life is. The menu of the good life is written by us. It has us at the center. And we employ God to do our bidding. If he does, we will thank him and proclaim his goodness. Yet this is self-centered religiosity that bears little resemblance to the faith of the Bible. Still we find it so easy to set ourselves up as sovereign. It's so natural to shop horizontally for what will only ever be found vertically, and then to question why God failed to deliver.

As Psalm 103:2 and 5 say, the "good things" we enjoy come in a person, and his name is Jesus. Yes, it is true—Jesus is the "good life" that you need, no matter what is on your wish list.

> Bless the Lord, O my soul,
>   and forget not all his benefits, . . .
> who satisfies you with good
>   so that your youth is renewed like the eagle's. (Ps. 103:2, 5)

Reflect: What do your most regular prayer requests say about your heart and your vision for the "good life"?

JUNE 25

Discouragement focuses more on the broken glories of creation than it does on the restoring glories of God's character, presence, and promises.

They were standing on the borders of the land that God had promised them. It stretched out before them with beauty and abundance. But the children of Israel were not jumping up and down in celebration and anticipation, ready to get going. They were doing quite the opposite. They were digging in their heels and refusing to move at all. They stood there grumbling against the Lord, saying: "Because the LORD hated us he has brought us out of the land of Egypt, to give us into the hands of the Amorites, to destroy us. . . . 'The people are greater and taller than we. The cities are great and fortified up to heaven'" (Deut. 1:27–28).

These people were just like us. They were about to be given what they did not deserve and could not earn. Why? Because the one who had redeemed them from bondage was not just a deliverer of freedom. He was also a giver of life. But they would not move. Why? Because to them it all seemed like a cruel setup; the big, spiritual bait and switch. They had been promised a land of their own, but what they got was a place filled with people who didn't want them there. What in the world was God doing anyway?

Yet their disappointed thinking had a fatal flaw in it. What they saw as blocking God's plan was actually part of his plan. God knows what you are facing too. He sees the impossible brokenness that is all around you. He is not in a panic, wondering how he'll ever pull off his plan with all these obstacles in the way. Don't be discouraged. God has you exactly where he wants you. He knows just how to take what makes you afraid and use it to build your faith. He is not surprised by the troubles you face, and he surely has no intention of leaving you to face those things on your own. He can defeat what you can't. And he intends these troubles to be tools of grace that transform you.

> Have I not commanded you? Be strong and courageous. Do not be frightened, and do not be dismayed, for the LORD your God is with you wherever you go." (Josh. 1:9)

Reflect: What's stressing you out right now? How does today's devotional change the way you should think about your troubles?

JUNE 26

When you think you're righteous, you expect others to be righteous as well, so you become demanding, judgmental, and constantly disappointed.

So much of our disappointment in relationships is not because we have an unrealistic view of others. It's because we have a distorted view of ourselves. Confused? Let me explain.

Late on a Thursday night, one of your parents comes to your room to ask you something. They can barely open the door because there are dirty clothes, spoiled food items, and pieces of sports gear everywhere. Your mom or dad explodes: "I never thought one of my children would turn out to be such a slob. I should take every piece of your junk and lock it away and leave you in an empty room until you put on your big-boy pants and grow up. Why, in my day, I never would have thought of treating my stuff this way." Now, unpack this statement with me. As your parent is venting, what are you thinking? Good chance you're not saying to yourself: "My, this is helpful. This is a truly wise person who is saying very helpful things to me. I am so thankful that this person is my parent." No, that's not what you're thinking. In fact, if you took a moment, you're probably thinking that this is one of the least helpful things for changing your life.

Perhaps this would never happen with your room or your parents. But don't we all adopt this kind of attitude? If we're honest, we all know how easy it is to feel self-righteous. And then it doesn't take much before self-righteousness permits us to be angry and unkind to someone else. When you unleash on someone like this, you're saying, "If you were as righteous as me, you wouldn't live like this." When you assign to yourself righteousness that you don't have, you expect the people around you to be as righteous as you think you are, and you greet them with judgment when they aren't (see Matt. 23:1–12).

In contrast, you deal with others with grace when you walk around with the humble realization of how deeply you need grace. When you admit that there are few struggles in others that don't exist in some way in your life as well, you encourage them with God's grace rather than hammering them with the law.

> Whoever exalts himself will be humbled, and whoever humbles himself will be exalted. (Matt. 23:12)

Reflect: Do you silently compare yourself with others? What could you do instead?

JUNE 27

There is a significant difference between amazement and faith. God doesn't just want to blow your mind; he wants to rule your heart.

Here's an important distinction. Faith engages and even amazes your mind, but true biblical faith also radically rearranges the way you approach everything in life. Amazement is what you experience when you are taken beyond what you can explain. Amazement is a step in the faith process, but there is a huge difference between amazement and faith.

Pretend you're standing next to me on a pier on the Jersey Shore. We're looking at one of those amusement park contraptions that is essentially a 50-foot-high slingshot, into which they strap some otherwise sane human being and launch him back and forth over the Atlantic Ocean in the night. Now, that ride amazes both of us, but we're not about to strap in and let ourselves be launched into the night. Amazed? Yes, but we will not put our faith in that thing. In the same way:

- You can be amazed by the grand sweep of the redemptive story in Scripture and not be living by faith.
- You can be amazed by the exquisite logic of the theology of the word of God and not be living by faith.
- You can be amazed by the great worship music you participate in every Sunday and not be living by faith.
- You can be amazed by the love of your small group and not be living by faith.
- You can be amazed by the wonderful biblical preaching and teaching that you hear and not be living by faith.
- You can be amazed by the grace of the cross of Jesus and not be living by faith.

There is a significant, yes, even profound difference between amazement and faith. God will not leave us in a state of amazement. He works by grace to craft us into people of settled, hopeful, courageous, active, celebratory, God-glorifying faith. He will settle for nothing less. He is not satisfied with the wonder of our minds. He works so that we really will "believe that he exists and that he rewards those who seek him" (Heb. 11:6). You can't work that faith up in yourself. It is a gift of his grace. The cross makes that gift available to you right here, right now.

This people honors me with their lips,
  but their heart is far from me. (Matt. 15:8)

Reflect: How is your Sunday morning worship different from your Friday night living?

JUNE 28

If God is in control of every aspect of your world and his grace covers all your sin, why would you ever give way to fear?

There are many things I wish were true about me:

- I wish I could say that worry never interrupts my sleep, but I can't.
- I wish I could say that I never give way to envy, but I can't.
- I wish I could say that I am always aware that God is near, but I can't.
- I wish I could say that I never dread what's around the corner, but I can't.
- I wish I could say that all that I do is done out of faith and not fear, but I can't.

You see, I have come to be very aware that although I know the Bible and its truth well, the battle between fear and faith still goes on in my heart. Here's what this means for real life. For the Christian, fear should be an artifact of a former civilization, right? So why does fear still haunt the life of a believer in the hallways, kitchens, bedrooms, family rooms, workrooms, and vans of everyday life?

Fear lives and rules in the heart of a believer who has forgotten God's sovereignty and grace. If left to myself, I *should* be afraid. There are many trials, temptations, dangers, and enemies in this fallen world that are bigger and more powerful than me. But the message of the gospel is that I haven't been left to myself. God rules with perfect wisdom over all the circumstances and locations that would make me afraid. In grace, he blesses me with what I need to face whatever he's put on my plate. I am never—in anything, anywhere, at any time—by myself. I never move beyond the reach of his authority. He is never surprised by where I end up or by what I am facing. He never leaves me to the limited resources of my own wisdom, strength, and righteousness. He will never abandon me out of weariness or frustration. I do not need to be afraid. When you forget God's sovereignty and his grace, you give room in your heart for fear to do its nasty, debilitating work.

> Fear not, nor be afraid;
>   have I not told you from of old and declared it?
>   And you are my witnesses!
> Is there a God besides me?
>   There is no Rock; I know not any. (Isa. 44:8)

Reflect: Pray right now for grace to remember God's sovereignty all throughout your day and week. Your Savior loves to hear and answer.

JUNE 29

If you're God's child, when you sin, you can run toward God and not away from him because all your sin is covered by the blood of Jesus.

The beginning of the Bible and its end feature two starkly contrasting scenes! In the beginning scene, we see Adam and Eve quickly clothing themselves and hiding from God. They feel the guilt and shame that's the sad result of their sin (Genesis 3). Before, they were blessed with an unhindered relationship with the Lord, Creator, and King of the universe. They were blessed with a garden lush with every good thing. They really did have it all. They were made by God and hardwired to enjoy eternal fellowship with him. So how could they try to hide from the one who was the reason for their entire existence? It is too sad to grasp, but the answer to the question is clear: sin, with its weight of guilt and shame, separated them from God and drove them from the garden of his presence. The bond was broken; how would it ever be repaired?

The second scene is the marriage supper of the Lamb (Rev. 19:6–10). It too is a gathering of sinners, but they aren't cowering in shame and guilt. They aren't dreading his presence or anger. No, these sinners are celebrating because the bond that was broken in the garden has been restored. They have been wed to their Savior forever. Forever they will be in his presence. Never again will they hide. Never again will they be driven away. Their fellowship will never end. They are accepted because of him. There is no sin that separates them. It is a scene of such outrageous beauty that describing it would stretch human language beyond its limits.

What made the difference between these two scenes? Not human wisdom, strength, position, or righteousness. The difference is captured in one gloriously transformational word: *grace*. Grace in the person and work—the life, death, and resurrection—of Jesus is what made the difference. If you're God's child, stop hiding behind the trees of your shame. Step out into the light. There's a celebration in your future!

> And I heard a loud voice from the throne saying, "Behold, the dwelling place of God is with man. He will dwell with them, and they will be his people, and God himself will be with them as their God." (Rev. 21:3)

Reflect: What does this grace say to you in moments when you feel cynical?

JUNE 30

If the righteousness of Christ allows me to stand before a holy God utterly unafraid, why should I be haunted by what you think of me?

So many people live with a great big gap right in the middle of their gospel, and they don't know it. I did for years. Most Christians have a basic understanding of salvation past. (That is, you know about the grace of forgiveness that you've received because of the broken body and shed blood of the Lamb, the Lord Jesus Christ.) And most Christians tend to look forward with anticipation toward salvation future. (That is, you anticipate the grace of eternal peace and harmony lived in the presence of the triune God.) But, sadly, many, many Christians have little understanding of salvation present. (That is, we don't grasp the benefits of the work of Jesus Christ right here, right now.) It is vitally important that we understand the *nowism* of the gospel of the Lord Jesus Christ.

Jesus died for the tough conversation that you need to have with your parent, your sibling, or your friend. He died for the tensions in your broken and dysfunctional family. He died for the sexual temptation that seems to get the better of you. He died for the materialism that seems to kidnap you. He died for your fear of the opinions of others or for the darkness of your depression. He died so that, between your past conversion and your future resurrection, you would have everything you need to live as he intended.

When you begin to understand this, it really does change the way you think. And it changes the way you live. If he has given you his full and complete acceptance, even on your worst day, then why should you seek your inner peace from the acceptance of a flawed human being? If he is with you, providing whatever you need, why should you fear what's around the corner? His present grace frees us from so much of the fear and control that distorts our lives and relationships. Why? Because once you know what he thinks of you, you are free to worry less about what the person next to you thinks. That's a freedom many of us could use!

> Since, therefore, we have now been justified by his blood, much more shall we be saved by him from the wrath of God. (Rom. 5:9)

Reflect: How does fear grab your heart most often? Meditate on that fear, God's present help, and Romans 5:9.

JULY 1

Does discouragement preach to you a false gospel that causes you to forget that your future has already been written into the pages of God's book?

It is discouraging to face:

- your struggle with sin;
- the disloyalty of a friend;
- the disappointment of your parents;
- the temptations that seem to be all around you;
- the injustice that lives in this fallen world;
- the pain and worry of physical sickness; and
- the death of your dreams.

Yes, it's hard to face all of these things. It's easy to lose your way. It's tempting to wonder what God is doing, if he cares, and if he hears your prayers. It's hard to hold on to his promises. It's hard to stay committed to good spiritual habits. It's hard not to give in to discouragement and give way to the desire to quit.

But in the face of discouragement, there is one thing that you need to remember. It is captured in just a few powerful words from Psalm 139: "Your eyes saw my unformed substance; in your book were written, every one of them, the days that were formed for me, when as yet there were none of them" (139:16). When trouble comes your way and discouragement begins to grip your heart, it's vital to remember that every single day of your life was written into God's book before you lived any of them. None of those disappointments are a surprise to your Lord. He carefully authored the content of every one of your days with his own hand. He controlled every twist and turn of the plot that is your story. Nothing will happen to you that he has not written into his book. And he has already determined how your story will end.

You see, what discourages you doesn't surprise him. Why? Because he authored it all with a glorious combination of wisdom and grace. Nothing is out of his control. Your Savior is sovereign. He knows what is best and will do what is best. This is where rest and courage are to be found when discouragement shakes the resolve of your heart.

> The LORD knows the days of the blameless,
>   and their heritage will remain forever;
> they are not put to shame in evil times;
>   in the days of famine they have abundance. (Ps. 37:18–19)

Reflect: Are you bitter about specific areas or disappointments in your life? How do God's wisdom and grace help, even without fixing the problems?

JULY 2

Corporate worship is designed to turn your heart from the shadow glories of creation to the one glory that will satisfy it.

The words below, from Deuteronomy 6, were a warning to the children of Israel. Yet as you read them, remember that they are words we all need to hear and heed.

This side of eternity, having lots of stuff can be dangerous. It's not that material things are bad in and of themselves. God intentionally designed his world to be a beautiful place. It's not that it's wrong to enjoy the material world around us. God gave us the capacity and desire to enjoy this beauty. The problem with material things is not found in the material things; it's found in us. Our problem with the material world is a heart problem. The warning can be stated in a few words: *Be careful when you're full that you do not forget.* The sight, sound, touch, taste, and splendor of these created glories tempt us to think that life is found in having these things and to think we have everything that we need because we have them. These things weaken our God awareness and our God hunger. So we are then set up to give our hearts to the worship of what is created rather than the worship of the one who created it all.

The physical world is full of many glories, but the pursuit of these glories must not rule my heart. Why? Because they have zero ability to offer me the life that I so desperately need. Life is only ever found in what all those earth-bound glories point to—a God of awesome glory who is the source and giver of life. He gives life that satisfies and remains forever. Because he is a God of grace, he showers glories on me so that those glories would lead me to him.

> And when the Lord your God brings you into the land . . . with great and good cities that you did not build, and houses full of all good things that you did not fill, and cisterns that you did not dig, and vineyards and olive trees that you did not plant—and when you eat and are full, then take care lest you forget the Lord, who brought you out of the land of Egypt, out of the house of slavery. It is the Lord your God you shall fear. (Deut. 6:10–13)

Reflect: What practical steps could you take today (like making notes or using an app) to help you better remember the Lord today?

JULY 3

Jesus paid it all! There are no bills due for your sin!
You are now free to simply trust and obey.

Stop trying to earn something from God. Stop trying to gain more of his acceptance. Stop trying to win his allegiance. Stop trying to morally buy your way out of his anger. Just stop trying.

So many Christians load onto their shoulders a burden that they do not have to bear. They get up every morning and pick up the heavy load of trying to achieve something with God. Yet it simply cannot work. Instead, it leads to one of two places. It can lead to the scary pride of self-righteousness. This is where you have no problem judging people you don't think who have achieved a level of righteousness you think that they should have. Or it can lead to fear and discouragement. This is a culture of people who don't run to God with their sin because they're afraid of him.

Paul wipes out this distorted, debilitating "buy your way into grace" culture with a striking economy of words: "Now it is evident that no one is justified before God by the law" (Gal. 3:11). No one is ever accepted by God because he or she has kept the law. No one. Here's why. First, it's impossible to buy your way into God's favor because sin makes you a lawbreaker. And, second, your bills were fully and completely paid in the single payment of the cross of Jesus Christ. There is no payment plan because the cross means that everything's already paid for once and forever in one single payment.

So stop trying to measure up so you can get something from God. Stop hiding from him when you mess up. Stop comparing yourself to other people. Stop naming the good things you do as righteousness. Just stop asking the law to do what only grace can achieve. Then start resting in the fact that you don't have any moral bills due because Jesus paid them all on the cross. And when you sin, don't pretend you didn't, don't panic, and don't hide. Run to Jesus and receive mercy in your time of need, the kind of mercy he paid for you to have.

> But he was pierced for our transgressions;
> he was crushed for our iniquities;
> upon him was the chastisement that brought us peace,
> and with his wounds we are healed. (Isa. 53:5)

Reflect: Which sentence above struck closest to your heart? Why?

JULY 4

When you're weary with the battle, remember that the one who is your strength never takes a break, never needs sleep, never grows weary.

Life in this fallen world is wearisome. Sometimes your friendships are exhausting as you cultivate a friendship with other sinners. Sometimes you don't feel like being nice to "that person" who seems to be able to look at everything and find a reason to complain. Sometimes you just get exhausted with dealing with your heart—you know, those desires you shouldn't have and those thoughts you shouldn't think. Sometimes you have to drag yourself to your church service or your small group. Sometimes you'd just like to get off the Christianity treadmill and zone out, but you can't. You wake up the next day and you have to do it all over again—another temptation, another misunderstanding, another conflict with another friend, or another moment when you feel the emotional temperature change.

When you're weary and feeling weak, run to the Psalms; there's grace to be found there. The psalm below confronts you and me with two truths that we must always remember. First, we are not in this battle alone. We have a keeper, and our safety is his commitment. Second, the one who is our keeper never, ever takes a break. His keeping care is 24/7 forever and ever. The inexhaustible keeper is your help and strength; when weary, run to him.

> I lift up my eyes to the hills.
> From where does my help come?
> My help comes from the Lord,
> who made heaven and earth.
>
> He will not let your foot be moved;
> he who keeps you will not slumber.
> Behold, he who keeps Israel
> will neither slumber nor sleep.
>
> The Lord is your keeper;
> the Lord is your shade on your right hand.
> The sun shall not strike you by day,
> nor the moon by night.
>
> The Lord will keep you from all evil;
> he will keep your life.
> The Lord will keep
> your going out and your coming in
> from this time forth and forevermore. (Psalm 121)

Reflect: Which part of this psalm is most difficult for you to accept? Why?

JULY 5

Weakness is the window to strength. Confessing your inability produces hunger for the power that is only ever found in Jesus.

Our problem is not our weakness. God's grace is up to the task. Our problem is our delusions of strength that keep us from seeking the grace to strengthen us in our weakness. We just don't like to be weak. We don't want others to see us that way. So we act as if we can handle things that we can't handle, and we don't seek the help that's available. It is all a failed quest for independence.

But we are not independent. None of us are. We were not created to be independent. We were formed to be dependent on the one who made us. And we were re-created in Jesus Christ to be dependent on his grace. God does not expect of you what you do not have. He knows who you are. He is never shocked or dismayed by your weakness. He has moved toward you in grace because you are weak. He knows we would have no hope in life and death without him. The person who is shocked and dismayed by your weakness is you. It bothers and embarrasses you. It causes you to playact in public and to deceive yourself in private. Your weakness will drive you crazy unless you understand the gospel of Jesus.

What is that message? It is the story of a strong and able Savior who showers his powerful grace on people who are fundamentally weak. He confronts you with your weakness so you will run to him for strength. He calls you to mountains too big to climb. Why? So that in your inability, you will look to him. Perhaps it's not such a bad thing to come to the end of your rope—if at the end of your rope you find a strong and willing Savior.

So don't be afraid to cry out in weakness. Because when you affirm your weakness, you are teaching your heart to celebrate the grace that can make you strong.

> The Lord is my strength and my song,
>   and he has become my salvation;
> this is my God, and I will praise him,
>   my father's God, and I will exalt him. (Ex. 15:2)

Reflect: Sometime in the next week, you'll be confronted with your weakness. When you are, how will you respond? Will you work to convince yourself you're strong? Or will you run to the one who is?

JULY 6

The grace you've been given is not just the grace of forgiveness and acceptance; it's also the grace of empowerment. So get up and follow.

In the life of the believer, God has promised to provide and empower; your job is to follow him by faith where you live every day. You don't wait for the provision before you move. God has not promised that you will see it beforehand. Instead, you move forward in the certainty that he is with you, for you, and in you. This God of awesome power will give you power to do what is needed. This is his reliable promise to you.

And what kind of power does he have? Let me refer you to one of the strangest verses in all of Scripture, one that paints a dramatic picture of the awe-inspiring power of God. It's found in Exodus 11. God is delivering his people from their captivity in Egypt, and all the firstborn of Egypt are going to die, including cattle. God says that as the result of this, there will be a great cry throughout Egypt like there has never been before. Then he says, "But not a dog shall growl against any of the people of Israel, either man or beast, that you may know that the LORD makes a distinction between Egypt and Israel" (11:7). What kind of power does God have? He has the power to silence the growl of every dog in Egypt. But there is more. He also has the power to cause the dogs to distinguish between Israelites and Egyptians. The dogs will wail against the Egyptians and be silent in the presence of Israelites. How is this possible? All because there is a God who rules all things. He even has the power to direct individual animals to do what he wants them to do.

Yes, your God has awesome power, distinguishing power. He knows who his people are, where they are, what they need, and when they need it. He also knows what needs to be delivered and what needs to be controlled for his will to be done. He always gives the power that his people need.

> Say therefore to the people of Israel, "I am the LORD, and I will bring you out from under the burdens of the Egyptians, and I will deliver you from slavery to them, and I will redeem you with an outstretched arm and with great acts of judgment." (Ex. 6:6)

Reflect: Do you feel like you are one of God's special children? Why or why not?

JULY 7

As God's child, you don't sit and wait for hope. No, grace makes it possible for you to get up and live in hope.

Perhaps one of the dirty secrets of the church is how much we do out of fear and not faith. We tell ourselves that what we're facing is too big and requires too much of us. We stand at the bottom of mountains of trouble and give up before we've taken the first step of the climb. We wait for hope to come in some noticeable, seeable way, but it never seems to arrive. We want to believe that God is there and that he really does care. Yet it seems that we've been left to ourselves. With each passing day, it seems harder to have hope for our families, for our churches, for our friendships, or just for the ability to survive all the trouble with our faith and sanity intact.

We fail to understand that we don't have a hope problem; we have a sight problem. Here's how: Hope has already come. "What?" you say. "Where?"

Hope isn't a thing, a set of circumstances, or a set of ideas. Hope is a person, and his name is Jesus. He came to earth to face what you face and to defeat what defeats you so that you would have hope. Your salvation means that you are now in a personal relationship with the one who is hope. You don't have a hope problem; you have been given hope that is both real and constant. The issue is whether you see it. In the verse below, Paul prays that we will have well-working spiritual vision. Why? So that we will "see" the hope that we have already been given in Christ. What is this hope? It is a rich inheritance. Jesus died and left us, who are weak, a rich inheritance of grace. You see, you don't really have a hope problem; you have a vision problem, and for that there's enlightening grace.

> Having the *eyes of your hearts* enlightened, that you may know what is the hope to which he has called you, what are the riches of his glorious inheritance in the saints, and what is the immeasurable greatness of his power toward us who believe, according to the working of his great might. (Eph. 1:18–19)

Reflect: What has captured your vision this week? Ask God to open your eyes to the beautiful hope of the gospel of Jesus Christ.

JULY 8

You always approach life with a mindset of some kind. Scripture says there are only two possibilities: "on earth" or "above."

I sat next to him on the Chinatown bus, the cheapest way to get home from New York City. I was tired and didn't really want to talk; if I could have found a completely empty seat, I would have gone for it. However, the seat next to this man in his late twenties was the only one open. It wasn't long before he asked me where I was from and what I did. I told him I lived in Philly and that I was a pastor and an author. He asked me what I wrote, and I told him that I wrote about everyday life issues from the perspective of the Bible. He responded: "I don't believe in the Bible, and I'm surprised that people still do. In fact, I don't think there is any such thing as truth that you can lay on someone else." I said, "But you just did—you just very confidently laid a truth on me." From there, we launched into a conversation that stretched to an hour and a half.

As I thought later about our conversation, I was struck by the utter lack of even a hint of neutrality in anything he or I said. Everything we said flowed out of who we thought we were, what we thought about God, what we thought about the nature of and purpose for life, and what we understood about the nature of truth and about the future.

So it is with you. Here are the practical questions: What set of values determines your schedule? What view of life determines how you make decisions? How does your thinking shape what you do and say every day? According to the verses below, you have only two choices: (1) You've got an "on earth" way of thinking that is all about this right here, right now physical moment. Or (2) you've got an "above" way of thinking that looks at life from the vantage point of the grand redemptive story. More specifically, this perspective keeps the person and work of the Lord Jesus Christ in view. What's your choice?

> If then you have been raised with Christ, seek the things that are above, where Christ is, seated at the right hand of God. Set your minds on things that are above, not on things that are on earth. (Col. 3:1–2)

Reflect: In everyday life, how are you viewing your life through the lens of the radical truths of the gospel of Jesus Christ?

JULY 9

The scary deception of sin is that, at the point of sinning, sin doesn't look all that sinful.

We lose sight of the sinfulness of sin or the evil of evil. When we do, we are vulnerable to the seductive lies of temptation. Perhaps this is one of the reasons why there are stories like this in the Bible. A man brought his son, who was being tormented by an evil spirit, to Jesus.

> And when the spirit saw [Jesus], immediately it convulsed the boy, and he fell on the ground and rolled about, foaming at the mouth. And Jesus asked his father, "How long has this been happening to him?" And he said, "From childhood. And it has often cast him into fire and into water, to destroy him. But if you can do anything, have compassion on us and help us." And Jesus said to him, "'If you can'! All things are possible for one who believes." Immediately the father of the child cried out and said, "I believe; help my unbelief!" And when Jesus saw that a crowd came running together, he rebuked the unclean spirit, saying to it, "You mute and deaf spirit, I command you, come out of him and never enter him again." And after crying out and convulsing him terribly, it came out, and the boy was like a corpse, so that most of them said, "He is dead." But Jesus took him by the hand and lifted him up, and he arose. (Mark 9:20–27)

In stories like these, God is lovingly confronting us with two things. First, we see the shocking evil of evil. Second, we realize the only place where deliverance from evil can be found. Examine the graphic descriptions of what evil is doing to this boy. Nothing good ever happens when evil is in control of a person's heart. Sin really is a scary, horrible thing. Evil is ugly and destructive, and must never be minimized. This story is meant to put a holy dread in your heart. But it is also meant to assure you that delivering grace is a reality. No matter how powerful the evil of evil is, God's delivering power is greater.

> To open their eyes, so that they may turn from darkness to light and from the power of Satan to God, that they may receive forgiveness of sins and a place among those who are sanctified by faith in me. (Acts 26:18)

Reflect: Do you live with this balance of hating sin and relying on the grace of Jesus Christ? Which is stronger for you? Why?

JULY 10

You once desired it, but now you're persuaded that you need it. Once you've named it a need, it has you.

It may be the sloppiest, most all-inclusive word in human language: *need*. We put far too many things into our "need" category. We need a heavenly Father who knows what we need (see Matthew 6) because we get *want* and *need* confused all the time.

When this happens, a need-driven addiction (spiritual slavery) often develops. It all starts with *desire* ("I want . . ."). There is nothing evil about desire itself. Yet it is very hard for sinners to hold desire with an open hand. It doesn't take long for our desires to morph into *demands* ("I must . . ."). The thing that was once a desire is now taking hold of us. We're less willing to live without it. We're more and more convinced that we have to have it. Then demand morphs into *need* ("I will . . ."). Now, we are convinced that we cannot live without it. That means it's now in control of our hearts. We think about it all the time. We are fearful when we're without it. We plot how to keep it in our lives.

But the cycle of slavery doesn't end there. Need forms *expectation* as to what God ought to do ("You should . . ."). You see, if you're convinced it's a need, you will think you're entitled to it. Then you will judge God's love by his willingness to deliver it. Expectation then leads to *disappointment* if God doesn't deliver ("You didn't . . ."). We can't believe that God would say that he loves us yet not meet this "need." The fact is, God has been faithful to all that he's promised us, but this desire that morphed into a need is not something he's promised to give us. So disappointment then leads us to some kind of *anger* ("Because you didn't, I will . . ."). Because we now judge God as unfaithful, we quit trusting him as we should. We let go of the good habits of our faith. Isn't it good to know that Jesus came to free us from our idolatry?

> But if we have food and clothing, with these we will be content. But those who desire to be rich fall into temptation, into a snare, into many senseless and harmful desires that plunge people into ruin and destruction. (1 Tim. 6:8–9)

Reflect: Which phase of this addiction development felt most familiar to you? Why? Confess it to the Lord of all grace and help.

JULY 11

God is at the center of his universe, and when you put yourself there, it only ends in relational brokenness and personal disappointment.

There is someone at the center of all things. There is someone who rules over heaven and earth. There is someone who controls the forces of physical nature. There is someone who authors the plot details of the story of every human being who has lived. There is someone who is worthy of honor, dominion, and power. There is someone who is deserving of the complete allegiance and unending worship of everyone.

The Bible is very clear when it proclaims who is at the center, and it is not us:

- In the beginning, God . . . (Gen. 1:1)
- You are my Son; today I have begotten you. Ask of me, and I will make the nations your heritage, and the ends of the earth your possession. (Ps. 2:7–8)
- For to us a child is born, to us a son is given; and the government shall be upon his shoulder, and his name shall be called Wonderful Counselor, Mighty God, Everlasting Father, Prince of Peace. (Isa. 9:6)
- He does according to his will among the host of heaven and among the inhabitants of the earth; and none can stay his hand or say to him, "What have you done?" (Dan. 4:35)
- For from him and through him and to him are all things. To him be glory forever. Amen. (Rom. 11:36)
- For by him all things were created, in heaven and on earth, visible and invisible, whether thrones or dominions or rulers or authorities—all things were created through him and for him. And he is before all things, and in him all things hold together. (Col. 1:16–17)

Yet the message of the garden of Eden is that sin makes us quest for God's position. We want life to work according to our will and conform to our plans. This desire to be at the center never goes anywhere good, personally or relationally. Self-centeredness is at the core of sin's dysfunction, another powerful evidence of our need for rescuing grace.

Worthy are you, our Lord and God,
    to receive glory and honor and power,
for you created all things,
    and by your will they existed and were created. (Rev. 4:11)

Reflect: What do your social media feeds reveal about what might be at the center of your life?

JULY 12

Life in this fallen world is hard. That's why you need a community of love.

Your walk with God is designed by God to be a community project. Anonymous, consumerist, isolated, independent, self-sufficient, "Jesus and me" Christianity describes distant distortions of the faith of the New Testament. You and I simply were not created ("It is not good that the man should be alone," Gen. 2:18) or re-created in Jesus Christ ("For the body does not consist of one member but of many," 1 Cor. 12:14) to live all by ourselves. The biblical word pictures of temple (stones joined together to be a place where God dwells) and body (each member dependent on the function of the other) destroy any idea that healthy Christianity can live outside of essential community.

Yet many, many believers live their lives with a huge gap between their public church personas and the details of their private existence. We are skilled at brief, non-personal conversations about the weather, sports, and politics. We live in long-term networks of endlessly casual relationships. No one really knows us beneath the well-crafted public display. And because they don't know us, they cannot minister to us because no one can minister to that which he does not know.

And if we think we know ourselves, and we think we're okay, we're forgetting the blinding power of sin. That's why church is, for many of us, nothing more than a thing to attend on Sunday. Church provides a wholesome buffet of activities for us. But the Bible is clear. The church is a community that's meant to enlighten and protect. It is meant to motivate and encourage. It is meant to rescue and restore. It is meant to instill hope and courage. It is meant to confront and rebuke. It is meant to be a visible representation of the grace of Jesus that is your hope. It is not a luxury. It is a spiritual necessity. When *each part* is working properly, the body of Christ grows to maturity in Christ (see Ephesians 4). We each need to live in an intentional, Christ-centered, grace-driven redemptive community.

> For as in one body we have many members, and the members do not all have the same function, so we, though many, are one body in Christ, and individually members one of another. (Rom. 12:4–5)

Reflect: What limitations do you experience in online church interactions?

JULY 13

You don't work in the hope of getting an identity; you work in celebration of the identity that, in Christ, you have been given.

In Christ. These are two of the most important words in the Bible's vocabulary. These two words that by grace we have been united to Christ, is a dominant theme in the apostle Paul's writing; he uses the phrase "in Christ" thirty-three times. All of the graces of the gospel flow to us because we are "in Christ." We are justified and forgiven because we are in Christ. We are being sanctified and have every need supplied because we are in Christ. We are adopted children, objects of the Father's love because we are in Christ. We have eternal hope because we are in Christ.

No longer aliens, no longer enemies, no longer condemned—but by grace we are in Christ, the children of God, objects of the Father's love, justified, forgiven, righteous, eternally loved, and united to God and one another. Because we are in Christ, we stand in the life-giving rain of justifying mercies, an eternal shower that nothing in heaven or on earth can ever stop. What better gift could ever be given than the gift of the person, work, and justifying grace of the Lord Jesus Christ?[9]

Identity:
No need to search for
myself.
No need to grasp for
meaning
for my life
or purpose
for what I do.
No need to hope for
inner peace,
that sense of well-being
for which every heart
longs.
No need to hope that
someone or something
will make me
happy
or give me joy.
I no longer need any
of these things because
grace
has connected me to you
and you have named me
your child.

> For in Christ Jesus you are all sons of God, through faith. For as many of you as were baptized into Christ have put on Christ. There is neither Jew nor Greek, there is neither slave nor free, there is no male and female, for you are all one in Christ Jesus. (Gal. 3:26–28)

Reflect: Take a few minutes, stop reading, and celebrate that you are "in Christ."

JULY 14

You don't get wisdom by experience or research. You get wisdom by means of relationship. Grace makes that relationship possible.

Sin reduces all of us to fools. Sadly, we think we can spend what we want to satisfy our desires without getting into hopeless debt. We think we can rebel against authority, and it will be all right in the end. We think we can be selfish and demanding in our relationships, and our loved ones will still want to be near us. We think that we can step over God's boundaries without consequences. Shockingly, there are more times than most of us recognize or would be willing to admit when we think we're smarter than God.

To sinners (and that includes us all), wisdom is not natural. It is one of humanity's most profoundly important quests. It is hard for us to gain wisdom by research or experience because they are filtered and interpreted by our own foolish hearts! It is here where the Bible greets us with a radical, counterintuitive message. You can't buy wisdom. You can't get it by hard work or lots of experience. No, wisdom is the result of *rescue* and *relationship*.

To be wise, you first need to be rescued from you. You need to be given a new heart, one that is needy, humble, seeking, and ready to get from above what you can't find on this earth. And then you need to be brought into a relationship with the one who *is* wisdom. Colossians 2:3 says of Jesus, "in [him] are hidden all the treasures of wisdom and knowledge." Think of this: grace has connected you to the one who is wisdom. Grace has caused wisdom to live inside you. This means that wisdom is always with you and is always available to you.

The one who is wisdom now guides you, protects you, and convicts you. Wisdom teaches and matures you, encourages and comforts you. Wisdom works to change your thoughts and redirect your desires. Today you will once again demonstrate your need for wisdom's work. Don't resist. Wisdom has come to be with you forever.

> Yes, if you call out for insight
>   and raise your voice for understanding,
> if you seek it like silver
>   and search for it as for hidden treasures,
> then you will understand the fear of the LORD
>   and find the knowledge of God. (Prov. 2:3–5)

Reflect: How can you reach out to the Lord, and perhaps to a trusted adult, asking for wisdom with a thankful heart?

JULY 15

You were hardwired to depend on God, so your dreams of self-reliance and self-sufficiency will prove to be more nightmares than dreams.

Why is it so hard for so many of us to ask for help? Why do children resist the instruction of their parents? Why do we hate to be told what to do by our teachers or bosses? Why do we work so hard to present ourselves as more ready, knowledgeable, and capable than we really are? Why do we tell people that we're okay when we're not? Why?

The answer seems too straightforward and simplistic, but the answer to each of the questions above is *sin*. Self-reliance and self-sufficiency are what sin does to the heart. Hosea 10:13 captures this very powerfully: "You have plowed iniquity; you have reaped injustice; you have eaten the fruit of lies. Because you have trusted in your own way and in the multitude of your warriors." Don't miss the cause-and-effect structure of this passage. The prophet essentially asks: "Why have you experienced moral impurity? Why have you endured injustice? Why have you accepted what is not true?" There is only one possible answer to these questions, and it's not the one we want to hear. All of these things happened, the prophet says, because you wanted and trusted your own way. You've relied upon your own strength.

It is hard to accept, but vital to humbly admit. Bad things happen when we attempt to live as we were not created to live. Sin causes us to deny our need for God and others. Sin causes us to assign to ourselves the wisdom, strength, and righteousness we do not have. Sin is shockingly proud and self-assured. And because sin does this to all of us, it is dark, deceitful, and dangerous. Self-reliance as your fundamental approach to life will never lead to anything good. Sin always leads to death of some kind in some way. So we need to be rescued from our quest for independence and brought into relationship with the one who really does have everything we need. And that's exactly what the grace of Jesus does for us!

> Who is wise and understanding among you? By his good conduct let him show his works in the meekness of wisdom. But if you have bitter jealousy and selfish ambition in your hearts, do not boast and be false to the truth. (James 3:13–14)

Reflect: Think about the last time you responded to someone defensively. How did your words and attitude actually display your self-sufficiency?

JULY 16

Justification is the only foundation for personal transformation. Personal transformation never results in justification.

You could not find a more confronting, humbling, and encouraging passage than the one from Titus below. First, it *confronts* us with this reality—there is no way we can win acceptance with God by our own efforts. Our relationship with God is always the result of his initiative and not ours. Why does he exercise his sovereign initiative in this way? Because there is no other way. It is God's grace that causes us to reject ungodliness, to run from worldly passions, and to live in self-controlled and upright ways. Justification is never God recognizing and responding to our purity and righteousness. What you and I bring to our relationship with God is desperate spiritual and moral need.

This passage is also *humbling*. We come to him dirtied and burdened by our worldliness, ungodliness, and lack of self-control. We need the power of his justifying and transforming grace to wash us clean and empower us to live in the way that we were created to live. And none of these things would happen to us if he had not willingly given himself for us. Why? Because we had no inclination or ability to do them on our own. So you and I are left with no reason to boast and every reason to worship.

And you and I have every reason to be *encouraged* because this Redeemer has not acted on our behalf just once. He has acted, he is acting, and he will continue to act until we stand before him as his people, completely pure forever and ever. You see, if you and I could have done these things for ourselves, the life, sacrifice, death, and resurrection of Jesus would not have been necessary. The most precious of things in our lives, our relationship with God, we did not earn. It is the eternal, transforming gift of his grace.

> For the grace of God has appeared, bringing salvation for all people, training us to renounce ungodliness and worldly passions, and to live self-controlled, upright, and godly lives in the present age, waiting for our blessed hope, the appearing of the glory of our great God and Savior Jesus Christ, who gave himself up for us to redeem us from all lawlessness and to purify for himself a people for his own possession who are zealous for good works. (Titus 2:11–14)

Reflect: If you are justified by God, how should that acceptance influence the way you perceive other people's opinion of you?

JULY 17

Sin causes me to be all too convinced of my righteousness and too focused on your sin.

It's a searing rebuke. Revelation 3:15–19 contains hard words that capture the scary self-righteousness of sin. Here's the problem: you and I like to think that no one has a clearer, more accurate view of us than we do. We're all way too trusting of ourselves. We do this because we don't take seriously what the Bible says about the dynamic of spiritual blindness. If sin is deceitful (and it is), if sin blinds (and it does), then as long as sin still lurks inside me, there will be patches of spiritual blindness. I simply will not see myself with the accuracy that I think I do. In the language of poverty and riches, the passage basically says, "You look at yourself and you think you're okay, but you're far from okay."

Not only does sin blind, but as sinners, we participate in our own blindness. We all swindle ourselves into thinking that what we're doing is okay when, in fact, it's not okay in the eyes of God. The spiritual reality is that we're like naked, homeless people, but we see ourselves as wealthy and well-dressed. It's an embarrassing and humbling word picture.

Perhaps your eyes are more closed than you think they are. Perhaps you don't know yourself as well as you think you do. Pray for the sweet, loving, sight-giving, convicting ministry of the Holy Spirit. His presence in you is a grace. Spiritual clear-sightedness always leads to personal grief and confession not condemnation of your neighbor.

> I know your works: you are neither cold nor hot. Would that you were either cold or hot! So, because you are lukewarm, and neither hot nor cold, I will spit you out of my mouth. For you say, I am rich, I have prospered, and I need nothing, not realizing that you are wretched, pitiable, poor, blind, and naked. I counsel you to buy from me gold refined by fire, so that you may be rich, and white garments so that you may clothe yourself and the shame of your nakedness may not be seen, and salve to anoint your eyes, so that you may see. Those whom I love, I reprove and discipline, so be zealous and repent. (Rev. 3:15–19)

Reflect: Did you find yourself becoming defensive as you read today's devotional? Take a moment to pray and ask the Lord to help you take in the warning.

JULY 18

God's grace calls you to suffer and it calls you to wait, but it never calls you to stand in your own strength or to stand alone.

The Bible never denies reality. The Bible never plays it safe. The Bible never offers you a romanticized view of the world. The Bible never tricks you into thinking that things are better than they are. The Bible is straightforward and honest but not void of hope. While it is very candid about the hardships of life in this broken world, the Bible is also gloriously hopeful. The honesty does not crush the hope, but neither does the hope negate the honesty. Psalm 28 offers a good example of the important harmony of these two themes:

> To you, O Lord, I call;
> my rock, be not deaf to me,
> lest, if you be silent to me,
> I become like those who go down to the pit.
> Hear the voice of my pleas for mercy,
> when I cry to you for help,
> when I lift up my hands
> toward your most holy sanctuary.
>
> Do not drag me off with the wicked,
> with the workers of evil,
> who speak peace with their neighbors
> while evil is in their hearts. . . .
>
> Blessed be the Lord!
> For he has heard the voice of my pleas for mercy. . . .
>
> The Lord is the strength of his people;
> he is the saving refuge of his anointed.
> Oh, save your people and bless your heritage!
> Be their shepherd and carry them forever. (Ps. 28:1–3, 6, 8–9)

This psalm of trouble ends up being a psalm of shining hope. That's the story of the life of every believer because you and I are never alone in our trouble. The "saving refuge" is always with us!

> Preserve me, O God, for in you I take refuge. (Ps. 16:1)

Reflect: When life is hard, where do you most often turn for relief and refuge? Why?

JULY 19

God puts you in hard moments when you cry out for his comfort so that your heart becomes tender to those near you who need the same comfort.

Sometimes we are quicker to judge than to comfort. This hit me not too long ago on the streets of Philadelphia, where I live. I walked by a young homeless person who was begging on the street, and I immediately thought, "I wonder what you did to get yourself here." Criticism came more quickly to me than compassion. Hard-heartedness is more natural for us than I think we like to admit. It is a form of self-righteousness that, in some ways, still lives inside all of us. When we have named ourselves as strong, wise, capable, mature, and righteous, we tend to look down on those who have not achieved what we think we have.

So God humbles us. He puts us in situations where our own weakness, foolishness, and immaturity are exposed. I remember how I struggled with the sovereignty of God in the painful days after my father's death. I had previously prided myself in how well I understood and could communicate this important doctrine. Yet there I was, grappling with God's plan. At street level, my dad's story made no sense to me. I wondered what in the world God was doing. It all looked chaotic and out of control. It was humbling to admit my struggle. However, doing so caused me to be much more patient with others who struggle with God's rule in hard moments in their lives.

The hard moments are not just for your growth in grace, but for your call to be a tool of that same grace in the life of another sufferer. In difficulty, God is softening your heart and sharpening your edges. God intends for you to give away the comfort, hope, and grace you've been given. What a plan!

> Blessed be the God and Father of our Lord Jesus Christ, the Father of mercies and God of all comfort, who comforts us in all our affliction, so that we may be able to comfort those who are in any affliction, with the comfort with which we ourselves are comforted by God. . . . If we are afflicted, it is for your comfort and salvation; and if we are comforted, it is for your comfort. (2 Cor. 1:3–4, 6)

Reflect: When you look down on someone else, someone not like you, what does this reveal about your own heart?

JULY 20

Grace doesn't help you just to do different things but to become a totally different person by changing you at the level of your heart.

I want to refer you right now to one of the Bible's best-known prayers of confession. The problem is that it's so familiar to most of us that we've quit giving it serious study. Yet for us to enjoy the rescue that it offers, we must examine its words and take its truths to heart. The confession is David's from Psalm 51:

Have mercy on me, O God,
    according to your steadfast love;
according to your abundant mercy
    blot out my transgressions.
Wash me thoroughly from my iniquity,
    and cleanse me from my sin!

For I know my transgressions,
    and my sin is ever before me.
Against you, you only, have I sinned
    and done what is evil in your sight,
so that you may be justified in your words
    and blameless in your judgment. . . .
Purge me with hyssop, and I shall be clean;
    wash me, and I shall be whiter than snow.
Let me hear joy and gladness;
    let the bones that you have broken rejoice.
Hide your face from my sins,
    and blot out all my iniquities.
Create in me a clean heart, O God,
    and renew a right spirit within me. (Ps. 51:1–4, 7–10)

Look carefully at the words of David's prayer. This is not only a prayer of confession—it is also a cry for change. He admits that he came into the world with his problem. He confesses that his problem is not external but internal. So he cries out for what every sinner needs: a new heart. It is something only God can create. It is the focus of his work of grace. He wants more than reformed behavior. He sent his Son to die for you so that you would have a new heart, one that is constantly being renewed. If your heart is your problem, then the grace of heart change is your only hope.

And I will give them one heart, and a new spirit I will put within them. I will remove the heart of stone from their flesh and give them a heart of flesh. (Ezek. 11:19)

Reflect: Do you feel your biggest problems are around you or in you?

JULY 21

You simply can't debate it—God's way is better than your way. His plan is infinitely better than any plan you would have for yourself.

I was so discouraged. I was through. I had planned my exit and was pretty certain about where I would land next. The plan looked good to me, much better than what I had been going through. I had been chasing my ministry dream, but I didn't know it. Nothing had worked out according to my little self-oriented plan. The dream had become a nightmare. So I thought the wisest thing to do was to get out quickly and make a fresh start. I had already written the next chapter of my story. But I had forgotten that someone else was the author. The problem was that God had a much, much better plan for me.

At the end of the service where I announced my resignation, the oldest man in our congregation asked if he could speak to me, then said: "We know you're discouraged, and we know you're a bit immature, but we haven't asked you to leave. Where is the church going to get mature pastors if the immature ones leave?" God had interrupted my plan. I knew immediately that he was right. I was running because my dream had blown up in my face. And I knew right there, right then that I could not leave. I went home and told my wife that we couldn't leave. So I called my elders and asked to take back my resignation.

I stayed for many more years—years of growth in both grace and ministry. Nothing I have experienced since would have happened if I had left. I was going to jump ship and leave pastoral ministry. But thankfully I am not the author of my own personal story.

Your story isn't an autobiography either. Your story is a biography of wisdom and grace written by another. Every turn he writes into your story is right. Every twist of the plot is for the best. Every new character or unexpected event is a tool of his grace. Each new chapter advances his purpose. God's ways are better. How could they not be? He is infinite in wisdom and grace!

Whoever is wise, let him understand these things;
    whoever is discerning, let him know them;
for the ways of the LORD are right. (Hos. 14:9)

Reflect: What pressures in your life right now make you want to quit? How do God's wisdom and grace challenge your perspective?

JULY 22

Corporate worship is designed to move the meditation of your heart from self-centered complaint to God-glorifying praise.

Every day of your life you will find reasons to complain, and you'll also have reasons to be thankful. These two completely different ways of viewing the world, complaint and gratitude, pull at the heart of each of us. Why? Because they're rooted in two completely different ways of viewing yourself.

Which one is your default setting? Do you find it easier to complain than to give thanks? Are you easily irritated and quickly impatient? Do boring things get under your skin? Are you humbled by the myriad things in your life that you regularly enjoy but that you don't deserve? How often do you whisper thanks to God or communicate thanks to those around you?

I made a strong statement above. I said that the lifestyle of complaint and that of gratitude are both rooted in the way you view yourself. Here's what I mean. Complaint really is an identity issue. If you have placed yourself in the center of your world, if you have reduced your active concerns down to your wants, your needs, and your feelings, if it really is all about you, then you will live with an entitled, "I deserve _____" attitude. And if you do, you will have constant reason to complain. Why? You will grumble because the reality is that you are not at the center. The universe doesn't operate to satisfy your desires. This is a dark and discouraging way to live. But there's another way. If you humbly admit that as a sinner you deserve nothing but God's wrath, that in acts of outrageous grace he has turned his face of mercy and kindness toward you, and that every good thing in your life is an undeserved blessing, then you will find reasons to be grateful everywhere you look. Feelings of need and thankfulness—rather than entitlement and disappointment—will fill your heart.

This is where the regular gathering of God's people for worship serves to shift your focus. You'll move from complaint to gratitude by being reminded of the beautiful and faithful mercy of God toward you. As the gospel puts you in your place, it also puts praise in your mouth. And that is a very good thing.

> Rejoice in the Lord always; again I will say, rejoice. (Phil. 4:4)

Reflect: When you think about how you've talked to the people closest to you over the last week, would you say it's been more grumbling or gratitude?

JULY 23

God will call you to do what you cannot do but will provide everything you need to do it.

Noah didn't have the power to get all those animals into that ark. But the Lord provided what was necessary for it to happen.

Joseph didn't have the ability to preserve his life and put himself in a position of power in Egypt. But the Lord made it happen.

Moses didn't have what it took to free the Israelites from their slavery in Egypt. But the Lord empowered him to lead them to the promised land.

The Israelites didn't have a way to get across the Red Sea. But the Lord parted the waters for them.

Those Israelites had no means of feeding and sustaining themselves in the wilderness. But the Lord provided everything they needed.

The children of Israel had no means of defeating the walled city of Jericho. But the Lord gave them victory.

David had no personal power to overcome Goliath. But the Lord gave him courage and strength that day.

Shadrach, Meshach, and Abednego had no ability to keep themselves from burning up in that fiery furnace. But the Lord preserved their lives.

The disciples had no means of feeding the hungry crowd that had gathered to hear Jesus. But he fed them well from a little boy's lunch.

Paul had no ability to preserve himself and those who were with him from shipwreck. But the Lord exercised his power so that none were lost.

You and I have no natural abilities to rise and do what God calls us to do. But he refuses to leave us to our own resources. He is not so unwise, unkind, or unfaithful as to ever call us to a task without enabling us to do it. I am not able to love my wife the way Jesus loves the church, but I am not left by God to my own character and strength. I am not able to keep my heart pure, so God fills me with his empowering Spirit. As the verse below reminds us, we have been given everything we need for life and godliness. The God who calls us to a radical new way of living meets us with radical empowering grace.

> His divine power has granted to us all things that pertain to life and godliness, through the knowledge of him who called us to his own glory and excellence. (2 Pet. 1:3)

Reflect: Have courage. Be active. Your Savior really is your strength.

JULY 24

Don't be discouraged today. No matter how alone you feel, you've been blessed with the Father's love.

Do you feel alone today? Are there ways in which you feel alienated and unloved? Do you feel misrepresented or misunderstood? Do you feel passed by and taken for granted? Do you feel broken and in need of repair? Does it seem that there's no one to share your heart with? When the waves of loneliness and discouragement roll over you, where do you run, where do you hide?

I love the depiction of God's tender care in Isaiah 42:3: "A bruised reed he will not break, and a faintly burning wick he will not quench." What a beautiful word picture in two parts! First, imagine walking through the brush and coming across a young tree with a bent and almost broken limb hanging at a rather odd angle. You spontaneously complete the job, ripping the limb completely off. Your heavenly Father would never think of breaking you the rest of the way. He comes to you in grace to comfort, strengthen, encourage, and restore. He is near you when it seems no one else is. He will heal your wounds when no one around you seems to see how wounded you are. If you are his child, it is impossible for you to be alone and unloved because your heavenly Father is with you and reaches out to you in tender, restoring love.

Next, imagine that the little flame on the candle that is giving you light is faintly flickering and about to die. In an act of impatience and frustration, you reach out with your finger and snuff it out. Your heavenly Father would never think of doing that to you. When your hope is fading and your faith is weak, he is not impatient. He does not grow frustrated. His beautiful mercy breathes life into your heart and vitality into your soul. He is slow to anger and abounding in mercy. He really is the Father of comfort. He is the ever-faithful friend. Yes, life can be very hard, people can be very cruel, and there are times when you are left alone. Yet you are never completely abandoned because your Father is with you in tender, restorative love.

> He can deal gently with the ignorant and wayward, since he himself is beset with weakness. (Heb. 5:2)

Reflect: What situations make you feel most alone? Which of the two truths (above) is most comforting to you? Why?

JULY 25

Today you'll wonder if you'll have enough, or you'll tell yourself, "The Lord will provide," and in faith you'll move forward.

To live the way you're supposed to live, you have to know your address. You have to know where you are. For example, if you live in the suburbs, you know you'll have a big yard that will require attention. If you live in the inner city, you may need to be aware of the dangers on the streets at night. If you live in an old house, you can be sure that you'll need to hone your carpentry, electricity, and plumbing skills. The same is true spiritually. It is essential that you understand the implications of knowing where you live—or you'll find yourself confused and unprepared over and over again.

Where do we live? You and I live between the "already" and the "not yet." Jesus has already made the ultimate sacrifice. The Holy Spirit has already come to live inside you. But the work of God in you, for you, and through you has not yet been completed—not yet. This means that sin has not yet been fully eliminated. You are not yet all that grace will transform you to be. So the spiritual war still goes on.

That means you need to understand that you live in a moral war zone, and the battles are fought on the turf of your heart. Your life is lived every day in the middle of a war for control of your soul. It's a war of doubt and faith. It's a war of anxiety and trust. It's a war of hope and despair. It's a war of allegiance and disloyalty. It's a war.

Perhaps the frontline of that war is this question: "Will the Lord do what he has promised?" Will the Lord provide? Can I step out in faith and courage, knowing that the Lord is with me and will provide what I need when I need it? Or do I have to worry that, when push comes to shove, I won't have enough? Should I be afraid, or is God trustworthy? You won't always feel his nearness, but you can rest assured he will never abandon you.

> I have been young, and now am old,
> yet I have not seen the righteous forsaken
> or his children begging for bread. (Ps. 37:25)

Reflect: When you feel the battle in your heart erupt, how will you respond? What will you believe? What promise that God has made should you tell yourself?

JULY 26

Why would you be afraid when in Christ you have been completely accepted, eternally forgiven, and richly supplied?

What are the three questions that everyone has asked and is in some way haunted by?

1. Will I be loved?
2. Will people tolerate me once they really get to know me?
3. Will I have what I need to live?

In some way, every person who has ever lived is on a hunt for love and scared to death that he won't find it. That's why a good love story is always so popular. In some way, everyone fears judgment and failing to measure up. That's why mercy and forgiveness stories hit us so deeply. In some way, everyone is afraid of being poor. We're afraid that success will escape our grasp, and we'll end up as beggars on the street. This is why we all love a "rags-to-riches story."

Isn't it amazing that each of these fundamental human fears is addressed and solved by the gospel of the Lord Jesus Christ? First, the gospel is the world's best love story. It is a story of a God of love who sends the Son of his love to make a sacrifice of love for a people who do not deserve his love so they can be welcomed into his arms of love and become a community of love that takes his love to those in desperate need of that love. Second, the gospel of Jesus Christ is the world's most amazing forgiveness story. It is the story of one who was willing to die for crimes he did not commit so that the people who committed those crimes would be completely forgiven of every wrong. Third, the gospel of Jesus Christ is also the greatest of all provision stories. It is a story of God giving everything to impoverished rebels who deserve nothing.

If you are God's child, you don't have to be haunted by these deep questions of life. Because of Jesus Christ, you are loved; because of him, you are forgiven; and because of him, you have everything that you need.

> The eyes of all look to you,
> and you give them their food in due season.
> You open your hand;
> you satisfy the desire of every living thing.
> The Lord is righteous in all his ways
> and kind in all his works. (Ps. 145:15–17)

Reflect: Which of the three questions resonates with you most? How can you apply Psalm 145:15–17 to that question in your life today?

JULY 27

Since God forgives by grace, it makes no sense to hide, excuse, or shift the blame when you are faced with your sin.

So often when faced with our sin, we immediately excuse ourselves or shift the blame. When our consciences bother us, it's tempting to hide the wrong that we have done like Adam and Eve hiding from God in the garden. Or we try to convince ourselves that what we did was not so bad after all. But hiding and blaming—while possible in this broken world—make one big, sad, irrational lie.

Why would you and I work so hard to hide or deny what has been fully, completely, and eternally forgiven? Why would we work so hard to pretend that we are something less than sinners when the message of the gospel is that Jesus loves and accepts sinners? Why would we hide in guilt when Jesus has fully borne our guilt? Why would we care what others will think of us if we're honest about our sin when the one who holds our destiny in his hands has accepted us as if we had never sinned? Why sing the truths of the gospel on Sunday and functionally deny the gospel during the week in street-level acts of denial, excusing, and blame? Why would you defend yourself when a loved one points out a wrong or excuse yourself when you are caught? Why, in the face of wrong, would you work to soften the pain of conviction by debating the Holy Spirit's gracious prompting?

Paul encouraged the believers in Colossae to "continue in the faith, stable and steadfast, not shifting from the hope of the gospel that you heard" (Col. 1:23). Forsake excuses, denial, and all other acts of gospel irrationality that minimize your sin. That way, you will never forget the awesome hope that you have been given in Jesus.

> Indeed, I count everything as loss because of the surpassing worth of knowing Christ Jesus my Lord. For his sake I have suffered the loss of all things and count them as rubbish, in order that I may gain Christ and be found in him, not having a righteousness of my own that comes from the law, but that which comes through faith in Christ, the righteousness from God that depends on faith. (Phil. 3:8–9)

Reflect: Why do you not want others to think of you as needy? How does honesty and confession actually lead to hope not fear?

JULY 28

Grace frees you from faking what you don't have and boasting about what you didn't earn.

Faking is a big part of the culture of fallen humanity. Maybe you fake it when you tell a story in such a way that it makes you way more of a hero than you really were. Maybe you fake it when you buy clothes that are more expensive than you can responsibly afford. Maybe you fake it when you try to work your way into certain friendships. Or maybe your fakery is your unwillingness to confess to the person next to you that you struggle with the same area of sin that he or she has just confessed to. Maybe your fakery is in the big difference between the polished version of you online or in public and the messier details of your private life.

So here is a question that you need to wrestle with. Is there someplace where, to yourself or others, you pretend to be something that you're not or where you boast about something you didn't actually do? I think there are artifacts of fakery in the lives of everyone of us. Here's why I say that. Because there is a desire in all of our hearts to be more independently wise, righteous, and strong than we really are.

"For by grace you have been saved through faith. And this is not your own doing; it is the gift of God, not a result of works, so that no one may boast" (Eph. 2:8–9). Praise God that his grace offers you what you did not earn and forgives you for the wrongs you actually did. In grace, your identity is not in what you have achieved or in what the people around you think of what you have achieved. No, as a result of grace, your identity is rooted in what Jesus has done for you. Grace allows you to live free of the fabricated identity of human fakery once and for all. Grace means you can rest in the honest and stable identity you have found in Jesus and his eternal work on your behalf.

> Beware of practicing your righteousness before other people in order to be seen by them, for then you will have no reward from your Father who is in heaven. (Matt. 6:1)

Reflect: Grace invites you to be real and honest. Where do you need to bring the public and private aspects of your life into the light of grace?

JULY 29

Fish were designed to swim, the sun to shine, and you to worship God. Grace welcomes you back to what you were designed for—worship.

If someone were to ask you why God has given grace—what is its ultimate goal—what would you answer? God's grace can make you more financially wise. God's grace can make you a better citizen and neighbor. God's grace can cause you to be more responsible with the use of your body and more sexually pure. God's grace can help you to make better decisions in life. God's grace can enable you to be more honest with yourself and more forgiving in your dealings with others. God's grace can make you less anxious and more courageous. God's grace can give you a reason to get up in the morning even when things aren't going well. God's grace can pilot you through disappointment and give you joy even when you're suffering. God's grace can help you to know you are loved even when you're alone and to know you have strength even when you are weak. All of these things are the beautiful harvest of grace. All of these are things for which we should be eternally thankful. But none of these good gifts is the ultimate goal of God's grace.

Here is the bottom line: sin kidnapped our worship, and grace works to restore it to its rightful owner—God. Ultimately, grace helps us realize and restore God to his rightful place in our hearts. The goal of grace is worship. Focus on the following words from the book of Romans:

> For the wrath of God is revealed from heaven against all ungodliness and unrighteousness of men, who by their unrighteousness suppress the truth. For what can be known about God is plain to them, because God has shown it to them. For his invisible attributes, namely, his eternal power and divine nature, have been clearly perceived, ever since the creation of the world, in the things that have been made. So they are without excuse. For although they knew God, they did not honor him as God or give thanks to him, but they became futile in their thinking, and their foolish hearts were darkened. Claiming to be wise, they became fools, and exchanged the glory of the immortal God for images resembling mortal man and birds and animals and creeping things. (Rom. 1:18–23)

Reflect: Think about three areas in your life where you're enjoying God's grace and blessing. How can you respond to those gifts by giving worship to the giver?

JULY 30

What could be a greater, higher honor than to be a chosen instrument for the most important renewal project in the universe—redemption?

We have an unbiblical view of ministry. We think that ministry should allow us to live comfortably as Christian consumers. The work of evangelism, the spiritual growth work of the church, and the cause of worldwide missions, was never designed by the Redeemer to be shouldered by a small collection of paid religious professionals. Does God set people apart for ministry? Of course he does! But their role is not just to do ministry. In addition, they're to mobilize, train, and equip all of God's people to spread his amazing grace wherever they are. It is sad that so many of God's people spend their lives searching for some significant endeavor to give themselves to. The truth is that they have been chosen to be part of the most powerfully transformative work in the history of the universe.

The fact of the matter is that since we have been bought with the blood of Jesus, our lives don't belong to us anymore; they are his possession for his use. This means that for every Christian our life *is* ministry and ministry *is* our life.

There is no real separation between life and ministry. That means we live, work, relate, play, and relax with a ministry mentality. It means I am always thinking about how to be part of what God is doing in the locations where he places me. This means my connection to the work of the body of Christ is not that I'm the attender of something, but rather that I am a participant in something along with everyone else. The greatest honor of my life is that I have been chosen to be both a recipient and an instrument. This is what grace alone can do.

> And Jesus came and said to them, "All authority in heaven and on earth has been given to me. Go therefore and make disciples of all nations, baptizing them in the name of the Father and of the Son and of the Holy Spirit, teaching them to observe all that I have commanded you. And behold, I am with you always, to the end of the age." (Matt. 28:18–20)

Reflect: How can this truth—that you are a recipient and instrument of grace—give your life deeper meaning than anything you could have found on your own?

JULY 31

Grace not only forgives you, but enables you to live for something hugely bigger than yourself. Why go back to your little kingdom of one?

Your spiritual life is all about inner motivations. It's all about kingdoms. It's all about warfare. It's way bigger than the surface Christianity to which it is often reduced. You could read your Bible every day—and the entire Bible each year—and still live for yourself. You could be faithful to attend every event at your church and still live for your little kingdom. You could regularly give your hard-earned money to Christian causes and still not live with God's kingdom in view. You could participate in ministries to the poor and needy and still not live for the big kingdom. You could do all of these things, and the trajectory of your life could still be more toward the kingdom of self than the kingdom of God.

In the same way, there was something deeply defective, something tragically missing in the religion of the Pharisees. That is why Jesus said something so strong and striking about the religion of the Pharisees. Here's a sampling:

> Woe to you, scribes and Pharisees, hypocrites! For you clean the outside of the cup and the plate, but inside they are full of greed and self-indulgence. You blind Pharisee! First clean the inside of the cup and the plate, that the outside also may be clean. (Matt. 23:25–26)

The public religious acts of the Pharisees were not the result of deep devotion in their hearts toward God and the work of his kingdom. No, they did these things in the absence of that devotion. That means they didn't do them for God and his kingdom at all. They did them in allegiance to the kingdom of self, for the purpose of personal power and public acclaim. They were acts of righteousness that were actually not righteous. Why? Because they did not come from hearts of worship. True Christianity is always a matter of the submission of the heart to God, something that only rescuing grace can produce.

> No one can serve two masters, for either he will hate the one and love the other, or he will be devoted to the one and despise the other. You cannot serve God and money. (Matt. 6:24)

Reflect: What do your spending habits reveal about your heart and the kingdom you love?

AUGUST 1

Hope for the believer is not a dream of what could be but a confident expectation of a guaranteed result that shapes one's life.

We constantly speak in hope language:

- "I hope my team wins."
- "I hope he isn't mad at me."
- "I hope God really does answer prayer."
- "I sure hope it doesn't rain tomorrow."
- "I hope this sickness isn't something serious."

If you are a human being, you hope. You attach your security, your sense of peace and rest to something every day. The question is not whether you hope, but what holds your hope. Take a moment to think about hope with me:

- *You hope in something.* From the little hope of the young child for a snack or toy to the profound hope of the young adult for meaning and purpose, we all hope. We all place our hope in someone or something, and we ask that person or that thing to deliver something to us.
- *Hope is a lifestyle.* Your hope shapes the way you live. A lack of hope causes you to feel stuck and unmotivated. Confident hope makes you decisive and courageous. Wobbly hope makes you timid and indecisive. Hope is not just something you do with your brain. You always live your hope in some way.
- *Most of our hopes disappoint us.* All of us place our hope in things in this fallen world that simply can't deliver. Your physical possessions, abilities, health, and friends won't give you inner peace. When our hopes disappoint us, it is a sign that we've put our hopes in the wrong things.
- *Hope in God is sure hope.* When you hope in the Lord, you not only hope in the one who created and controls the universe. But you also hope in one who is glorious in grace and abounding in love. Now that's well-placed hope that will never disappoint.

And now, O Lord, for what do I wait?
My hope is in you. (Ps. 39:7)

Reflect: What situation has recently caused you to feel stuck or indecisive? What does that reveal about your hope? Ask the Lord to help you transfer that hope to him.

AUGUST 2

Yes, you're weak, you're often foolish, and you tend to want your own way, but God's redeeming grace is greater.

Perhaps Isaiah 53:6 is the most accurate diagnostic passage in the Bible: "All we like sheep have gone astray; we have turned—every one—to his own way; and the Lord has laid on him the iniquity of us all." Here's the diagnosis: *All have gone astray, each turning to his own way*. There are no exceptions. It is an accurate description of the heart and life of every person who has ever lived. You and I must forsake our attempts to convince ourselves and others that we are exceptions. We all wander away from the Creator's plan for us. We all find ways to step outside of his boundaries. We all do things that he does not want us to do, and we all fail to do what he has called us to do.

Here's another important element of the diagnosis. We're all like sheep, and like sheep, we wander. There's something inside us, something with which we were born, that causes us to wander away from the good and wise will of the great shepherd. The Bible names it—sin. Sin is a matter of our nature before it is ever played out in our behavior. And what does that sin do to us? It causes us to make life all about us, to want little more than our own way, and to live like we're the kings over our own lives.

With this diagnosis, what's the cure for people like us? Well, trying harder or being smarter won't work for us because our problem is deeper than behavior. Systems of self-help won't work because we are our own biggest problem. There is only one place to find a cure. It is only ever found in God's redeeming grace. The grace that placed our sin on the Savior—so that we could be both forgiven and delivered—is more powerful than our sinful natures. Our cure is not a system; it is a person, and his name is Jesus!

> As a shepherd seeks out his flock when he is among his sheep that have been scattered, so will I seek out my sheep, and I will rescue them from all places where they have been scattered on a day of clouds and thick darkness. (Ezek. 34:12)

Reflect: What do movies today typically encourage you to do for your problems? Instead of following that advice, run to Jesus right now. He really is all that you need.

AUGUST 3

The purpose of the cross is to completely decimate your loyalty to the most seductive and powerful of all idols—the idol of self.

You see it in the whines of a little boy. You see it in the entitlement of the young adult. You see it in the needless argument of the married couple over something unimportant. And you see it in the bitterness of the old man. None of us has escaped this disease. It is a personal and moral disaster, yet its power draws all of us in. We see it in others and deny it in ourselves. It ruins our vacations and holidays. It makes us spend ourselves into hopeless debt, to fall into paralyzing addiction, and to eat more than we ever should. It turns friends and families against each other.

What is this thing that kidnaps us all? It is the selfishness of sin. We make it all about us. A good day is a day that is pleasurable or easy for me. A good church has the worship, programs, and preaching that satisfy me. A good job is one that keeps me happy and engaged. We put ourselves in the center of the story.

But the first four words of the Bible confront us with the inescapable reality that it is *not* all about us. These words confront us with the truth that life comes from, is controlled by, and exists for another. We will never be at the center because God is. It will never be about us because it's about him. We won't rule because he rules. Life will not submit to us because ultimately all things will submit to him. He is at center stage. He is the spot-lit character.

Life is not to be found in putting ourselves at the center. That only leads to dysfunction, disappointment, and brokenness. Jesus came to destroy our misplaced loyalty. Why? So that we would find freedom from our bondage to ourselves and know the peace that passes understanding. When Adam and Eve's rebellion becomes our own delusion, we also share their hope. For the sin of "me-ism" there is the rescuing grace of God!

The Lord God has sworn by himself, declares the Lord, the God of hosts:

> "I abhor the pride of Jacob
> and hate his strongholds,
> and I will deliver up the city and all that is in it." (Amos 6:8)

Reflect: Where do you see selfishness in other people? Will you ask the Lord to show you that kind of selfishness in your own life?

AUGUST 4

When nothing else or no one else in your life remains and is faithful, you can rest assured that God will be both.

I love the honesty of the Bible. I love that faith in God doesn't require you and me to tamper with reality. When you read Psalm 90, how's this for honesty? "The years of our life are seventy, or even by reason of strength eighty; yet their span is but toil and trouble; they are soon gone, and we fly away" (90:10). The psalmist is saying: "Your life will be short and will be marked by difficulty." Not very good news is it? But it's true. You live with flawed people who think, say, and do wrong things. You live in a place where corruption, immorality, injustice, pollution, and disease still live and do their ugly work. You live in an environment that does not function according to God's original design.

In all this, you are tempted to feel alone, forsaken, poor, and unable. In your trouble, some people around you are insensitive and unloving. And the people who are sensitive and loving have little power to erase your trouble. This is why this honest psalm starts with the most important declaration that anyone who faces trouble could ever hear: "Lord, you have been our dwelling place in all generations. Before the mountains were brought forth, or ever you had formed the earth and the world, from everlasting to everlasting you are God" (90:1–2).

If you are God's child, you are not alone. Glorious grace has connected you to the one whose power and love don't shift with the times. Grace has connected you and me to the one who is the ultimate dwelling place, the ultimate place to which we can run. This means that I am never left just to my own resources. I am never left to figure out and deal with life on my own. As God's child, I must never see myself as poor or forsaken. Grace has opened to me the door to find hope and refuge in the one who rules everything that would cause me to feel alone.

In the day of my trouble I call upon you,
for you answer me.

There is none like you among the gods, O Lord,
nor are there any works like yours. (Ps. 86:7–8)

Reflect: When you feel all alone, where does your mind naturally go next? How does this verse challenge that thinking with what is real and true?

AUGUST 5

Today you will convince yourself that you're smarter than God and will write your own rules—or will humbly submit to his wise call.

You and I step over God's boundaries because there are moments when we think we're smarter than God. We tell ourselves that what he says is wrong, isn't so wrong after all. We tell ourselves that our way is better than God's way. The big lie that fuels all this is believing that there is real life to be found on the other side of God's wise boundaries for us. This was the lie that was first told, embraced, and acted upon in that terrible moment in the garden of Eden. Human beings have fallen into believing that lie ever since.

The psalmist says: "I will never forget your precepts, for by them you have given me life. . . . I have more understanding than all my teachers, for your testimonies are my meditation. . . . The unfolding of your words gives light; it imparts understanding to the simple" (Ps. 119:93, 99, 130). There it is—God's precepts give life. Yet you will think that you can spend more than you make and your finances will work out in the end. Or I will come to believe that I can permit myself to lust without doing damage to my heart. In a thousand ways, we tell ourselves that somehow this moment is an exception to God's rules. This reveals that our wandering hearts don't always love what God says is good, right, true, lovely, and pure. Sometimes what God says is evil doesn't appear evil to us. In those moments, we are a danger to ourselves because we have bought into what is completely impossible—that we know more and are wiser than God. It is the height of the delusion of sin. It is a dangerous and destructive moral insanity. And it never results in the life that we are seeking.

This "I'm-smarter-than-God" temptation stands as another argument for our daily need for grace. It is yet another place where we need to be delivered from ourselves. It reminds us again that none of us has outlived our need for the rescuing mercy of an ever-present and ever-willing Redeemer. Run to that mercy once again today.

> There is a way that seems right to a man,
> but its end is the way to death. (Prov. 16:25)

Reflect: What boundaries that God has set would you change if you could? Why? What does this say about your delusions of wisdom?

AUGUST 6

Truth requires you to love, and love requires you to be truthful.

Contrary to popular opinion, love and truth don't stand in opposition to one another. In fact, you can't really have one without the other. To love truth, you have to be committed to love. And to love love, you have to be committed to truth. The most loving person who ever lived—so loving that he died a cruel and bloody public death for crimes that others committed—was at the same time the most honest truth-speaker that the world has ever known.

The biblical call to love will never force you to trim, deny, or bend the truth. And the biblical call to truth will never ask you to abandon God's call to love your neighbor. We see this graphically displayed in a very well-known moment in the life of Jesus Christ (see Luke 18:18–24). A rich ruler comes to Jesus to ask him about eternal life. In a moment of complete honesty, Jesus exposes the central idolatry of this man's heart. Jesus tells this man the bad news he needs to hear if he is ever to want the good news he desperately needs. And in the face of Jesus's honesty, the man walks away, and as he does, Jesus looks at him with sadness. You see, Jesus isn't being cold and indifferent. His sadness at the end of the conversation exposes the love that motivated the words he had said. Those hard words are words of grace, spoken by the Savior of love, spoken to redeem.

Truth isn't mean and love isn't dishonest. They both long for the spiritual welfare of another. Today you are called to loving honesty and honest love. You will be tempted to let one or the other slip from your hands. Pray for the help of the one who remained fully committed to both, even to death. His grace is your only hope of staying true to his righteous agenda.

> Love is patient and kind; love does not envy or boast; it is not arrogant or rude. It does not insist on its own way; it is not irritable or resentful; it does not rejoice at wrongdoing, but rejoices with the truth. (1 Cor. 13:4–6)

Reflect: Which do you think social media is worse at creating a space for—truthful speech or loving acceptance? Why?

AUGUST 7

Mercy is what we have been given and what we are called to give. It is my commitment to suffer with you, just as Christ suffered for me.

How is it possible that we who have been blessed with eternal and undeserved love, could be so regularly unloving to those around us? Why, instead of offering grace, do we judge and criticize so naturally in response to the sin, weakness, and failure of others? Why do we find it so hard to forgive when we have been forgiven at the price of the suffering and death of Jesus? Why can we walk past suffering with little compassion when our lives have been rescued by the tender compassion of the Savior? Why do we resist serving one another when the Lord of all things willingly came and served us even to the point of his death?

The answer to each of these questions is humbling. We don't always respond to others as the Savior has responded to us. Why? Because we don't share his heart. Our hearts are not always ruled by what ruled his heart. We don't always find joy in what brought him joy. As a result, we lack the mercy that drove and shaped his life.

Our selfish hearts are often more committed to our own kingdom purposes than his. We want the lavish riches of grace for ourselves, but do not want to have to make sacrifices of grace for others. We see this in the self-righteous anger of a parent, in the bitter unforgiveness of a friend, in the nasty comments made online, in divisions in the body of Christ, or in our unfaithfulness in our relationships. The war of kingdoms rages in our hearts, and one of the first casualties is mercy. It is sad but true—our refusal to give grace to others reveals how much we still need grace ourselves. Yet the weakness in our love demonstrates how our only hope rests in a God who loves us even on our very worst days. Given our struggles to live the gospel in our relationships with others, picture how much we need the rich gospel ourselves. And it all argues that we still don't deserve the favor that we are given daily. And it's this grace that we are called to give to others who are as undeserving as we are.

> This is my commandment, that you love one another as I have loved you. (John 15:12)

Reflect: In what areas of your life do you find it easiest to show grace? In what areas is it hardest? What does this say about your own need for grace?

AUGUST 8

For the believer, obedience is not a pain but a joy. Each act of obedience celebrates the grace that motivates and empowers it.

I remember my brother Tedd saying it to me, but I didn't realize how right he was: "Obedience is its own reward." Whenever you or I obey, in every act of obedience, it reveals God's grace at work. As you read the list below, you'll see what a miracle of amazing grace it is that any of us ever chooses to obey God:

- Sinners tend not to esteem authority.
- Sinners like to write their own rules.
- Sinners tend to believe in their own autonomy.
- Sinners tend to think they're wiser than they are.
- Sinners tend to have a moral code that is formed more by their desires than by God's law.
- Sinners tend to think that they don't need what they don't desire.
- Sinners tend to be self-focused and self-excusing.
- Sinners tend to crave what God has prohibited.
- Sinners tend to opt for short-term pleasure over long-term gain.

Miraculous grace enables obedience. Because all of the above statements are true, it is even more of a miracle that we can find joy in obeying someone whom we cannot see, hear, or touch. Any time we desire, in word, thought, or action, to do what pleases God, we are being rescued, transformed, and empowered by his grace. You see, your obedience celebrates grace even in moments when you aren't consciously celebrating it yourself. Each moment of submission to the will of God celebrates this reality: "For sin will have no dominion over you, since you are not under law but under grace" (Rom. 6:14).

So smile when you obey; you are experiencing the riches of grace. Give thanks when you submit; you are being rescued by grace. Celebrate when you make the right choice; you are being transformed by grace. Sing for joy when you serve God's purposes; you have just given evidence of the presence of redeeming grace!

> But God, being rich in mercy, because of the great love with which he loved us, even when we were dead in our trespasses, made us alive together with Christ—by grace you have been saved. (Eph. 2:4–5)

Reflect: Where have you recently seen the miracle of God's grace in someone else's life? How can you encourage them by telling them what you've observed?

AUGUST 9

Love is more than being nice to people. It's loving God above all else so that you love people as he commands you to.

Relationships are first fixed vertically before they are ever fixed horizontally. Paul captures this dynamic in surprising words in Galatians 5: "For the whole law is fulfilled in one word: 'You shall love your neighbor as yourself'" (5:14). Now, think this through with me. Is it not the command to love God (Mark 12:28–30) that must always be first and foremost in our hearts? But that's not what Paul writes. He says the entire law is fulfilled in this: "Love your neighbor as yourself" (Gal. 5:14). What? How does that fulfill all that God has called us to as his children?

Paul is on to something very important here. First, he knows that only people who love God above all else will ever love their neighbors as themselves. In my marriage, I have had to make this confession—my problem isn't first that I have failed to love Luella in the way that I should. No, my deeper problem is that I have not loved God as I should. And because I haven't, I make it all about me and therefore do not love Luella in the way that I should.

Paul also knows a second thing: that one of the ways our lack of love for God is revealed is by the lack of active love that exists in our relationships. John says it this way: "If anyone says, 'I love God,' and hates his brother, he is a liar; for he who does not love his brother whom he has seen cannot love God whom he has not seen" (1 John 4:20). Love for others really begins, continues, and is daily motivated by love for God. When his purposes are more important than your desires, when his glory is more valuable to you than your temporary moments of glory, and when his agenda activates you more than your plan for you, then you will be freed from your bondage to self-love and be freed to love others. Our relationships need more than horizontal fixing. They need vertical rescue, and for that there is the ever-sufficient grace of a willing and patient Savior.

> Love does no wrong to a neighbor; therefore love is the fulfilling of the law. (Rom. 13:10)

Reflect: Slowly read 1 Corinthians 13:4–7. How do your actions and attitudes compare with this biblical description of love for other people?

AUGUST 10

God knows everything from beyond origin to beyond destiny. You have ___ years of sin-tainted human experience. Why debate him? God's smarter!

It's really amazing how much I don't know:

- I don't know how bees could ever fly.
- I don't know why I do all the things I do.
- I don't know what tomorrow will bring.
- I don't know how long my life will be.
- I don't know so many things about art, science, and politics.
- I don't know why I wake up happy on some days and morose on others.
- I don't know many things about origins and many things about destiny.
- I don't know many things about the operation of my own body and brain.
- I don't know why weeds overtake flowers.
- I don't know why God brings certain things into my life.

This is just a brief, spontaneous list of some of the things I don't know. If I were to take the time, I could fill hundreds of pages with lists of things I don't know, and there would still be lots of things not listed. Why? Simply because I don't know that I don't know them.

In light of this, it is stunning to know that God knows absolutely everything. Yes, you read it right—*everything*. His grasp of everything has no beginning and no end. He is never confused. He never has to live with misunderstanding. There is nothing that ever surprises him or leaves him perplexed. He never has trouble reconciling one truth with another. He never has to deal with gaps in his knowledge. He never has to relearn something. He never has to admit that what he thought was wrong. No one ever showed him the path of understanding or taught him knowledge (Isa. 40:14).

So run from any thought that you are smarter. Consume his wisdom. And be thankful for the grace that rescues you from your own foolishness and connects you to one who defines what is wise.

> Who has measured the Spirit of the Lord,
>   or what man shows him his counsel?
> Whom did he consult,
>   and who made him understand?
> Who taught him the path of justice,
>   and taught him knowledge,
>   and showed him the way of understanding? (Isa. 40:13–14)

Reflect: What puzzling thing is really stressing you out right now? How does that all change, when you realize not one bit of that thing puzzles God at all?

AUGUST 11

You disobey not because you lack the God-given grace to obey, but because you love something more than the God who's given you that grace.

Your disobedience is never God's fault. Yet, as much as we know that God is not responsible for our behavior, we have subtle ways of shifting the blame to him. We say:

- "If only my youth leader was more available in times of need, then I would've . . ."
- "If only I had had a better job at the time, I wouldn't have . . ."
- "If only my parents had been better models for me, I could've . . ."
- "If only I had come to Christ earlier in my life, I'm sure I would've . . ."
- "If only there weren't so much pornography on the internet, I wouldn't have been tempted to . . ."
- "If only I weren't so busy, I could take more time to . . ."

Whenever you blame other people for your circumstances or your actions, you are, in fact, blaming God. You are saying that God didn't give you what you needed. You are essentially saying: "My problem isn't a heart problem; my problem is a *poverty of grace* problem. If only God had given me ______, I wouldn't have had to do what I did." This is the same argument first made in the garden of Eden after the rebellion of Adam and Eve (Gen. 3:12–13). Adam: "The woman you gave me made me do it." Eve: "The devil made me do it."

It is hard for us to accept that our words and behavior are not caused by what's outside us, but by what's inside us (see Luke 6:43–45). But the Scriptures are clear that every wrong you and I do flows out of the thoughts and desires of our hearts. Have you convinced yourself that you're not your problem, but people and situations are? If so, then you're not going to be excited about God's provision of powerful forgiving and transforming grace. Why? Because, frankly, you don't think you need it. It is only when you admit and confess this that you begin to feel the need for and get excited about God's grace.

> The good person out of the good treasure of his heart produces good, and the evil person out of his evil treasure produces evil, for out of the abundance of the heart his mouth speaks. (Luke 6:45)

Reflect: How would you fill in the blank—"If only God had ________"?

AUGUST 12

Remember, what is out of your control exists under the careful control of the one who is all-knowing, all-wise, all-good.

Too much of our emotional energy is sapped by worry. Too many of us are captured by discouragement. Too many of us are paralyzed by regret or anxiety. Too many of us wonder where God is and what he is doing. Too many of us feel alone and misunderstood. Too many of us envy the lives of others. Too many of us, when we are thinking about our lives that feel out of control, leave out the ultimate explanatory fact—the existence, character, and plan of God.

Many of us need the worldview presented in the book of Daniel. Daniel's world is a world of injustice, oppression, idolatry, danger, political corruption, war, and various other kinds of trouble. But it is not a world that is out of control. In fact, in the face of all the trouble, Daniel offers us a world that, in every way and at every point, is under the control of one who is powerful and wise, and who holds the events of human history in the palms of his hands. Events happen according to his plan. History and the lives of individuals are shaped by his purpose. It is a world under rule.

You face many things that make you feel unprepared, small, or weak. But you must not give way to thinking that your life is out of control. You need to remind yourself of the truths that Daniel confronts us all with—that over all the trouble that hurts and confuses us is God. He's the God of glorious wisdom, power, and grace who rules every moment of every situation. No, you will not always see his hand. You often won't understand what he is doing. At times, you will wish that life could be different. There will be moments when you will feel unprepared for what is on your plate. In these moments, look up and remember that above it all there is a throne. And on that throne sits a God of unimaginable majesty, ruling all for his glory and for your good.

> For he is the living God,
>   enduring forever;
> his kingdom shall never be destroyed,
>   and his dominion shall be to the end.
> He delivers and rescues;
>   he works signs and wonders
>   in heaven and on earth. (Dan. 6:26–27)

Reflect: Write down two encouragements from Daniel that you can use to fight anxiety when you feel unprepared today?

AUGUST 13

Self-righteousness is being more concerned for, and motivated by, the knowledge of others' sin than your own.

Here's a spiritual version of the old question, "Which came first, the chicken or the egg?" Is self-righteousness the reason for personal spiritual blindness? Or is personal spiritual blindness the root of self-righteousness? Whatever the case, they motivate and strengthen each other. And this presents a grave danger to anyone who still has sin living inside him or her. (And that's all of us.)

I've seen this operate so powerfully in relationships. One person comes to counseling with a long list of the other person's sins, weaknesses, and failures (but with little awareness or concern for his/her own). And when I talk to the other person, he or she comes with a detailed list of the other person's wrongs (but with little reference to his/her own). When I ask each one what's the problem in the relationship, do you know what they never say? "I'm the problem." They talk about the other person.

Be honest right here, right now as you are reading this devotion. Whose sin bugs you more: your own or that of someone near you? Who are you desperate to see change: you or someone else in your life? Jesus directly addresses this self-righteousness/spiritual blindness/judging of others dynamic in Matthew 7:1–5 (see below). He reminds us that self-righteousness means you don't see yourself or the other person with accuracy. It means you see his or her speck as a log and your log as a speck. So you are condemning of him or her, and you are excusing of yourself. This troubling dynamic is another powerful argument for our desperate need for rescuing grace. You see, it takes grace for you to realize how much you still need grace.

> Why do you see the speck that is in your brother's eye, but do not notice the log that is in your own eye? Or how can you say to your brother, "Let me take the speck out of your eye," when there is the log in your own eye? You hypocrite, first take the log out of your own eye, and then you will see clearly to take the speck out of your brother's eye. (Matt. 7:3–5)

Reflect: Think about someone who has recently irritated you. Then, as you think about that person, ask God to help you learn about yourself, to see yourself more clearly.

AUGUST 14

Could there be a greater comfort known to man than these six hope-giving words: "His mercies are new every morning"?

Post those six words on the mirror that you look into each morning. Tape them on your door. Put them somewhere where you will see them every day. Don't allow yourself to view yourself, your circumstances, your daily joys and struggles, or God, other people, or the meaning and purpose of life without this gorgeous redemptive reality: mercy.

Mercy is the theme of God's story. Mercy is the thread that runs through all of Scripture. Mercy is the reason for Jesus's coming. Mercy is what your desperate heart needs. Mercy is the healer your relationships need. Mercy is what gives you comfort in weakness and hope in times of trial. Mercy not only meets you in your struggle, but guarantees that someday your struggle will end. Mercy is what this sin-broken world groans for. If God offered us only justice, no one would run to him. It is the knowledge of his mercy that makes us honestly face ourselves and gladly run to him. And it is mercy that we will sing about and celebrate a million years into eternity.

I love the words of Lamentations 3:22–23: "The steadfast love of the Lord never ceases; his mercies never come to an end; they are new every morning; great is your faithfulness." Let these amazing words sink in. If you are God's child, they describe your identity and your hope. They enable you to face and admit how messed up you really are. They allow you to extend mercy to the failing people around you. And they allow you to be comforted by God's presence rather than be terrified at the thought that he is near.

Not only does God lavish on you love that will never cease, but the mercy he extends to you and to me is renewed each new morning. It is not tired, stale, irrelevant, worn out, ill-fitting, yesterday mercy. No, God's mercy is *new morning mercy*. Yes, we all get the same mercy, but it doesn't come to all of us in the same size and shape. God knows who you are, where you are, and what you're facing. And he meets you with just the right mercies for the moment.

Gracious is the Lord, and righteous;
our God is merciful. (Ps. 116:5)

Reflect: Don't allow yourself to think about your day as devoid of new morning mercies.

AUGUST 15

Don't complain to someone else, cry out to God. He'll never turn a deaf ear to the cries of his people.

Your life really is shaped by the cries of your heart. If your cry is a complaint, you will find yourself with other complainers because misery loves company. As a result, your heart will grow more discouraged and hardened. If you cry to people instead of God, what will happen? You will ask those people to do what only God can do. They will feel overwhelmed and unable, and you will grow more desperate. If you silence your cries, crying only to yourself, you will feel increasingly alone. And then, without anyone who cares and understands, you'll feel more and more helpless. In contrast, the good news of the gospel is that you don't have to muffle your cries. You don't have to be ashamed that you need to cry, and you surely don't have to feel that God is too grand, too far off, or too busy to listen to your measly little cries for help.

I think one reason why God put Psalms in the Bible is to give us courage to cry and to teach us when to cry:

> Why, O Lord, do you stand far away?
> Why do you hide yourself in times of trouble? (Ps. 10:1)

> How long, O Lord? Will you forget me forever?
> How long will you hide your face from me? (Ps. 13:1)

> Contend, O Lord, with those who contend with me;
> fight against those who fight against me! (Ps. 35:1)

> My tears have been my food
> day and night,
> while they say to me all the day long,
> "Where is your God?" (Ps. 42:3)

> O God, you have rejected us, broken our defenses;
> you have been angry; oh, restore us. (Ps. 60:1)

There are many more passages like these in the Psalms. They are there to encourage you to cry to the one who will never turn a deaf ear to your cries and who has the power and willingness to meet you in your need.

> Answer me when I call, O God of my righteousness!
> You have given me relief when I was in distress.
> Be gracious to me and hear my prayer! (Ps. 4:1)

Reflect: Do you feel like you have no one to talk to? Pour out your heart to God today.

AUGUST 16

Your little kingdom will look very attractive to you today, but it is the very kingdom from which grace works unrelentingly to rescue you.

The Bible really is a story of kingdoms in conflict. It's about the battle that rages on the field of your heart. Each kingdom demands your loyalty. Each kingdom promises you life. One kingdom, the big one, leads you to the King of kings. The little kingdom sets you up as king. The big kingdom of glory and grace is gorgeous from every perspective. Yet it doesn't always look that way to you. The little kingdom is deceptive and dark, but it often appears to you as beautiful and life-giving.

So it makes sense that Jesus came to earth as a King to establish his kingdom. But he didn't give his life to set up a physical, political kingdom. He came to set up a much better, much greater kingdom. He came to dethrone all other rule and set up his grace-infused, life-giving reign in your heart. He came to free you and me from our bondage to our own self-serving kingdom purposes. He didn't come to help us make our little kingdom purposes work but to invite us to a much, much better kingdom.

So tell yourself again today that there is a King, but he is not you. Tell yourself that there is a kingdom that will protect and satisfy your heart, but it is not yours. Quite apart from anything you could have done or earned, you have been given a kingdom. Its price was the suffering and death of the King. But he conquered death so that by grace he could establish his rule, and he will continue to rule until the last enemy of your soul and of his kingdom has been defeated. Then he will invite you into the final kingdom, where peace and righteousness will reign forever. Why would you ever want to go back to the delusional hopes of your little kingdom?

> And if it is evil in your eyes to serve the Lord, choose this day whom you will serve, whether the gods your fathers served in the region beyond the River, or the gods of the Amorites in whose land you dwell. But as for me and my house, we will serve the Lord. (Josh. 24:15)

Reflect: Today you will either pray that God's kingdom will come and that his will be done or you will work to make sure that your will and your way win the day. Ask the Lord to help you.

AUGUST 17

One of the most basic sins in relationships is inattention; we make greater commitments to our gardens than to the people we say we love.

You simply cannot let that relationship coast and expect that it will be okay. It's like planting a garden. You clear the land, you break up the soil, and you plant, water, and nurture your flowers, but at that point, you do not have the liberty of walking away. Your work has not ended; in fact, it has just begun. Why? Because you have planted your flowers in impure soil and in a less-than-perfect environment. Weeds will immediately begin to grow, and if you don't attend to them, they will soon dominate the turf and choke out your beautiful flowers.

So it is with relationships. Once a relationship is planted, weeds quickly sprout. Weeds of conflict, control, bitterness, unforgiveness, anger, selfishness, pride, greed, jealousy, impatience, and self-righteousness grow and choke the life out of the relationship. Daily attention is needed. Here's why. Every person in a relationship brings something dangerous and destructive into that relationship. The Bible names this thing *sin*. As long as sin lives in us, it has the power to wreak havoc on our relationships. So we cannot neglect the daily nurture that they need. A good relationship is a good relationship because the people in the relationship never quit working on the relationship.

Does this make you want to run away from relationships? Well, you don't need to be afraid. Because if you're God's child, you bring something else into your relationships that should give you hope. Peter reminds married couples in 1 Peter 3:7 that they are joint heirs of the *grace of life*. Because you've inherited grace, there is hope for your relationships; there are resources for the struggle. This big, expansive, powerful grace motivates and empowers the hard work that every relationship requires. Day after day, knowing the grace you have been given, you rid your relationships of the weeds of selfishness and sin so that flowers of peace and love may grow. And in the end, you don't celebrate how good you are at relationships. No, you celebrate the giver of that grace.

> And God is able to make all grace abound to you, so that having all sufficiency in all things at all times, you may abound in every good work. (2 Cor. 9:8)

Reflect: Pray for God, through his massive grace, to give you the resources you need to truly love difficult friends today.

AUGUST 18

If you're God's child, the gospel isn't an aspect of your life, it is your life; that is, it is the window through which you look at everything.

Sadly, thousands and thousands of sincere believers have a huge hole right smack dab in the middle of their gospel. They celebrate the forgiveness they have been given and their welcome into God's family. And they look with hope to the future, when they will be with the Lord forever. Yet they don't understand the radical, mind-changing, and life-altering *nowism* of the gospel of the Lord Jesus Christ.

For a believer, nothing in his or her life is unchanged by the gospel. If you look at life from the vantage point of the present benefits of the person, work, presence, and promises of the Lord Jesus Christ, nothing in your life looks the same. The apostle Peter encourages people to live in a radical new way because they have been given "all things that pertain to life and godliness" (2 Pet. 1:3). This means we aren't left to our own maturity, character, ingenuity, righteousness, wisdom, or power. Not only that, but the gospel redefines how we understand our whole story, how we think about the meaning of life, how we understand the human struggle, where we get our identity, where we look for peace and security, what we consider in life to be dangerous, what we see as successful living, and so on. Jesus changes everything in life. Nothing remains the same.

Now, if you don't know this, you may celebrate your salvation, but for help with your money, friendships, fear, addictions, decisions, and such, you don't look to the gospel. You open Amazon.com and scan for the latest self-help book that addresses your topic of concern. You do this because you've forgotten who you are as a child of God. You've forgotten the glorious warehouse of spiritual wisdom that you have been given. You think that there is something you need that you haven't yet found. Yet the reality is you have already been given every single thing you need—right now—to be what you're supposed to be and to do what you're supposed to do.

> Now we have received not the spirit of the world, but the Spirit who is from God, that we might understand the things freely given us by God. (1 Cor. 2:12)

Reflect: The gospel gives you everything and changes everything in your life. Do your goals for self-improvement show you actually believe that?

AUGUST 19

God's care comes in many forms. Fellowship is God caring enough to put people in your life to encourage, rebuke, and comfort you.

Read the passage below carefully, and when you've finished reading it, read it again. This passage immediately confronts us with the fact that our relationships belong to God for his use, his purpose. We cannot allow ourselves to have an owner's view of our relationships, as if they exist for the sole purpose to make us happy. Something big, important, and transformational is being said here about us and our relationships.

First, this passage defines our *need*. We were not designed to live on our own. Independent, self-focused living never goes anywhere good. We must all accept the truth that we were not designed to live the Christian life on our own. Here's why: because relationships are an irreplaceable tool in his redemptive hands.

Second, this passage defines our *identity*. The passage offers a list of traits—characteristics that look like Jesus. And the best word for that living like him is *ambassador*. Every believer has this identity: we're ambassadors of the Savior King. Now, you know that the only thing an ambassador does is represent the king who sent him. This means that Jesus makes his invisible presence visible through his people, who represent him in one another's lives. You are the look on Christ's face. You are the tones of his voice. You are the touch of his hands. You are the physical representative of his grace. This is your mission in every relationship of your life—to make the grace of the invisible King visible.

Third, this defines our *calling*—to ask again and again, "What of the person and work of Jesus does this person need to see in this particular moment of his or her life?" Now, none of us is up to this task. So the Redeemer who sent us also comes with us and enables us. Through his strength, we will have the grace we need to represent him well.

> Put on then, as God's chosen ones, holy and beloved, compassionate hearts, kindness, humility, meekness, and patience, bearing with one another and, if one has a complaint against another, forgiving each other; as the Lord has forgiven you, so you also must forgive. And above all these put on love, which binds everything together in perfect harmony. (Col. 3:12–14)

Reflect: How would being Christ's ambassador change the way you text or talk to your friends today?

AUGUST 20

Corporate worship is meant to so enthrall you with God's grace that you want to be an instrument of that grace in the lives of others.

I understand why people, who get hurt and disappointed by others, decide to live in isolation or limit themselves to comfortable and casual relationships. I understand why people say to themselves, "I've been taken once, and I won't be taken again." I understand why adult children choose to live a great distance away from their parents. I understand why many people dread the family gatherings that accompany the holidays. I understand why people hide their hurt and refuse to talk about painful topics with one another. I understand that none of us have ever lived in one single relationship that hasn't disappointed us in some way. I understand that relationships are hard.

But there is one other thing that I understand. It is that, for the believer, relationships are not a lifestyle option. No, they are—for the time period between your salvation and your final resurrection—an essential piece of God's calling. Biblical faith is fundamentally relational. It is shaped and driven by two primary communities. First and foremost is our community with God. This is the whole reason for our existence. Life is found in community with the Creator. Then, second, there is God's call to live in self-sacrificing love of your neighbor. God wants you to be a tool of God's work in your neighbor's heart and life. You and I just don't have the choice of opting out. We are relational beings who have been called to lifelong community with God and others.

We need help to face the often overwhelming call to relationships. Part of God's purpose in corporate worship is to correct your vision about those relationships. If you're not looking at your relationships through the lens of God's amazing grace, you're not seeing those relationships accurately. So when you meet to worship, gathering after gathering is intended to so enthrall you with the grandeur of God's grace that you can't think of anything better than being a tool of that grace in the lives of others.

> Let love be genuine. Abhor what is evil; hold fast to what is good. Love one another with brotherly affection. Outdo one another in showing honor. (Rom. 12:9–10)

Reflect: When it comes to your relationships, where do you tend to hide or go along with the crowd? Stop and pray for God to use your words today in meaningful ways.

AUGUST 21

You're not called to work for God's acceptance; you're called to trust the one who completed that work on your behalf.

Even though we've been told again and again that it's impossible, we try to work for what we have already been given. It causes us to be either insanely proud or irrationally fearful. Some of us boast about what we did not earn or achieve on our own. Or spend our lives feeling like we could never measure up. We wonder what God really thinks of us, and the thought of his presence produces more fear than comfort in our hearts. It all gets to the very heart of the message of the gospel.

Jesus lived the perfect life you and I never, ever could have lived. And now his righteousness has been credited to our accounts. He died the death that we should have died. His death satisfied the Father's anger with our sin. He rose again, conquering sin and death so that we would know life eternal too. All of this was done so that the gulf between us and God would be bridged, so that we would be fully and eternally accepted into his family. Never again would we face his rejection, never again need to pay the penalty for our sins, and never again try to measure up to his standard in order to experience his love. What needed to be done, Jesus did. The work is complete.

Now, having said that, it is true that you have been called to give yourself to the work of God's kingdom and to daily obey the commands of the King. But the work you do is never to be done in order to earn something. The work you're called to do is to be done in celebration of all Christ achieved on your behalf. So you don't have to wonder if you've worked enough. You don't have to fear that you'll mess up and get booted out of the family. The bridge of impossibility has been walked by Christ. The job is done. Your relationship with God is eternally secure. Now, in thankfulness, go out and do his work.

> But if it is by grace, it is no longer on the basis of works; otherwise grace would no longer be grace. (Rom. 11:6)

Reflect: You might have an "earning" mindset, if you envy what you think others have and wish you could do what you think they've achieved. Pray about its effect in your life and seek God's grace.

AUGUST 22

Don't be satisfied with anything less than all God's powerful grace is able to produce in you and through you.

I know it's my problem, and I suspect it's yours too—we're just too easily satisfied. It's not that we want too much from God. No, the reality is that often we are willing to settle for too little. We are content with a little bit of change, a little bit of growth, a little bit of maturity. We settle for a little bit of biblical understanding and theological knowledge.

If our families are livable, if our school isn't terrible, if our friendships aren't a disaster, and if we have nice stuff, good churches, and good health, most of us are satisfied. But God is not satisfied. He knows that we will continue to need his transforming grace until sin is no more. We will continue to need his deliverance and protection as long as we are still susceptible to temptation in this fallen world. Our Savior loves us enough to continue to be dissatisfied even in those moments when we are all too satisfied. He will not abandon the work of his hands. He will not turn from his grace. He will not forsake his saving zeal.

So you'll find yourself in situations you do not like. You'll find yourself having to deal with things you didn't plan. You'll find yourself dealing with trouble you never thought would enter your door. You'll face the unplanned, the unexpected, and the unwanted. Here's why. Your Lord will be using all these hard and uncomfortable moments to wrench you out of your satisfaction. He is working to create heart-and-life change that will not be created any other way. Your Lord exposes your weaknesses so that you will cry out for what he knows you need, but what you have been willing to live without.

So be thankful for all that grace has done for you but be dissatisfied. Don't quit before grace has completed its work. Cry out for more rescue and transformation. And be grateful that your Savior continues to work even in those moments when you don't value the work that you so desperately need.

> And I am sure of this, that he who began a good work in you will bring it to completion at the day of Jesus Christ. (Phil. 1:6)

Reflect: How do you usually view the unplanned, unexpected, and unwanted events in your life? Because of God and his grace, how can you think about them?

AUGUST 23

Don't waste your time in envy. You always have what you need because God's faithfulness is never tainted by partiality.

It is so tempting, when you are suffering, to look around and compare what you are enduring to what others seem to be enjoying. And as you do this, it's so easy to fall into wanting someone else's life. But envy never produces a good harvest. Envy adds layers of trouble to the trouble you're already facing. And worst of all, envy steals away the hope that you only find when you're convinced of the presence and goodness of God. Envy does all this because envy never tells you the truth. It distorts your view of your life, the life of others, and the character of God. Envy whispers dangerous and debilitating lies into your ears. Envy points out all the bad things and puts its hand over your eyes so that you can't see the good things. Envy is a punch in the stomach when you're already out of breath. It's bad news when you already feel that you can't bear anything more. Envy is the enemy of hope.[10]

In a world of
justice gone bad,
where disloyalty brings
daily pain,
where government is
corrupt,
and even faithful friends
come up short;
where the haves get more
and the have-nots wonder why;
and where it is very
tempting
to look over the fence
at someone else's life
and wonder why
so much good
has fallen on him,
it is so good to know that you
never play favorites.
You lavish riches of grace
on each and every one
of your children.
You meet every child's
every need,
and you do it with unbroken
faithfulness.
So I will quit keeping score.
I will not judge your goodness.
No, I will rest in the bounty of your
mercy.

Fret not yourself because of evildoers;
be not envious of wrongdoers!
For they will soon fade like the grass
and wither like the green herb.

Trust in the Lord, and do good;
dwell in the land and befriend faithfulness.
Delight yourself in the Lord,
and he will give you the desires of your heart. (Ps. 37:1–4)

Reflect: How has envy been lying to you? How has social media amplified that lie?

AUGUST 24

Yes, you live in a world where evil still exists, but the one who conquered sin and death is still with you.

It is the disastrous duo—the evil outside us and the evil that still remains inside us. It is not just that we live in a world where evil still exists. No, the danger of the external evil is made incredibly greater by the evil that lives inside us. You see, it is only ever the evil inside you that magnetizes you to the evil outside you. Sin is only ever attractive to a sinner. It really is true, "To the pure, all things are pure" (Titus 1:15). The problem is that none of us is yet completely pure. Yes, by the operation of powerful grace, we are purer than we once were. But here is our dilemma: our purification from sin is a lifelong process and not a single event. That process takes place within a dramatically broken world where evil lurks around every corner. And so, there is not a day in our lives when internal and external evil do not intersect somehow, some way.

Are you discouraged as you read this? Well, you must remember that you have not been sent out into this world on your own. You have not been asked to journey through this dark world all by yourself. As Jesus was sending his disciples out into this dark world to bring the message of the gospel to those enshrouded by evil external and controlled by evil internal, he said something that really changes everything: "And behold, I am with you always, to the end of the age" (Matt. 28:20).

Jesus doesn't send us out with a pack of principles and promises. No, he does so much more. He knows that we'll never make it unless he is with us in every moment of every situation, location, and relationship. He is not a rescue squad that leaps into action in our moment of trouble. He's there with us in trouble because he's been there with us all along. In our struggle with evil, he gives us the only gift that will help us—himself! *He* is the best gift of his grace.

> Therefore the Lord himself will give you a sign. Behold, the virgin shall conceive and bear a son, and shall call his name Immanuel. (Isa. 7:14)

Reflect: Which seems harder to deal with—the evil you see around you or within you? Who can you remind today that Jesus is with them, just like he is with you?

AUGUST 25

Real faith never calls you to swindle yourself into thinking that things are better than they are. Biblical faith is shockingly honest and hopeful.

Biblical faith is not about wearing a fake smile while you live in a constant state of religious denial. It's not about praying in religious phrases because somehow that makes you feel more spiritual. It's not about priding yourself on your ability to keep God's rules or because you're on pace to read through the whole Bible again this year. It's not about cleaning yourself up on Sunday so your public image hides the real details of your private spiritual life. If you are doing, saying, or thinking religious things that are meant to hide you from reality, you are not living biblical Christianity. The faith of the Bible will never call you to deny reality in any way. The faith of the Bible is so in awe of the grandeur and glory of God that it is able to look at the darkest of realities in life and not be afraid.

Abraham did not need to deny reality in order to leave his home without knowing for sure where God was taking him. Noah did not need to deny reality in order to spend 120 years building that ark. The children of Israel did not need to deny reality in order to walk around Jericho for seven days. David did not need to deny reality in order to face Goliath in battle. Peter didn't need to deny reality in order to stand before the Sanhedrin and refuse to quit preaching the gospel. You see, it wasn't an immaturity of faith that propelled these people. No, it was the clarity of faith that caused them to do what they did.

It is only when you look at this dark world through the lens of the existence, power, authority, wisdom, faithfulness, love, and grace of the King of kings and Lord of lords that you see reality with clarity. You cannot ever understand what you are facing if you omit the fact of facts—the existence of God.

> So we are always of good courage. We know that while we are at home in the body we are away from the Lord, for we walk by faith, not by sight. (2 Cor. 5:6–7)

Reflect: Are you lacking faith? Run to the one who freely gives it as his gift of grace to you.

AUGUST 26

Why fear when God has already given you, in Christ, everything you need to be what you're supposed to be and to do what you're called to do?

I think it's one of the dirty secrets of the church: we do many things out of fear and not faith. Fear happens when I look at myself, assess my resources, and conclude that I do not have what it takes to handle what God is putting before me. Fear in a believer is a function of forgetfulness. To the degree that you forget who God is, who you are as his child, and what grace you've been given, fear is your default emotion. I am deeply persuaded that the only solution to fear is fear. In other words, fear is defeated only by a bigger, greater fear. Here's what I mean. When the fear of God overwhelms and controls your heart, it protects you from the paralyzing and debilitating fear of other things. It's only when God looms hugely larger than anything you could ever face that your heart is able to experience peace. Meditate on these passages:

> Even though I walk through the valley of the shadow of death,
> I will fear no evil,
> for you are with me. (Ps. 23:4)

> The Lord is my light and my salvation;
> whom shall I fear? (Ps. 27:1)

> The fear of the Lord leads to life,
> and whoever has it rests satisfied. (Prov. 19:23)

> Fear not, for I am with you;
> be not dismayed, for I am your God;
> I will strengthen you, I will help you,
> I will uphold you with my righteous right hand. (Isa. 41:10)

> Blessed is the one who fears the Lord always. (Prov. 28:14)

So how can you enter the experience of vertical fear (fear of God) overwhelming and quieting horizontal fear (fear of anything else)? Well, first run to God in prayer. Ask him to give you the eyes to see and a heart to remember his awesome glory. Then require yourself to quit meditating on your problems and instead begin meditating on the glory of the God who has become your Father and who is always with you. No, you should not deny your problems. Yet if you obsess about them, they will loom larger and larger, and you will grow more and more afraid.

> I sought the Lord, and he answered me
> and delivered me from all my fears. (Ps. 34:4)

Reflect: Today what fearful reality should you face while also meditating on God's glory?

AUGUST 27

God calls you to live a wise and righteous life, then he connects you to the one who is wisdom and righteousness—the Lord Jesus Christ.

Who do you think you are? I'm serious. What's the identity (or identities) that you assign to yourself that defines who you are and what you're supposed to be doing? Even more important, who do you tell yourself that God is? And how does that shape the way you think about and respond to the opportunities, responsibilities, and temptations of everyday life? The gospel of Jesus Christ is one big, massive identity story.

The Bible pulls back the curtains and reveals to us the one who sits at the center of all things. The Bible tells us that God is the Creator, controller, and King over all things. It tells us that God is boundless in authority, wisdom, and power. However, the Bible also tells us that this high and mighty one is slow to anger and plenteous in love; that he is merciful, tender, kind, and forgiving. It tells us that he is the long-suffering giver of amazing grace.

But the Bible also reveals your identity. It tells you that you are the creation of this awesome God. It also reveals that because of sin you are a fallen creation. You were created by God to be dependent on him. Yet sin makes you rebellious. Sin makes you quest for independence and self-sufficiency. Sin makes you love what is foolish, while thinking that you're wise. Sin makes you think you're capable of what you cannot do. Sin makes you think you're righteous when really your heart is corrupt. Sin convinces you that you are okay when actually you're heading for disaster. The Bible lovingly confronts you with everything you are not. It does so in order that you would run after everything you could be. The Bible forces you to face your foolishness and failure so you would run to one who *is* wisdom and righteousness, and find your hope and identity in him.

This is what the gospel is about. The cross makes a way for the one who is everything that you're not to become for you and in you everything that you need.

> You are in Christ Jesus, who became to us wisdom from God, righteousness and sanctification and redemption. (1 Cor. 1:30)

Reflect: How might God be calling you to do—only through the grace of Christ—what you cannot do on your own?

AUGUST 28

God's grace calls you to submit. But it offers you true freedom like you've never known before.

I think we misunderstand true freedom. Freedom that satisfies your heart is never found in setting yourself up as your own authority. True freedom is not found in doing whatever you want. True freedom is not found in resisting the call to submit to any authority but your own. True freedom is never found in writing your own moral code. True freedom is not the result of finally deciding on your own identity. When you attempt to do these things, you never enjoy freedom; you only end up in another form of captivity.

Why is this true? Because you and I were born into a world of authority. First, there is the overarching authority of God. Nothing exists that does not sit under his sovereign and unshakable rule. If God created this world (and he did), and if he owns what he created (and he does), then you and I do not have independence from his rule. This means that as his creatures, we were created to live in willing submission to his will for us. Here's the point: freedom is never found in spinning free of his authority. No, freedom is found in the willing submission of our hearts to his authority. Then, second, there are all the levels of human authority that God put on earth to make his invisible authority visible. This means that personal freedom is not found in resisting human authority either. Freedom and authority are not enemies.

The bottom line is that you and I always exist under some kind of authority. Yet none of us is wise enough, strong enough, or good enough to rule ourselves well. We are no more hardwired to rule our own lives than a beagle is hardwired to live in a water-filled aquarium. Self-rule never leads anywhere good. God doesn't give you grace so you can live how you want. His agenda for grace is to transform you into a person who humbly recognizes your need for authority. Grace leads you to celebrate the holy, loving, and benevolent authority of God.

> But now that you have been set free from sin and have become slaves of God, the fruit you get leads to sanctification and its end, eternal life. (Rom. 6:22)

Reflect: If God knows what is best and gives what is best always, how does that change your view of his authority in your life?

AUGUST 29

The transformative power of grace will be one of the divine wonders that we will celebrate forever when eternity is our final home.

The Bible is not a collection of stories about human heroes. No, the Bible is the story of a hero Redeemer who, by his powerful grace, transforms weak and ordinary people. Think with me of the characters who walk across the pages of Scripture:

- Moses wasn't a natural-born leader. He begged God to send someone else to Egypt, yet by transforming grace, there was no prophet like him in all of Israel.
- Gideon was convinced God had the wrong guy, that he didn't really mean to call Gideon to lead the Israelite army against the Midianites. Yet when Gideon obeyed, he witnessed the awesome power of the God who had called him.
- David was the least likely son of Jesse to rise to the throne of Israel, but God's grace gave him a heart of courage.
- Peter was so fearful that he denied that he knew Jesus, but he became the man who stood before the Sanhedrin and essentially said, "You can threaten to kill me, but I will not stop preaching the gospel" (see Acts 4:19–20).
- Paul was the least likely of the apostles. He had murderous hatred for the followers of Jesus. Yet by grace he became the most eloquent spokesman of the gospel.

The Bible does not celebrate the steely spirit of a bunch of heroic characters. No, the Bible puts before us people who were just like you and me. They were weak and fearful. They doubted God as much as they trusted him. They sometimes followed God's way and at other times demanded their own ways. These were not natural-born heroes. Yet they all accomplished great things. They helped advance God's purpose. What made the difference? You can answer the question with one word: *grace*. Grace transformed their hearts. Grace gave them the desire, power, and wisdom to do what they would not have been able to do on their own. Grace means that when God calls you, he goes with you. Grace supplies what you need for the task at hand. They weren't naturals; no, they were transformed!

> Then he said to me, "This is the word of the LORD to Zerubbabel: Not by might, nor by power, but by my Spirit, says the LORD of hosts." (Zech. 4:6)

Reflect: What weakness in your life makes you wonder if God could use you? How can you trust his grace today to take the next step in following his call?

AUGUST 30

Grace smashes your pride, but it gives you more reason for confidence than you have ever had before.

Nebuchadnezzar was the arrogant king of the conquering nation of Babylon. He had devastated Judah and taken its people as his captive servants. Then he commanded everyone in his kingdom to worship an idol or face death. Listen to the extent of his pride: "Is not this great Babylon, which I have built by my mighty power as a royal residence and for the glory of my majesty?" (Dan. 4:30). But while the words were still in his mouth, he was dramatically humiliated by the Lord. By the power of God, Nebuchadnezzar was "driven from among men and ate grass like an ox, and his body was wet with the dew of heaven till his hair grew as long as eagles' feathers, and his nails were like birds' claws" (4:33). The pride of the king had been destroyed by the finger of God. We don't know for sure how long Nebuchadnezzar was in that humiliated state, like an animal. Yet we do know that when his senses returned, his choking arrogance had been replaced with confidence. Are you confused at the distinction? Well, read these words below and compare them to what Nebuchadnezzar had said before.

Nebuchadnezzar was confident in the position and power he had been given, but the old pride had been broken. What he once took credit for building, he now praised God for establishing. Nebuchadnezzar did not minimize the splendor of his reign. Yet he no longer said, "This is from me, about me, and for me." You see, pride takes credit for what it could not achieve on its own. While confidence stands strong because it recognizes the power and presence of one greater. Only divine grace can lead you from one to the other.

> At the same time my reason returned to me, and for the glory of my kingdom, my majesty and splendor returned to me. My counselors and my lords sought me, and I was established in my kingdom, and still more greatness was added to me. Now I, Nebuchadnezzar, praise and extol and honor the King of heaven, for all his works are right and his ways are just; and those who walk in pride he is able to humble. (Dan. 4:36–37)

Reflect: What ability do you have that you take pride in? How can you, instead, give credit to the God who gave it to you?

AUGUST 31

If you're God's child, you are blessed with the convicting ministry of the Holy Spirit. The question is, are you listening?

It is possible to be a believer in the Lord Jesus Christ, saved by his blood, and still have a hard heart. So the warning of Hebrews 3:12–13 is much needed by all of us: "Take care, brothers, lest there be in any of you an evil, unbelieving heart, leading you to fall away from the living God. But exhort one another every day, as long as it is called 'today,' that none of you may be hardened by the deceitfulness of sin."

It is tempting to not listen to the protective promptings of the Holy Spirit. Why? Because you think you have a more accurate view of yourself than you really have. Sin is deceitful, so there are places in our lives where we think we're better off spiritually than we actually are.

It is tempting to resist the convicting ministry of the Holy Spirit because few of us actually believe that we need help. As a result, we have not opened ourselves up to one of the primary tools the Holy Spirit uses to convict us: other believers.

It is tempting to harden your heart against the Holy Spirit's conviction by arguing for your own righteousness whenever one of your sins, weaknesses, or failures is revealed.

It is tempting to refuse to listen to the convicting voice of the Spirit by comparing yourself to other believers and arguing that you are surely more righteous than they are.

It is tempting to run from the Spirit's restoring and protective work by rewriting your history. As a result, you swindle yourself into believing that your wrongs are not so wrong after all.

It is tempting to resist the Spirit's loving work of conviction by confusing skill, experience, and success with personal maturity.

But be comforted. You serve a dissatisfied Redeemer. He will not turn from his work of grace even when you fail to recognize it and you work to resist it.

> And I will ask the Father, and he will give you another Helper, to be with you forever, even the Spirit of truth, whom the world cannot receive, because it neither sees him nor knows him. You know him, for he dwells with you and will be in you. (John 14:16–17)

Reflect: With patient grace, Jesus once more calls you to listen. How are you hearing what his Spirit is saying to you today through his word?

SEPTEMBER 1

Don't be disheartened because you feel weak. By grace your Savior lives inside you, and he is your strength.

Where do you run when you're discouraged or faced with your weakness or failure? I run to Romans 8:1–11. In those moments, this passage has been my friend and comforter again and again:

> There is therefore now no condemnation for those who are in Christ Jesus. For the law of the Spirit of life has set you free in Christ Jesus from the law of sin and death. For God has done what the law, weakened by the flesh, could not do. By sending his own Son in the likeness of sinful flesh and for sin, he condemned sin in the flesh, in order that the righteous requirement of the law might be fulfilled in us, who walk not according to the flesh but according to the Spirit. (Rom. 8:1–4)

Think about this passage. First, we will never again face condemnation for our sin. Jesus bore every aspect of our penalty. Even on days of evident weakness and repeated failure, we will not be punished for our sin. So in those moments, we don't have to hide or run *from* the Lord. Instead, we can run *to* him for his help and forgiveness.

Second, sin can leave us weak, lame, and unable. It makes it impossible for us to keep God's law. It wasn't enough for God to forgive us, although that forgiveness is a glorious thing. God also comes to live inside us by his Spirit (see Rom. 8:9–10). His Spirit gives us new life and empowers us to desire and do what we would be unable to do without his indwelling presence. This means that you do not have to fear or deny your weakness. You can face your weakness with joy. Here's why: because you know that you have been given grace for that weakness. This grace that is not a thing but a person—the Holy Spirit.

> You, however, are not in the flesh but in the Spirit, if in fact the Spirit of God dwells in you. Anyone who does not have the Spirit of Christ does not belong to him. But if Christ is in you, although the body is dead because of sin, the Spirit is life because of righteousness. (Rom. 8:9–10)

Reflect: Where do you feel inadequate and weak? Throughout the day, in those moments of weakness, pause and seek the Spirit's help.

SEPTEMBER 2

Grace causes us to be alive to God and causes our eyes to be open to spiritual realities we once had no capacity to see.

> Now we have received not the spirit of the world, but the Spirit who is from God, that we might understand the things freely given us by God. And we impart this in words not taught by human wisdom but taught by the Spirit, interpreting spiritual truths to those who are spiritual.
>
> The natural person does not accept the things of the Spirit of God, for they are folly to him, and he is not able to understand them because they are spiritually discerned. The spiritual person judges all things, but is himself to be judged by no one. "For who has understood the mind of the Lord so as to instruct him?" But we have the mind of Christ. (1 Cor. 2:12–16)

This really is one of those "that says it all" passages. It confronts us with our inability. We really don't see and understand the things of God. That means on our own we're not prepared for knowing God or for living life as he designed it to be lived. Despite our best experience and research, you and I simply cannot know all that we need to know in order to be what we're supposed to be. Yet God first reveals the wisdom we need in his grand redemptive book, the Bible. Then he opens our eyes and our hearts so that we can receive and understand what he has revealed. Without this ministry of illumining grace, these things would be at worst completely concealed from us and at best a whole lot of foolishness to us. We need Christ to come to us by his Spirit to reveal his mind to us so that we can think his thoughts after him.

All of this is vitally important because one of the things that sin does is turn us all into fools. Sin brings with it a functional insanity from which we all need to be delivered. So here in 1 Corinthians 2 we're reminded about God's delivering grace. It opens the understanding of our hearts so that we may know God, know his grace, and seek and receive the life that only he can give.

> Open my eyes, that I may behold
>   wondrous things out of your law. (Ps. 119:18)

Reflect: What sources of wisdom and understanding have you sought most this week—the internet and friends, or God's word and Spirit?

SEPTEMBER 3

Hope is more than wishing things will work out. It is resting in the God who holds all things in his wise and powerful hands.

We use the word *hope* in a variety of ways. Sometimes we're talking about a wish about something over which we have no control. We say, "I hope it doesn't rain on the day of the picnic." Sometimes we also use the word *hope* to say what we think should happen. We say, "I hope he will choose to be honest this time." So because the word *hope* is used in a variety of ways, it's important to understand how the Bible uses this word.

Biblical hope is more than a wish or expectation, although it includes those. So what is biblical hope? It is *confidently expecting a guaranteed result that changes the way you live*. Let's pull this definition apart.

First, it *confidently hopes*. Biblical hope is confident because it is not based on your wisdom, faithfulness, or power. Instead, it's rooted in the awesome power, love, faithfulness, grace, patience, and wisdom of God. Because God is who he is and will never, ever change, when you hope in him, it's hope well placed and secure.

Hope is also *expecting a guaranteed result*. It is being sure that God will do all that he has planned and promised to do. You see, his promises are only as good as the extent of his rule. Yet since he rules everything everywhere, I know that resting in the promises of his grace will never leave me empty and embarrassed. I may not understand what is happening, but I can have hope. Here's why: my hope does not rest on my understanding but on God's goodness and his rule.

Finally, true hope *changes the way you live*. When you have hope that is guaranteed, you live with real confidence. That courage causes you to make choices of faith that would seem foolish to someone who does not have your hope. If you're God's child, hope has invaded your life by grace, and his name is Jesus!

> The war horse is a false hope for salvation,
> and by its great might it cannot rescue.
>
> Behold, the eye of the Lord is on those who fear him,
> on those who hope in his steadfast love,
> that he may deliver their soul from death
> and keep them alive in famine. (Ps. 33:17–19)

Reflect: Where have people crushed your hopes? How can God's goodness and power restore your hope?

SEPTEMBER 4

Sin is more than bad behavior. It's a heart condition that results in bad behavior. That's why we can't independently defeat sin.

In his teaching that we call "the Sermon on the Mount" (Matthew 5–7), Jesus powerfully makes the point that sin is a heart problem. Yet we still find it difficult to accept. We want to hold on to two operational falsehoods. First, we believe that sin is simply a matter of bad behavior. Maybe we want to deny that sin is some dark defect in our character. If we work hard enough, we can free ourselves from sinful acts. But sin is not just a matter of behavior.

Here's the second operational falsehood. We all like to think that our sin is caused more by what is outside us than what is inside us. If you ask the little boy on the playground at school why he hit the little girl, he probably won't talk about himself. He will blame someone or something outside himself. We don't want to face the fact that sin is caused by what's inside us.

So Jesus confronts our misperceptions about what sin is and what causes us to sin. He says:

> You have heard that it was said to those of old, "You shall not murder; and whoever murders will be liable to judgment." But I say to you that everyone who is angry with his brother will be liable to judgment. (Matt. 5:21–22)
>
> You have heard that it was said, "You shall not commit adultery." But I say to you that everyone who looks at a woman with lustful intent has already committed adultery with her in his heart. (5:27–28)

With these words, Jesus is explaining to us the law's original intent. God's law is meant to address and expose the heart. Why? Because sin is always a matter of the heart before it's an action of the body. It's hatred within my heart that causes me to use my body to harm someone else. It's the lustful desires of my heart that lead me to sexual sin. This is why the delivering grace of Christ is essential. You can escape many things, but you cannot escape your heart. In gorgeous mercy, God delivers you from you.

As it is written:

> "None is righteous, no, not one." (Rom. 3:10)

Reflect: We all tend to want to think that we are more righteous than we actually are. Where do you see this tendency in your life?

SEPTEMBER 5

God's care is sure, but will you run to him in your time of need or look elsewhere for hope and comfort?

By his promises, God invites us to run to him:

> [Cast] all your anxieties on him, because he cares for you. (1 Pet. 5:7)

> He has said, "I will never leave you nor forsake you." (Heb. 13:5)

> The LORD is my light and my salvation;
> whom shall I fear?
> The LORD is the stronghold of my life;
> of whom shall I be afraid? (Ps. 27:1)

> And my God will supply every need of yours according to his riches in glory in Christ Jesus. (Phil. 4:19)

These are just a small sampling of God's words of invitation and welcome. He really is the "Father of mercies and God of all comfort" (2 Cor. 1:3).

He can do for you what no one else can do. He has power that no one else possesses. He is able and willing to meet you in your moments of need, even when you created the problem.

He will never mock you in your weakness. He will not stand idly by and sarcastically say, "I told you so." He finds no joy in your suffering. He is full of compassion. He abounds in mercy. He will never walk away disgusted. He will never use your weakness against you. He has no favorites and shows no partiality. He never grows tired. He never becomes impatient. He will never quit because he's had enough.

He will never refuse to give you what he's promised because you've messed up so badly. He is just as faithful to all of his promises on your very worst day as he is on your very best day. He doesn't ask you to earn his compassion or to do things to gain his mercy. He knows how weak and fickle your heart is. Yet he continues to move toward you with grace that won't quit. He delights to meet your needs. He finds joy in bringing peace to your heart. He really is everything that you need. Why would you run anywhere else in your time of weakness or trouble?

> Cast your burden on the LORD,
> and he will sustain you;
> he will never permit
> the righteous to be moved. (Ps. 55:22)

Reflect: When you feel stressed out or alone, where do you tend to run for help or relief?

SEPTEMBER 6

What kind of Jesus do you want? Do you want a Jesus, who will make you feel better? He will be only your sovereign Savior King.

What do you define as blessing? What do you identify as a sign of God's care? When you say, "If only I had ______, then I'd be content," what goes in the blank? What tempts you to be disappointed with your life? Be honest—what do you want from God? Or maybe this is a more provocative way of saying it—what kind of Messiah do you want Jesus to be?

I think many of us are just not on Jesus's agenda page. What we dream of is not the same as what he has promised us. Perhaps many of us struggle with disappointment with God because, we don't prize what God values. Could it be that many of us want nothing more than a Jesus, who will make us feel better and make our lives easier? And if he delivers, of course we'll give him thanks.

Perhaps many of us crave *success* more than we crave redemption. We are willing to do almost anything to be successful. Meanwhile, we neglect the things that God says have eternal value.

Perhaps many of us value *acceptance* more than we value redemption. We find more joy from being accepted by the people around us than we do in God's abounding love.

Perhaps many of us desire *comfort* and *pleasure* more than we desire redemption. If our lives could just be easier and more predictable, we would be satisfied.

Perhaps many of us want *material things* more than we want redemption. We tend to judge the quality of our lives by the size of the piles of stuff we have acquired.

Now, none of these things is inherently evil. It is not wrong to desire any of them. The question is this: "What set of desires rules my heart?" Maybe your struggle of faith comes from the fact that you don't really value what your Savior is working to produce in your heart and life. Your Messiah is faithful; he is your sovereign Savior King.

For where your treasure is, there will your heart be also. (Luke 12:34)

Reflect: How do the desires that rule your heart affect how you evaluate your life and how you make decisions? Most importantly, how do your heart-desires influence the way you think about the goodness and faithfulness of God?

SEPTEMBER 7

Do you want the "vacation-planner Jesus," who'll take you to a place where life is more pleasurable? He will be only your sovereign Savior King.

If you judge God's goodness by the amount of suffering in your life, you will end up concluding that he is not good. If you judge God's love by how much disappointment and grief you have had to deal with, you will end up questioning his love. Here is the bottom line: *you will suffer because your suffering is an essential part of God's good plan for you.*

When suffering has entered your door, it does not indicate that God's plan has failed. These difficult moments do not mean that he has forgotten you. These painful moments do not reveal that he is unfaithful to his promises. Here's what you and I need to understand and live in light of: these difficult moments of life are not the failure of God's plan. These moments are part of his plan. They are placed in our lives as tools of his ongoing work of rescuing, transforming, and delivering grace. Why are they in our lives? Because God values holiness more than he values our temporal definition of happiness. He is not working to give us that temporary emotional high. God is working to produce something much better—eternal joy.

The reality is that God has not agreed to give me that catalog of things that I think will make me happy. He is not working to make my journey as easy as it could possibly be.

No, walking with Jesus is not the grand vacation, a life free of responsibility and trial. Walking with Jesus is not like that. Here's why. Because life with him is not a destination (as a vacation would be). He is not "vacation-planner Jesus"; he is our sovereign Savior King. Thus, this present life is meant by God to be a time of preparation for the final glorious destination that will be our eternal home. So our right-now life is not a paradise. Right now, God in grace is working to prepare us—through the difficulties of life—for what is guaranteed to each and every one of his children.

> And now I commend you to God and to the word of his grace, which is able to build you up and to give you the inheritance among all those who are sanctified. (Acts 20:32)

Reflect: How is your final destination (glory with Christ) better than what you've been wanting God to give you?

SEPTEMBER 8

Maybe you want the "suggestion-box Jesus," whose law is more advice than command. He will be nothing less than the sovereign Savior King.

Consider how these passages portray God's law:

> The law of the LORD is perfect,
> reviving the soul;
> the testimony of the LORD is sure,
> making wise the simple;
> the precepts of the LORD are right,
> rejoicing the heart;
> the commandment of the LORD is pure,
> enlightening the eyes;
> the fear of the LORD is clean,
> enduring forever;
> the rules of the LORD are true,
> and righteous altogether. (Ps. 19:7–9)

God's law is not a curse; it is a grace. God's law is not a burden; it is a gift of his love. Immediately after redeeming his children from the slavery of Egypt, God took them to Mount Sinai to give them his law. He did this because they were the children of his love, the objects of his redemption. As your Creator, God knows you. He knows the world you live in and he knows the plans he has for you. Because he knows all of these things, he is infinitely more qualified to set the boundaries of your living than you are. He is your sovereign Savior King, not the "suggestion-box Jesus." His grace works in you a heart of submission. In grace to you, he creates a heart that esteems his authority and finds joy in his law.

> Oh how I love your law!
> It is my meditation all the day.
> Your commandment makes me wiser than my enemies,
> for it is ever with me.
> I have more understanding than all my teachers,
> for your testimonies are my meditation. (Ps. 119:97–99)

Reflect: Where have you bought into the insanity that you might be smarter than God and his law?

SEPTEMBER 9

Maybe today you want the "district-attorney Jesus," who'll get all those people who've made your life hard. He will be only your sovereign Savior King.

Have you ever wanted revenge? God has placed a desire for justice in each of our hearts. So when we face injustice, it's very tempting to want to take justice into our own hands. We see it in the little child, who, when hit, immediately hits back. We see it in ourselves when we've been publicly embarrassed by a friend. We not only cut that friend out of our life, but look for a way to heap embarrassment on him as well. We really do find it easier to make war than to make peace. And we often wish that God would make war with others on our behalf.

Consider how Paul approaches this topic in Romans 12:18–21:

> If possible, so far as it depends on you, live peaceably with all. Beloved, never avenge yourselves, but leave it to the wrath of God, for it is written, "Vengeance is mine, I will repay, says the Lord." To the contrary, "if your enemy is hungry, feed him; if he is thirsty, give him something to drink; for by so doing you will heap burning coals on his head." Do not be overcome by evil, but overcome evil with good.

The foundation of this passage is God's promise that he will exercise his righteous justice. This doesn't mean that Jesus is your district attorney. God does not promise that he will do it according to your schedule. He does not promise that he will abandon his mercy for his justice. But he does promise to repay. When Paul says, "Leave it to the wrath of God," he is essentially saying, "Stop trying to do God's job, and trust him to do what he has promised he will do." You can trust him because he is your sovereign Savior King.

> You have heard that it was said, "An eye for an eye and a tooth for a tooth." But I say to you, Do not resist the one who is evil. But if anyone slaps you on the right cheek, turn to him the other also. (Matt. 5:38–39)

Reflect: None of us has the strength of character to live the way described above. Even the evil that is done to us exposes how much we need God's grace. Thank God that his grace is yours for the taking!

SEPTEMBER 10

Perhaps today you long for the "Match.com Jesus," who will give you someone to love. He will be to you what you need, your sovereign Savior King.

We were designed to be social beings. We were made to live in vertical community with God and horizontal community with others. But we can only know the true joys of human love, if love for God first rules our hearts. If love for God isn't the place where you find your rest, you will need human relationships too much. And you'll be asking people to do for you what only your Savior can do. This never works because there are no perfect people in your life.

And there's more: if God is not in his rightful place in my heart and life, guess who I will insert in his place? The answer, of course, is me. I make my relationships all about me. Rather than love for God shaping my relationships and motivating what I say and do, love of self drives me.

So when I look for help to "Match.com Jesus," I'm actually asking God to replace himself with other messiahs in my life—messiahs I can see, hear, and touch. This is the source of so much relational dysfunction and heartache.

But this picture is also a primary argument for how much we need grace. Sin does make us focus on us too much. Sin does cause us to forget God and elevate people in our lives to the role of savior. Sin does cause us to question the goodness of God because he hasn't placed these perfect little messiahs in our lives.

For this struggle, there is amazing, patient grace. God bestows on us his eternal transforming love so that, through his love, we will become people who find our rest in his love. And because we do, we are then able to love others well.

> Jesus answered, "The most important is, 'Hear, O Israel: The Lord our God, the Lord is one. And you shall love the Lord your God with all your heart and with all your soul and with all your mind and with all your strength.' The second is this: 'You shall love your neighbor as yourself.' There is no other commandment greater than these." (Mark 12:29–31)

Reflect: Do you want to use loving God to have loving relationships with people? Or do you truly love God first and people second?

SEPTEMBER 11

Maybe today you want the "Amazon.com Jesus," who will deliver all your golden dreams. He will be nothing less than your sovereign Savior King.

We are all dreamers. Everyone in some way wishes, "If only I had this, I would be content and able to stop looking for the next thing." We all chase a vision of what we would like life to be. We all dream and imagine. Now, this ability is not evil in and of itself. Yet if we combine it with the selfishness of sin, it will surely get us into trouble.

Here's what happens: you have a dream, and then your heart gets captured by your dream. It becomes your definition of "life." What was once a desire has morphed into a demand, and it won't be long before you view that demand as a need. Then it becomes the thing that you are unwilling to live without. Soon you're unhappy, not because life has been hard or God has been unfaithful, but because this thing that rules your heart lies beyond your grasp. You are despondent and discouraged. You envy people who seem to have captured their dreams. You wonder why you've been singled out. You wonder why God has forgotten you. Dream? Yes, but when your dream becomes a ruling thing, it wreaks havoc on your spiritual life.

As your dreams gobble up more of your heart, pay attention to what happens to your relationship with God. God is no longer your source of courage, hope, or joy. Awe of God is no longer the reason you do everything you do. Sadly, God has been reduced to a delivery system. Your Savior has become "Amazon.com Jesus." If he delivers, you'll worship and serve him. Yet if he fails to deliver, you will question his goodness and love, and you'll have little motivation to offer your life to him.

However, there is grace for this struggle—grace that battles for your heart, grace that is more powerful than any dream. Own the dangerous dreams of your fickle heart and run to the grace that is yours in Jesus.

> But I have this against you, that you have abandoned the love you had at first. Remember therefore from where you have fallen; repent, and do the works you did at first. If not, I will come to you and remove your lampstand from its place, unless you repent. (Rev. 2:4–5)

Reflect: Ask God to help you to hold onto your dreams—with open hands.

SEPTEMBER 12

Grace means you can never say that it's too hard, that you've been left on your own, or that you simply don't have enough.

A hundred times a day, you are constantly trying to make sense out of the situations and experiences of your life. Every one of us is an archaeologist; we dig through the mounds of our own little lives to make sense of the "civilization" that has shaped us. Because we all have this inner drive for life to make sense, we are all in a constant conversation with ourselves. You really do talk to yourself a hundred times a day. Most of us have learned that it's best not to move our lips or people will think that we're crazy. But we all do it.

The things you say to you about yourself, about God, and about life are very, very important. Why? Because they shape the way you act and react to the things that God places in your life. In those silent and private conversations that you have with you, you're either remembering God's grace or you're not.

When you remember God's grace, you tell yourself that you're not alone, that you have been graced with all that you need for what God has called you to be and to do. When you remember God's grace, you are also reminded of his presence and his promises. Ultimately, human rest is not found in measuring the size of your righteousness, strength, and wisdom against the size of the situation you're facing. No, rest is found when you compare the size of what you're facing to the person, presence, character, power, and grace of God.

What is God's best gift of grace? The answer is easy—himself. God knew that our need would be so great that the only gift that would meet our need would not be an it or a thing. No, grace means that he meets our deepest need with the greatest gift—he gives himself. So today, as you're having that conversation with yourself one more time, remind yourself of that gift. Rest in the fact that because you have been given the gift of gifts, you are never alone and never without the resources that you need.

The Lord is my shepherd; I shall not want. (Ps. 23:1)

Reflect: What kind of things does your inner voice usually tell you? As you think about what you've read, how will you talk back to that voice today?

SEPTEMBER 13

Prayer is abandoning all other objects of worship and giving myself to the daily worship of God alone.

Prayer is an act of worship. It is profoundly more than bringing to God our grocery lists of wants and needs. Here are five ways in which prayer is rooted in worship:

- *Prayer acknowledges God's existence.* Prayer begins and ends with the recognition that there is something more ultimate in the universe than you. Prayer places emphasis firmly on the first four words of the Bible: "In the beginning, God . . ." (Gen. 1:1). So prayer is an acknowledgment of God as Creator and Sovereign. It would make no sense to pray if you thought God was your equal.
- *Prayer bows to God's glory.* This is the constant requirement of prayer. Prayer recognizes that there is a glory in this universe greater than your own glory or the brilliant glories of the physical created world. Prayer is recognition that no created glory can or will ever satisfy the heart of the one who prays. It flows from the understanding that only when you live for the glory of God can your heart rest content.
- *Prayer submits to God's plan.* Prayer is not bringing your list and asking God to sign on the bottom. Prayer recognizes that the one who made the world, including you, knows what is best for you. As the psalmist says, "The rules of the LORD are true, and righteous altogether" (Ps. 19:9). Prayer is handing God a blank sheet that you have already signed and trusting him to fill it out as he sees fit.
- *Prayer rests in God's provision.* True prayer isn't spoken in a panic, but in a spirit of trust and rest. You know that the one to whom you pray is near, faithful, and willing to meet your every need.
- *Prayer celebrates God's grace.* True prayer arises when you are blown away by grace. It's this grace that gives you the desire to pray, the confidence that God welcomes your prayers, and the promise that he will answer.

Prayer is laying down your idols and kneeling before God in humble and joyful worship.

> I cry aloud to God,
> aloud to God, and he will hear me. (Ps. 77:1)

Reflect: Which of these aspects of your prayer life is God challenging you to grow in the most?

SEPTEMBER 14

The disappointments of relationships are many, but his grace is sufficient—in fact, it is made perfect in your weakness.

Why are our relationships such a struggle? Why is it so hard to live in peace and harmony with people we say we love? Why do we experience so much irritation, hurt, and impatience?

The answer to these questions is both clear and hard to accept. Here's why our relationships are a struggle. Because we all carry something into our relationships that is destructive to them. The Bible names it: sin.

Sin causes us to be self-absorbed and self-focused because it causes us to live for ourselves (see 2 Cor. 5:15). Sin makes us more demanding than serving, more accusing than forgiving, more defensive than approachable, and more critical than understanding and patient. So you and I shouldn't be surprised that our relationships are marked by problems. Because of all the sin that we drag into our relationships, what should surprise us is that our relationships survive at all!

Yet you don't need to abandon hope for all your relationships. Why? Because there is grace for this struggle. The hope for your relationships is not to be found in you or in the others in your relationships. Hope is found in a third person who has invaded your relationships by his grace. You are never alone in your relationships. He is with you. He is in you. He is for you. He offers you grace that is up to the task even when you're not.

James 4 begins with one of the New Testament's most honest discussions of conflict in our relationships. This passage is honest and direct about what we all face and why we face it. Yet the passage doesn't leave us there. In the middle of this passage is this little phrase that changes everything: "But he gives more grace" (4:6). There is grace for every hurtful moment. There is grace for every time you sin or are sinned against. And the grace that you are given for your relationships will never, ever run out.

> What causes quarrels and what causes fights among you? Is it not this, that your passions are at war within you? (James 4:1)

Reflect: There is always more grace for what is coming around the corner. So you can give yourself to love, to forgive, to confess, to confront, to trust, and to persevere even when things are hard because "he gives more grace" (James 4:6).

SEPTEMBER 15

You will face loss, trouble, and disappointment, but nothing has the power to separate you from your Redeemer's unrelenting love.

As I've said before, I really do love the honesty of the Bible. I don't want to feel like I've got to close my eyes to things and make believe that life is better than it really is. The Bible is filled with brutally honest stories of flawed people and broken situations. Unsurprisingly, the Bible requires us all to be honest as well.

John 13–17 recounts Jesus's last hours with his disciples before his crucifixion. He is preparing them for life without his physical presence. He is warning them of the things they will face in this broken world. This passage is way more than "Goodbye, I love you." It is honest to the point of being scary. Jesus says, "If they persecuted me, they will also persecute you" (15:20). He says, "The hour is coming when whoever kills you will think he is offering service to God" (16:2). It's not a very bright picture of the disciples' future. His words are probably enough to make the disciples panic, but this passage is also dyed with amazing grace. Jesus assures them that he will not leave them like a bunch of orphans (14:18). He comforts them with the promise of the ongoing ministry of the Holy Spirit (14:25–27). John 16:33 spells out their hope (and ours): "I have said these things to you, that in me you may have peace. In the world you will have tribulation. But take heart; I have overcome the world." There will be times when you feel that you simply don't have what it takes to deal with what you're facing. You will be tempted to think that you have been singled out to endure particular difficulty. But in all of this there is real reason for peace and hope. It's not the peace that comes when life seems to be working well, when the people around you seem to appreciate you, or when your health and finances are good. Real peace is found in knowing that grace has connected you to the one who has overcome everything that could cause your heart to be troubled, and nothing can sever that connection.

> What then shall we say to these things? If God is for us, who can be against us? (Rom. 8:31)

Reflect: What situations make you feel like life is out of control? In what ways is that never true?

SEPTEMBER 16

Every time you work to make a wrong you've done look right, you deny the gospel of the grace of the Lord Jesus Christ.

When you are confronted with a wrong, caught in a wrong, or rise to your own defense even when you know what you did was wrong—you aren't just being self-righteous, and you aren't just deceiving yourself. You are fighting the Holy Spirit. At that moment he is gracing you with insight, conviction, protection, and rescue. In grace, he is blowing through your walls of spiritual blindness and self-righteousness to help you to see yourself as you actually are. When that happens, he's helping you seek the grace that is yours in Christ Jesus.

These moments of painful internal discomfort are not bad things. They are very good things. They are evidences of the tender, patient care of your Savior. He works again and again to give sight to your eyes and tenderness to your heart. Why? So that you will be progressively freed from the hold of sin on your thoughts, desires, attitudes, and actions. These moments of personal conviction are always moments of beautiful grace in action. But you and I don't always see them as grace. We tend to hate being confronted. We tend to have a hard time admitting when we are wrong. So instead, we act contrary to the gospel. We deny our wrongs and argue for our righteousness, seemingly afraid of where humble confession will lead us.

We do not need to fear facing our sin and spiritual need. There really is nothing that we will ever need to admit and honestly face that hasn't been fully addressed by the grace that is ours because of the life, death, and resurrection of Jesus. There is nothing that we could ever do that is outside that grace. There is nothing that we could ever do that would cause God to turn his back on us. There is no reason for us to deny and defend. Why? Because every sin has been carried to the cross by Jesus. Open your heart to the Spirit's work. To defend yourself against his painful promptings never takes you anywhere good.

> But if we walk in the light, as he is in the light, we have fellowship with one another, and the blood of Jesus his Son cleanses us from all sin. (1 John 1:7)

Reflect: What areas of your life do you need to bring into the light of God's grace today?

SEPTEMBER 17

This isn't paradise. You can't make it into paradise. Paradise is coming, and your place was secured for you on the cross of Jesus Christ.

We all try to turn this present world into the paradise we dream of. Why do we all attempt this impossible task? Because deep in the heart of every human being, we all long for paradise. We all desire for things to be the way the Creator intended them to be. We all feel the pain of living in a world gone bad. We all zigzag from disappointment to disappointment because reality never seems to rise to the level of our dreams. Each of us tries to turn this moment into the paradise it will never be. And each of us faces the frustration that results from our failed attempts.

The cry of an infant who is dealing with a pain he doesn't understand is a cry for paradise. The tears of a little boy who has been mocked on the playground are tears for paradise. The anger of a teenager whose iPad has been stolen is a cry for paradise. The frustration of a young professional with a boss who never seems to be satisfied is a cry for paradise. We all groan, and those groanings are cries for a better world.

But here's what you have to face. God, for your good and his glory, has chosen to keep you for a while in this broken-down world. He has chosen to use the hardships of this world to complete his work in you. He does not leave you alone. He does not leave you without resources. He blesses you with his new morning mercies. But he has you right where he wants you. This means your church, your family, and your friendships will never be the paradise that you want them to be in this world.

But more needs to be said. In his grace, God has also granted you a place in paradise. If you're God's child, the final chapter of your story will take place in an eternal paradise beyond your wildest dreams. Listen to the words of Jesus:

> In my Father's house are many rooms. If it were not so, would I have told you that I go to prepare a place for you? (John 14:2)

Reflect: As you face the hardships of today, remember that grace has purchased you a ticket for the paradise that is to come.

SEPTEMBER 18

Today, remember that this moment isn't intended to be a destination, but it is what God's using to prepare you for your final destination.

If you live with a destination mentality, you are going to be regularly disappointed. If you live with a destination mentality, you will struggle to believe that God is loving, good, faithful, and kind. If you live with a destination mentality, it will be easier for you to complain than to be content. If you live with a destination mentality, you will be tempted to envy the life of someone else.

Living with a destination mentality means that you load all your hopes and dreams, into this present moment. It means that no matter what your theology says about eternity, you live as if this is all there is. And because you are living as if this is all there is, you try to turn this present moment in this fallen world into the paradise that it will never be. Yes, if you are God's child, you have been promised a paradise beyond your ability to conceive. Yet this sin-broken world, populated by sin-scarred people, will never be the paradise that we tend to long for.

Yet there is meaning and purpose in everything we are going through. In a real way, God is using all the difficulties of life in this fallen world to change and mature us, making us ready for the world that is to come.

Yet it's not just that this is a time of preparation. The fact that we are guaranteed a place in the life that is to come tells us about the present: who we are and what we have been given. Who are we? We are pilgrims on a journey with a glorious destination assured. What have we been given? Well, the guarantee of the future grace of eternity assures us that we will have all the grace we need in the present. So don't try to turn today into paradise. Instead, thank God that you are being prepared by grace for the paradise that will be your forever home.

> For we know that if the tent that is our earthly home is destroyed, we have a building from God, a house not made with hands, eternal in the heavens. For in this tent we groan, longing to put on our heavenly dwelling. (2 Cor. 5:1–2)

Reflect: How would you usually answer this question: What would make your life a paradise for you? How does today's devotional challenge you?

SEPTEMBER 19

Corporate worship is designed to make you thankful, not just for possessions and accomplishments but also for what you've been given in Christ.

I carried all the seductions and attractions of life in a fallen world into worship that morning. I needed to have my values reoriented and my celebration recalibrated. I needed to be not just thankful for the ease, comforts, and accomplishments of life, but thankful for things of eternal value. I needed to see, remember, cry out for, and celebrate grace once again. It was the second song of the worship service that gave the sadness of sin and the joy of grace back to my heart:

No list of sins I have not done, no list of virtues I pursue,
no list of those I am not like can earn myself a place with you.
O God! Be merciful to me. I am a sinner through and through.
My only hope of righteousness is not in me, but only you.

No humble dress, no fervent prayer, no lifted hands, no tearful song,
no recitation of the truth, can justify a single wrong.
My righteousness is Jesus' life. My debt was paid by Jesus' death.
My weary load was borne by Him, and He alone can give me rest.

No separation from the world, no work I do, no gift I give
can cleanse my conscience, cleanse my hands, I cannot cause my soul to live.
But Jesus died and rose again. The pow'r of death is overthrown!
My God is merciful to me and merciful in Christ alone.[11]

As I listened to my brothers and sisters sing and as I took in each phrase, I began to remember the impossibility of my sin and the totality of the solution that is found only in Jesus Christ. Forgetfulness seems like a minor thing. We forget little things every day. But forgetfulness is not a minor thing when it comes to grace. It robs you of worship, identity, humility, courage, and hope. Thank God he ordained for us to gather and remember.

I will remember the deeds of the Lord;
    yes, I will remember your wonders of old. (Ps. 77:11)

Reflect: In what ways does technology distract you most easily and cause you to forget about God and his grace?

SEPTEMBER 20

Hopelessness is the doorway to hope. You have to give up on yourself before you will be excited about the hope that is yours in Christ Jesus.

- We tend to give ourselves far too much credit.
- We tend to think we have more wisdom than we do.
- We tend to pride ourselves on having the "right" character.
- We tend to think of ourselves as being more patient than we are.
- We tend to think we are submissive and obedient.
- We simply tend to see ourselves as more godly than we are.

Here's the problem with this tendency: when you think of yourself as more righteous or mature than you are, you don't seek the grace that is your only hope. We don't think we devalue grace, but that's exactly what many of us do. You see, only people who acknowledge how deep their need is and who admit that they have no ability to meet that need get excited about the grace that meets every one of their spiritual needs.

On the other hand, we don't like to think of ourselves as needy. So we tend to minimize our sin. Sadly, many of us are far more concerned about the sin of others than our own. We pay far more attention to the spiritual needs of others than our own. We minimize our sin and see ourselves as righteous. So we don't cry out for and run after the rescuing and transforming grace that is ours as the children of God. As long as we still have hope in our own ability to be righteous on our own—we won't run after the grace that is offered us in Christ Jesus.

Yes, it really is true that hopelessness is the doorway to hope. Seeing yourself, if left to yourself, as hopeless and helpless, initiates and ignites your pursuit of God's grace. The fact is that we all give daily evidence of our continuing need for grace. Simply put, we have no ability to make it on our own. We still stand in desperate need of divine help.

> Therefore let anyone who thinks that he stands take heed lest he fall. (1 Cor. 10:12)

Reflect: In what situations, or around what people, do you most regularly give yourself too much credit? Are you willing to admit your neediness today and run to where grace can be found?

SEPTEMBER 21

Good is not good enough; complete conformity to Christ's image is the plan of grace.

Most of us are just too easily satisfied. Our personal goals, wishes, and dreams fall far short of God's plans and purposes for us. God will settle for nothing less than each of us being completely conformed to the likeness of his Son. He will finally and completely defeat sin and death. He will not abandon his purpose for any reason. Our problem is that often we don't share his mind or buy into his purpose. Other mentalities capture us:

- *The consumer mentality.* Here we're like religious shoppers. We're looking for a religious experience that is comfortable and meets our felt needs. When we're dissatisfied, we have no problem in moving.
- *The "good is good enough" mentality.* Here we're satisfied with a little bit of biblical literacy or theological knowledge, slightly better relationships, a little personal spiritual growth, and so on. We quit seeking, but God is far from being finished with transforming us.
- *The "this bad thing can work" mentality.* Here we work to make the best out of what God says is not good. So, for example, a teenager is satisfied to just tolerate his mom or dad; he learns to merely accommodate rather than working toward a truly godly relationship.
- *The "personal comfort vs. personal holiness" mentality.* Here what captures our hearts is the craving for a life that is comfortable, pleasurable, predictable, and problem free. We tend to judge God's goodness based on how well life is working for us not on how he's making us more holy.
- *The "event vs. process" mentality.* Here we are just impatient. We sort of want God to do the good things he has promised us, but we don't want to have to persevere through a lifelong process.

Finally, then, brothers, we ask and urge you in the Lord Jesus, that as you received from us how you ought to walk and to please God, just as you are doing, that you do so more and more. (1 Thess. 4:1)

Reflect: Ask yourself today, "What do I really want from God?" Have you made the purposes of his grace your life purpose? Do you want what he wants? Or are you simply too easily satisfied?

SEPTEMBER 22

There is no need to be paralyzed by the opinions of another. God gives you the ultimate tool of self-assessment, the mirror of his word.

Her letter was twelve pages long. I didn't want to read it, but I knew I had to. She took me apart like a coroner doing an autopsy. Each paragraph was like a knife cutting into a different organ, searching for disease. The judgment was harsh and unrelenting. There was little grace while the examples of my failures in her eyes were many. When I got to the end of the letter, I sat at my desk stunned. I was her pastor, but she had no respect for me whatsoever. I couldn't believe what I had read, and I was paralyzed by the thought that others felt the same way. The next morning was worse. I woke up with a knot in the pit of my stomach. I wanted to run, to quit.

Now, no opinions of people should have that power, but often they do. Without knowing it, we put our identity and inner peace in the hands of other people. We ride the roller coaster of their views of us. We begin to do things because we know they will please the people whose opinion and acceptance of us mean too much. I think "fear of man" is a bigger motivation for many of us than we tend to admit.

The gospel of Jesus Christ frees us from this by presenting to us the only reliable standard of self-evaluation—the perfect mirror of the word of God. Then it frees me from seeking my identity horizontally because I am given an eternal identity in Christ. It also frees me from being worried about being known or exposed. How? Because I know that nothing could ever be exposed about me that hasn't already been covered by the precious blood of Jesus. Finally, I am not haunted by what you think of me because I don't look to you for my inner sense of well-being. I can go to bed in peace knowing that the one person who knows me thoroughly, will never turn his back on me. Now, that's a reality that can free you from your bondage to the opinion of others.

The fear of man lays a snare,
but whoever trusts in the LORD is safe. (Prov. 29:25)

Reflect: Where do you feel anxiety about other peoples' opinion of you? Which truths did you need to hear most?

SEPTEMBER 23

God's care comes in many forms. In his patience, God cares enough to give ample time for his grace to do its transforming work.

When was the last time you reflected on the amazing patience of your heavenly Father? Do you know that without God's incredibly patient heart, you and I would have no hope? God's patience is what gives time for his grace to do its work.

When I read through the Old Testament, I am blown away by the extent of God's patience. I have often thought that if I had been in control, given the degree of my impatience, Adam and Eve would've disobeyed in the morning, and Jesus would've come in the afternoon and then died and risen again that evening. But God's ways are not like my ways. Year laps upon year, decade upon decade, century upon century until literally thousands of years pass before Jesus comes to deal with the disaster of the fall. Yet Scripture says that Jesus comes at just the right moment (Rom. 5:6). This means that for all those years, God is preparing the world for the coming of the Savior.

I am also impressed by God's patience with Israel. God didn't just send one prophet to give his people one warning. No, amazing patience, he sends prophet after prophet, giving his children opportunity after opportunity to respond to his mercy.

I am also convicted by the patience of Jesus with his disciples. They never seem to get it quite right. Even as he is ascending, they are asking the wrong questions. But Jesus doesn't give up on them. He gives time for his grace to transform this group of arrogant and confused men.

How can you and I not be grateful for God's patience with us? He doesn't demand of us instant maturity. It is his tender willingness to wait that allows his powerful grace to finish its transforming work. Thank God today for that patience. And as you are thanking him, pray that he will make you more like him—willing to give time for his mercy to do its work.

> But do not overlook this one fact, beloved, that with the Lord one day is as a thousand years, and a thousand years as one day. The Lord is not slow to fulfill his promise as some count slowness, but is patient toward you, not wishing that any should perish, but that all should reach repentance. (2 Pet. 3:8–9)

Reflect: How might technology be contributing to your feeling even more impatient?

SEPTEMBER 24

We wander. God pursues and reconciles. We stumble and fall. God forgives and restores. We grow tired and weary. God empowers us by his grace.

When it comes to our relationship with God and our growth in grace, you and I don't have much we can take credit for. Instead, we give daily proof of our ongoing need for that grace. And if we followed Jesus for a thousand years, we would need his grace as much for the next day as we did the first day that we believed.

He is the sun that gives us light. He is the refuge where we can hide. He is the water that nourishes us and the bread that feeds us. He is the solid rock on which we stand. He is the captain who defends us against the enemy. He is wisdom, blessing us with the insight of truth. He is the Lamb that bore the penalty for our sin. He is the high priest who daily brings our case to the Father. He is the faithful friend who will not forsake us even in our worst moments. He is the one who makes us aware of our sin and brings conviction to our hearts. He is the Shepherd who seeks us when we have wandered and are lost and brings us back to the fold of his care. All of these are necessary ingredients of our spiritual lives. Yet we could provide none of them for ourselves. We are like babies, unable to meet our own needs and completely dependent on the love of our Father for life, sustenance, and health.

Taking credit for what only grace can produce is the height of spiritual arrogance. If you think that the grace you once needed is no longer essential, you've created a recipe for disaster. We are not spiritually independent in any way. We cannot go it on our own. There really is no good thing that we have that we have not received from God's gracious hand.

So there is no reason to boast. There is nothing we can take credit for. All praise, honor, worship, and service go to God and God alone. He sought us. He birthed us. He sustains us. He matures us. He protects us. And he will finally deliver us. To him be the glory. Amen.

> Yet for us there is one God, the Father, from whom are all things and for whom we exist, and one Lord, Jesus Christ, through whom are all things and through whom we exist. (1 Cor. 8:6)

Reflect: How do your prayer habits reflect dependence on God and not yourself?

SEPTEMBER 25

Discouragement focuses more on the broken glories of creation than on the restoring glories of God's character, presence, and promises.

What captures your mind dominates the desires of your heart. That which dominates your meditation shapes the way you view yourself, life, and God, and your view of those things shapes the choices you make and the actions you take.

Is your meditation kidnapped by:

- the disloyalty of that good friend?
- the sorry state of your finances?
- disappointment with your church?
- the dysfunction of your family?
- the daily struggles of school?
- your crazy and demanding schedule?
- physical sickness?

Remember biblical faith—that is, true faith in the existence, presence, promises, and provisions of God—never requires you to deny reality in any way. It is not biblical faith to try to convince yourself that things are better than they actually are. It is not biblical faith to work to make yourself feel good about what is not good. Biblical faith looks reality in the face and does not flinch.

On the other hand, there is a crucial difference between facing hard realities and allowing those realities to dominate the meditation of your heart (see God's counsel to Joshua in Josh. 1:1–9). Here's what biblical faith does: it examines reality, but it makes the Lord its meditation. The more you meditate on your problems, the bigger and more unbeatable they seem to be. Meditating on God in the midst of your trouble reminds you once again that the God to whom grace has connected you is infinitely greater than any problem you could ever experience. Then your responses are shaped by his glory and not by the seeming size of your problems.

I remember the days of old;
  I meditate on all that you have done;
  I ponder the work of your hands.
I stretch out my hands to you;
  my soul thirsts for you like a parched land.

Answer me quickly, O Lord!
  My spirit fails!
Hide not your face from me,
  lest I be like those who go down to the pit. (Ps. 143:5–7)

Reflect: What practical steps can you take to help you meditate on God more consistently, even when you face difficulties?

SEPTEMBER 26

True faith lives on the basis of two unshakable realities—that God really does exist and that he always rewards those who seek him.

There is nothing more important, more central, more heart engaging, and more formative than my belief in and my relationship with my Savior and Lord. It is not only the center of my worldview, but he is the source of all of my hope in this life and in the life to come. I love him with all my heart, and everything I do is shaped by the worship of him . . . but not always.

What do I mean "but not always"? There are moments when you and I think, desire, speak, or act as if God doesn't exist. Sometimes we're practical atheists, and we all need to confess this struggle. It's so important that we have hearts ready to confess our moments of practical atheism as God, in his convicting grace, reveals them to us.

We profess to have given our lives over to belief in the existence, glory, power, and grace of the God of the Bible. So we need to cry out for his protecting, rescuing, and enabling grace. That's the only way to have fewer and fewer moments in our lives where we insert ourselves in the center and act as if he doesn't exist.[12]

Grace has positioned me
on two foundation stones
that have redefined
my identity,
redirected my purpose,
reshaped my desires,
rescued my thoughts,
and reformed my living.
I have new reason
to get up in the morning
and face my day
with courage,
hope
joy,
confidence,
and rest.
Your grace has changed
everything,
for it has made me
sure
that you exist
and that
you reward
"those who seek" you (Heb. 11:6).

> And without faith it is impossible to please him, for whoever would draw near to God must believe that he exists and that he rewards those who seek him. (Heb. 11:6)

Reflect: Where are you susceptible to acting, reacting, or responding as if God didn't exist?

SEPTEMBER 27

There is no need to fear what God will ask of you because in the asking is always the promise of grace to empower your heart and hands.

Consider God's call to Moses to lead the Israelites out of their cruel captivity in Egypt. In Moses's reply, we see a reflection of how we often respond when God asks something of us:

> Then the Lord said, . . . "And now, behold, the cry of the people of Israel has come to me, and I have also seen the oppression with which the Egyptians oppress them. Come, I will send you to Pharaoh that you may bring my people, the children of Israel, out of Egypt." But Moses said to God, "Who am I that I should go to Pharaoh and bring the children of Israel out of Egypt?" He said, "But I will be with you, and this shall be the sign for you, that I have sent you: when you have brought the people out of Egypt, you shall serve God on this mountain." (Ex. 3:7, 9–12)

Throughout this amazing encounter with the Lord, Moses does what we often do as we evaluate what God has put on our plates and how he has called us to respond. Moses omits the ultimate fact that changes everything about how we should think and respond to God's call. That fact is not the difficulty of the calling or your perceived ability to answer that call. It is not the size of the situation or the size of your wisdom and strength. This life-changing fact is that the God of glory and grace, who calls his people to do his will on earth, always goes with them as they obey his calling. He never sends without going too. When he sends you, he doesn't give you a bunch of stuff to help you along the way. He always gives you himself because *he* is what you need and he alone can give you what is required.

> Be strong and courageous. Do not fear or be in dread of them, for it is the Lord your God who goes with you. He will not leave you or forsake you. (Deut. 31:6)

Reflect: Remember today that when and where God sends, he goes too! Why is this important? How is it meaningful to you?

SEPTEMBER 28

Laziness is rooted in self-love. It's taking ourselves off the hook, opting for the comfortable instead of the best. Grace isn't lazy.

As long as sin lives inside us, laziness will be an issue for us all. Before you quit reading, let me explain. Second Corinthians 5:15 says that Jesus came so that "those who live might no longer live for themselves." Paul is arguing here that the life and sacrifice of Jesus were necessary because the DNA of sin is selfishness. Sin causes me to ignore God's existence and his rightful claim on every area of my life. Because God is not in his rightful place in my living, that is, in the center of it all, I then insert myself in that place. My life becomes all about me. I reduce my focus down to the small space of my wants, my needs, and my feelings. The desires of my heart are gobbled up by my ease, my comfort, my pleasure, and my success.

As a result, I work to avoid anything that is uncomfortable. I tend to curse hard work, the need to serve others, the call to persevere, the requirement of daily labor, the call to engage myself in the work of a bigger kingdom than my own.

Sin also makes us all work avoiders. But the fact of the matter is that we were created to work, and not just for the good of our own lives but also in willing and joyful submission to the one who created us. Work is not a curse. Before the fall, Adam and Eve were instructed to work. So work is part of our created identity. It is true that work has been made more difficult because we now labor in a seriously broken world. Yet this also reveals our daily need for grace. Until grace has completed its work, we will tend to find work more of a burden than a calling and a joy. Grace and grace alone is able to make otherwise lazy people industrious workers to the glory of God.

> For you yourselves know how you ought to imitate us, because we were not idle when we were with you, nor did we eat anyone's bread without paying for it, but with toil and labor we worked night and day, that we might not be a burden to any of you. (2 Thess. 3:7–8)

Reflect: What hard situation do you find yourself avoiding? Pause and ask yourself why.

SEPTEMBER 29

God calls you to grow in your faith and then feeds you with the growth-producing nutrients of his grace and truth.

Are you growing in your faith? Do you care if you're not? Have you stopped feeding on the spiritual food of God's grace? Do you hunger for grace to continue to do its transforming work? Does your relationship with God really shape the way you think about and act in your friendships, in your schooling, in your hobbies, in your online activities, in your private pursuits, or in your secret thoughts and desires?

When I think on this topic, my mind immediately runs to the two passages listed below. As you read them, be honest—which passage best describes you? Are you that ravenous baby who can't get enough of his mother's milk? Or are you the person who should be mature enough to digest solid food but isn't ready? Remember, you don't have to defend yourself or deny the evidence. The cross of Jesus welcomes you to be honest because all the places where you need to be honest have been covered by the blood of Jesus.

> So put away all malice and all deceit and hypocrisy and envy and all slander. Like newborn infants, long for the pure spiritual milk, that by it you may grow up into salvation—if indeed you have tasted that the Lord is good.
>
> As you come to him, a living stone rejected by men but in the sight of God chosen and precious, you yourselves like living stones are being built up as a spiritual house, to be a holy priesthood, to offer spiritual sacrifices acceptable to God through Jesus Christ. (1 Pet. 2:1–5)

> About this we have much to say, and it is hard to explain, since you have become dull of hearing. For though by this time you ought to be teachers, you need someone to teach you again the basic principles of the oracles of God. You need milk, not solid food, for everyone who lives on milk is unskilled in the word of righteousness, since he is a child. But solid food is for the mature, for those who have their powers of discernment trained by constant practice to distinguish good from evil. (Heb. 5:11–14)

Reflect: Are you pursuing the grace that you've been given? Consider that you regularly demonstrate that you are not yet a grace graduate.

SEPTEMBER 30

The life we couldn't live, he lived for us. The death we should have died, he died for us. The new life we need, he gives to us.

Only the amazing grace of God has the power to transport us from death to life. No human effort could accomplish this. Salvation is simply beyond our grasp. A relationship with God stands outside our reach. Moral perfection is a mountain too high for us to climb. Living to God's glory exceeds our finest motivation. Righteousness and wisdom fall outside the scope of our natural abilities. We all fall short of God's standard and are all deserving of his penalty.

If you don't understand and accept the gravity of your condition, the Bible, and particularly the work of Christ, will make no sense to you at all. Why did God go to the history-shaping extent of sending his Son to earth? Why was it necessary for Jesus to live a completely perfect life? Why was it important for him to walk in our shoes and experience the full range of the temptations that we face? Why was it vital for him to suffer and die? Why did there absolutely have to be a resurrection? Why? The answers to these questions can be found by tracing a thread that runs throughout the Bible.

There had to be a Savior because we have no ability whatsoever to save ourselves. We can escape situations, locations, and relationships, but we cannot escape ourselves. We cannot run from who we are, what we have done, and what we deserve. The only hope is that God in love and grace will move toward us, doing for us what we cannot do for ourselves.

So God sent his Son to be the second Adam. He would face the temptations that Adam faced, but he would not fall. He would obey perfectly where Adam disobeyed. The second Adam would die in Adam's and his descendants' place. He would meet God's moral requirement and satisfy his anger, and in so doing, he would open the way again for us to have an eternal relationship with God. Everything Jesus did, he did as a substitute. Everything he did, he did for you.

> For if, because of one man's trespass, death reigned through that one man, much more will those who receive the abundance of grace and the free gift of righteousness reign in life through the one man Jesus Christ. (Rom. 5:17)

Reflect: What defines you and your daily experience more—you and your life, or Jesus and his life?

OCTOBER 1

Because he is zealous to rescue you from you, God's care can be violent. He rips you from what is dangerous to give you what is better.

When you think of God's care, what picture comes into your mind? When you consider God's grace, what mental images does the term *grace* conjure up? Could it be that there are times in your life when you are crying out for the grace of God even though you're getting it? God's grace does not always come in the form of comfort and encouragement. Could it be that the "care" that we often cry out for is not the care that we really need?

There was a cycle in the life of the children of Israel that is very instructive. Remember that they were people just like us. And the accounts about them were written for our example and instruction, so that, by grace, we would not fall into the same errors. Carefully examine the description below. You'll read how God sent his people the violent grace of trouble in order to rescue their hearts from idolatry. Yet all that his children wanted was the situational grace of freedom from their enemies. When they got it, they turned back to their sinful ways.

> And the people of Israel did what was evil in the sight of the LORD and served the Baals. And they abandoned the LORD, the God of their fathers, who had brought them out of the land of Egypt. They went after other gods, from among the gods of the peoples who were around them, and bowed down to them. . . . So the anger of the LORD was kindled against Israel, and he gave them over to plunderers, who plundered them. And he sold them into the hand of their surrounding enemies, so that they could no longer withstand their enemies. . . .
>
> Then the LORD raised up judges, who saved them out of the hand of those who plundered them. . . . Whenever the LORD raised up judges for them, the LORD was with the judge, and he saved them from the hand of their enemies all the days of the judge. For the LORD was moved to pity by their groaning because of those who afflicted and oppressed them. But whenever the judge died, they turned back and were more corrupt than their fathers, going after other gods, serving them and bowing down to them. They did not drop any of their practices or their stubborn ways. (Judg. 2:11–19)

Reflect: Today, what kind of grace do you long for from the hands of your Messiah?

OCTOBER 2

You simply must not underestimate sin, and you simply cannot overestimate grace.

Think for a moment: Whose sin do you tend to minimize? Your friends'? Your family members'? Your father's or mother's? For most of us, the problem is not that we underestimate the sin of others. No, we tend to do the opposite. We're typically all too focused on the failure of others. We find it all too easy to point out their flaws. We're all tempted to keep a running record of the specific sins of the people around us. If we're honest, we tend to be hyperaware of the weaknesses of those living near us while we appear to be functionally blind to our own. For this reason, we begin to forget that we are more like them than unlike them.

Now, this dynamic is not okay. When you're blind to your own sin, you're also blind to your own spiritual need. And such a denial always leads you to devalue and resist God's grace.

Here's the problem—we are all very good at doing both. We're all very good at looking at our sin and naming it less than sin, and we all tend to degrade what grace has done, is doing, and will do. In contrast, what we're talking about here are the two sides of a healthy Christian life. You confess that although you are in Christ, the presence of sin is still within you. However, it is being progressively defeated. How? Only because God's glorious grace can do for you what you could never do for yourself.

Admitting your sin doesn't lead you somewhere dark and depressing. Why? Because you can celebrate a grace that is greater than your sin. Confession of sin without the celebration of grace leads to guilt, self-loathing, timidity, and spiritual paralysis. Embracing grace without admitting your sin leads to confident theological "always rightism," but doesn't change your heart and life. So today, refuse to minimize sin, reject the temptation to devalue grace, and run to Jesus weeping and celebrating at the same time.

> My little children, I am writing these things to you so that you may not sin. But if anyone does sin, we have an advocate with the Father, Jesus Christ the righteous. (1 John 2:1)

Reflect: Which is usually bigger in your mind—the sin of others, your own sin, or the grace of Jesus?

OCTOBER 3

You don't have to understand everything in your life because the Lord of wisdom and grace understands it all.

It is a paradox that many of us don't handle well. We were created by God to be rational human beings, and we carry around with us a desire to know and understand. Yet we must not forget that we will never experience inner peace simply because all our questions have been answered. Biblical faith is not irrational, but it takes us beyond our ability to reason. We believe in our identity as God's image-bearers and the truthfulness of his word. We also recognize that it's important to study, to learn, to examine, to evaluate, and to know. But we do not trust our reason more than we trust God. We do not reject what God says is true when it doesn't make sense to us. We know that God's secret will leaves us with mysteries in our lives.

So you ask, "Where is peace to be found?" This question is answered clearly and powerfully in Isaiah 26:3–4. Peace is never found in trying to figure out the secret will of God. It's not to be found in personal planning or attempting to control the circumstances and people in your life. Peace is found in trusting the person who controls all the things that you don't understand and who knows no mystery because he has planned it all. How do you experience this remarkable peace—the kind of peace that doesn't fade away when disappointments come, when people are difficult, or when circumstances are hard? You experience it by keeping your mind stayed on the Lord. The more you meditate on his glory, his power, his wisdom, his grace, his faithfulness, his righteousness, his patience, his zeal to redeem, and his commitment to his eternal promises to you, the more you can deal with mystery in your life. Why? Because you know the one behind the mystery is gloriously good, worthy not only of your trust but also the worship of your heart.

> You keep him in perfect peace
>   whose mind is stayed on you,
>   because he trusts in you.
> Trust in the LORD forever,
>   for the LORD GOD is an everlasting rock. (Isa. 26:3–4)

Reflect: Even in younger years, peace is not found in figuring out your life but in worship of the one who has everything figured out already.

OCTOBER 4

Our struggle with sin is so deep that it was not enough for God to forgive us, so he also unzipped us and got inside of us by his Spirit.

Perhaps all good theology is meant to be both humbling and comforting at the same time. Why is this? Because God's goal in giving us theology is a radically transformed life. And the theology of the Holy Spirit in the New Testament is particularly humbling.

Having said this, why is the indwelling presence of the Holy Spirit presented as an absolute gift that every believer needs? The answer is because sin does not leave us merely *guilty*; it also renders us *unable*. Sin kidnaps our desires and distorts our thoughts. It controls our behavior and saps our resolve. It leaves us lame, weak, and unable. Our struggle with sin is so deep that only God living inside us can give us the power to please him with our living. So God doesn't just forgive us, call us to do what is right, and promise us a final home with him; he comes to us in between. He gets inside us, working within us because there is no possibility that we will desire and do what is right without the inner working of his power.

How humbling! Not only can we not take credit for our salvation because it is all the result of God's justifying grace, we also cannot take credit for any aspect or any instance of our obedience. Why? Because apart from the Spirit's presence, we would have neither the motivation nor the power to obey. Yes, we are new creatures in Christ, and yes, we are alive in him, but without the Spirit, we would have no power to defeat sin.

Where's the comfort in this? Here it is: if you're God's child, you already have the Holy Spirit inside you. You don't have to hope and pray that he will be there for you. He has come, and his convicting and enabling grace is his moment-by-moment gift to you.

> So if there is any encouragement in Christ, any comfort from love, any participation in the Spirit, any affection and sympathy, complete my joy by being of the same mind, having the same love, being in full accord and of one mind. (Phil. 2:1–2)

Reflect: Does your sin tend to make you think of yourself more as guilty or as unable? Why? And how is Christ and his grace more than enough?

OCTOBER 5

Faith in God is more than believing the right things. It's living the right way because you believe the right things.

What you believe in your heart and mind is an essential ingredient of faith, but it does not summarize all that faith is. True biblical faith is always something that you live. Faith is also not just mental assent to a collection of truths. Faith *is* deeply theological, but it is much more than that. So if your faith does not reshape your life, it is not true faith. This is why Hebrews 11 focuses more on what people did with their lives than on the details of their theology.

As you read the passage below, notice how the writer of Hebrews defines faith. He immediately gives three examples of how real faith in God transforms the way that you live. First, faith redirects and recaptures the *worship* of your heart (Abel). Second, it produces in you a heart of *obedience* (Enoch). Third, faith causes you to submit to the *calling* of God (Noah).

Now think about it: everyone's life is shaped by what he worships, by the rules that she obeys, and by the life-calling that we follow. True, living, biblical faith causes you to submit all three of these shaping influences to God. He becomes the object of the worship of your heart. His rules define the moral boundaries of your life. And his kingdom work becomes your joyful calling. Hebrews 11:1–7 is a say-it-all description of what faith is and what faith does:

> Now faith is the assurance of things hoped for, the conviction of things not seen. For by it the people of old received their commendation. . . . By faith Abel offered to God a more acceptable sacrifice than Cain, through which he was commended as righteous, God commending him by accepting his gifts. . . . By faith Enoch was taken up so that he should not see death, and he was not found, because God had taken him. Now before he was taken he was commended as having pleased God. And without faith it is impossible to please him, for whoever would draw near to God must believe that he exists and that he rewards those who seek him. By faith Noah, being warned by God concerning events as yet unseen, in reverent fear constructed an ark for the saving of his household. By this he condemned the world and became an heir of the righteousness that comes by faith. (Heb. 11:1–2, 4–7)

Reflect: Remember, you can't conjure up life-shaping faith. No, God gives it as a gift of his grace.

OCTOBER 6

Without eternity in the center of our thinking, our picture of life is like a jigsaw puzzle missing a central piece.

Everyone wants life to make sense. We all pick our lives apart, trying to make sense of them. We all develop our own systems of theology, biblical or otherwise. We all carry around with us worldviews that shape the way we think, desire, talk, and act.

So God, knowing that we are hardwired to make sense of our lives, has given us his word. In it, he reveals who he is, he defines who we are, he explains the meaning and purpose of life, he unfolds the greatest of humanity's problems—sin—and he points us to the hope of his amazing grace. He doesn't tell us everything because we would not be able to understand everything or deal with it in our daily lives. Yet he does give us all we need so we can live as we were created to live.

Essential to this biblical worldview is eternity. The Bible confronts us with the reality that this is not all there is. You and I are eternal beings who will spend eternity somewhere. It will either be in the presence of God forever and ever or separated from him in a place of eternal punishment forever and ever.

The reality of eternity infuses the here and now with seriousness and hope. The way you live now is important because there is an eternity to follow. You simply cannot hold to an "all that's important is the pleasures of the moment" view of life and believe in eternity at the same time. In light of eternity, it makes no sense to forget God and live for yourself. Eternity requires you to take life seriously.

But eternity also fills this moment with hope. Because I know that this is not all there is, I also know that the sin, trials, and sufferings of the present will not last forever. For God's children, eternity promises that sin will die, suffering will end, our trials will be no more, and we will live with God in perfect peace forever and ever and ever.

> Truly, truly, I say to you, an hour is coming, and is now here, when the dead will hear the voice of the Son of God, and those who hear will live. (John 5:25)

Reflect: When was the last time you and your friends talked about how eternity changes the way you look at your life circumstances?

OCTOBER 7

A thing I can't live without, such that I doubt God's love when it is absent, becomes a functional God-replacement, directing my heart more than he does.

Be honest—what do you tell yourself that you can't live without? What are the "if-onlys" that you carry around with you that shape the way you think about yourself, about life, and about the goodness of God?

In Colossians 3, the apostle Paul knows that even though his readers are God's children, the spiritual war is not yet over for them. So he tells them: "If then you have been raised with Christ, seek the things that are above, where Christ is, seated at the right hand of God. Set your minds on things that are above, not on things that are on earth" (3:1–2). Paul is reminding them that the heart is always living under the rule of either "things that are above" or "things that are on earth."

At street level, you and I are either worshiping and serving the creation or the Creator. There are times when we get it right, and the deepest motivation and joy of our hearts is to live in a way that pleases God. But there are other times when we tell ourselves that there is some created thing that we have to have. When this happens, we functionally forget God and give ourselves to getting this thing that has captured our thoughts and shaped our desires.

This "above" or "earth" struggle will be fought in all of the situations, locations, and relationships of your daily life. It is not wrong to celebrate created glories. But they must not be allowed to rule your heart and, in ruling your heart, to become your functional God-replacement. Only grace can free us from our bondage to things that will never give us what God alone can give: life.

> As for the rich in this present age, charge them not to be haughty, nor to set their hopes on the uncertainty of riches, but on God, who richly provides us with everything to enjoy. They are to do good, to be rich in good works, to be generous and ready to share, thus storing up treasure for themselves as a good foundation for the future, so that they may take hold of that which is truly life. (1 Tim. 6:17–19)

Reflect: When you look back with joy at how things have gone in a certain situation or relationship, what gives you that joy?

OCTOBER 8

Corporate worship reminds you that hope is not a situation, location, idea, or thing. Hope is a person, and his name is Jesus.

Everyone craves hope. It's the thing that fuels what we do. It's what gets you through the tough times and keeps you from quitting. It's hard to be happy when you don't have any of it.

Now, the radical message of the Bible is that sturdy hope, hope that won't ever fail you, is only found vertically. The horizontal situations, locations, experiences, and relationships of everyday life are dangerous places to look for hope. Why? First, everywhere you could look horizontally has been affected by the fall in some way. There are simply no perfectly ideal situations, no paradise locations, no completely satisfying experiences, and surely no perfect people this side of eternity. Add to this the fact that none of them lasts. Every horizontal thing, this side of eternity, is in the process of decay. So hope that addresses your deepest needs, that gives you reason to continue no matter how hard life is, and that promises you eternal good is only ever found vertically.

Yet the message of the Bible is even more powerful and pointed. Reliable hope is more than found in Jesus. It *is* Jesus! In his life, death, and resurrection, your life is infused with hope. The grace of the cross doesn't just forgive and accept, but also gives you everything you need until you are needy no more. Because the one who is hope has infused my life with hope, I do not have to search for hope any longer and can now give myself to a life of good works. To find hope, find him.

> But when the goodness and loving kindness of God our Savior appeared, he saved us, not because of works done by us in righteousness, but according to his own mercy, by the washing of regeneration and renewal of the Holy Spirit, whom he poured out on us richly through Jesus Christ our Savior, so that being justified by his grace we might become heirs according to the hope of eternal life. The saying is trustworthy, and I want you to insist on these things, so that those who have believed in God may be careful to devote themselves to good works. (Titus 3:4–8)

Reflect: Do you know the hope described above? If not, a good first step toward finding it would be to gather with other believers this Lord's Day to worship the one who is your hope.

OCTOBER 9

Today you are called to abandon the purposes of your kingdom and give yourself to the will of a greater King. Grace makes it possible.

Life *is* war. When Paul ends the book of Ephesians by telling his readers to put on gospel armor and get ready for war, he's not introducing a new topic. No, he's summarizing everything he's said so far. Every application of what it means to live in light of the gospel of Jesus Christ must be lived out in the context of a great spiritual battle. What is this war about? This great spiritual war is not the wild experience of demons dancing on the table that we often think it is. No, it's the great war for the rulership of our hearts. With sin still living inside of us, we are still torn between our love for the oppressive little kingdom of self and the grand and glorious purposes of the kingdom of God. We still are tempted to want our own way and to write our own rules. We are tempted to have more excitement in the things of this world than we do with the reality that we have become the children of God.

Ephesians 6 also reminds you that you have been given ample grace for this battle.

> Finally, be strong in the Lord and in the strength of his might. Put on the whole armor of God, that you may be able to stand against the schemes of the devil. For we do not wrestle against flesh and blood, but against the rulers, against the authorities, against the cosmic powers over this present darkness, against the spiritual forces of evil in the heavenly places. Therefore take up the whole armor of God, that you may be able to withstand in the evil day, and having done all, to stand firm. (Eph. 6:10–13)

Reflect: What feels like your greatest battle in life right now? Which piece of armor feels like your greatest need in that battle?

OCTOBER 10

If you're God's child, you've been called to forsake your "my life" mentality and daily live with a moment-by-moment ministry mentality.

You begin to get close to what God has designed your life to be as one of his children when you understand that nothing that makes up you and your life belongs to you. The New Testament is quite clear about ministry (see 1 Cor. 12; Eph. 4:11–16; Col. 3:12–17): Our lives no longer belong to us. We don't own our physicality. We don't own our emotionality. We don't own our spirituality. We don't own our mentality. We don't own our psychology. We don't own our communicative abilities. We don't own our relationships. We don't own our gifts or our experiences. We don't even own our possessions in the deepest sense of what ownership means. Paul gets at this when he says at the end of a discussion of sexuality in 1 Corinthians 6, "You are not your own, for you were bought with a price" (6:19–20). You and all that makes up you were bought with a price, so you are owned by the one who paid that price.

But there is a second thing that the New Testament makes very clear. It is that God has called all his children to be instruments of his grace. It is what I call the "total involvement paradigm," that is, all God's people all of the time. Every one of God's children has been given a call to ministry, and every one must think of himself that way. Finally, the New Testament does not teach a separation between life and ministry. Every dimension of your life is a forum for ministry. Family is ministry. Friendship is ministry. School is ministry. Being a neighbor is ministry. The workplace is a place of ministry.

You have been called to represent a glorious Savior, who has graced you with everything you need to live with a ministry mentality.

> And we urge you, brothers, admonish the idle, encourage the fainthearted, help the weak, be patient with them all. (1 Thess. 5:14)

Reflect: How does the statement, "Be true to yourself," go against the view of ministry taught by the New Testament?

OCTOBER 11

God is not satisfied with you being a witness to his work of grace. He's called you to be an instrument of that grace to others.

All of God's children have a mind-boggling calling. Sadly, so many people who attend evangelical churches on Sunday have little life commitment to the work of those churches. Yet, we've all been called to be his ambassadors. Remember, the only thing an ambassador does is represent. God's plan is to make his invisible presence and his invisible grace visible through his people, who represent his presence and carry that grace to others. That's God's call to every one of his children. There are to be no self-satisfied recipients, no consumers. The body of Christ is designed by God to be an organic, constantly ministering community.

If the church is ever going to be this, then God's people need three things. First, we need *vision*. We need to be reminded again and again of our place in the work of the Redeemer. Next, we need *commitment*. We need to be encouraged to make specific and concrete decisions to better position ourselves for the work to which God has called us. Last, we need *training*. We need to understand what it really looks like to represent the grace of the Redeemer in the lives of the people whom he puts in our paths. We need to be trained not to see those relationships as belonging to us for our happiness. Instead, those relationships are more like workrooms in which the Lord can do his transforming work of grace.

What an amazing way to live! We have been chosen by God to be part of the most important work of the universe. We have been chosen to carry the life-changing message of the grace of the Savior King with us wherever we go. And we have been given the same grace to enable us to be the ambassadors that we have been chosen to be.

> But exhort one another every day, as long as it is called "today," that none of you may be hardened by the deceitfulness of sin. (Heb. 3:13)

Reflect: Take a few minutes to prayerfully plan how God might use you today, even in the lives of people you might at first find annoying.

OCTOBER 12

Prayer is abandoning a life of demand and complaint, recognizing undeserved blessing, and giving myself to a life of thankfulness.

When you think of prayer, what comes to mind? True prayer happens at the intersection of *surrender* and *celebration*. Prayer is profoundly more than handing a wish list to God. Wish-list prayers essentially say, "I know what's best for my life, and I'd appreciate it, God, if you would use your might to make it happen." This kind of prayer puts you at the center and, in a real way, reduces God down to the divine waiter. It's not him that you want. It's not his wisdom that you see yourself as needing. It's not his grace that your heart craves. This kind of prayer makes life all about your wants, your needs, and your feelings. In true prayer, you surrender your claim on your life to the greater and wiser plans and purposes of God.

Then prayer is celebration. In prayer, you bask in the wonder of what it means that you actually do have a heavenly Father. You find joy in the reality that he has chosen to give you his kingdom. You are blown away by the fact that he unleashes his almighty power to meet your needs. You celebrate forgiving, rescuing, transforming, enabling, and delivering grace. You find peace in the fact that grace means you are never left to the small resources of your own wisdom, righteousness, and strength. You rejoice in the fact that you no longer have to look for life in the people, situations, and locations around you, but you've been given life—life that is eternal.

Does true prayer include making requests of God? Sure it does. God encourages us to cast our cares on him because he really does care for us. But the requests of true prayer are always in the context of surrender and celebration. This keeps those requests from being selfish demands or bitter complaints. This kind of prayer is also a tool of God's grace in your life. As you put God in his proper place and celebrate your place as his child, prayer becomes a tool God uses to free you from your bondage to you. Now, that's grace!

And he said to them, "When you pray, say:

> 'Father, hallowed be your name.
> Your kingdom come.'" (Luke 11:2)

Reflect: Whenever you pick up your phone today, pause to offer two brief prayers: a brief prayer of surrender and a brief prayer of celebration.

OCTOBER 13

You can't hear him, but he's wiser; you can't see him, but he's more faithful; you can't touch him, but he's nearer than whatever else you'd trust.

On the surface, the passage provided below doesn't make any sense. If it weren't true, you would call the people involved "crazy." Stop and think about the radical nature of what this passage says about the deepest motivations of God's people. They have connected their deepest love, belief, joy, and faith to someone they have never seen, heard, or touched. They have staked the hopes and dreams of their lives to this invisible one. Their relationship to him is one of life-altering love. When they think of him, they experience joy, joy so deep that it cannot be expressed.

If it were not for the existence, character, and plan of God, none of this would make any sense at all. You would stand back, look at these "believers," and conclude that they were delusional—crazy. But they are not crazy. They are the blessed ones, the enlightened ones, the ones whose hearts have been opened to the most important thing that your heart could embrace.

This is what grace does. It rescues us from our spiritual blindness. Grace gives us the faith to be utterly assured of what we cannot see. It frees us from refusing to believe in anything we cannot experience with our physical senses. But grace does more. It connects us to the invisible one in an eternal love relationship. And he fills us with joy we have never known before and gives us rest of heart that we would have thought impossible.

And that grace is still rescuing us. Why? Because we still tend to forget what is important, real, and true. We still tend to look to the physical world for our comfort. We still fail to remember in given moments that we really do have a heavenly Father. Grace has done a wonderful thing for us and continues to do more and more.

> Though you have not seen him, you love him. Though you do not now see him, you believe in him and rejoice with joy that is inexpressible and filled with glory, obtaining the outcome of your faith, the salvation of your souls. (1 Pet. 1:8–9)

Reflect: How do you usually strengthen your relationships with your friends? How could you do something similar in your relationship to Christ?

OCTOBER 14

The battles of sanctification are many, but God's mercies are new morning after morning after morning.

The battle for your heart still goes on. Temptations exist all around you. The enemy lurks as a roaring lion. Falsehood battles with truth. The people of God live as an often misunderstood minority. Sickness and suffering enter your door. In weakness, you give way to what you should resist. You are sinned against by others. Hopes, dreams, and plans fail. There are times when you are tempted to wonder if it's all worth it. But in all this, God is still at work, molding you into the likeness of his Son.

Maybe you're reading and thinking, "Boy, Paul, this has been *very* encouraging so far." Well, let me ask you to reflect on something that is incredibly encouraging in the midst of the hardships.

Consider what the passage below says about who you are and what you have been given as a child of God. God's steadfast, faithful, never-failing love has been placed on you even though you never could have done anything to earn or deserve it. But there's more to say about this love. It never ceases. God will never give up on you. He will never walk away in disgust. He will never regret that he placed his love on you. He will love you just as much on your worst day as he does on your best day. This gift of love is yours forever.

But the passage says more. It announces that as God's child, you have been blessed with eternal mercies that are new every morning. Consider what this means. There are fresh mercies for you today. They're formfitted for all the things you will face—both those that you may know and worry about, and also those that you don't know about yet. God's mercy isn't generic. It meets you right where you are and gives you just what you need. Yes, life this side of forever can be hard, but you're not alone. You've been given sturdy love and new morning mercies—just what you need right here, right now.

> The steadfast love of the Lord never ceases;
> his mercies never come to an end;
> they are new every morning;
> great is your faithfulness. (Lam. 3:22–23)

Reflect: How have you seen God give fresh grace for the hardships or anxieties that you've had to face recently?

OCTOBER 15

Today a war of love will be fought on the turf of your heart.
Will you be ruled by love for God or for some other lover?

It's easy to give the right spiritual answer to the question above: "No doubt about it, my heart will be controlled by love for God above all else." The problem is that at street level, there is still a war of love in our hearts. We do lose our way. We forget God and tell ourselves that we must have ______. Love of the world and the things that are in the world still kidnaps our hearts. Yes, the battle still rages.

I wish I could say this is not true of me, but it is. Sometimes I want my comfort too much, and I become an irritable and grumbling man because I'm not getting what I think I deserve. Sometimes I want to be right too much, and I become aggressive and argumentative. Sometimes I want the respect and affection of others too much, and because I do, I am all too controlled by their opinions. Sometimes I crave the edible glories of creation too much, and I ingest more than I should.

I find that most of the things that battle for the love of my heart are not evil in and of themselves. The desires to be right, to be respected, to own possessions, to have some control, or to eat delicious things are not inherently evil. But here's the thing that you and I need to remember: a desire for a good thing becomes a bad thing when that desire becomes a ruling thing. When this happens, they take the place in our hearts that only God should have.

You see, we are always placing the love of our hearts on something. And it is important to remember that there are only two places where we can invest that life-shaping love—on the Creator or on the creation. It's not wrong to love God's glorious creation, but it's a spiritual disaster to be ruled by that love. So here is yet another argument for our need for grace. Because of our hearts, we all still need protecting and rescuing grace. Thank God that grace has been given!

> So flee youthful passions and pursue righteousness, faith, love, and peace, along with those who call on the Lord from a pure heart. (2 Tim. 2:22)

Reflect: How do your spending habits reflect your heart and what you love?

OCTOBER 16

The difficulties of your life are not in the way of God's plan; they are a tool of it. They're crafted to advance his work of grace.

Perhaps the two most important questions you could ask as a Christian are:

1. What in the world is God doing right here, right now?
2. How in the world should I respond to what God is doing?

The way that you answer these questions determines, in a real way, the character of your faith and the direction of your life. Consider how James answers these questions in the first part of his letter:

> Count it all joy, my brothers, when you meet trials of various kinds, for you know that the testing of your faith produces steadfastness. And let steadfastness have its full effect, that you may be perfect and complete, lacking in nothing. . . . Blessed is the man who remains steadfast under trial, for when he has stood the test he will receive the crown of life, which God has promised to those who love him. (James 1:2–4, 12)

What is God doing in the here and now? He is employing the difficulties of life as tools of grace to produce character in you that would not grow any other way. So your trials are not a sign that God has forgotten you or is being unfaithful to his promises. Rather, they stand as a reminder that he is committed to his grace and will not forsake it—it *will* complete its work.

No, God is not exercising his power to make your life easy. No, he's not at work trying to deliver your particular definition of happiness. He's giving you much more than that—eternally faithful, forgiving, and transforming grace.

And what should your response be? James says, "Remain steadfast under trial." So, don't become discouraged and give up. Don't listen to the lies of the enemy. Don't forsake your good habits of faith. Don't question God's goodness. Look at your trials and see grace. Behind those difficulties is an ever-present Redeemer who is completing his work.

> And have you forgotten the exhortation that addresses you as sons?
>
> "My son, do not regard lightly the discipline of the Lord,
> nor be weary when reproved by him.
> For the Lord disciplines the one he loves,
> and chastises every son whom he receives." (Heb. 12:5–6)

Reflect: How might God be using the rules and restrictions in your life to actually advance his gracious work of grace in your heart?

OCTOBER 17

Idolatry occurs when anything created to point you to God replaces God in the thoughts and desires of your heart.

This struggle goes all the way back to the beginning in the garden of Eden and has marked humanity ever since. What was designed to point us to God now replaces God in our hearts. It is the sad tragedy of sin. Sin is basically idolatrous. Because of it, we love something more than God. We look to what God made to do what only God can do. We worship the gift and neglect the giver.

Consider how the disobedience of Adam and Eve is described: "So when the woman saw that the tree was good for food, and that it was a delight to the eyes, and that the tree was to be desired to make one wise, she took of its fruit and ate, and she also gave some to her husband who was with her, and he ate" (Gen. 3:6). Eve knew the boundaries that God had set. Yes, the garden was a gorgeous place, with beautiful sounds, smells, sights, and tastes. But every wondrous physical thing that God created was intended to point to him. Every tree, flower, bird, stream, piece of fruit, and animal was meant to remind Adam and Eve of God's existence, presence, love, and authority.

When Eve ate the fruit, and Adam after her, they weren't confused about what God had commanded them. They knew that the tree was off limits, but at the moment of eating, they didn't care. By the time they had sunk their teeth into the succulent fruit, they had already given away the love and allegiance of their hearts. Love for God should have given them the motivation and ability to say no to temptation and run away from the tree. But their hearts, created for love of the Creator, had been kidnapped by love for the creation. It was the beginning of sin's disastrous exchange—worshiping and serving created things instead of the Creator (Rom. 1:25). Sadly, that exchange has taken place millions and millions of times since the garden. It is humanity's great spiritual dysfunction; we allow the creation to replace the Creator in our hearts. No wonder Jesus had to come. No wonder his grace is so essential. No wonder God knew that he could not leave us to ourselves, that he had to send a rescuing Redeemer.

Therefore, my beloved, flee from idolatry. (1 Cor. 10:14)

Reflect: What part of God's creation do you most often turn to for comfort or refuge from hardship? Why?

OCTOBER 18

Don't give way to discouragement, feelings of futility, or waves of fear because the Father has graciously chosen to give you the kingdom!

There are so many reasons to be discouraged in this fallen world, it's a wonder that anyone is happy. It's disheartening to be betrayed by a dear friend. It's disappointing to not win the award you worked so hard to achieve. It's depressing to face a sickness that you're not sure you'll ever overcome. It's disheartening to have to be concerned about crime, injustice, and corruption. It's hard to be mocked and rejected for your faith. It can seem as if everything in your life is in the process of decaying or in danger of going bad. People die, dreams die, flowers die, and marriages, churches, jobs, and friendships go bad. If you look around, this old world that God created isn't doing very well. In many ways, it's a hard, discouraging place to live.

But that's not all that is discouraging. It often seems as if you're powerless to make much change. You do everything you can to restore a friendship, but it just seems stuck. You know you don't have the power to change other people or situations.

So where is encouragement to be found? It's found in grace. You can read about it in the beautiful words of the passage below. With these words, everything changes. These words tell you that it's not you against a world gone bad. Yes, you are a citizen of this world, and you are touched by its brokenness. Yet you must remind yourself that you are the citizen of another kingdom. Your King rules over everything that would discourage and disappoint you. He also rules for your good and his glory. What is out of your control is under his rule. What you don't understand is under his careful administration. But there is more. While everything around you seems temporary, this kingdom will have no end. Long after the kingdoms of this world have been destroyed, you will reign with your King in his kingdom forever and ever and ever.

> Fear not, little flock, for it is your Father's good pleasure to give you the kingdom. (Luke 12:32)

Reflect: When you're feeling anxious or discouraged, how does Jesus's promise to give you his kingdom comfort and help you?

OCTOBER 19

By calling you to die daily, the gospel welcomes you to live eternally. Contrary to popular opinion, death really is the portal to life.

Death leads to life—something seems not right about this, but it is right. It makes perfect sense when you face the reality that you and I cannot live for ourselves and God at the same time. We cannot live for his kingdom and our kingdoms. We cannot write our own rules and submit to his rules. We cannot live for our glory and his glory. We cannot insert ourselves in the center of our worlds and have him at the center too.

You see, coming to Jesus is not a negotiation. Coming to Jesus is not an agreement. Coming to Jesus is not a contract. Coming to Jesus is a death—your death. He died so that you may live. Now he asks you to lose your life so that you may find life in him.

Here's why our death is essential for finding life. It's because we act as if we're smarter than God. We think our rules are better than his. We tell ourselves that present pleasure is better than eternal gain. And if someone doesn't rescue us from our delusions about our lives, we will lose our lives. Yes, we must die if we are ever going to live.

So grace is out to kill us. But in presiding over our deaths, grace gives us life—real, abundant, and eternal life. Don't fight the death of your old life. Instead, celebrate the new life that is yours by grace and grace alone. And remember that your Savior will continue to call you to die; it is the way of life.

> And he said to all, "If anyone would come after me, let him deny himself and take up his cross daily and follow me. For whoever would save his life will lose it, but whoever loses his life for my sake will save it. For what does it profit a man if he gains the whole world and loses or forfeits himself? For whoever is ashamed of me and of my words, of him will the Son of Man be ashamed when he comes in his glory and the glory of the Father and of the holy angels." (Luke 9:23–26)

Reflect: What promises of true life do you see promised through advertisements? How are they different than Jesus's promise to give you true life by his grace?

OCTOBER 20

Naming Jesus as Lord is the start of a theological commitment. Living as though he is Lord demands day-by-day forgiving, rescuing, and transforming grace.

In my early seminary days, I would take the subway home, run up the stairs to our third-floor apartment, and say to Luella: "I'm learning to think. I'm learning to think." It was much, much more than gathering together the academic truths of theology. It was profoundly more than getting to know my faith better. I was receiving more than advanced biblical literacy. I was being given a way to think about everything. And the whole system stood on four radical words, the first four words of the Bible: "In the beginning, God . . ." (Gen. 1:1).

I wasn't simply being educated. No, something deeper was happening. I was going through a process of heart and life transformation. The whole direction of my life, my thoughts about my identity, my definition of meaning and purpose, and where I would look for my inner sense of well-being were changing as well. All this provided the context for making decisions. It gave me reasons to get up in the morning. It confronted me with how much I needed grace.

This is what the theology found in Scripture is meant to do. The doctrines in the word of God are not supposed to produce what I call "theo-geeks." You know what I mean: egghead biblical academics, who think about things no one else does, who talk in a language no one else understands, and who don't do many people much good. Here's the thing we need to be reminded of again and again: the theology of the word of God was never intended to be an end in itself. Truth is a means to an end, and that end is a radically transformed life. The purpose of theology is not knowledge but holiness.

Now, think about what the Bible actually is. It's a grand story of redemption. Maybe it would be better to say that it's a story that includes God's essential notes. It is the story of Jesus, who came to offer the one thing you desperately need—grace. Theology that isn't zealous to promote forgiving and transforming grace, the kind of grace that changes your life, is simply bad theology.

> All Scripture is breathed out by God and profitable for teaching, for reproof, for correction, and for training in righteousness. (2 Tim. 3:16)

Reflect: How does today's devotional challenge the way you normally read the Bible or listen to Bible teaching?

OCTOBER 21

Corporate worship is designed to remind you of your identity in Christ so that you won't waste your time looking for identity elsewhere.

It's so easy to forget who you are in Christ and what you have been given as his child. It's so easy to shop horizontally for what you have already been given vertically. It's so easy to give in to fear or shame or guilt because you forget the present benefits of Jesus's finished work. It's so easy, in the hardships of life, to forget that nothing is powerful enough to separate you from God's love. When you are struggling, it's so easy to forget that if God gave you his Son, he will also give you everything else you need.

It's also easy to forget that every trial sent your way is sent by a Savior of grace as a tool of grace to advance the work of grace in your heart and life. It's so easy to forget that God really does live inside you in the powerful convicting, protecting, and enabling presence of the Holy Spirit. It's so easy to forget that God loves and accepts you no less on your worst day than he does on your best day.

It's so easy to feel weak in the face of temptation and give way to what grace has given you the power to resist. It's so easy to wonder if God is near and if he hears. It's so easy to question the goodness of God in times of trouble. When life seems out of control, it's so easy to forget that Jesus Christ rules over all things for his glory and for your good. It's so easy to forget who you are and look for identity elsewhere.

So God has ordained that we should gather again and again to remember again and again who we are and what we have been given. His church is a tool of grace, a vehicle for remembering, so that we may celebrate and grow.

> And let us consider how to stir up one another to love and good works, not neglecting to meet together, as is the habit of some, but encouraging one another, and all the more as you see the Day drawing near. (Heb. 10:24–25)

Reflect: How is your view of church different than the one described above? Why?

OCTOBER 22

We disobey. God convicts and restores. We doubt. God works to make us people of faith. We hunger. God feeds us with the bounty of his grace.

Other than the word *God*, there is no more important word that the human mind could consider and the mouth could speak than grace. Grace is a thunderous, expansive, powerful, and life-altering word. Grace is the ultimate spiritual game changer. It is the one thing that has the power to change you and everything about you. It is what all human beings need, no matter who they are or where they are. Men and women need grace, the young and old need grace, the rich and poor need grace, the popular and forgotten need grace, and the weak and powerful need grace. You could dig into grace every day of your life and not reach the bottom of its power and glory. Grace is the bottomless, treasure-laden mine of divine help. There simply is nothing comparable to God's grace.

In fact, your Bible is the cover-to-cover story of God's grace. Grace is why God sent his Son into this world to do for us what we could not do for ourselves—to transform us from what we are (sinners separated from him) into what we are becoming (Christlike and with him forever). John Newton, in his famous hymn, "Amazing Grace," really did choose the best word ever to describe God's grace: amazing.[13]

Plenteous grace
is what we're given;
grace that is
deeper,
fuller,
richer,
and greater
than our sin.
This grace does not
suspend operations
in the face of our
disobedience.
It will not
turn its back
in the face of our
doubt.
It will not stand
idly by
in the face of our
hunger.
No, this is
rich grace,
perseverant grace,
tender grace,
powerful grace.
There really is nothing
like it,
because it comes from the hand
of Jesus.

> But by the grace of God I am what I am, and his grace toward me was not in vain. On the contrary, I worked harder than any of them, though it was not I, but the grace of God that is with me. (1 Cor. 15:10)

Reflect: In what ways are online interactions often the exact opposite of grace? Why?

OCTOBER 23

We panic. God stays true to his sovereign plan. We wonder. God knows the end from the beginning. We pray. God answers with wisdom and grace.

There simply is no panic in heaven. God is never anxious. There is no confusion in the Trinity. God never wrings his hands and wishes he had made a better choice. God never worries about what is going to happen next. He never stresses over how things are going to turn out. God is never surprised or caught up short. He is never in a situation that overwhelms him. God never feels needy or unprepared. God never regrets that he did not do better. God never fails at a task. He never makes promises that he cannot keep. He never forgets what he said or what he wants to do next. God never contradicts himself. He is all-powerful, absolutely perfect in every way, faithful to every word, sovereign over all that is. He is the definition of love, and he is righteous, just, tender, and patient all at the same time. He is not dismayed or distracted by our panic and our questions. No, the sovereign move of his grace marches on!

So God is not discouraged in the face of our weakness and wondering. His plan is not thwarted by our spiritual ups and downs. He doesn't look at us and ask whether it's worth it. No, in the face of our ongoing struggles, his plan marches on. Why? It marches on because it is not based on our character but on his. Redemption does not rest on our resolve but on his. Salvation doesn't hang on our strength but on his. We have hope because it all comes from him and rests on him. It is humbling to admit, but it is the only place of hope. Nothing of our salvation depends on us. It all rests on his sovereign grace. Here is the bottom line: he is able, he is willing, and he is faithful. Grace supplies everything we need. Grace will win!

> In him we have obtained an inheritance, having been predestined according to the purpose of him who works all things according to the counsel of his will, so that we who were the first to hope in Christ might be to the praise of his glory. (Eph. 1:11–12)

Reflect: What doubts and uncertainties can you bring before the Lord today? Confess them to him and leave them in his capable hands.

OCTOBER 24

We are fearful. God's presence gives courage. We are alienated. His love draws us near. We are doubtful. His promises give us hope.

God meets us where we are. He does not wait for us to come to him; he comes to us. There is no better example of this than Jesus's response to Peter after Peter's denial. If there was someone on whom you would expect Jesus to turn his back forever, it would be the apostle Peter. How could he deny Jesus, even after being warned? Wasn't that unforgivable? No! Instead, Peter's denial is a shockingly concrete picture of how much we need the cross of Jesus Christ. The life, death, and resurrection of Jesus were necessary because we are people like Peter. We have no power in ourselves to be faithful, wise, good, and righteous. We cannot save ourselves. We are people in need of rescue.

So in amazing condescending grace, God meets us where we are, just as he did with Peter. He comes to us in our fear. He meets us in our doubt. He pursues us when we wander. He empowers us when we're weak. He restores us when we are unfaithful. When we deny him, he does not deny us. He sits down with us, assuring us again of his love, drawing out from us love for him, and sending us on our way to do the work he has chosen for us to do. This is the way of grace.

> When they had finished breakfast, Jesus said to Simon Peter, "Simon, son of John, do you love me more than these?" He said to him, "Yes, Lord; you know that I love you." He said to him, "Feed my lambs." He said to him a second time, "Simon, son of John, do you love me?" He said to him, "Yes, Lord; you know that I love you." He said to him, "Tend my sheep." He said to him the third time, "Simon, son of John, do you love me?" Peter was grieved because he said to him the third time, "Do you love me?" and he said to him, "Lord, you know everything; you know that I love you." Jesus said to him, "Feed my sheep. Truly, truly, I say to you, when you were young, you used to dress yourself and walk wherever you wanted, but when you are old, you will stretch out your hands, and another will dress you and carry you where you do not want to go." (This he said to show by what kind of death he was to glorify God.) And after saying this he said to him, "Follow me." (John 21:15–19)

Reflect: In what place of weakness in your life is Jesus meeting you today?

OCTOBER 25

God's agenda is change. Your need is change. The promise of grace is change. The hope of eternity is the completion of the work of change.

The more I travel from church to church, the more I engage with leaders, and the more I have opportunities to interview people in the seats, the more I grow convinced that the true crisis in the modern evangelical church is not dissatisfaction. Instead, it's the opposite. The problem is personal spiritual self-satisfaction.

We're all too satisfied with who we are, where we are, and what we're doing. We're satisfied with a little bit of Bible knowledge. We're satisfied with faithful attendance at the weekend services of our churches. We're satisfied with quick morning devotions. We're satisfied with a little ministry participation. We're satisfied that we don't act out most of our lust, and we don't communicate most of our envy. We're satisfied that in our disappointment with God, we don't walk away. We're satisfied to use most of our material resources to keep ourselves comfortable. We're satisfied to be mere consumers of the work of the church rather than committed participants in it. We're satisfied with hearts that occasionally wander and with thoughts that contradict what the Bible says is good and true. We're satisfied.

None of us is yet a grace graduate, but we're satisfied. We all give evidence that we still need to grow, but we're satisfied. And because we are satisfied, we are resistant to the grace that is our only hope. What happens if you are able to convince yourself that you are healthy, even though there may be indicators that you are not? The answer is: you're probably not going to go to the doctor asking for his help.

But here's what you and I need to remember: we serve a dissatisfied Redeemer. He knows we still need the transforming work of his powerful grace. Isn't it wonderful that, in gracious dissatisfaction, he will not relent until every microbe of sin is removed from every cell of every one of the hearts of his children?

> Not that I have already obtained this or am already perfect, but I press on to make it my own, because Christ Jesus has made me his own. (Phil. 3:12)

Reflect: Think about the differences between growing in your education (or personal improvement) and growing in Christ. How would you explain the phrase, "None of us is yet a grace graduate"?

OCTOBER 26

God justifies the ungodly. This means there really is hope for people like us.

I wish I could say that all my actions are godly, but they're not. I wish I could say that all my responses to the people in my life are motivated by love for God and for them, but they're not. I wish awe of God was the principal motivation for all I do, but often it isn't. I wish I could say that selfishness and greed are in my rearview mirror, but there's evidence that they're not. I wish I could say that materialism doesn't kidnap my heart anymore, but there are still times when it does. I wish I could say that there are never times when I am irritated or impatient, but I still struggle with both on occasion. I wish I could say that I always rest in the righteousness of Christ, but there are still times when I give way to the pride of parading my so-called righteousness before others. I wish I could say that the great spiritual battle is over for me, but there is regular evidence that it is not.

All this means that I value justifying grace. I celebrate that, in Christ, God found a way to be "just and the justifier" of the ungodly (Rom. 3:26). I am daily thankful for the perfect life of Jesus. I am thankful that he subjected himself to the temptations of this fallen world. I am thankful that on the cross he took my judgment and carried my guilt and shame. I am thankful that he burst out of that tomb, conquering death. I am thankful that his righteousness is attributed to my account. I am thankful that he fulfilled the law and satisfied the Father's anger.

So I am so very thankful that justifying grace ensures that I will forever be accepted as one of his righteous ones, even though I still don't measure up. Yes, today I have reason again to be thankful for justifying grace.

> You are severed from Christ, you who would be justified by the law; you have fallen away from grace. For through the Spirit, by faith, we ourselves eagerly wait for the hope of righteousness. (Gal. 5:4–5)

Reflect: In what ways do you see God's grace in putting you in your family, even though your family also doesn't measure up?

OCTOBER 27

Belief is not simply a function of the brain. No, it's an investment of the heart that fundamentally changes the way that you live.

During seminary I had filled my brain with the details of the theology of the word of God. I could hold my own in almost any theological debate. I thought of myself as a man of faith. I had committed many passages of Scripture to memory, so I looked at myself as spiritually mature. Because I had ministry gifts, I thought I was living a life of faith. But my faith was like a luxury car with no engine. It was beautiful on the outside. Yet it lacked the power necessary to do what it was meant to do. This house of spiritual cards was about to come down.

I worked hard to deny the evidence. I pointed to my acts of righteousness to pump air into my delusion. But God would not turn away. I was a very angry man, but I denied that anger and its roots in my heart. I was a very proud man, but I refused to see it. I was controlling, but I said it was just me using my God-given leadership gifts. But things didn't get better, they got worse. My wife, Luella, confronted me again and again about my anger. People in our congregation confronted me about my pride. God used ministry and family brokenness to begin to craft in me mature faith. I am a very different man today, but the craftsman God is still at work, maturing the faith that only his grace can produce.

God is faithful and will do what is necessary to craft real faith in us. Trusting our own strength and wisdom is natural, but faith is not natural for us. So in sanctifying grace, God works to turn baby believers into mature people of faith. He will not relent until that work is complete. Nothing can stop him. Here's what you need to understand: your faith is not your hope. The only source of hope for fickle-faith sinners is his zealous grace.

> My son, do not despise the Lord's discipline
>   or be weary of his reproof,
> for the Lord reproves him whom he loves,
>   as a father the son in whom he delights. (Prov. 3:11–12)

Reflect: Where have you been resisting other people's attempts to help you see where you need to grow?

OCTOBER 28

Will your responses today be shaped more by fear of your inability or by celebration of Christ's sufficiency?

No one just lives life as a neutral observer. No one is objective. No one is passive. You and I always bring an interpretive grid for how we view ourselves, our behavior, others, God, and life. For the believer, the gospel of the person and work of Jesus is intended to be that life-altering interpretive grid. This is what Paul means when he says, "Let the word of Christ dwell in you richly" (Col. 3:16).

Why does he say "word of Christ"? What Paul means is the gospel. The overarching message of the Bible is the gospel of Jesus Christ. The Bible is not a series of stories. The Bible is not a textbook of theology. The Bible is the grand biography of the Lord Jesus Christ. Perhaps it is more accurate to say that the Bible is the annotated story of the Lord Jesus Christ. In other words, it's his story with God's essential explanatory and application notes. You simply cannot make sense of Scripture without the person and work—the grace—of the Lord Jesus Christ.

So where does all of this lead us? You have two ways of looking at life. You can look at all your internal and external challenges from the perspective of your track record and catalog of abilities. Or you can look at them from the vantage point of the sufficiency of the work of Jesus on your behalf. The gospel of Jesus Christ must not be just an aspect of your theology. It must not be relegated to the "religious" dimension of your life. Your relationship with God through Jesus Christ *is* your life. It touches and alters every aspect of your existence. It redefines your identity. It completely reshapes your purpose and your destiny. So the work of Jesus on your behalf must be the window through which you look at everything in your life.

> See to it that no one takes you captive by philosophy and empty deceit, according to human tradition, according to the elemental spirits of the world, and not according to Christ. (Col. 2:8)

Reflect: Don't give way to the fear of inability when the work of Jesus has supplied you with everything you need.

OCTOBER 29

If you trust only when you understand, you'll live with lots of doubt. God's wisdom is bigger than anything your mind can conceive.

You will never reach true, sturdy, and lasting peace of heart by means of understanding. "Why not?" you may ask. Because there will always be things in your life that you do not understand. God reveals in his word all the things that you need to know. Yet he does not tell you all the things that could be known. You and I simply are not able to contain in our limited brains all of God's plans for us and all of the reasons for those plans.

Now, here's the rub: God created you to be a rational human being. He designed you to think, that is, to strive to make sense out of your life and your world. That is not a bad thing in itself. In fact, it is a very good thing. Your ability to think, interpret, examine, define, explain, and understand is meant to drive you to God. So biblical faith is not irrational, but it will take you beyond your ability to reason. You and I never could have started at the fall of Adam and Eve and used reason to predict the coming of Jesus and his death on the cross. Old Testament believers knew that God was going to deal with sin and give new life to his people because God told them that this was what he was going to do. But they did not know that the death of the Son of God would be the means by which this would happen.

In the same way, we can be assured of all that God has told us in his word. Yet, there will be mysteries and surprises in our lives. If you and I question God's goodness and love every time he acts in a way that is unexpected, we will end up concluding that he is not good. If we refuse to rest when we don't understand, we will end up living lives of distress.

You rest not because you know, but because the one who knows it all is the definition of what is wise and what is good.

> For the foolishness of God is wiser than men, and the weakness of God is stronger than men. (1 Cor. 1:25)

Reflect: How does the vastness of the internet, with all its information and options, push you away from the rest that God wants you to find in him?

OCTOBER 30

People make good friends and loved ones, but they make bad messiahs. Life is only ever found in Jesus.

We tend to put people in the place of God and ask them to do for us what only he can do. We ask our loved ones to give us identity. We ask them to heal our hurts. We ask them to cause us to be happy. But they will simply never, ever rise to the level of our expectations. In our relationships, we often try to drink from a dry well, and then we wonder why we come up thirsty. No human being can be your personal Savior.

Here is the bottom line, so powerfully captured by the passage below: *Jesus is life*. As Creator, he gave physical life to our bodies. As eternal God, he is the source of the life of everything that lives. But there is more. As Savior, he is the one who alone gives spiritual life to our dead hearts. The passage says we are not born again by human blood, by human flesh, or by human will, but by God. It is *his* fullness that we receive; life-giving grace upon life-giving grace.

So don't put the burden of life onto another person. It will only crush that person and disappoint you. Besides, you don't need him or her to give you life because you've already been given life in the person and work of Jesus.

> In the beginning was the Word, and the Word was with God, and the Word was God. He was in the beginning with God. All things were made through him, and without him was not any thing made that was made. In him was life, and the life was the light of men. The light shines in the darkness, and the darkness has not overcome it. . . . And the Word became flesh and dwelt among us, and we have seen his glory, glory as of the only Son from the Father, full of grace and truth. . . . For from his fullness we have all received, grace upon grace. For the law was given through Moses; grace and truth came through Jesus Christ. No one has ever seen God; the only God, who is at the Father's side, he has made him known. (John 1:1–5, 14, 16–18)

Reflect: Whose approval do you fear to lose the most? What does that reveal to you?

OCTOBER 31

Be aware that the kingdom of self is a costume kingdom. It does a perversely brilliant job of masquerading as the kingdom of God.

Spiritual fakery is one of the chief tools of the enemy. It is one of the key ingredients of spiritual blindness. This is why we read the warning in Matthew 7:15: "Beware of false prophets, who come to you in sheep's clothing but inwardly are ravenous wolves." The kingdom of self is very skilled at wearing the clothing of the kingdom of God.

- A focus on material things can masquerade as good stewardship of your possessions.
- Loving personal control can masquerade as using God-given leadership gifts.
- Anger can masquerade as having a heart for what is right.
- Self-righteous legalism can masquerade as loving God's law.
- Caring for what people think can masquerade as caring for others.
- Selfish attention-seeking can masquerade as being candid about your needs.
- Judgment and criticism can masquerade as a commitment to honesty.
- Theological pride can masquerade as a commitment to God's truth.
- Lust can masquerade as a celebration of the beauty of God's creation.
- Gossip can masquerade as a prayerful concern for others.

The kingdom of self is a costume kingdom. This is because one of the enemy's most useful tools is to use wrong to imitate right. It is scary to think of the number of times we think we are serving God when we're actually serving ourselves, or the number of times we think we are worshiping God when we're actually giving worship to some aspect of the creation.

Yet the masquerading idols have no power to deliver to our hungry hearts what Jesus alone can give us. Only God can give us insight into our hearts and free us from our bondage to the little costume kingdom of one.

> Woe to you, scribes and Pharisees, hypocrites! For you clean the outside of the cup and the plate, but inside they are full of greed and self-indulgence. You blind Pharisee! First clean the inside of the cup and the plate, that the outside also may be clean. (Matt. 23:25–26)

Reflect: How is it actually a loving work of grace for Jesus to unmask our costume kingdom of self?

NOVEMBER 1

Yes, God disciplines his children, but rest assured, the full penalty for your sin has been borne by Christ and won't again be borne by you.

I'm a parent of four children, and I can honestly say that there weren't many moments in my children's lives when they seemed genuinely thankful for the faithful discipline of their parents. They tended to see discipline as vengeful, harsh, punitive, and unloving. (Sadly, human discipline often is like this.) Our children didn't seem to understand that our discipline wasn't a suspension of our love but a result of it. We didn't discipline them because we were upset that we were stuck with them in our family, but because they were unshakably part of the family. We didn't discipline them in order to remind them that they hadn't quite yet been good enough to earn our love, but rather because they were the objects of our love.

I think we have the same difficulty with the loving disciplinary zeal of our heavenly Father. He disciplines us not to teach us how far we have to go to become his children, but because we *are* his children. His discipline, therefore, is never the result of his rejection, but the fruit of his acceptance. Since our penalty was fully and completely paid by Jesus on the cross, it needn't be paid by us ever again!

Think with me for a moment. It is only when you understand the completeness of your *justification* (that your penalty has been paid and you have been made eternally right with God by the life and death of Jesus) that you are able to rest in the ongoing discipline of your *sanctification*.

So you can expect his discipline, but you do not have to fear his anger. You will experience his correction, but you will never face his rejection. He disciplines all his children in order to produce a harvest of righteousness, but he will never punish you for your sin.

> For Christ also suffered *once* for sins, the righteous for the unrighteous, that he might bring us to God, being put to death in the flesh but made alive in the spirit. (1 Pet. 3:18)

Reflect: How do you think God feels about you today? What does the Bible say about how he feels about you?

NOVEMBER 2

The cross of Jesus Christ stands as a beacon of hope in a world gone bad. Life, hope, forgiveness, and change really are possible!

The cross is not the sad symbol of a plan gone wrong. It isn't the grand symbol of redemption's embarrassment. The cross shouldn't make you ashamed. No, it should stand at the epicenter of your boasting. Hear the words of the apostle Paul: "But far be it from me to boast except in the cross of our Lord Jesus Christ, by which the world has been crucified to me, and I to the world" (Gal. 6:14). The place where they executed criminals seems to be the last place to go to find hope. The scene where they killed the world's only innocent man doesn't seem to be a place that excites celebration. But such is the paradox of grace. Hopelessness is the entrance to hope. Weakness is the place to find strength. Injustice is where mercy flows. Life comes to those who deserve death. Defeat is actually a victory. The end is really a beginning. Out of sorrow comes eternal celebration. The tomb is the place where new life begins.

The impossible paradoxes of redemption become the regular moves of transforming grace. Hope is sung to suffering's tune. Life is played on death's instruments. Grace doesn't play by the law's score. God composes hope from tragedy's notes. So we look at Calvary and we don't sing a dirge. Instead, we sing a song of triumph and celebration, of hope and salvation. Satan's players have not been able to drown out salvation's song. The songs of hope by the company of the redeemed will never end. They grow in volume, celebration, and glory. The cross is the subject of those songs, and its life-giving mercy is the chorus.

It is the cross of Jesus Christ that gives you reason to hope, sing, celebrate, and live. It was never the interruption of God's saving plan, but the essential means of accomplishing it. It was never a defeat. It was always a victory.

And they sang a new song, saying,

> "Worthy are you to take the scroll
>   and to open its seals,
> for you were slain, and by your blood you ransomed people for God
>   from every tribe and language and people and nation,
> and you have made them a kingdom and priests to our God,
>   and they shall reign on the earth." (Rev. 5:9–10)

Reflect: How does the cross shine light into the darkest areas of your life?

NOVEMBER 3

How do you measure your capability—by your previous successes and failures or by the boundless resource of grace that's yours in Christ?

It is something every human being does many times a day. Most of the time, we do it unconsciously. The way we do it says a lot about who we think we are and what we think we are facing. What am I talking about? Measuring your capability. We are always assessing what we bring to the table to deal and comparing it with what is currently on our plates.

Now, it's not stupid or crazy to measure your potential by examining your track record. How have you done so far? What are the things that tend to trip you up? What are the weaknesses that have been exposed? What have you learned that will help you do better the next time? These are all good questions as far as they go, but they lack something that is dramatically important. They lack the gospel of Jesus Christ. You see, the message of God's grace is that you haven't been left to your track record or your own spiritual resources. Rather, in Christ, you have been given both a new identity and new potential.

God knew exactly what you would face as you journeyed through this fallen world. He knew that temptation would greet you every day. He knew that sorrow and suffering would get you down. So he gave you exactly what you need so that you can be what you're supposed to be and do what he has called you to do even in the broken surroundings where you live. What did he give you? He gave you himself! God's best gift of grace is himself. He comes to us. He makes us the place where he lives. This means that divine power resides inside us. Our potential as God's children is much more than our natural gifts and track records predict because Immanuel, the Lamb, the Savior, the Lord almighty, the sovereign King has made us his residence. How could this new potential be more radically and powerfully stated than in the apostle Paul's words below?

It is no longer I who live, but Christ who lives in me. (Gal. 2:20)

Reflect: A new identity and a wildly new potential is yours in Christ. How can you go out and live as if you really believe it today?

NOVEMBER 4

If you're God's child, don't ever tell yourself that you are alone—for you, "alone" is a redemptive impossibility.

Walking away from the funeral of a loved one, you can feel very alone. Dealing with long-term sickness or personal rejection are very lonely experiences. Standing for what is right in a culture that mocks the morals you hold dear can make you feel fearful and alone. Loneliness of some kind is the universal experience of people living this side of eternity. Sin brought alienation and separation into the world. It first broke the fellowship between God and man. As a result, sin also shattered the fellowship between people and their family members, friends, and neighbors. This aloneness is spiritual, emotional, relational, and cultural. It's nearly impossible to escape.

The drama of human aloneness is captured by the apostle Paul in the passage below, but there is more. He also captures how the grace of Jesus Christ reconciles us to God and, in so doing, reconciles us to one another so that we will never again be alone. As you read, let the words sink in: from (a) "having no hope and without God in the world" to (b) "reconcile[d] . . . to God" and "being built together into a dwelling place for God by the Spirit" (Eph. 2:22). What is this movement of grace? We have gone from being hopeless and alone to being reconciled and inhabited by God, and therefore never alone again!

> Remember that you were at that time separated from Christ, . . . having no hope and without God in the world. But now in Christ Jesus you who once were far off have been brought near by the blood of Christ. For he himself is our peace, who has made us both one and has broken down in his flesh the dividing wall of hostility by abolishing the law of commandments expressed in ordinances, that he might create in himself one new man in place of the two, so making peace, and might reconcile us both to God in one body through the cross, thereby killing the hostility. . . . So then you are . . . built on the foundation of the apostles and prophets, Christ Jesus himself being the cornerstone, in whom the whole structure, being joined together, grows into a holy temple in the Lord. In him you also are being built together into a dwelling place for God by the Spirit. (Eph. 2:12–17, 19–22)

Reflect: Don't forget to remind yourself again today that as God's child you simply cannot be alone, no matter what you feel.

NOVEMBER 5

You will never turn any created thing into your personal messiah. There is one true Messiah, and life can be found only in him.

I wish I could say that I never look for life where it can't be found, but the temptation to do this still haunts me. As much as we all know that there is only one true God, we still hunt for God-replacements. We all still tend to look horizontally for what we will only ever find vertically. There are times when we ask creation to be our Savior:

- We attach our identity to the respect of other people.
- We draw too much of our sense of well-being from our physical appearance.
- We think material possessions have the power to make us happy.
- We attach our meaning and purpose to our achievements.
- We base our identity on our education.
- We look to food and drink to satisfy and calm us.
- We continually say, "If only I had _____, then my life would be _____."

The list is really endless. There is nothing in creation that you can't try to turn into your personal messiah. Yet it never, ever works. The creation can never, ever give you what the Creator alone can. It makes no sense at all to desperately look for what you have already been given by your Savior.

All the good and glorious created things that God puts in our lives are things he has designed and placed there for a reason. They exist to point us to the only place where life can ever be found—in him. You know how this works from driving around or from taking a trip: a sign points you to a thing, but the sign is not the thing. Creation points us to the Creator, but it can never give us what the Creator can give. All the good situations, locations, possessions, relationships, achievements, and natural beauties of this physical world are wonderful blessings from the hand of God. However, they have no ability to give you the one thing that your heart desperately desires—life. This is what Jesus himself taught:

> I am the way, and the truth, and the life. (John 14:6)

Reflect: With these words from John 14, Jesus ends our need to search. Since he is life, why is there no need to look for it anywhere else?

NOVEMBER 6

God loves too much to be willing to forsake his glorious kingdom of grace for your self-absorbed little kingdom of one.

On this side of our final destination, sin causes us all to set ourselves up as sovereigns over our kingdoms of one. We all want our will to be done. So God gives us his grace. Is his grace given to give you what you need to be your own king? Does he give grace so your little kingdom purposes will happen? No, God's grace dethrones you from your little kingdom. His grace welcomes you to a much better kingdom than you could ever want for yourself. But in this kingdom, you will never be at the center. Because in this kingdom, all things are for God and God alone.

The dynamic of kingdoms in conflict is powerfully demonstrated in the passage below. In the most piercing way yet, Jesus talks to the disciples about his coming death. Clearly the disciples do not fully grasp what he is saying. There is no display of grief or even concern on their part. No, they quickly move on to the topic that is really important to them. After Christ tells them about the violent death that is to come for him, they immediately begin to argue about who is the greatest. In this moment, their tiny kingdoms collide with God's kingdom of grace. These kingdoms collide today as well. Only grace can make us love God's kingdom more than our own.

> "The Son of Man is going to be delivered into the hands of men, and they will kill him. And when he is killed, after three days he will rise." But they did not understand the saying, and were afraid to ask him.
>
> And they came to Capernaum. And when he was in the house he asked them, "What were you discussing on the way?" But they kept silent, for on the way they had argued with one another about who was the greatest. And he sat down and called the twelve. And he said to them, "If anyone would be first, he must be last of all and servant of all." And he took a child and put him in the midst of them, and taking him in his arms, he said to them, "Whoever receives one such child in my name receives me, and whoever receives me, receives not me but him who sent me." (Mark 9:31–37)

Reflect: Think about the past few days—what have your words revealed about the true desires of your heart and your kingdom?

NOVEMBER 7

God calls you to deny yourself and then blesses you with the indwelling Holy Spirit so you have the power to say no.

Sin presents as beautiful what God calls ugly. As a result, reaching out for what God forbids gives momentary pleasure. But it quickly fades. So you reach out again, hungry for more. Each time you need more to achieve the pleasure you are craving. Whether it's gluttony, pornography, materialism, gossip, thievery, or the lust for appreciation, control, or success—whatever satisfied you yesterday doesn't do so today. So you have to have more and more.

Before long you can't stop thinking about what you want. What you once were convinced was harmless and under your control, now controls you. You are addicted to what God has forbidden. Yet you will do your best to convince yourself that you're not. Sin is never harmless; it is a cruel slave master, out to kidnap your heart and control your life.

The addicting and enslaving power of sin should make each of us thankful for the power of the Messiah Jesus to "proclaim liberty to the captives, and the opening of the prison to those who are bound" (Isa. 61:1). He is our only hope of escape from the bondage-inducing power of sin. Stop right now and examine your life. Where are you finding it hard to say no to your desires? Do you need to run to your Savior for his bondage-breaking grace? He is able, he is willing, and he will not turn you away.[14]

You have called me to say
no.
Not no to you
or no to others,
but no to myself.
I must say no to
selfish desires,
wrong thoughts, and
dangerous emotions.
I must say no to
the world's values,
sin's temptations, and
my desire to control
what only God can rule.
But left to myself,
I have
little desire
or power
to say
no.
So you have given me
exactly what I need.
It's the only thing
that will solve my
problem.
You have given me
your Spirit.
So, when necessary,
I am able
to say
no.

Little children, keep yourselves from idols. (1 John 5:21)

Reflect: Where do you think that your desires are a bit out of control? Why?

NOVEMBER 8

Today you can give way to fear-producing "what-ifs" or rest in the sovereign care of your wise and gracious Savior King.

Here's the bottom line: if you're God's child, your life is never, ever out of control. It's not spinning wildly in every direction with no intelligent direction. It's not controlled by random and impersonal luck. Yes, vast pieces of your existence are out of your control. But you must not conclude that your life is out of control.

There are two reasons for this. First, the story that is your life has been included, by grace, in the greater story of redemption. This story is about God's age-old commitment to call a people to himself, to fix everything that sin has broken, to conquer sin and death, to establish a new heaven and a new earth, and to invite all his children to live there with him forever. This huge story was set in motion before the earth was created, it is unstoppable, and it will never have an end. So because your story is woven into the fabric of the redemption story, there is meaning, purpose, and direction to every part of it. The story of redemption carries your story along. The goal of redemption guarantees your destiny. No, you won't understand all that you face. And yes, God's plans will confuse you at points. Yet your story has been infused with meaning and purpose. Why? Because it's been included in God's story of redemption and restoration.

But the fact that your life is under control is even more personal than that. God has appointed his Son, the Lord Jesus Christ, to be "head over all things to the church" (Eph. 1:22). Right now, Jesus is ruling over all things. That means that every situation, relationship, and location of your life is ruled by King Jesus. You cannot be in a place that is not under his rule. The phrase "to the church" is better translated "for the church." This means that not only is everything under the careful rule of the risen Lord Jesus, but he rules over all things for your help and benefit. Since his story is unstoppable and his rule is good, there is grand and gracious control over every aspect of your life.

> And we know that for those who love God all things work together for good, for those who are called according to his purpose. (Rom. 8:28)

Reflect: Think about what you have planned for the next 24 hours. Take a few moments to acknowledge to Jesus that he is in control of all the moments of your day.

NOVEMBER 9

While sin is still a sad and ever-present reality in each of our lives, it is simply no match for the grace of the Lord Jesus Christ.

True biblical faith never requires that you deny reality. If you have to turn your back on what is real and true in order to have some temporary personal peace, you may feel better. Yet that's not the faith of the Bible. This realism applies to sin. There's a great temptation to deny or at least to minimize our sin. However, you don't reflect the message of the gospel by denying your own spiritual struggles.

This is not to say you should make your sin the focus of your meditation. When you treat yourself as an unworthy, impure, and incapable spiritual worm, you're denying the amazing grace of the gospel of Jesus Christ. You must not allow yourself to wonder if he loves you. You must not see yourself as unworthy of his care. You must not work to measure up in his sight. You must not beat yourself up when you fail. You must not give yourself to acts of payment and penance after you have messed up in God's eyes. You must never run from God in fear as you think of the remaining sin you see in yourself every day.

What you and I must meditate on every day is the absolute perfection and completeness of the work of the Lord Jesus Christ. He was perfect in his life, perfect in his death, and perfect in his resurrection. There is nothing we could ever think, desire, say, or do that could in any way add to the forgiveness and acceptance that we have received from God based on Christ's work. You are perfect in the eyes of God because the perfect righteousness of Jesus has been attributed to your spiritual account. You measure up in his eyes even on those days when you don't measure up because Jesus measured up on your behalf. Yes, you should acknowledge the sad reality of remaining sin, but you must not make that sin your meditation. Meditate on and celebrate the amazing grace that has completely changed your identity, potential, and destiny.

> You know that he appeared in order to take away sins, and in him there is no sin. (1 John 3:5)

Reflect: What about yourself do you tend to meditate on most? Think of two ways you can meditate more on Christ today than on yourself.

NOVEMBER 10

God is not satisfied with informing you about the work of his kingdom. He transforms you to participate in the work of his kingdom.

God has not revealed his truth to you so that you can sit in the audience. God has called all his children to participate in the work of his kingdom. He really does mean to employ all his children in his work of redemption. Yes, you read that right—all his children. The *total involvement paradigm* is his normal plan for the church.

Clearly, the Bible says that the body of Christ grows as every part does its part (Eph. 4:11–16). Scripture even says that every one of God's children should be prepared to teach and warn others (Col. 3:12–17). This sounds radical, doesn't it? Yet they were not radical in the context in which they were given. Paul is just explaining God's normal plan for his people and his church. They appear radical to us because we have drifted so far from what God expects for his church. Many, many Christians' church attendance is the spiritual edition of going to a concert. They go to experience the religious performance of ministry professionals. Their relationship to the church is self-focused ("Here's the kind of church I want to attend") and passive ("I'm so thankful for the good work our church staff does").

But God's plan for his church is very different. He has called all his children to be his ambassadors. Here's the plan: a God of grace makes his invisible grace visible by sending his people of grace to reflect his grace to people who need grace. You have been called to be the look on his face, the tone of his voice, and the touch of his hand. Using your mentality, your personality, your emotionality, your physicality, your possessions, and all your relationships, you are to represent his presence and his love. You are placed where you are to make his mercy and faithfulness visible and concrete.

Yet you and I have no ability to represent God well. So all this drives us to him to receive the grace we need to represent his grace in the lives of others. What a plan!

> Therefore, we are ambassadors for Christ, God making his appeal through us. We implore you on behalf of Christ, be reconciled to God. (2 Cor. 5:20)

Reflect: If you're an ambassador, what do your texts or social media posts reveal about what you represent?

NOVEMBER 11

You don't wait for grace and then do what God has told you to do. You get enabling grace in motion.

God's grace provides everything you require. God's grace is form fitted for your moment of need. God, in grace, doesn't just forgive you, he also gives you his grace as you follow him and at the moment when you need it.

However, it's always been hard for the people of God to rest in this reality. Take for example the children of Israel, when they found themselves at the Red Sea with the angry army of Egypt bearing down on them. Even though they have just experienced God's miracles that secured their escape from the slavery of Egypt, the children of Israel, are in a complete panic. They're stuck between the Red Sea and the Egyptian army, with no means of changing their circumstances! They are convinced that Moses has dragged them out into the wilderness to die. But God knows exactly what he is doing. He has manufactured this whole situation to demonstrate his glory to his people and to defeat the Egyptian army. What he does not do is tell them what is going to happen beforehand. Why? Because he is working in them, as he works in us, to craft them into people of strong faith.

> When Pharaoh drew near, the people of Israel lifted up their eyes, and behold, the Egyptians were marching after them, and they feared greatly. . . . The Lord said to Moses, "Why do you cry to me? Tell the people of Israel to go forward. Lift up your staff, and stretch out your hand over the sea and divide it, that the people of Israel may go through the sea on dry ground. And I will harden the hearts of the Egyptians so that they shall go in after them, and I will get glory over Pharaoh and all his host, his chariots, and his horsemen. And the Egyptians shall know that I am the Lord, when I have gotten glory over Pharaoh, his chariots, and his horsemen." (Ex. 14:10, 15–18)

Reflect: What fears have been regularly invading your thoughts? How can you redirect those anxious thoughts into prayers to the Lord for his grace?

NOVEMBER 12

You will never find fulfillment of heart on the far side of rebellion. True rest of heart is always found in submission to the Savior.

Today is my birthday. I mention this not because I hope you will log on to Amazon.com and rush me a gift (although Amazon's delivery system is quite efficient, if you're so inclined). I have walked with the Lord and studied his word for many, many years; longer than I would like to admit. Over the years, I have gained a high level of biblical knowledge and a solid understanding of theology. I have surely grown in my faith. I have an understanding of God's grace that for many of my years I did not have. What God has called me to do has taken me to almost every continent to fellowship and serve with God's people there. I love to worship, and I love to sit under Christ-centered, grace-filled preaching. I'm married to a godly wife who encourages my faith. This birthday, like many others, stimulates me to count my blessings, and they really are many. But there is one thing today that confronts me as it did the year before: I am not a grace graduate.

I am still tempted to think that my way is better. No, not in big, grand, public sins, but in the more acceptable sins of pride, impatience, failure to be gentle, loving myself more than my neighbor, and loving pieces of the creation more than I should. It is embarrassing to admit that all of this is fueled by a grand delusion that I thought I had conquered long ago. It is the lie that was first told in the garden and that has been repeated a billion times since. Believing this lie not only turns you into a fool. It also makes you a rebel against your heavenly Father. What is this lie? It is the lie that life can be found outside of the Creator. We all want lasting rest and sturdy peace of heart. But we forget that real peace and rest are always found when we give our hearts in submission to the Savior. This is my prayer for myself today and for all who read this devotion.

> Submit yourselves therefore to God. Resist the devil, and he will flee from you. (James 4:7)

Reflect: Make this prayer your own; find true rest as you pray to the Lord: "May your kingdom come in all that I think, desire, and say today."

NOVEMBER 13

Prayer is abandoning my righteousness, admitting my need for forgiveness, and resting in the grace of the cross of Jesus Christ.

It is a shocking prayer that the Pharisee speaks in Christ's parable (below). It isn't shocking just because he compares himself to sinners worse than him. We are all tempted to do the same. It isn't shocking just because he lists his good works in his prayer. We all make ourselves feel better about our spiritual state by cataloging the good things we've done.

What's shocking about this prayer is that it is not a prayer at all! What he says is not prayerlike in posture, attitude, or content. In shocking self-confidence, he essentially looks God in the face and says: "I don't need you. I don't need your forgiveness. I don't need your strengthening. I don't need your wisdom. I'm doing quite well on my own." If you essentially tell God that you don't need him, your words maybe sound religious, but they're not prayer.

Real prayer rises from an attitude that the Puritans labeled *importunity*. That means being troubled and frightened into crying out for help. It is a condition of heart that exists only because of grace. It's grace that causes you to acknowledge your sin. It's grace that opens your heart to the help that only God can give. Real prayer is motivated by that grace and acknowledges your need for that grace. Prayer isn't an announcement of personal righteousness but a cry for help that rests in the righteousness of another.

> He also told this parable to some who trusted in themselves that they were righteous, and treated others with contempt: "Two men went up into the temple to pray, one a Pharisee and the other a tax collector. The Pharisee, standing by himself, prayed thus: 'God, I thank you that I am not like other men, extortioners, unjust, adulterers, or even like this tax collector. I fast twice a week; I give tithes of all that I get.' But the tax collector, standing far off, would not even lift up his eyes to heaven, but beat his breast, saying, 'God, be merciful to me, a sinner!' I tell you, this man went down to his house justified, rather than the other. For everyone who exalts himself will be humbled, but the one who humbles himself will be exalted." (Luke 18:9–14)

Reflect: Have you prayed today?

NOVEMBER 14

We dream of having perfect relationships, but in reality, relationships are messy. God has mercy for that mess.

I have been married for many years. I have a wonderful wife. (I have hoped for years that she won't realize what a bad deal she got!) From a distance, you would conclude that we basically have a problem-free marriage. But our relationship is still messy. We typically spend Mondays together. We love these days and enjoy the ability to spend them with one another. But somewhere in the middle of one recent Monday, a misunderstanding erupted between us. We both got a bit defensive. The tension was obvious. Too much silence followed until we asked one another's forgiveness. "Too minor to worry about," you say, but these are the moments we live in.

I tell people all the time that we don't just live in big, important moments. We make only a few grand decisions in our entire lives. We live in little moments, so the character of our relationships is not set in three or four big moments but in ten thousand little moments of life.

The reality is that you and I have never had a relationship in our lives that hasn't disappointed us in some way. This is true because we all carry into each of our relationships something that is destructive to them. It's something that can make us impatient, self-serving, irritable, proud, critical, and demanding. This relationally destructive thing is sin. Second Corinthians 5:15 tells us that Jesus came so that "those who live might no longer live for themselves." Yes, it is true—the DNA of sin is selfishness. It reduces the field of our normal concern down to our wants, our needs, and our feelings. It makes us unwilling to overlook minor offenses. It makes us hold onto what we should have long since forgiven. The mess of relationships is the mess of sin.

Admitting that the mess of relationships is the mess of sin is a major step toward hope. It is the very "me-ism" of sin from which Jesus came to deliver us by his life, death, and resurrection. This means there is grace for every messy moment. You enter into that grace by admitting just how much you need it.

> Be kind to one another, tenderhearted, forgiving one another, as God in Christ forgave you. (Eph. 4:32)

Reflect: What do the little moments of your relationships look like? How are you dealing with the messiness that lives there?

NOVEMBER 15

Today you have hope, not because people like you or because situations are easy, but because God has placed his unshakable love on you.

Looking to the fallen world to give you hope to continue just doesn't work very well. Think about the address where you live:

- You live with fallen people who inevitably disappoint you in some way.
- You live in a broken world where corruption and injustice are commonplace.
- You face temptation somehow, some way, every day.
- Storms and pollution complicate your life.
- Satan prowls, doing his evil work.
- War and strife pit nation against nation.
- Partiality and prejudice divide us.

Sin creates constant instability and unpredictability around us. Why? Because our world simply does not function the way its Creator intended. There are times when life works well and seems easy. Yet there are many other times when sickness, a betrayal, an injustice, the corruption of a leader, a crime against you, or the death of a loved one makes life very hard.

It is so good to know that you don't have to frantically look for sturdy hope horizontally, where it just can't be found. No, you are freed from this search because powerful grace has connected you to hope. You see, hope is not a situation, a location, a feeling, or a relationship. Hope is a person, and his name is Jesus. He died so that you can know life, real life.

He is present with you so that you are guaranteed to have everything you need. He forgives you of all your sins. He empowers you to do much better. He never leaves you or turns his back on you. He always responds to you in tender compassion and righteous justice. He never mocks your weaknesses or throws your sin in your face. He never makes you feel guilty for needing his good gifts. Jesus is your hope as you live in a world where hope is a rare commodity. And remember, you are connected to him forever. This means there will be a day when you won't have to hope anymore because the paradise you have hoped for will be the eternal reality in which you live.

> Why are you cast down, O my soul,
> and why are you in turmoil within me?
> Hope in God; for I shall again praise him,
> my salvation and my God. (Ps. 42:5–6)

Reflect: Can you think of five ways that Jesus is different (better) than your friends?

NOVEMBER 16

If you're God's child, you are loved today even if, in your human relationships, you are completely alone.

So how do you respond, where do you run, what do you tell yourself when, in this broken world, you are left alone? In some way, it happens to us all. We're made to live in community with God and with one another. Yet we find ourselves alienated and alone. That means that aloneness cuts deep and hurts a lot. We were made to live in self-sacrificing love and peace with one another. Harsh words, disloyal acts, mean motives, and violent moments were never supposed to infect and destroy our relationships. But immediately after Adam and Eve disobeyed God, tension and accusation erupted between them. Then it became really bad really fast. Cain, the son of Adam and Eve, murdered his brother in a fit of sibling jealousy.

Since sin has infected our world, wrong still infects our relationships. This aloneness takes many forms:

- Friends turn their backs on friends.
- Husbands and wives divorce.
- Neighbors move away.
- Employees get fired.
- Children reject their parents.
- Churches divide.
- Friends and relatives lose contact.
- Death takes dear ones from us.

Yes, somewhere in your life, you will be left alone. But it is in this experience of aloneness that you must remember the gospel of Jesus Christ. As he faced death, Jesus reminded his disciples: "Behold, the hour is coming, indeed it has come, when you will be scattered, each to his own home, and will leave me alone. Yet I am not alone, for the Father is with me" (John 16:32). Yes, people and circumstances leave you alone. Yet it is impossible for one of God's children to be completely abandoned. Why? Because we have a Father in heaven who is always with us and who will not leave us, no matter what.

> For the LORD will not forsake his people;
> he will not abandon his heritage. (Ps. 94:14)

Reflect: Remind yourself today that, as God's child, no matter how many people have walked out of your life, true aloneness is a thing of your past.

NOVEMBER 17

Since sin is deeper than bad behavior, trying to do better isn't a solution. Only grace that changes the heart can rescue us.

Sometimes disappointment will lead you to self-reformation. And sometimes grief will lead you to heartfelt confession. I think that we often confuse the two. The first person believes in personal strength and the possibility of self-rescue. The second has given up on his own righteousness and cries out for the help of another. One gets up in the morning and tells himself that he'll do better today, but the other starts the day with a plea for grace. One targets a change in behavior, and the other confesses to a wandering heart.

These two are polar opposites. People who acknowledge that they've done wrong and then immediately lay out plans to do better unwittingly deny what the gospel of Jesus Christ says about them. They deny how real change takes place and where help can be found. What they have neglected is confession.

When you confess your sins to God, you don't just admit that you have sinned. No, you also confess that you have no power to deliver yourself from the sin you have just confessed. True confession always combines an admission of wrong with a plea for help. The heart then, encouraged by the forgiveness of Jesus, longs to live in a new, better way (repentance).

Without this, there is no godward confession, no recognition of desperate need for his rescue. Instead, it's an "I can save myself" way of dealing with sin, and it never results in lasting change. It never produces humility of heart. It never stimulates further worship and service of the Savior. It simply does not work. The whole story of the gospel in Scripture is a story of people who are desperately trapped in sin and have no hope except the rescuing grace of the Redeemer.

> And the son said to him, "Father, I have sinned against heaven and before you. I am no longer worthy to be called your son." But the father said to his servants, "Bring quickly the best robe, and put it on him, and put a ring on his hand, and shoes on his feet. And bring the fattened calf and kill it, and let us eat and celebrate. For this my son was dead, and is alive again; he was lost, and is found." And they began to celebrate. (Luke 15:21–24)

Reflect: When your sin is revealed today, which of the two pathways mentioned above will you take? Take a moment to pray and ask the Lord to prepare you for today by his grace.

NOVEMBER 18

God is holy, but we're not. Jesus became our righteousness so that we can stand before God, holy in him.

Sin left us in a desperate condition. Yet we tend to want to think that sin is not so sinful. Yet one little phrase in the passage below forcefully declares why our only hope is the righteousness of the Lord Jesus Christ. Here it is: "every intention of the thoughts of his heart was only evil continually" (Gen. 6:5).

God wasn't grieved because the people he had made occasionally did wrong things or once in a while had bad thoughts or motives. This would have been bad enough, but the effect of sin on people was total. It distorted everything people desired, thought, said, and did. It is humbling to grasp, but the result of sin is that there is nothing righteous about us. There is nothing that we can hold before God as a reason to quiet his grief and engender his acceptance. Nothing.

But this passage tells us more. It lays out the pattern by which God would deal with sin—judgment and redemption. He would wipe out people from the face of the earth in an act of righteous judgment. However, he would also redeem one man and his family, and renew his covenant promises to them. The redemption of Noah was to be a finger that pointed to another redemption, one following the same pattern. God would send his Son, the Lord Jesus Christ. Jesus would be righteous in every way, yet judgment would fall on him. He would experience the full weight of God's anger over sin, even to death, so that we wouldn't have to. His resurrection would guarantee us life. His righteousness is our only hope because sin renders us all deeply unrighteous.

> The LORD saw that the wickedness of man was great in the earth, and that every intention of the thoughts of his heart was only evil continually. And the LORD regretted that he had made man on the earth, and it grieved him to his heart. So the LORD said, "I will blot out man whom I have created from the face of the land, man and animals and creeping things and birds of the heavens, for I am sorry that I have made them." But Noah found favor in the eyes of the LORD. (Gen. 6:5–8)

Reflect: When you think about how sin affects the people closest to you, just like it affects you, how does that change your attitude toward them?

NOVEMBER 19

You must never let your enthusiasm for the gift replace your worship of and service for the giver.

God asks a stinging question of the children of Israel at the beginning of the book of Jeremiah. His question should cause all of us to search our own hearts. What we celebrate as a blessing from God can also become an idol that rules and directs our hearts. It happens too easily and so subtly. The genuine obedience that was the fruit of grace morphs into self-righteous pride that I parade before other people. The house that I once viewed as an undeserved gift of God becomes an idol that gobbles up the thoughts and desires of my heart. That relationship that I once saw as a blessing from God's good hand replaces him as the source of my identity.

I replaced God as the center of my spiritual hope. More than that, I also put my hope in things that are empty and cannot and will not ever deliver. I have replaced the fountain of living water with wells that are completely dry. What's scary is that I may not even know that I've done it. Here is the biblical principle—it's not that I desire only evil things. No, the struggle is more subtle than that. It's that good things can replace the giver of those things in my heart. A desire for a good thing becomes a bad thing when that desire becomes a ruling thing. It's not wrong to desire biblical knowledge, personal comfort, or the respect of others, but these things must not rule our hearts. Here is another reason for how much we need grace. We all still have wandering hearts. We are all still tempted to put the gift in the place that the giver alone should occupy.

> Has a nation changed its gods,
>   even though they are no gods?
> But my people have changed their glory
>   for that which does not profit.
> Be appalled, O heavens, at this;
>   be shocked, be utterly desolate,
>   declares the LORD,
> for my people have committed two evils:
> they have forsaken me,
>   the fountain of living waters,
> and hewed out cisterns for themselves,
>   broken cisterns that can hold no water. (Jer. 2:11–13)

Reflect: What good things have become too important to you?

NOVEMBER 20

No need to deny, rationalize, or otherwise excuse away evidence of your sin. God wouldn't have sent his Son if your sin were not real.

- "I think you misunderstood me."
- "I wasn't angry, just emphasizing an important point."
- "It wasn't lust; I'm just someone who enjoys beauty."
- "I wasn't feeling well."
- "I just have a strong personality."
- "I think you're being too judgmental."
- "No harm, no foul."
- "It wasn't a lie, just another way of looking at things."
- "Sometimes you have to choose the better of two evils."
- "I was planning on giving it back."
- "It wasn't gossip. I was just asking them to pray."
- "I had to defend myself."

The list could go on and on. We're all so skilled at convincing ourselves that our sin is less than sin. In the end, it's a scandal of self-righteous unbelief. Why? Because we're refusing to take God at his word when he says that we are in a bad condition apart from his grace. In contrast, all you really need to convince yourself of the depth and seriousness of your sin is the cross of Jesus Christ. Why would God go to the extent that he did to sacrifice his one and only Son, unless the moral tragedy of sin is real? It is so real that God's real Son had to come in a real birth, live a real life of perfection, die a real death, and walk away from a real tomb so that you could have real forgiveness and real hope in the face of your real sin. When sin is real, real grace is the only hope!

> Rejoice not over me, O my enemy;
>   when I fall, I shall rise;
> when I sit in darkness,
>   the LORD will be a light to me.
> I will bear the indignation of the LORD
>   because I have sinned against him,
> until he pleads my cause
>   and executes judgment for me.
> He will bring me out to the light;
>   I shall look upon his vindication. (Mic. 7:8–9)

Reflect: Which of the listed comments above hit closest to home? Why?

NOVEMBER 21

Corporate worship is designed to keep you humble by reminding you of your need and thankful by reminding you of God's gift.

To the unbelieving world, it's just a bunch of foolishness. *Sin? Who cares? Grace? Who needs it? God's moral law? I'll make up my own rules, thank you. Heaven? Hell? Nobody believes that stuff anymore. Right and wrong? Who knows? True and false? Who has the right to decide? Just be happy and don't hurt anyone else.* You and I live in a world that tells us it's all foolishness. That's why we need to be reminded again and again.

Isn't it good that God devised a plan so that we would regularly gather at church and remember what the world around us ignores or mocks? As we remember, our hearts fill once again with gratitude and are moved once again to worship. We leave with a fresh knowledge that grace isn't foolishness. Instead, it's the foundation of our hope. There's no way I could say it better than the apostle Paul:

> For the word of the cross is folly to those who are perishing, but to us who are being saved it is the power of God. For it is written,
>
> "I will destroy the wisdom of the wise,
> and the discernment of the discerning I will thwart. . . ."
>
> For since, in the wisdom of God, the world did not know God through wisdom, it pleased God through the folly of what we preach to save those who believe. . . .
>
> For consider your calling, brothers: not many of you were wise according to worldly standards, not many were powerful, not many were of noble birth. But God chose what is foolish in the world to shame the wise; God chose what is weak in the world to shame the strong; God chose what is low and despised in the world, even things that are not, to bring to nothing things that are, so that no human being might boast in the presence of God. (1 Cor. 1:18–19, 21, 26–29)

Reflect: How has some aspect of church recently strengthened your faith in God? Why?

NOVEMBER 22

How could you not have all that you need when your Savior has promised not to withhold any good thing from you?

Need—it's a very interesting word. It's one of the most frequently used words in human culture. It's also one of the words used most sloppily. We use it to refer to all the things we're convinced we just can't live without. Most of us think of ourselves as needy in some way, and most of us worry that our needs will never be met. And sometimes we wonder if God will really provide what we need. It's tempting to look over the fences at the lives of others and conclude that their needs have been met, which leads us to wonder why ours haven't. Yes, *need* is an interesting and troubling word.

The problem is that, if *need* means "essential for life," most of the things we load into our need category aren't really needs. They're actually desires that have become so important to us that we can't conceive of being happy without them. Here are three things that happen when you name something a need:

- If you are convinced that something is a need, you feel *entitled* to it. This means you are sure it's your right to have it.
- If you are convinced something is a need, you think that it's your right to *demand* it. You do not feel uncomfortable about asking for it again and again.
- If you are convinced that something is a need, you *judge* the love of God by his willingness to deliver it.

This is the scary pathway down which this concept of "need" leads you. If you believe God isn't delivering your "need," you begin to question his goodness. Here's what's so deadly about that. You don't tend to run for help to someone you doubt. So misnamed "needs" can devastate your communion with God. I am persuaded that many people struggle with doubts about the goodness and faithfulness of God for this very reason. Yet here's what's true: God has committed himself to meet every one of your needs. That's why it's so comforting to know that you have a heavenly Father who knows exactly what you need and is actively delivering.

> For the Lord God is a sun and shield;
> the Lord bestows favor and honor.
> No good thing does he withhold
> from those who walk uprightly. (Ps. 84:11)

Reflect: What is it that you think you need that might be causing you to question God?

NOVEMBER 23

Obedience is an act of thankful worship, not a fearful means of trying to gain favor with God.

There is simply nothing you can do to gain God's favor. You have to accept this and remember it. You will never be righteous enough for long enough to satisfy God's holy requirements. Your thoughts and desires will never be pure enough. Your words and actions will never be clean enough. The bar is too high for you and me to ever reach. There are no exceptions. We all live under the same weight of the law and the same inability of sin. We're all more naturally proud than humble. We all find envy more natural than contentment. We all covet what others have. We more naturally bend the truth than protect it. We condemn with our words rather than giving grace. We lay down evidence every day that we will never independently reach God's standard.

Here is your "that says it all" statement: "For by the works of the law no human being will be justified in his sight" (Rom. 3:20). And why is this true? It's true because "all have sinned and fall short of the glory of God" (Rom. 3:23). The language is all-inclusive. It leaves no room whatsoever for exceptions. It is devastatingly humbling news that all people need to accept. But this hard-to-accept news is the doorway not to gloomy self-hatred but to eternal hope and joy. It's only when you accept who you are that you begin to understand the need for God's gift. Let's put the bad news and the good news together, as Paul does in Romans 3. He writes, "all have sinned and fall short of the glory of God," but that is not the end of the story. He goes on to say that we "are justified by his grace as a gift, through the redemption that is in Christ Jesus, whom God put forward as a propitiation by his blood, to be received by faith" (3:24–25).

A propitiation is an atoning sacrifice. The sacrifice of Jesus satisfied the wrath of God. It reconciled God and everyone who places their faith in him. You don't need to obey to gain God's favor. Christ has gained God's favor on your behalf.

> For God has consigned all to disobedience, that he may have mercy on all. (Rom. 11:32)

Reflect: How do you most often measure how well you're doing? In what ways does this push you toward (or away) from God's grace?

NOVEMBER 24

It is dangerous to live without your heart being captured by awe of God because awe of God is quickly replaced by awe of you.

I love the visual arts, great music, and food of all kinds. A beautiful, well-executed painting leaves me in awe. A band's well-constructed album leaves me amazed and wanting more. The memory of a great restaurant leaves me wanting to recreate dishes and plan another visit. None of these things are wrong in themselves. God intended us to be in awe of his creation. Yet that awe cannot and should not be an end in itself.

At this point in my life, I wish I could say that every moment I enjoy some created thing prompts deeper worship of the Creator. Yet my life reveals that I give my heart to the worship of the thing that has been made rather than the one who made it. I spend when I don't really have a need, envy what someone else has, or eat when I'm not really that hungry.

I need to spend more time gazing upon the beauty of the Lord. I need awe of him to recapture, refocus, and redirect my heart again and again. And I need to remember that the war for the awe of my heart still wages inside me.[15]

It is a daily battle,
one that is free of
physical weapons,
political parties,
and national boundaries.
It is a battle that has been raging
since the garden
and will not stop until the war
is finally won.
This battle is not fought
between people,
it is fought
within people.
It is a much greater danger
to each of us
than war between nations
will ever be.
It is a battle of awe.

We were created to live in
a real,
heart-gripping,
agenda-setting,
behavior-forming
awe of God.
But other awes kidnap our hearts.
Awe of creation,
awe of other people,
and awe of ourselves
shove the awe of God
out of our hearts.
So we need grace
to see again,
to tremble again,
and to bow down again
at the feet of the one
who deserves our awe.

Let all the earth fear the LORD;
let all the inhabitants of the world stand in awe of him! (Ps. 33:8)

Reflect: What does your browsing history say about your heart and what holds you in awe? How does God's awe-inspiring grace draw you to him at this moment?

NOVEMBER 25

The question is not whether you will worship, but rather what you will worship—your glorious Creator or something he created.

I disappointed myself yesterday. I failed. Let me unpack this moment for you. As I was reading and enjoying my peace and comfort, my wife, Luella, interrupted me to ask me a question. Immediately I snapped at her that I was busy and didn't need to be disturbed. She walked away quietly, only to come back a few moments later to ask, "Can you explain why you responded to me as you did?" The minute she said this, I was crushed, filled with grief. I had done it again. I had been the husband that I don't want to be. I had treated a person that I say I love with irritation and impatience.

Now, why did this happen? It is humbling to admit, but my problem wasn't a relationship problem, it wasn't a schedule problem, and it wasn't just a misunderstanding. No, I did what I did because I still have a worship problem. You see, you and I can keep the second greatest commandment ("You shall love your neighbor as yourself," Mark 12:31) only if we keep the Great Commandment ("You shall love the Lord your God," 12:30). If God is not in his rightful place, guess who we insert in his place? In that regretful moment with Luella, I gave way to the most seductive, addictive, and deceptive of all idols—the idol of self.

The idolatry that defeats us is usually not the worship of formal religious idols. Instead, we turn to a whole catalog of God-replacements, the main one? The self. So I am in desperate need of a Redeemer who not only can protect me from external idols but also can rescue me again and again from me. The purpose of the cross of Christ was not only to forgive us for our idolatry, but also to reclaim us for the one thing that every human being was created to do—worship of God. This is the grace we all need.

And Jesus answered him, "It is written,

> 'You shall worship the Lord your God,
> and him only shall you serve.'" (Luke 4:8)

Reflect: Everything we do and say is rooted in worship. Think through how your recent choices flow from worship. The question is not *if* we worship but *what* we give our hearts to worship.

NOVEMBER 26

Can you tell the story of redemption in one sentence? Sin has driven us out of the garden, but grace drives us right into the Father's arms.

It is the most unexpected plot twist in human history. You wouldn't have predicted it. What am I talking about? God's announcement of how he would deal with sin.

Adam and Eve had it all: they were perfect people living in a perfect world and enjoying a perfect relationship with God. There was no tension between them and no separation between them and God. There was no pollution or disease, no injustice or corruption, and no hatred or violence. Life for Adam and Eve was complete in every way.

But it wasn't enough for them. They wanted more. So they ate the fruit that God had forbidden. It was an "in your face" act of self-centered rebellion. It was evil and ugly. God had every right to judge them, and he did. Yet shockingly, that judgment would not be the end of the story. If the story of Adam and Eve were a movie, we would expect God's judgment, and then fade to black. But the God who was writing the script is a God of glorious grace.

Grace leads the biblical story in a very different direction than we would anticipate. Immediately after the rebellion of Adam and Eve, God announced he was not only going to judge sin, he was going to defeat it forever. He said to the serpent: "I will put enmity between you and the woman, and between your offspring and her offspring; he shall bruise your head, and you shall bruise his heel" (Gen. 3:15). Who is the offspring that God was talking about? It is the son of Mary, the son of David, the Son of Man, the Son of God, Jesus of Nazareth, the Messiah. Where did this bruising take place? It took place on that hill called Golgotha, outside the walls of Jerusalem. On the cross, Jesus was bruised, but the enemy was defeated forever. Yes, this is a radical, unexpected story of astounding mercy granted to rebels, of amazing grace bestowed upon fools. It is the story that gets me up in the morning, and I hope it does the same for you.

> For God so loved the world, that he gave his only Son, that whoever believes in him should not perish but have eternal life. (John 3:16)

Reflect: How is God's grace writing the story of your life in ways you never expected?

NOVEMBER 27

Today you'll envy the blessings of another or you'll bask in the wonder of the amazing grace you have been given.

I wish I could say that I am always content. I wish I could say that I never complain. I wish I could say that I never want what others have. I wish I could say that I am better at counting my blessings than I am at assessing what I don't have. I wish my heart would finally be satisfied. These are all wishes because they are not yet completely true of me. Envy still lurks in my heart. One of the dark results of sin is that it still resides there.

Why does the Bible speak so strongly against envy? Here it is: when envy rules your heart, the love of God doesn't. Envy assumes that you deserve blessings that you don't deserve. When your heart is ruled by envy, the attitude of "I am blessed" gets replaced with the attitude of "I deserve." Envy is selfish to the core. Envy always puts you in the center of the world. It makes everything all about you. It causes you to examine life from the sole perspective of your wants, needs, and feelings.

Sadly, envy causes you to question the goodness, faithfulness, and wisdom of God. Envy accuses God of not knowing what he's doing or of not being faithful to what he's promised to do. When you are convinced that a blessing that another person has ought to belong to you, you don't just have a problem with that person, you have a problem with God. When you begin to question God's goodness, you quit going to him for help. Why? Because you don't seek the help of someone you've come to doubt.

Envy also assumes that you have a clearer understanding of what is best than God does. Furthermore, envy causes you to forget God's amazing rescuing, transforming, empowering, and delivering grace. You become so preoccupied with what you do not have that you no longer recognize or celebrate his loving commands or his enormous blessings of grace—blessings that we could never have earned, achieved, or deserved.

The only solution to envy is God's rescuing grace—grace that turns self-centered sinners into joyful and contented worshipers of God.

> A tranquil heart gives life to the flesh,
> but envy makes the bones rot. (Prov. 14:30)

Reflect: Where are you most easily tempted to envy—when you're online, around other people, or alone with your thoughts? Why?

NOVEMBER 28

The person next to you doesn't need the gospel more than you do; he just needs it differently than you do. All people sin and fall short.

We are all in the same desperate condition. None of us is better off than any other. None of us is more righteous. None of us is more deserving. None of us has anything to point to that would commend us to God. We all need to be rescued from the dark rebellion of our own hearts. We are sinners. And there's only one hope for us all—the amazing, forgiving, rescuing, transforming, and delivering grace of Jesus. The problem is that we often don't see it that way.

Part of this blindness is our tendency to be more irritated by the sin of the people next to us than our own. Because we are blind to our own sin and our eyes are open to theirs, we tend to see our neighbors as bigger sinners than we are. In this way, false spiritual comparisons put you in spiritual danger. Because they make you think that you're better off than you are and weaken your resolve to seek and celebrate redeeming grace. Instead, we must cry out for grace to deliver us from this tendency.

Yes, we all stand before God deserving of his anger. How grateful we ought to be that Christ bore our penalty so that we could bask in God's grace.

> What then? Are we Jews any better off? No, not at all. For we have already charged that all, both Jews and Greeks, are under sin, as it is written:
>
> "None is righteous, no, not one;
> no one understands;
> no one seeks for God.
> All have turned aside; together they have become worthless;
> no one does good,
> not even one." . . .
>
> But now the righteousness of God has been manifested apart from the law, although the Law and the Prophets bear witness to it—the righteousness of God through faith in Jesus Christ for all who believe. For there is no distinction: for all have sinned and fall short of the glory of God. (Rom. 3:9–12, 21–23)

Reflect: Ask a friend or family member to help you identify spiritual blind spots in your life: "Where do you think I don't see myself as God sees me?"

NOVEMBER 29

Your world is dramatically broken and you are still riddled with flaws, but Jesus is present, gracious, and faithful.

You and I have two big problems. First, we live in a dramatically broken world that does not function the way God intended. You will not live in this fallen world without suffering in some way. Perhaps it will be a situation of heart-breaking injustice. Maybe you'll be the victim of betrayal. Maybe a disease will weaken your body. But even if none of these things comes your way, you'll suffer the hardship of living in a world where things simply don't work in the way that God designed. But that's not all. You'll also be required to deal with the endless temptations that wait for you around every corner. What God says is ugly will be presented to you as beautiful. Seductive voices will whisper untruths in your ears. So if you don't take the fallenness of your world seriously, you'll live with unrealistic expectations and be easily tempted.

But we have a second and even more fundamental problem. It is far more troublesome than the evil that is outside us. It's the evil inside us. If you're God's child, the power of sin has been broken in God's justifying grace. Yet the presence of sin still remains. It's being progressively eradicated by sanctifying grace, but sin still lives inside you. Your trouble is never just around you, it is also in you. So if you embrace the theology of the heart that is in Scripture, you know that sin is first a heart problem before it is ever a behavior problem.

Never forget: it is only the evil inside us that ever hooks us to the evil outside us. Sin makes me susceptible to the lure of temptation. Temptation appeals to the sinful desires of my heart, to my selfishness and greed. Temptation targets my laziness and impatience. Temptation hooks my materialism and discontent.

But as the verses below remind us, Jesus is present, in his grace, to help us overcome both of these problems.

> As for you, O Lord, you will not restrain
> your mercy from me;
> your steadfast love and your faithfulness will
> ever preserve me!
> For evils have encompassed me
> beyond number;
> my iniquities have overtaken me,
> and I cannot see;
> they are more than the hairs of my head;
> my heart fails me. (Ps. 40:11–12)

Reflect: When you make excuses for your sinful "mistakes," what part of reality does that deny? How does God's grace for sin give you hope today?

NOVEMBER 30

You were created to be dependent. God welcomes your dependency with his grace, so why would you want to go it on your own?

Wrapped into the devious temptation of the serpent in the garden were two foundational lies. These lies have been believed by every person who has ever lived, ever since childhood.

The first lie is the lie of *independence*. This lie tells you that your life belongs to you, and that you have the right to live your life as you please. It is an attractive and seductive lie. Believing this lie makes a little child protest when he's told to go to bed or to eat his peas. However, the doctrine of creation destroys the lie of independence. I am a painter; it's a hobby I love. Once I have composed, painted, and completed a painting, it belongs to me. Why? Because I created it. So since God created you and me, we belong to him. We don't own our mentality, our spirituality, our emotionality, our psychology, our personality, or our physicality. We do not have a natural right to do with our physical and spiritual selves whatever we desire to do. Independence is a life-destroying lie.

The second lie is the lie of *self-sufficiency*. This lie tells you that you have everything within yourself to be what you're supposed to be and to do what you're supposed to do. This lie explains why a little child struggling to tie his shoelaces will slap away his mom's hand when she tries to help, even though he has no idea how to make a bow. However, the doctrine of creation destroys this lie as well. The flower you plant in your garden is not self-sufficient. If it is not weeded and not watered, it will not grow. Immediately after creating Adam and Eve, God began to talk to them because he knew they had no capacity to figure life out on their own. The lie of self-sufficiency is also life-destroying because it causes us to resist the help of our Creator—the very help we were designed to need and he is willing to give. Going it on your own simply does not work. The self-made man is always poorly made. What grace that God has shown us how much we need grace!

> Abide in me, and I in you. As the branch cannot bear fruit by itself, unless it abides in the vine, neither can you, unless you abide in me. (John 15:4)

Reflect: Which of these two lies do you most often believe? Where specifically do you see this happening in your life? Why?

DECEMBER 1

You have one place of hope, security, and rest. It is found in these words: "God is love."

It is something every human being does. It separates us from the rest of creation. It causes us much anxiety and much joy. It shapes the decisions that we make. It calms our fears or leaves us scared and feeling alone. It exposes the fact that we are deeply spiritual beings. It is one of our most foundational quests. As different as we are one from another, in this way we are all the same. We all are looking for something in which to place our hope. We're all in search of security.

I don't know if you've thought about this, but there are only two places to look for hope. You can search for it horizontally. This happens when you think that something in creation will give you the security, peace, and inner sense of well-being that you seek. Or you can seek it vertically. This happens as you entrust your life into the loving hands of your Creator.

People put their hope in creation all the time. They seek satisfaction of heart in the love of other human beings or in the success of their careers. They think their hearts will be satisfied by certain achievements or possessions. But none of these things has the power to satisfy your heart. They are all meant to point you to the one place where your heart will find secure rest. You and I need to face this reality—creation will never be our savior!

So where is hope to be found, hope that will never disappoint or shame you? It really is found in three of the most glorious words ever penned in human language. These words can end your frantic search and give your weary heart rest: "God is love" (1 John 4:16). Because he is love and because he has placed his love on you, you have security and hope, even in those scary moments when it feels as if you have neither. The one who is love sent his Son of love to be a sacrifice of love so you and I could be rescued by his love and rest in that love forever and ever.

Anyone who does not love does not know God, because God is love. (1 John 4:8)

Reflect: Analyze your anxiety. In what situations do you find yourself most restless? At those times, how might you be putting your hope in creation?

DECEMBER 2

If you are not fully formed into the image of Jesus, your Redeemer is neither satisfied nor finished, and neither should you be.

We don't talk about it much. It's not the typical way we think about our Redeemer. Yet it is an observation that not only gives you hope, but defines for you what your Lord is doing right here, right now. Here it is—you serve a dissatisfied Redeemer. You ought to be very thankful that your Lord isn't easily satisfied. Jesus does not walk away from what he has begun until it is perfectly finished. He does not grow bored, tired, discouraged, or distracted. He isn't irritated by how long his work is taking. He never wishes that he hadn't begun in the first place. He never tries to rush what takes time. He never contemplates calling it all off.

Your Redeemer is zealous for one goal—the final renewal of all things. Ultimate salvation from sin and all it has broken is his constant pursuit. He will not be satisfied until the last enemy is under his feet and the final kingdom has come. Yes, there is great hope for you in the dissatisfaction of your Redeemer.

Our problem is that we are all too easily satisfied. We're satisfied with a little bit of Bible knowledge, occasional moments of service, and a measure of personal spiritual growth. Sadly, we're satisfied with being a little bit better, when God's goal is that we be completely remolded into his image. In fact, it's even worse than that: we actually begin to think that we can find our satisfaction in this created world. So while our Redeemer, in glorious dissatisfaction, still works to redeem us from us, we are out chasing other lovers. We begin to believe that they can do for us what he alone can do. We begin to invest our time, energy, and hope in things that can never deliver.

Hope is not found in the places where our hearts look for satisfaction, but in the dissatisfaction of our Redeemer. He will complete his work even when we don't care that he does.

> From of old no one has heard
>   or perceived by the ear,
> no eye has seen a God besides you,
>   who acts for those who wait for him. (Isa. 64:4)

Reflect: How is Jesus's dissatisfaction different than your own natural dissatisfaction with the shortcomings of situations or people around you?

DECEMBER 3

Corporate worship is a regular, gracious reminder that it's not about you. You've been born into a life that is a celebration of another.

Corporate worship is a celebration that serves as a very important reminder for us all. We gather together to celebrate the One who created, controls, and sits at the center of all things. Every biblical worship service is guided and shaped by the words of Romans 11:33–36, and the final verse says it all.

This verse is not only a prescription for every worship service, but also a powerful statement about what life is all about. Life is not about us. It is not about our wants, our needs, or our feelings. It is not about our comfort, pleasure, and ease. It's not about how many of our dreams we actually get to experience. It's not about our successes and achievements. It's not about how well our relationships are working.

It's not wrong to desire personal happiness, peace, a healthy body, and healthy relationships. The issue is this—these things must not rule our hearts. Why? Because when they do, they place us at the center of our world. It is sad that many people, even professing Christians, live in a way that is God-forgetting and God-replacing. As a result, we reduce God to little more than the delivery system for our catalog of self-oriented dreams.

So corporate worship calls us back, again and again, to remember and to celebrate. It calls us to remember that all that exists, including us, is from God. Everything exists through him and points to him. He is the beginning, the center, and the end of all things. It is only by grace that we celebrate a lordship other than our own. Corporate worship points us to our need for and the availability of that grace.

> Oh, the depth of the riches and wisdom and knowledge of God! How unsearchable are his judgments and how inscrutable his ways!
>
> "For who has known the mind of the Lord,
>   or who has been his counselor?"
> "Or who has given a gift to him
>   that he might be repaid?"
>
> For from him and through him and to him are all things. To him be glory forever. Amen. (Rom. 11:33–36)

Reflect: What do you enjoy about life right now? Take a few minutes to give God praise and worship for creating and providing such blessings.

DECEMBER 4

You were designed for it. You have missed the point without it. What is it? Living every day for the glory of the Father.

I have written about it much, and I will continue to write about it as long as I am able. It is an important and practical concern that touches everything that we think, desire, say, and do. It reaches to the deepest levels of human motivation. It sits at the epicenter of our spiritual struggles. It is at the heart of why we were created. It expresses God's will for everyone who has ever taken a breath. And it is the reason Jesus had to come.

Life is all about glory. Sin is all about glory. Grace is all about glory. Spirituality is all about glory. Heaven and hell are all about glory. Submission and rebellion are all about glory. Love and hatred are all about glory. Contentment and craving are both motivated by glory. Every word you speak and every action you take is directed by glory. Glory causes you to want some things and despise others. Glory makes you arrogant and causes you to be humble. Glory makes your heart glad or causes it to be eaten with envy. Glory makes you constantly thankful for a Savior or causes you to forget he exists.

We human beings were hardwired for glory for at least two reasons. First, God intended us to be able to take in all the glories of creation. Second, God intended those glories to point us to the one glory that is truly glorious and alone able to satisfy our hearts: the glory of God. This means that we are always living in pursuit of some kind of glory. Either our hearts have been captured by the temporary glories of the created world or by grace they have been captured by the eternally satisfying glory of God. We are always living for some kind of glory.

Jesus came to liberate us from our addiction to glories that will never satisfy our hearts. He willingly died so that we would find our satisfaction in and live for the glory of God. Jesus not only revealed God's glory on earth; he died so that that glory would be the final resting place of our hearts.

> So, whether you eat or drink, or whatever you do, do all to the glory of God. (1 Cor. 10:31)

Reflect: What truths about God put your heart in a state of awe? Who can you tell about that today?

DECEMBER 5

You can't live to meet all your needs and live to serve Christ at the same time. Live as his disciple; he's got your true needs covered.

We place many things in our "I just can't live without" category. Yet many of them are not things we actually require for life. These things may be wonderful to enjoy and sweet blessings from a loving Father. However, they are not needs and must not be named as such. When we call them needs, we tell ourselves that we have to have them. We're saying that we cannot live without them and that we have a right to demand them. So we end up evaluating the love of God on the basis of how many "needs" he has delivered. As we do this, we become so focused and anxious about our "needs," that we have little personal time left for the larger pursuits of the kingdom of God.

Instead, Philippians 4 reminds us we can quit worrying about our catalog of "I must haves." By grace, you are freed to give yourself to the work of God's kingdom when

- you are convinced that God will give you the strength you need to face whatever he has ordained you to face ("I can do all things through him who strengthens me," 4:13), and
- you really do believe that God is actively committed to meeting every one of your true needs ("And my God will supply every need of yours according to his riches in glory in Christ Jesus," 4:19).

When grace causes your heart to rest in these truths, you no longer live a need-obsessed life. You are then free to give yourself to the worship and service of God.

> Not that I am speaking of being in need, for I have learned in whatever situation I am to be content. I know how to be brought low, and I know how to abound. In any and every circumstance, I have learned the secret of facing plenty and hunger, abundance and need. I can do all things through him who strengthens me. Yet it was kind of you to share my trouble. . . . And my God will supply every need of yours according to his riches in glory in Christ Jesus. To our God and Father be glory forever and ever. Amen. (Phil. 4:11–14, 19–20)

Reflect: What is in your "I just can't live without" category? Will you surrender that to God and trust him for his grace?

DECEMBER 6

Every day you need it. You simply can't live without it. What is it? The heart-convicting ministry of the Holy Spirit.

I love the hymn "Come, Thou Fount of Every Blessing," especially the honesty of its third verse:

> O to grace how great a debtor
> daily I'm constrained to be!
> Let thy goodness, like a fetter,
> bind my wandering heart to thee.
> Prone to wander, Lord, I feel it,
> prone to leave the God I love;
> here's my heart, O take and seal it,
> seal it for thy courts above.[16]

Here is an honest, excuse-free expression of the spiritual struggle we experience in everyday life. It's what causes us to lose our way. It's what leads us to live in a way that contradicts what we say we believe. It's what makes us susceptible to temptation. We would like to think that our hearts are perfectly faithful and true, but they are not. We would like to think that nothing could lure us away from our loyalty to our Lord. We would like to think that our moral commitments are unshakable. We would like to think that what God says is wrong would not be attractive to us. But the problem is that we still have fickle hearts.

Our biggest problem is not that we live with flawed people who bring trouble our way. Our great difficulty is not that we live in a fallen world filled with temptation. The big issue for us is not that we live in a world where we face difficulty, suffering, and grief. No, our big difficulty is that sin still resides in our hearts. The less-than-perfect people, the temptations around us, and the broken world in which we live are problems for us. Why? Because we have this problem in our hearts. So what we need most is not a change of location or relationship but a fundamental rescue of heart. In his grace, that is exactly what God, through the person of the Holy Spirit, provides for us.

> And he said, "What comes out of a person is what defiles him. For from within, out of the heart of man, come evil thoughts, sexual immorality, theft, murder, adultery, coveting, wickedness, deceit, sensuality, envy, slander, pride, foolishness. All these evil things come from within, and they defile a person." (Mark 7:20–23)

Reflect: It's only ever the sin inside us that hooks us to the sin outside of us.

DECEMBER 7

No one knows you more deeply and fully than your Savior, so no one offers you help formfitted for your deepest needs like he does.

The passage below is one of the most comforting parts of the New Testament. Hebrews 4:14–16 calls us to live with hope, encouragement, courage, and confidence. Why? Because you have a high priest who is both exalted at the Father's throne and also sympathetic to your weaknesses. But why is he so understanding? Because he hears and answers you knowing exactly what you are going through. He came to earth and faced the full range of the sufferings and temptations that we face. He knows what it is like to be homeless, hungry, and rejected. He is acquainted with disease and physical pain. He knows the power of accusation and injustice. He faced the siren voice of temptation. He knows what it is like to be forsaken by loved ones. He understands suffering and death. He stared evil in the face. He knows us and has a firsthand understanding of what we deal with day in and day out.

The word translated as "weaknesses" in this passage is profound. It's almost untranslatable. It is used in many ways. It's probably best understood as "the human condition." Our high priest Jesus understands what it is like to be a human being in this fallen world because, in an act of shocking, condescending love, he took on human flesh and lived with us as a man. Now, as the resurrected and ascended man, he sits next to the Father as our high priest. This means that our struggles and prayers are not greeted with harshness, condemnation, or impatience but with understanding and sympathy.

So we can be confident that he hears us with the sympathy of shared experience. Because he does, he will provide for us exactly what we need. Now, that's amazing grace!

> Since then we have a great high priest who has passed through the heavens, Jesus, the Son of God, let us hold fast our confession. For we do not have a high priest who is unable to sympathize with our weaknesses, but one who in every respect has been tempted as we are, yet without sin. Let us then with confidence draw near to the throne of grace, that we may receive mercy and find grace to help in time of need. (Heb. 4:14–16)

Reflect: How do you tend to respond to the weaknesses you see in the people you interact with?

DECEMBER 8

If Christ is your life, you are free from the desperate quest to find life in situations, locations, and relationships.

It is a wonderful freedom that we just don't think about enough. It liberates you from the stress, fear, and anxiety that so many people live with every day. It is a sweet gift of grace that you could have never found on your own. You never could have earned or achieved it.

You have been given Christ, and in being given Christ, you have been given life. You don't need to search for meaning and purpose. You don't need to search for identity or the inner sense of well-being that every person wants. You don't have to wonder if you'll ever be loved. You don't have to worry that your life and work will result in nothing. You don't have to worry about your future. You don't have to worry about whether your wrongs will be forgiven and your weaknesses greeted with patience and grace. You don't have to worry because you have a Savior who has invaded your life with his grace and has made you the place where he dwells.

So you have been freed from the endless quest that consumes so many people. They hope their marriages will give them the happiness they have not yet found. They look to their jobs to give them identity. They look to people and possessions to give them peace. They don't know it, but they are asking the situations, locations, and relationships of everyday life to be their saviors. Sadly, they're drinking from wells that are dry, and they're eating bread that will never satisfy. The situations, locations, and relationships of daily life are wonderful to enjoy. Yet we must understand that they will never, ever satisfy our hearts. For that, we have been given a true Savior, the Lord Jesus Christ.

So instead of wasting time on that endless quest for life, you have been invited to enter into God's rest for the rest of your life. Rest in your identity as his child. Rest in his eternal love. Rest in his powerful grace. Rest in his constant presence and faithful provision. Rest in his patience and forgiveness. Rest.

> So then, there remains a Sabbath rest for the people of God, for whoever has entered God's rest has also rested from his works as God did from his. (Heb. 4:9–10)

Reflect: What do your recent Google searches reveal about what you're searching for in life?

DECEMBER 9

God harnessed the forces of nature and controlled the events of history to redeem you. Will he abandon you now in your moment of need?

The Bible isn't a catalog of interesting characters. It isn't a manual of theology. It isn't a book of helpful wisdom principles. One story, with one hero, forms the cord that holds the whole Bible together. The Bible is essentially the story of redemption. This grand redemptive story, with God's essential explanatory notes, is the main content of the word of God.

The Bible displays the extent to which God has gone in order to provide salvation for us. He really controlled every event in human history—and harnessed the forces of nature—so that at a certain time his Son would come and live, suffer, die, and rise again to provide salvation for us. This stunning story provides a way to understand everything you face in your life in this broken world.

If God went to such lengths as to control the events of the world and to sacrifice his one and only Son, would it make any sense at all for him to abandon you? Would it make any sense for him to turn his back on you now? Would it make any sense for him to ignore you in your hour of need? Would you spend a great amount of personal effort and sacrifice to secure something of value and then not work to keep, maintain, and protect it?

You are precious in God's sight. So don't let any evil enemy whisper lies into your ear. Don't let him tell you that you are alone, that you're left to your own resources, or that God doesn't hear or care. Don't let yourself doubt God's presence and his goodness. Don't let yourself wonder if you'll make it through. God unleashed his power to make you his own. He will continue to unleash his power to keep and protect you until you are with him forever in that place where you will need his protection no more because the final enemy will be under his feet.

> He who did not spare his own Son but gave him up for us all, how will he not also with him graciously give us all things? (Rom. 8:32)

Reflect: Take a few minutes to write out and apply the logic of these verses in your words. "Because God paid the greatest price—giving his own Son—then he will also _____."

DECEMBER 10

It is a grace to be willing to listen to and consider criticism. It takes grace to quiet the mind and settle the heart to hear.

We are not naturally open to criticism. Most of us don't like to be confronted. It is natural for us to rise to our own defenses when we are questioned. It is natural for us to be more focused on the sin of others than our own. It is natural for us to see our wrongs as less than wrong. It is natural for us to swindle ourselves into believing that we are far more righteous than we really are. For sinners, self-righteousness is more natural than humility.

In short, it is more natural for us to have hard hearts that are resistant to change than hearts that are open, humble, and crying out for change. So if you are open to loving confrontation, if you are ready to admit your sin and ask for forgiveness, if you are thankful for those who have loved you enough to help you see what you would not see on your own, then you know that you have been visited by the grace of Jesus. Why? Because none of these attitudes are natural for us apart from divine intervention.

It takes powerful redeeming grace to remove the hearts of stone from us and replace them with hearts of flesh. That's the Bible's way to talk about hearts that are sensitive to sin, sensitive to the grace of conviction, sensitive to the need for change, and resting in the forgiveness that's found only in Jesus. It takes grace to give us the courage to look at ourselves in the searching mirror of Scripture. It takes grace for us to let go of excuses, rationalizations, and blame-shifting. It takes grace for us to be able to stand as sinners before a holy God and admit that there are ways in which we are still rebels against his lordship and his commands.

Confession is not intuitive for sinners. Humility is not our natural first response. So if you are willing to say, "God, show me my heart," and willing to speak these words, "Please forgive me," then you know that you have been showered with amazing grace. And this grace has already changed your heart and promises more change to come.

The sacrifices of God are a broken spirit;
a broken and contrite heart, O God, you will not despise. (Ps. 51:17)

Reflect: How can you prepare, now, for times later today when you may likely receive advice or criticism?

DECEMBER 11

If obedience is a personal act of worship, then disobedience is personal too. Every sin is a violation of a relationship—a sin against God.

We often misunderstand what sin is about. When we do this, we minimize how horrible it really is. If you unwittingly devalue destructive sin, you will also devalue rescuing grace.

The first way we devalue sin is to think that sin is about behavior and behavior alone. But that is not what the Bible teaches. Sin is first and foremost a matter of the heart (see Jesus's teaching in the Sermon on the Mount, Matthew 5–7). Since you live out of the heart (see Luke 6:43–45), sin always originates there. Sin is always a matter of the thoughts, desires, motives, and choices of the heart. Sin is a matter of the heart that expresses itself in the behavior of the body. This is precisely why we need rescuing grace. We can run from a certain situation, location, or relationship. Yet we have no ability whatsoever to escape our hearts. That requires rescuing grace.

Second, we tend to think of sin as the breaking of a set of abstract rules. But sin is much more than that. Sin is the breaking of a relationship that results in breaking God's rules. Every sin is an assault on God's rightful place. Every sin is a betrayal of him. Every sin denies his authority. Every sin replaces him with something else. Every sin quests for his power and his glory. Every sin is after his throne.

Sin is personal and relational, even if you are not conscious of it at the moment when you are sinning. That is why it is right for David, who has just committed adultery and murder, to say, "Against you, you only, have I sinned and done what is evil in your sight" (Ps. 51:4). David is not minimizing the horrible wrongs he did against Bathsheba, Uriah, and the people of Israel. He is confessing the core of what sin is about. Sin questions God's goodness, wisdom, faithfulness, and love. Sin challenges God's personal rule. Sin is personal, and that is why Jesus suffered and died so that you and I would receive forgiving grace.

> David said to Nathan, "I have sinned against the LORD." And Nathan said to David, "The LORD also has put away your sin; you shall not die. (2 Sam. 12:13)

Reflect: After you sin, do you find yourself more concerned with God or with the consequences of your sin?

DECEMBER 12

No matter how people treat you today, if you're God's child, you're being loved right now by an ever-present, ever-loving Redeemer.

Here's something incredibly encouraging to think about as we make our way through a world that is marked by hatred, violence, injustice, racism, betrayal, disloyalty, selfishness, abuse, and many other forms of relational sin and brokenness. It's something we need to remember in those moments when we've been sinned against in some way. Read carefully what I am going to write next: Jesus was willing to be despised. He was willing to endure rejection. He was willing to face hatred and violence. He was even willing to have the Father turn his back on him. Why was he willing to do all this? He did it willingly so that, as his children, you and I would be able to live knowing that we are perfectly and eternally loved by him. He endured rejection so that we, no matter what we face, would know God's accepting love forever and ever and ever. How amazing is this grace!

> Who has believed what he has heard from us?
>   And to whom has the arm of the Lord been revealed?
> For he grew up before him like a young plant,
>   and like a root out of dry ground;
> he had no form or majesty that we should look at him,
>   and no beauty that we should desire him.
> He was despised and rejected by men,
>   a man of sorrows and acquainted with grief;
> and as one from whom men hide their faces
>   he was despised, and we esteemed him not.
>
> Surely he has borne our griefs
>   and carried our sorrows;
> yet we esteemed him stricken,
>   smitten by God, and afflicted. (Isa. 53:1–4)

Reflect: How do you tend to handle rejection? What does that response look like in your life? Why?

DECEMBER 13

Don't buy the false gospel of self-reliance. If you could make it without help, Jesus would not have needed to come.

It is a seductive lie. It's told again and again. There is nothing new in its message. It was told first in the garden of Eden and hasn't ceased being told since. It is told in many forms:

- "No one knows you better than you know yourself."
- "You really don't need the ministry of others in your life."
- "You used to struggle with sin but not anymore."
- "Since you know the Bible so well, you're probably okay."
- "Look at your track record; you've come a long way."
- "Your little sins aren't really that sinful."

The voices of self-reliance are so deceptive. In some way, they greet you every day, tempting you to rely on yourself and not on God. It sounds attractive to us all because we don't like to think of ourselves as weak and needy. We don't like to think of ourselves as dependent or foolish. We like the story of the self-made man; you know, the person who made it on his own with no one to thank but himself.

But the message of the gospel is devastatingly humbling. It tells me that I am in a hopeless, impossible, and irreversible state apart from divine intervention. Even Adam and Eve could not make it on their own. Even though they were perfect people living in a perfect world and in a perfect relationship with God, they did not have the ability to go it on their own. So immediately after creating them, God began talking to them. He knew they would not figure life out on their own. They were dependent on the words of God in order to make proper sense out of life. They needed God's counsel and his help. Now, that was the state of people before sin entered the world. How much more is it true of us!

Self-reliance is a lie that leads you nowhere good. You do not have what you need inside yourself to live as you were created to live. So a God of tender grace comes to you in the person of his Son. He offers you everything you need for life and godliness. In grace, he is ever with you because he knows you'll never make it on your own.

> Not that we are sufficient in ourselves to claim anything as coming from us, but our sufficiency is from God. (2 Cor. 3:5)

Reflect: Where are you most tempted to think you've got things under control? Where do you tend to feel most inadequate? What makes the difference?

DECEMBER 14

What does it mean to be an ambassador of the King? It means reflecting his message, his methods, and his character wherever he's placed us.

It really is a very different way of looking at life. It's a very different guide for deciding who you are and how you should act, react, and respond. It is a radical way of living, quite different from the common cultural worldview that has you at the very center. This view says that life is all about your pursuit of happiness. When someone or something makes you unhappy, it says that the world is not operating the way it is supposed to operate.

But the Bible presents a polar opposite worldview, one that forms the identity and lifestyle of every believer. Scripture asserts that you were bought with a price (the life and death of Jesus), so you don't belong to you anymore (actually, because of creation, you never did belong to you).

God has a purpose for you. It is that you would live as one of his representatives; that is, that you would live in a way that represents your Savior King. This means you represent his *message*, his *methods*, and his *character*. Representing the King's message means that you look at every situation and relationship in life through the lens of the truth of Scripture. Representing his methods means that, for the people and world around you, you seek to be a tool of the kind of change he intends. And representing his character simply means asking yourself again and again, "What of the person, work, and character of the Lord Jesus Christ does this person need to see in the situation right now?"

In summary, God has called each of us to be an *ambassador*. God's grace has rescued you, but there's more. His grace has included you in much bigger and more beautiful purposes for your life than you would have ever chosen on your own.

> But he who is joined to the Lord becomes one spirit with him. Flee from sexual immorality. Every other sin a person commits is outside the body, but the sexually immoral person sins against his own body. Or do you not know that your body is a temple of the Holy Spirit within you, whom you have from God? You are not your own, for you were bought with a price. So glorify God in your body. (1 Cor. 6:17–20)

Reflect: Take extra time today to look at this passage from 1 Corinthians 6. How does it apply today's truth to the physical human body?

DECEMBER 15

As God's child, live today with the surety, hope, and courage that come from knowing that your standing before God is secure.

You want to be sure. You want to be secure. You want to have hope. You want to live with courage. You don't want to be weakened by fear, paralyzed by doubt, or filled with the anxiety of wondering what's next. You want to know that your life means something. You want to know that you're not alone. You don't want to feel unprepared, weak, or unable. You don't ever want to think that it's all been for naught. Yes, you want to stand on the firm foundation of security. And that means you will look to something to give it to you.

The fact of the matter is that in a world where things break, die, get corrupted, or otherwise fade away, security is found only vertically. If you're God's child, your standing before him is secure, and because it is, you have security in life right here, right now; in death; and in eternity.

- You have the security of knowing that you don't have to hide or pretend because every one of your sins and weaknesses has been covered by Jesus's blood.
- You don't have to worry that you'll be left alone because your Savior has made you the place where he dwells.
- You don't have to live with regret because all your past sins have been forgiven by his grace.
- You don't have to search for identity, meaning, or purpose because he has made you his child and called you to his purpose.
- You don't have to worry about the future because all the mysteries of what is to come are held in his sovereign hands.
- You don't have to fear trouble, difficulty, or suffering because your Savior uses all these things for your good and his glory.
- You don't have to hope that your labors are worth something because the work you do in his name is never in vain.
- You don't have to fear being punished because your Savior took your punishment and satisfied God's anger.

> We have this as a sure and steadfast anchor of the soul, a hope that enters into the inner place behind the curtain. (Heb. 6:19)

Reflect: You stand before God sure and secure. And because you do, your life right now is blessed with every kind of security you could ever want. Thank and praise him!

DECEMBER 16

It's futile to try to establish your own sovereignty. People don't want you as their king, and God won't forsake his holy throne.

If you really do believe that your world is not out of control or driven by chance, but rather that it is under the careful control of God Almighty, then you will live with peace of heart, confidence, and hope. Think of how different life looks when you really do believe that there is no situation, location, or relationship that isn't ruled by King Jesus.

It is encouraging to know that our world is not out of control, no matter how chaotic and confusing it may seem, but under the wise and careful control of the Lord almighty. It is sweet to know that the one who rules everything all of the time is our Father by grace. It is comforting to know that because he rules, nothing can stop the march of his life-producing, sin-defeating grace. It lifts burdens off your shoulders to remember that your sanity is not found in figuring everything out, but in trusting the one who has it all figured out from before origins to beyond destiny. It's spiritually healthy to wake up every morning and worship God as sovereign.[17]

I often give way to the fantasy
that I have the
wisdom and power
to control
people,
places,
and things in my life
that seem to be out of control.
I insert myself in
the center
and make it all about me.
But I don't need to control
because you have
every situation,
every location,
and every person
under your wise control.
You rule over all things
for my sake
and for your glory.
So once again you call me
to surrender control
and rest
in your sovereign care.

Daniel answered and said:

> "Blessed be the name of God forever and ever,
> to whom belong wisdom and might." (Dan. 2:20)

Reflect: In both hard times and easy times, it is glorious to know that God rules and we don't. How does this truth strengthen your heart today?

DECEMBER 17

Every time you desire to do and choose to do what is right in God's eyes, you celebrate the grace that is yours in Christ Jesus.

It's hard to admit, but doing what is right isn't natural for us. Sin turns us all into self-appointed sovereigns over our own little kingdoms. Sin makes us all self-absorbed and self-focused. Sin seduces us into thinking we are somehow, some way smarter than God. Sin makes us all want to write our own rules. Sin makes us resistant to criticism and change. Sin makes our eyes and our hearts wander. Sin causes us to crave material things more than spiritual provision. All of this means that sin causes us to step over God's wise boundaries in thought, desire, word, and action again and again. This is what's natural for a sinner.

So when you have a hunger to know what is right in God's eyes, when you care about his glory, when you willingly submit to his will, when you forsake your plan for his plan, and when you find joy in surrendering to his lordship, you know that you have been visited by rescuing grace. In the passage below, notice how Paul talks about our submission to the will of the Father.

The passage is a call to a faith-filled life of submission and obedience. It is a call to be serious about the life that grace has made possible for you. It is a call to follow the example of the Lord Jesus Christ. But then Paul reminds you that if you follow, if you obey, and if you do what is right in the eyes of your Savior, you can take no credit whatsoever. This is because your right desires and your right actions exist only because of his ever-active grace. Paul is saying that we do the right that we do because grace is at that moment rescuing us from ourselves.

Every moment of our obedience is an evidence of and a celebration of grace. We live in God's sight not in our own strength but only by grace.

> Therefore, my beloved, as you have always obeyed, so now, not only as in my presence but much more in my absence, work out your own salvation with fear and trembling, for it is God who works in you, both to will and to work for his good pleasure. (Phil. 2:12–13)

Reflect: Where do you feel most in need of God's grace today? Good news—his grace is completely sufficient for you right now!

DECEMBER 18

Don't be discouraged as you face your problems. You have more than strength and wisdom. You have the empowering grace of Jesus.

The passage below contains some of Jesus's final words to his disciples before facing his death on the cross. Here's what this passage tells you:

- *In your troubles, you don't have to act as though things are okay when they're not okay.* Jesus welcomes us to honesty. Biblical faith never asks us to deny the harsh realities of life in this fallen world. God invites our cries and welcomes us to run to him in our grief. This passage is a compassionate and honest warning about the inescapable troubles that we all face.
- *In your troubles, you need to remember that what you're experiencing is part of God's plan.* Jesus is telling his disciples that it is the plan of God to keep them in a world that is terribly broken and doesn't function in the way that God intended. You and I should never think that the troubles that we face indicate that God's plan and his promises have failed. No, this present suffering exists under his rule and according to his wise and loving plan.
- *In your troubles, you are invited to remember that you are never alone.* Here Jesus speaks personally. Even when forsaken by his followers, he says it is impossible for him to be alone. How? Because his Father is with him. In the same way, as God's children, you and I are never left alone in our troublesome circumstances. God, in power, wisdom, and grace, is always with us. This means that in times of trouble, we are never left with the personal resources of our own power.
- *In your troubles, you need to know that your troubles may overcome you, but they cannot overcome the Savior who protects and keeps you.* You may be discouraged and confused in your troubles, but your Lord never is. This means your troubles don't determine your destiny; he does!

> Behold, the hour is coming, indeed it has come, when you will be scattered, each to his own home, and will leave me alone. Yet I am not alone, for the Father is with me. I have said these things to you, that in me you may have peace. In the world you will have tribulation. But take heart; I have overcome the world. (John 16:32–33)

Reflect: Which truth from today's devotional was most encouraging? Why? Where today can you share how God is encouraging you?

DECEMBER 19

I know that, like me, you want the present to be a more comfortable destination, but it isn't that. It's an uncomfortable preparation for a comfortable destination.

I would drag myself out of bed each morning and get dressed with feelings of dread. Once again I would arrive at the locker room, where the lingering smell reminded me of yesterday's sweat and ointment for bruises. As we slowly put on our equipment, our desire to be there mixed with our knowledge of the hardship that was before us. On the field, under the blazing sun and after a series of grueling drills, you wanted to vomit, to have just a moment to breathe, or to walk off the field and quit altogether. Evenings were taken up with ingesting a huge amount of food, taking a scalding-hot bath, receiving a rubdown, and getting to bed early. Morning came quickly and the routine started all over again.

This was the daily routine of the two-a-day summer football practices. It was a grueling but amazingly efficient way of preparing us for the season to come. It taught us to work through pain. It taught us the importance of getting each play right. It taught us how to work together and the importance of following the commands of the coach. Those two-a-day practices were hard, but they were for our good. And they weren't our destination but a preparation for the destination of the football season that was to come.

Yes, your life is hard right now. You are being called to do difficult things under the heat of the sun of this fallen world. You are called to say no to feelings of discouragement and the desire to quit. You are called to work with others who are going through the same hardship and you are called to submit to the wise commands of your Savior King. You will face hardship tomorrow and the day to follow. Yes, there will be moments of comfort along the way—times of rest, healing, and retreat—but they will be followed by more hardship. You must face these repeated hardships because this is not your destination. Today, thank God that he has a home waiting for you and that he loves you enough to use hardship to make you ready for your welcome to your final home.

> For this light momentary affliction is preparing for us an eternal weight of glory beyond all comparison. (2 Cor. 4:17)

Reflect: Your preparation won't last forever, but your destination will have no end.

DECEMBER 20

God calls you to make war with sin every day, and then he fights on your behalf with divine power even when you don't have the sense to.

I wish I could say that sin always appears horribly ugly and destructive to me, but it doesn't. I wish I could say that I always hate what God hates, but I don't. I wish I could say that I always love to do what is right, but I don't. I wish I could say that I never think that my way is better than God's way, but I can't.

Here's the danger for me and for you: sin doesn't always look *sinful* to us. It's hard to admit it, but sometimes sin actually looks beautiful to us. The man lusting after the woman in the mall doesn't actually see something ugly and dangerous. No, he sees beauty. The child who is rebelling against the will of her parents doesn't see the danger that she's placing herself in because she is captivated by the thrill of her temporary independence. Part of the deceptive power of sin in my heart is its ability to look beautiful when it is actually terribly ugly.

So we need help, but this help doesn't come to us first in a theology or a set of commands or principles. Instead, help comes to us in a person. God knew that my struggle with sin would be so great that it would not be enough to forgive me. So he also gets inside me by his Spirit, who is a warrior Spirit. By grace he does battle with my sin even in moments when I don't care to. His redemptive zeal is unstoppable. Think of Peter, who denied any knowledge of Christ. Was it the end of his story? No, but not because Peter had the sense to pursue Jesus. Instead, it was because Jesus, in unrelenting, forgiving grace, pursued Peter (see John 18:12–14, 17–18, 25–27; 21:15–19).

In our battle with sin, are we called to wrestle, run, fight, and pray? Yes, but our hope is not in our ability to do these things. Our hope is in the God of grace, who will war with sin until sin is no more. He never grows tired, never gets frustrated, and never gives up. Now, that's hope!

> For you say, I am rich, I have prospered, and I need nothing, not realizing that you are wretched, pitiable, poor, blind, and naked. (Rev. 3:17)

Reflect: The next time you're scrolling online, in your mind, try to label each post, picture, or story as God would identify it.

DECEMBER 21

Jesus willingly lived without an earthly home so that by grace we would be guaranteed a place in the Father's home forever.

It is an amazing story, one that becomes no less amazing with every retelling. The King of kings and Lord of lords leaves the splendor of glory to come to a shattered earth to suffer and die for self-oriented rebels. The Messiah is not born in a palace, but in a stable. He lives without a small luxury even animals enjoy—a home (Matt. 8:20). He is despised and rejected, then subjected to a bloody and painful death. And he does it all willingly: so that those rebels will be forgiven, so that those separated from God will have a home with him forever, and so that grace will be supplied to people in desperate need of it.

The words from the wonderful old Christmas hymn "Thou Didst Leave Thy Throne" capture so well the stunning contrast between Jesus's suffering and our resultant blessing:

Thou didst leave Thy throne and Thy kingly crown,
When Thou camest to earth for me;
But in Bethlehem's home was there found no room
For Thy holy nativity.

Heaven's arches rang when the angels sang,
Proclaiming Thy royal degree;
But of lowly birth didst Thou come to earth,
And in great humility.

The foxes found rest, and the birds their nest
In the shade of the forest tree;
But Thy couch was the sod, O Thou Son of God,
In the deserts of Galilee.

Thou camest, O Lord, with the living Word,
That should set Thy people free;
But with mocking scorn and with crown of thorn,
They bore Thee to Calvary.

When the heav'ns shall ring, and her choirs shall sing,
At Thy coming to victory,
Let Thy voice call me home, saying "Yet there is room,
There is room at My side for thee."[18]

For you know the grace of our Lord Jesus Christ, that though he was rich, yet for your sake he became poor, so that you by his poverty might become rich. (2 Cor. 8:9)

Reflect: This Christmas, remember that you have an eternal home because, in amazing grace, Jesus was willing to leave his home and have no home.

DECEMBER 22

Jesus faced separation from his Father in the here and now so that we would know the Father's acceptance now and for all eternity.

Jesus knew what he was facing. He knew the price that needed to be paid. He knew what it would mean to stand in our place. He was quite aware of the spiritual math: suffering for a moment = acceptance for all of eternity. And he was willing.

Why? Because unlike anything else, God had created human beings in his image and for loving and worshipful community with him. This relationship had been broken in an outrageous act of rebellion and sedition. Not only had Adam and Eve stepped over God's clear boundaries, but they had also quested for his position. So in the saddest moment in human history, they had been driven out of the garden and away from God's presence.

From the vantage point of creation, it was all very unthinkable. People living separate from God? This was like fish without water, honey that is not sweet, or a sun that provides no heat. Human beings were not made to function on our own and to live based on our own wisdom or resources. We were created to live in a constant, life-giving connection to God. People's separation from God was a functional and moral disaster.

So this tragic gap between God and man had to be bridged, and there was only one way. Jesus would have to come to earth as the second Adam and live a perfect life in our place. He would have to bear the punishment for our rebellion and endure the unthinkable—the Father's rejection. It happened at that horrible ninth hour on the day of his crucifixion, when, in a loud voice, he cried, " 'Eloi, Eloi, lema sabachthani?' which means 'My God, my God, why have you forsaken me?' " (Mark 15:34). This was Jesus's most painful moment of anguish as he took on himself the tragedy of our separation from God.

This moment really is the center of the Christmas story. He came to be the temporarily separated Son so that we can be the eternally accepted children of God. Now, that's a story worth celebrating!

> "And I, when I am lifted up from the earth, will draw all people to myself." He said this to show by what kind of death he was going to die. (John 12:32–33)

Reflect: Are there broken relationships in your life that need your humble attention and God's grace?

DECEMBER 23

Jesus endured human injustice in the here and now so that we would be blessed with divine mercy for all eternity.

Is it possible that the celebration of grace could collide more directly with the horror of sin than at the birth of the baby Jesus? The Christmas story is this—that the baby in the manger was the Son of the Most High God. He willingly came to a place where such unthinkable violence and injustice exists. He would die a violent death at the hands of evil men. Followers would weep that the Messiah was dead, but he would rise again and complete the work that he came to earth to do.

As we sit beneath a beautifully decorated tree and eat the rich food of celebration, we must not let ourselves forget the horror and violence both at the end, and also at the beginning of the Christmas story. The story that ends with the violent murder of the Son of God, begins with a horrible slaughter of children. The tragic slaughter at the start depicts how much the earth needs grace. The murder at the *end* is the moment when that grace is given. As you celebrate this season, remember that the pathway to your celebration was the death of the one you celebrate and be thankful.

> Now when [the wise men] had departed, behold, an angel of the Lord appeared to Joseph in a dream and said, "Rise, take the child and his mother, and flee to Egypt, and remain there until I tell you, for Herod is about to search for the child, to destroy him." And he rose and took the child and his mother by night and departed to Egypt and remained there until the death of Herod. This was to fulfill what the Lord had spoken by the prophet, "Out of Egypt I called my son."
>
> Then Herod, when he saw that he had been tricked by the wise men, became furious, and he sent and killed all the male children in Bethlehem and in all that region who were two years old or under, according to the time that he had ascertained from the wise men. Then was fulfilled what was spoken by the prophet Jeremiah:
>
> "A voice was heard in Ramah,
> weeping and loud lamentation,
> Rachel weeping for her children;
> she refused to be comforted, because they are no more."
> (Matt. 2:13–18)

Reflect: When you feel discouragement during the Christmas season, how does the grace of Christ and his coming to earth help you?

DECEMBER 24

Jesus willingly entered the darkness so that we could live in the light of his presence forever.

The Christmas story really is a light story. No, not the lights that decorate the city where you live. Not the lights that you have carefully hung on the tree in your living room. Nor the candles that you have placed in your windows. No, this story is about the light coming into a world that had been sadly cast into darkness. Under the cloak of rebellion and sin, the world had become a dark place. In the darkness of immorality, injustice, violence, greed, self-righteousness, thievery, racism, and a host of other evils, the world was desperate for light. Everyone was part of the problem and everyone suffered from the problem. Yet no one could solve the problem.

God's solution was the only way. He sent the one who is light to be the light that would light the world by his grace. He came into the darkness so that we could know light and life forever. Here is the Christmas story—only light can defeat the darkness, and light has come!

> The true light, which gives light to everyone, was coming into the world. He was in the world, and the world was made through him, yet the world did not know him. He came to his own, and his own people did not receive him. But to all who did receive him, who believed in his name, he gave the right to become children of God, who were born, not of blood nor of the will of the flesh nor of the will of man, but of God. (John 1:9–14)

Reflect: Where have you felt the joy and relief of coming into the light of Jesus and his grace and truth?

DECEMBER 25

Jesus was despised and rejected in the here and now so that you would have the Father's love and acceptance forever.

The words you are about to read, below, should be included in every celebration of Christmas. They express the glorious story of the coming of the Christ child to earth—and its result. He experienced the manger, the flight to Egypt, the daily suffering of hunger and homelessness, the rejection of the religious authorities, the disloyalty of the disciples, the unjust trial, the cruel death, and the tomb so that you would have what these words express. He came and endured all these things for you and me. Why? So that we would have forever what we never could have earned, deserved, or achieved on our own: salvation by grace for the glory of God!

So sit in front of your Christmas tree and read this Bible passage out loud to your friends or family. Together you can remember what the Christmas story is all about. Remember that Jesus willingly endured constant rejection and life-ending injustice so that you and I would experience the unalterable, unshakable, undefeatable love of God forever. Remember that he deserved to be loved, but was rejected so that we who deserve to be rejected would be eternally loved. The promise of the Christmas story is unshakable love and every need met. Now, that's worth celebrating!

> Have this mind among yourselves, which is yours in Christ Jesus, who, though he was in the form of God, did not count equality with God a thing to be grasped, but emptied himself, by taking the form of a servant, being born in the likeness of men. And being found in human form, he humbled himself by becoming obedient to the point of death, even death on a cross. Therefore God has highly exalted him and bestowed on him the name that is above every name, so that at the name of Jesus every knee should bow, in heaven and on earth and under the earth, and every tongue confess that Jesus Christ is Lord, to the glory of God the Father. (Phil. 2:5–11)

Reflect: What situations in your life have been tempting you to question God's love? How are these situations leading you astray?

DECEMBER 26

Jesus endured suffering in the here and now so that you and I could escape suffering for eternity.

It didn't start with the cross; from the very first breath he took until he ascended, Jesus suffered.

- He suffered an uncomfortable and unsanitary birth in a stable.
- He suffered the terror of fleeing for his life as an infant.
- He suffered the trials of growing and learning as a boy.
- He suffered powerful temptation.
- He suffered exposure to disease.
- He suffered homelessness and hunger.
- He suffered sadness and grief.
- He suffered disloyalty and betrayal.
- He suffered disrespect and mockery.
- He suffered physical pain and the emotional pain of the rejection of his Father.
- He suffered punishment for the sins of others.
- He suffered injustice and violence.
- He suffered death.
- He suffered the full range of the hardships of life in this fallen world.

His calling, his mission, was to suffer, and suffer he did. His suffering was wide-ranging and constant. For the Messiah, suffering was an everyday thing, even a moment-by-moment thing. And every act of his suffering was as a substitute. He suffered in our place. He suffered in every way that we do, so that he could be a Savior to us in our suffering and put an end to our suffering. He suffered every day, so that there would be a time when all suffering would end. So that we could live with him in a world where suffering is no more.

He did not come to earth in regal splendor. He did not come to earth to live in a palace and be given homage as King. Although he was the King of kings, he came as a suffering servant. In his suffering, he would save us from ourselves and finally from our suffering. His suffering is our salvation.

> My God, my God, why have you forsaken me?
>   Why are you so far from saving me, from the words of my groaning?
> O my God, I cry by day, but you do not answer,
>   and by night, but I find no rest. (Ps. 22:1–2)

Reflect: How does Jesus's suffering give you hope in your suffering?

DECEMBER 27

Why give way to fear when, in Christ, it is impossible for you to ever be alone because you are now the temple in which God dwells?

It is far more than a "too good to be true" story. It is so amazing that it defies all normal human logic. It is the spiritual miracle of miracles! It is amazing enough that we are forgiven and accepted by God by grace and grace alone. It's the story of divine intervention, of divine substitution, of divine sacrifice, and of divine grace. It is a story of God sending his Son to live as we were meant to live, to die the death that each of us deserves, to satisfy God's righteous requirement and placate his anger, and to rise victorious over death. It is a story of forgiveness granted, acceptance secured, and righteousness given to those who could not have merited it on their own.

But as amazing as the grace of forgiveness and the acceptance of God are, there is still more amazing grace to this story. God knew that the dilemma of our sin was such a deep personal moral disaster, that it was not enough to forgive us. God knew we needed more. He knew that after our forgiveness and acceptance, we would need daily help. He knew we would need rescue, strength, wisdom, and deliverance. So he didn't just forgive us. He didn't just accept us. He came to us and made us the place where he dwells. Paul says it well: "It is no longer I who live, but Christ who lives in me" (Gal. 2:20).

I don't think that we talk about this enough. I don't think that we celebrate this reality enough. I don't think we let our hearts consider the wonder of this identity enough. By grace, we are the temple of the Most High God. By grace, he lives in us. By grace, he works within us to complete the labor of grace that he has begun. By grace, we are able to choose and do what is right, only because he lives in us and gives us the power to do so by his grace. He hasn't just forgiven us, he's taken up residence in us, and in that there is real hope.

> It is the Lord who goes before you. He will be with you; he will not leave you or forsake you. Do not fear or be dismayed. (Deut. 31:8)

Reflect: How does Jesus's presence in you affect the way you approach difficulties and temptations?

DECEMBER 28

Even pleasure preaches grace. Every day we all experience a symphony of pleasures we never could've earned the right to enjoy.

These are some of God's pleasant gifts to us:

- the sound of the birds in the spring
- the multihued display of a sunset
- the pristine blanket of new-fallen snow
- the tenderness of a kiss
- the smell of flowers in bloom
- the wide variety of tastes and textures of food
- the glory of a wonderful piece of music
- the enjoyment of a great drama
- the wonder of a master's painting

God created for us a world of amazing beauty where pleasures exist all around us. He created us with pleasure gateways (eyes, ears, mouths, noses, hands, brains, and so on), so that we could take in the pleasure. He blesses us with these good and beautiful things every day. That means that on your very worst day and on your very best day, you are blessed with pleasures that come right from the hand of God. That means you don't get these pleasures because you've earned or deserved them. Instead, he graces you with good things because he is good, not because you are.

Perhaps it's just a really good sandwich at lunch. You don't deserve the pleasure of that sandwich. You don't deserve a tongue that can take in its tastes and textures. You don't deserve a brain that can make sense of the whole experience. It is just another gift from the hands of God, who daily bestows on you what you do not deserve because he loves you. Maybe you look out your window and see that the leaves on your tree have turned fire red. The sight takes your breath away. Stop and be thankful that the God of amazing grace created that tree and your ability to see, understand, and enjoy it. He chose you to experience its pleasure at that moment because he is the God of tender, patient grace.

> For he makes his sun rise on the evil and on the good, and sends rain on the just and on the unjust. (Matt. 5:45)

Reflect: How is using a screen as a way to see the amazing world God has created inferior to seeing it firsthand? Why?

DECEMBER 29

Yes, change is possible, not because you have wisdom and strength, but because you've been blessed with the grace of Jesus.

You're not stuck. You're not encased in concrete. Your life is not a dead end. Why? Because the giver of transformative grace has made you and me the place where he dwells! If you were to ask what God is doing in your life, the answer could be given in one word: *change*.

First, there is that work of personal growth, which theologians call "progressive sanctification." It is God's lifelong commitment to actually make me what he declared me to be in justification—righteous. In every situation, location, and relationship of my life, God is employing people, places, and things as his tools for this transforming grace. He will not be content for me to be a little bit better. He will work by grace until I am finally and totally free of sin, that is, molded into the image of his perfectly righteous Son.

Second, there is environmental change. This zealous Savior is also a dissatisfied Creator. He is not content to leave this world in its present sin-scarred condition. So there will come a day when he will make all things new. He will return his world to the condition it was in before sin left it so damaged. Change really is the zeal of your Redeemer. Personal change (Titus 2:11–14) and environmental change (Rev. 21:1–5) are his holy zeal. So, when you are disappointed in yourself, grieved at the sin in your relationships, or upset with the condition of your world, what should you do? Cry out for change. When you do, you are crying for something that hits right at the center of the zeal of your Savior's grace.

Change doesn't mean that you'll get your wish list of things that you think will give you the good life. But you can rest assured that where real change is needed, there is a God of grace who knows just where that change needs to take place and offers you everything you need so that it can happen.

> Set your minds on things that are above, not on things that are on earth. For you have died, and your life is hidden with Christ in God. When Christ who is your life appears, then you also will appear with him in glory. (Col. 3:2–4)

Reflect: What areas that need change can you take—again—to God in prayer today?

DECEMBER 30

Corporate worship is designed to instill vertical hope where horizontal hope has been dashed.

One of the themes of this devotional is hope. Every human being is hardwired for and concerned about hope. We're all in a constant search for hope that delivers and lasts. We're all a bit discouraged and paralyzed when our hopes are dashed. When one hope dies, we grab hold of another hope as fast as we can.

The Bible is a hope story. It's about where not to look for hope and the only place where true hope can be found. The great hope drama of the Bible is summarized by a few very important words, included below, that are buried in the middle of the apostle Paul's letter to the Romans.

As you read, notice what Paul does in this passage:

- *He connects our hope to our justification.* We have hope because, by grace, we have been forgiven and accepted by the one who holds everything we need.
- *He connects our hope to our sufferings.* There is even hope in suffering because in that suffering the God who is our hope is doing good things in us and for us.
- *He says that our vertical hope (hope in God) will never put us to shame.* This means that all other forms of hope fail us in some way. Hope in created things never delivers what hope in the Creator can.
- *He connects our hope to the Holy Spirit who lives inside us.* Here is the ultimate reason that you and I have hope—God has made us the address where he lives.

Now, that's hope! As you worship God with other believers and hear the truths of his word proclaimed, your hope will be rekindled.

> Therefore, since we have been justified by faith, we have peace with God through our Lord Jesus Christ. Through him we have also obtained access by faith into this grace in which we stand, and we rejoice in hope of the glory of God. Not only that, but we rejoice in our sufferings, knowing that suffering produces endurance, and endurance produces character, and character produces hope, and hope does not put us to shame, because God's love has been poured into our hearts through the Holy Spirit who has been given to us. (Rom. 5:1–5)

Reflect: When you feel hopeless, how might you be attaching your expectations on a false hope?

DECEMBER 31

God's work in you is a process, not an event. It progresses not in three or four huge moments, but in ten thousand little moments of change.

Well, it's that season once again. It is the time for the annual ritual of dramatic New Year's resolutions! These goals are fueled by hope of immediate and significant personal life change.

But the reality is that few smokers have actually quit because of a single moment of resolve. Few obese people have become healthy because of one dramatic moment of commitment. And few people who were deeply in debt have changed their financial lifestyles because of a New Year's resolution.

Is change important? Is commitment essential? Of course! In various ways, all our lives are shaped by the commitments we make. But growth in grace—which has the gospel of Jesus Christ at its heart—simply doesn't rest its hope on big, dramatic moments of change.

Instead, personal heart and life change is always a process. And it takes place where you and I live every day. And where do we live? Well, we all have the same address. Our lives don't lurch from big moment to big moment. No, we all live in the utterly mundane.

Most of us won't be written up in history books. Most of us will make only three or four significant decisions in our lives, and several decades after we die, the people we leave behind will struggle to remember the things we did. You and I live in little moments that are profoundly important. Why? Precisely because these little moments form us. Yet because we devalue the little moments in which we live, we tend not to notice the sin that gets exposed there. We fail to seek the grace that is offered to us. You see, the character of a life is not set in two or three dramatic moments, but in ten thousand little moments. The character that is formed in those little moments shapes how we respond to the big moments of life. And what makes all of this character change possible? Relentless, transforming, little-moment grace!

> And we all, with unveiled face, beholding the glory of the Lord, are being transformed into the same image from one degree of glory to another. For this comes from the Lord who is the Spirit. (2 Cor. 3:18)

Reflect: Tomorrow, and throughout the new year, remember to wake up committed to live in the small moments of your daily life. Ask the Lord to give open eyes and humble, expectant hearts.

Bonus Chapter

Q&A FOR TEENS WITH PAUL TRIPP

During the teen years, you will move from having your parents think for you, or tell you what to think, to becoming a young adult, capable of thinking for yourself. In this bonus chapter, I have provided answers to questions about life that you will surely encounter. These answers are not designed to be comprehensive or specific. Yet Lord willing, they will help you to get started in learning how to think biblically about the everyday personal and cultural issues you will face as you continue to mature and eventually leave your home to build life on your own.

The stories, commands, wisdom, and principles found within the Bible have been recorded and preserved for you so that you can think, desire, choose, speak, and act in the way God intended in the context of your everyday life and culture. Although the Bible doesn't directly address many of the issues that you will have to face during your teen years, it does provide a body of wisdom that will help you decide how to respond to whatever comes your way.

As you grapple with the questions and answers that follow, may God bless you as you learn how to think through the issues of your generation in a way that is distinctively biblical.

PAUL DAVID TRIPP

May 26, 2023

Anxiety and Depression

I feel anxious, even depressed. It feels like I have a dark cloud of sadness that follows me nearly every day, or that I experience panic attacks. I know the Bible says, "Do not be anxious about anything" (Phil. 4:6) and "In your presence there is fullness of joy" (Ps. 16:11), but I just can't seem to get over my anxiety or depression. How can I find peace and happiness?

These experiences of fear, discouragement, depression, and anxiety are more normal than we tend to realize or are willing to talk honestly about. All of these emotions are pictured for us in God's word. Why are they normal? First, we live in a broken world that doesn't function the way God intended for it to function. Second, that brokenness is not just outside of us, but it's inside of us as well. Our minds, our emotions, and our physical bodies don't always function the way God designed for them to function when he created perfect people living in a perfect world. So the first thing you need to do when you're suffering with anxiety, fear, or depression is don't let shame drive you into silence and hiding.

One of the beautiful things the Bible tells us is that Jesus carried our shame (Heb. 12:2). Hanging naked on the cross, Jesus shamed shame so that we don't have to live in shame any longer. Don't act like you're okay when you're not. Don't put on a front, a happy face. Don't hide in shame. Be honest with yourself about what you're facing and then be honest with people around you. When I encounter people who are crippled by fear, crippled by anxiety, or paralyzed by depression, I encourage them to seek help. When you're dealing with these struggles and emotions, it's hard to get out of your own head. It's almost impossible to objectively step outside of yourself and tell yourself the things that you need to hear.

There may actually be physiological components to your anxiety or depression, so reach out for help and don't hide in shame. Don't allow yourself to think that you're abnormal or the only one struggling. These are the regular experiences of life in a fallen world. Because he loves us, God has provided help for us. He has designed for us to live in community, and as a teenager, it's really good for you to get a hold of this: a healthy life, spiritually and emotionally, is a community project. You can't do it on our own. You won't make it on your own. We all need help, so get help. Reach out for help, and don't hide in shame if you're struggling with fear, depression, or anxiety.

Sex and Marriage

A lot of my friends are having sex, or at least messing around. I know the Bible says I'm supposed to wait until marriage before sex, but if I told my friends I believed that, I'd be made fun of. What's actually so wrong or dangerous with sexual activity before marriage, and why does the Bible command us to wait?

God designed a world with all kinds of pleasures, and he created human beings to live in that world with what I call "pleasure gates"—our eyes, ears, nose, mouth, our ability to touch—so that we could enjoy those pleasures. Enjoying pleasure is not something God is against. In fact, when I enjoy pleasure God's way, it actually brings glory to God!

But any pleasure that God has created and designed for us to enjoy, whether it's sex, food, or entertainment, requires boundaries. You can't eat a piece of chocolate cake anytime you want without hurting your health. In the same way, sexual pleasure (which God designed for us to enjoy and pursue) requires boundaries. The question is: Who is going to define and set those boundaries?

Because God is my Creator, he knows everything about me. He knows everything about the way I am put together. He knows everything about what is wise for me and what is foolish for me, what is good for me, what is dangerous for me. There's no one who could know me better than God does. For example, when you buy a new car, what's in the glove box? An owner's manual. That manual is there to tell you how to best maintain that car, to keep it running on the road for as long as possible. Why is that manual reliable? Because the manual was written by the person who designed and manufactured your car. It's trustworthy.

In the same way, God has provided us with a manual of how we are to operate. It's called the Bible. He made us, he wrote the owner's manual, and it's the best thing you could ever trust. So, here's the decision you have to make, and this is very hard. You will either believe, "My culture and my friends and my desires (which are sinful, mind you!) are right, and they are best for me, so I will follow them." Or you will believe, "God knows best, and although it's hard because everybody seems to be going in the opposite direction, I'm going to trust in the perfect holiness, the perfect wisdom, the perfect love, and the perfect goodness of God. Even though it doesn't make sense and I don't have all the answers, I'm going to live the way God intended because he made me and knows me and wants what is best for me."

When it comes to your sexuality, do you believe that God's laws are good for you? They're not meant to crush or limit your pleasure. Because God is perfectly holy all the time and in every way, it's impossible for him to give you counsel, advice, and commands that are bad for you. What God commands of you is always good for you. God's boundaries for sex and sexual pleasure is never a restriction; it's an invitation for you to enjoy those pleasures in ways that God intended.

P.S.—If you're a teen who hasn't waited, or if you've been sexually active and now you're in a place where you're feeling shame and regret, let me say this: regret in the hands of God is a good and beautiful thing. God uses regret to draw us to himself. Why? Not so he can condemn us, but so he can wrap his arms of love and grace around us, offer us forgiveness, and give us divine power to take our lives in another direction. If you're feeling regret about your sexual life, don't run away from God. Run toward him. Your sin doesn't make you disgusting to God. Your sin excites his mercy and causes him to offer you the grace you need.

Pornography and Sexting

Lots of my friends are looking at pornography or sending sexual images and videos to each other. I've been asked to send these images and have been sent them without even asking. I know I shouldn't look at these things online or participate in sexting, but it seems impossible to avoid.

If you're going to stay pure in this sex-crazed culture and age of digital technology, then you have to be prepared to fight temptation 24/7. But it's not just about avoiding the sin and sex outside of you in the culture, on the internet, and circulating around in your friend group. It's always first about the sinful and selfish desires inside of your heart. It's only the sin inside us that every time magnetizes us to the sin outside us.

When Jesus teaches us to pray, "And lead us not into temptation, but deliver us from evil" (Matt. 6:13), he is calling us to admit that the evil that is the greatest danger to us is the evil inside each of us. If you want to stay pure, you need to be honest: while you might be able to escape the evil of a certain location, avoid an evil in a specific situation, or run from an evil person, you cannot run from the evil inside yourself. Only grace has the power to rescue you from you and to deliver you from the most threatening evil of all—the evil that still resides in your heart.

But of course, if you're going to fight temptation, then you have to be very careful and intentional with what you expose yourself to. Not everything on Netflix is going to help you to think correctly about sexuality. Not everything on TikTok or Instagram will be helpful for your eyes and your heart. Here's the question: If you want to be sexually pure, are you willing to say no to the popular things that everybody is participating in, watching, or talking about that will increase your temptation and make your struggle with purity even harder?

It's hard not to be laughing along with everybody else or talking with everybody else about what they saw the night before on that show or when sharing videos or reels or memes. Yet being pure means being willing to make sacrifices so that, by God's grace, you have greater control of your mind, thoughts, desires, and emotions.

Gender, Pronouns, and Sexual Identity

Some of my peers and adults around me are either changing their pronouns, their dress, their gender, or some other aspect of their sexual identity. Why can't love be love, and shouldn't Christians accept people for wanting to be their authentic selves? Is the Bible's teaching about one man and one woman outdated, harmful, and oppressive?

During this moment in our culture, where the conversation is focused on being your true authentic self, this is where the timelessness of the word of God is so helpful. God intended his word to be so powerfully truthful that it will never become outdated. "All flesh is grass, and all its beauty is like the flower of the field. The grass withers, the flower fades when the breath of the LORD blows on it; surely the people are grass. The grass withers, the flower fades, but the word of our God will stand forever" (Isa. 40:6–8). This is where you have to say, "I'm either going to listen to the word of God, to God's eternally wise and good and loving perspective," or I'm just going to say, "I want to be where my culture is."

The answer to the question, "What is my authentic self?" is found in the very first pages of the word of God. If there is a Creator—and there is—who designed us, created us, and put us together, then my authentic self is found in his creation, his design. If by his creative and sovereign design, I'm a biological male, no matter where my feelings take me, that is my authentic self. Why? Because that is the self the Creator designed for me to be. If he created me to be a biological female, then there's no more authentic self than the fact that I'm a female. Why? Because that's the self God designed for me to be.

If you go back to the beginning, it says God designed Adam and Eve male and female. It's very possible for your desires, emotions, and feelings to go all over the place. Yet that doesn't mean those emotions or desires are then the ruling definition of authenticity for you. Your emotions will lie to you. Your desires will lie to you. They will change, they will fade, they will blow with the winds of culture. But with the word of God that stands forever, you have a standard that you can run to and say, "Even though I feel this way, even though I'm pulled in this direction, even though I feel, at this period of time, more comfortable over here, God determines who my authentic self is. He's done that because he is my Creator, he loves me, and he knows what is best for me."

The Goodness of God and Hell

If God is truly good and loving, why do bad things happen? And how can a loving God send people to hell?

There are two things that are important to say to this huge question that theologians have debated for centuries. The first is that God, for our good and his glory, has designed for us to live in a terribly broken world. In Romans 8, the apostle Paul says, "For we know that the whole creation has been groaning together in the pains of childbirth until now. And not only the creation, but we ourselves, who have the firstfruits of the Spirit, groan inwardly as we wait eagerly for adoption as sons, the redemption of our bodies" (8:22–23). You groan when you're in pain, discouraged, or hopeless. We live in a broken, fallen, dysfunctional world, and it's impossible to live without that brokenness entering your door.

If you're not suffering now, you will someday, and if you're not suffering now, you're near someone who is. That's not because God hates us, it's not because he is uncaring, it's not because he is too weak to help us or his ear is not tuned to our cries for help (Isa. 59:1). It's because this messed up world is our address, and right here, right now, we don't get a ticket out of that brokenness.

There's a second thing that's important to understand (and I don't think this is a theological or philosophical cop-out): God will confuse you. God exists at a level beyond our understanding. I can remember when our children were three or four years old, and I would have to say, no to them. They would say, "But Daddy, why? Why not? Why can't I do that?" As their father, I knew that the explanation I could give was way beyond their ability to understand. So I would kneel down in front of them and say, "Does your Daddy love you?" (*Yes*) "Is your Daddy a monster who wants bad things to happen to you?" (*No*) Then I would say, "Daddy can't explain to you why he said no. Now you can either walk down the hallway and say, 'I have a bad Daddy because my Daddy says no to me,' or you can say, 'I don't understand why my Daddy said no, but I know my Daddy loves me and knows what is best for me.'"

Peace will never be found in understanding. Why? Because there are things you and I will experience that we will never understand. Peace is found in trusting the one who understands it all and who rules in a way that we won't fully understand but ultimately rules for our good. I know you probably want a more specific answer than that, but God never gives it. There are things that remain in his secret will because we would never be able to handle them if we understood them. God says, "I'm good. I love you. I know what is best. Trust me." It's in that trust that you find rest.

In the same thought, let's consider hell. The Scriptures are filled with themes of punishment and the consequences of sin. The most ultimate is hell. And just like the question above, why a loving God allows bad things to happen, there are two important keys to remember when asking about God and hell.

The first is this: human beings are not central in the biblical story, God is. This is God's story and God's world. You could argue that the most important words in the Bible are the first four, "In the beginning, God. . . ." (Gen. 1:1). If God was first on site, if God created all that we know, then everything is his and everything belongs to him. "For from him and through him and to him are all things. To him be glory forever. Amen" (Rom. 11:36). And so, whatever doctrine or reality we look at and ask hard questions about, whether it's human suffering or hell, we have to look at it from the centrality of the glory, holiness, and perfection of God. You'll never ever understand difficult doctrines unless you start there. This is God's world and his rules.

If that's true, and it is because the Bible declares it to be, then God has the right to do with this world whatever he wishes because it's his. In addition to my writing, I also like to paint. So when I put my hands, my brushes, and my paint to a canvas, it's my creation. I can do with it whatever I want because it belongs to me and that's the position of a creator.

There's a second key to remember: that human beings are unworthy. The mistake that people make is to think that people are good by nature and, therefore, that we deserve good things to happen to us. Meanwhile, the Bible declares the polar opposite.

One of the most shocking passages in all of the Bible is in Psalm 58:3, which says, "The wicked are estranged from the womb; they go astray from birth, speaking lies." Similarly, David writes in Psalm 51:5, "Behold, I was brought forth in iniquity, and in sin did my mother conceive me." There's never been a moment in my existence where I was good, never a moment from my very first breath, where I have had God in his rightful place. "As it is written: 'None is righteous, no, not one; no one understands; no one seeks for God. All have turned aside; together they have become worthless; no one does good, not even one' " (Rom. 3:10–12).

So hell is not this horrible place where an unloving God unjustly sends these good people who are in the center of the universe. Hell is actually the rightful state of everyone who has ever been born because everyone who was ever born rejects and rebels against the one who is central.

I don't actually struggle with the doctrine of hell. I struggle with how Paul Tripp could ever be freed from that destiny that I truly deserve. How could there be mercy this great? How could there be grace this huge? How could it be possible that people who shake their fists in the face of the one who created them and is central could wrap his arms of love around them and invite them to spend eternity in his presence? That's the doctrine that is crazy to me, made possible only by the cross of Jesus Christ.

Hell isn't crazy to me. It's heart-breaking, and we should never want anybody to ever be in hell, but hell makes sense to me. God's mercy given to me makes no sense except for the sacrifice, the payment, of Jesus. That's how I handle the doctrine of hell.

P.S.—These tough questions won't end after you leave the teenage years. You'll continue to have them, and you'll either let those questions drive you away from God or those questions will drive you toward him to find your rest in his wisdom and goodness.

Oh, the depth of the riches and wisdom and knowledge of God! How unsearchable are his judgments and how inscrutable his ways!

> "For who has known the mind of the Lord,
> or who has been his counselor?"
> "Or who has given a gift to him
> that he might be repaid?"

For from him and through him and to him are all things. To him be glory forever. Amen. (Rom. 11:33–36)

Boredom and Smart Phones

Lots of people say that teenagers spend way too much time on their phones or on social media, but I feel bored a lot. What else could I do?

If you feel bored, it's not because your environment is boring. We live in an amazing, multifaceted, endlessly interesting world. Not only that, God has given us the ability to think and create and imagine. You could argue that because of these things, no one should ever be able to claim that they are bored! It's not necessarily true that you live in a boring house or have a boring family or that school bores you. Boredom is actually an internal thing, a state of mind and a condition of the heart. If you feel bored, it's because there is something about the way you are dealing with life that makes it seem less interesting than it actually is.

One of the ways that teenagers today tend to deal with boredom is by numbing themselves with endless entertainment, screen time, social media, and chat apps. The smart phone seems to be the ultimate solution to boredom. Why? Because you can go down three thousand rabbit trails on social media or scroll through endless reels that will catch your interest for a moment or make you laugh. But think about this: none of these develops anything in you as a human being. Endless scrolling doesn't help you to think more deeply and more clearly. Constant screen time doesn't encourage you to be creative or help you discover the gifts God has given you or develop those gifts. I think social media and smart phones, at least in excess, have the ability to rob you of your humanity. You become at risk of being nothing more than a media sponge with a shorter and shorter attention span, and you lose the ability to think critically or create; all you do is just consume.

After God creates Adam and Eve, he tells them it's their job to do something with it. "And God blessed them. And God said to them, 'Be fruitful and multiply and fill the earth and subdue it, and have dominion over the fish of the sea and over the birds of the heavens and over every living thing that moves on the earth' " (Gen. 1:28). There's also an amazing Psalm that says, "The heavens are the LORD's heavens, but the earth he has given to the children of man" (Ps. 115:16). We've been placed by God to be the resident managers of earth. We're meant to steward the creation, to enhance its beauty, to protect it from danger, to nurture it.

I would encourage you to limit your daily consumption of things that don't make you a better human being, that don't make you think, that don't make you more creative. I was talking with my life, Luella, who is an art dealer and who has been in the art world for many years. We were discussing, with deep sadness, how the majority of humanity never realizes their creative potential. I think a lot of that is fear—fear of failure or fear of being made fun of—but today more than ever, it's because we don't give ourselves an opportunity to discover our creative potential.

Everybody has creative ability of some kind within them. There's an endless range of how you express that creativity, whether it's art, music, decoration, drama, writing, poetry, fashion, anything! Don't let smart phones and scrolling on social media suck the life out of you and the creative gifts that God has given you.

Social Media and Technology

I feel like I'm addicted to social media. I know what people (and reports) are saying about the dangers of social media, but it's how I stay connected with all my friends. Is it bad to be on social media?

I think that social media is like a hammer. With a hammer, you can build beautiful things, but you can also use a hammer to destroy something or harm someone. Social media is a tool; it can be used for enormous good, but it can also be harmful. It entirely depends on the hands of the person holding the tool and what their intention with the tool is.

Back in 2008, I realized that the way human culture would communicate was going to change, and that would be driven by these new internet media platforms. I signed up on Twitter and immediately realized what a powerful tool for the gospel this was going to be. I started to, and I still do to this day, tweet the gospel three times every morning and once on Sunday. That began to build and build and build, and I can honestly say that my entire ministry and the scope of my influence has been changed, for the good, by social media. In that way, I think Christians should "plunder the Egyptians" (Ex. 3:22), which means, take what the world has created and use it for the kingdom of God. I think there are powerful ways that Christians and the church can do that with social media and technology.

But of course, there are dangers. A good thing can become a dangerous thing if it becomes a ruling thing in your heart. I want to share four specific concerns that I have about social media and technology and our use of them.

Influence: Social media is filled with influencers, and whether you realize it or not, these influencers have significant moral authority over your life. It used to be that authority and influence was held only by institutional leaders, like teachers and preachers. These figures and their systems were certainly far from perfect, but they had at least gone through the ranks of an educational institution to earn that authority. Now, because of the power of social media, anyone with a smartphone can become an influencer, and they now have the ability to speak about all the important issues in your life without any accreditation, training, or accountability. So I would caution you when it comes to social media: Who are the influencers that you are listening to? How much moral authority are you letting them have over your life? Does what they are saying contradict the moral authority of the Bible, or do they encourage you to follow Jesus more?

Exposure: As soon as you start to scroll or chat on social media, you expose your eyes, your mind, and your heart to something. The question is, what? There was a time, before the internet and smart phones, where you would have to literally walk someplace or go to a physical store to find something that would expose your heart to the darker parts of the world. And there was always the risk that someone might see you or that you would get caught and embarrass yourself. That's not true anymore; it's right there in the palm of your hands, in the privacy of your room. With the tap of your screen, you can discover horrible things on the internet or social media. Even if you don't intend to search for something, within a few scrolls or clicks, you can end up in a place that you would be embarrassed if others saw your browsing history. So again, I would caution you when it comes to social media: What are you exposing your heart to? What is the impact that social media is having on the way you think about yourself, treat others, and approach life and faith?

Communication: Social media and chat apps are filled with so much ungodly, unhelpful, negative, disrespectful communication. The more time you spend on these platforms, the more likely it is that you will experience this or be tempted to participate in it. There's something about the fact that you're not standing in front of another person that makes you willing and able to say things that you would most likely not say if you were in person with them. What is your talk like on social media or chat apps? How much is helpful, positive, and building others up? And what about what others are saying to you? Are you reading terrible things that people are saying to you that put you in a dark place? There's something about the impersonal, anonymous nature of social media that allows you to communicate in a way that is much different than if you were face-to-face, and it's dangerous.

Time: I must admit, I hate the fact that my iPhone logs my screen time. I would rather not know! It can be pretty embarrassing and scary at the end of the day to see that I've been on my phone 3, 4, or 8 hours in a single day. I've seen these stats and thought, "It's impossible that I've spent that much time on my device." But it's real, and there's a way in which social media and these exciting tech devices are stealing our lives away from the things that God has called us to do. You only have 24 hours in a day and 7 days in a week. You'll never get 30 hours in a day or 10 days in a week. That means, if something is consuming your time, it's eating up time away from another area of your life. Stewardship of time is a bigger issue for us than ever before because of these powerful devices that we're carrying with us all the time.

To conclude, I'm going to say again how much I love social media. Why? Because I love what it's done for me and my team and our ability to get the gospel message to people around the world. When we post something, we'll have tens of thousands of views in just a few hours, and people will leave a comment in a language I can't read. What a beautiful tool that is, and what a tremendous opportunity to build the kingdom of God around the world. But social media and the tech devices we carry around can be equally as dangerous because of the seemingly unlimited access it has to influence us, expose us to evil, change the way we communicate, and eat up our time. May God help us to examine ourselves and to take these tools and use them for gospel good.

Career Planning and the Future

A lot of my friends seem to have a plan for their future or a career dream, but I don't know what I want to do with my life. How can I take steps for the future and understand God's will for my life?

When I look back on myself as a seventeen year old, facing the pressure of having to make significant life decisions like choosing a college and declaring a major and what I wanted to do with the rest of my life, I was totally unprepared to make those decisions. So it's very important that you surround yourself with lots of mature, wise voices. I'm also very thankful for those types of people in the lives of my children when they were teenagers. These were adults who cared about my kids and helped them to navigate that period of life when they were getting ready to leave the home and make decisions about where they would invest the rest of their lives.

It doesn't make any sense to make decisions during this period of life on your own. Your life has been designed by God to be a community project. You and I simply were not created, or re-created in Jesus Christ, to live all by ourselves. The Bible says, "It is not good that the man should be alone" (Gen. 2:18) and, "For the body does not consist of one member but of many" (1 Cor. 12:14). The biblical word-pictures of "temple" (stones joined together to be a place where God dwells) and "body" (each member dependent on the function of the other) remind us that community is essential.

There's something else that's important to remember. This process will be messy. Don't think you're not going to mess up. You don't have to make all these decisions at once or expect to get it right the first time. One of my sons went off to college on scholarships because he had done well in high school, but during his second year, he got a notice that his scholarship had been taken away because of low grades. He was upset, partially because of the scholarship, but more because he didn't know what he wanted to do with his life at that early stage. He said, "I don't know why I'm in college. I don't want to be here." So we told him to leave. Why throw away money on something you don't want to be doing? He worked for the next two years, mostly in a deli that he hated. I can remember once I picked him up from work and he said, "Dad, I know what I want to do now, and I want to go back to college." He just needed time and experience.

Of course, that was a rocky process, and as his parents, we were concerned about him. But when he went back to school, he wanted to be there, he knew what he was chasing, and he was a Dean's List student the rest of his time at college. Don't be so afraid of making mistakes that you either don't make any decision or that you make a decision too quickly. It's hard to know yourself and what you're good at and what you want to do at this age. That's why you want to surround yourself with wise counsel.

Culture and Evangelism

I'm finding it hard to be a public follower of Jesus and share my faith in a world that is increasingly hostile to Christians and biblical beliefs. How can I do that?

If I'm having a conversation with a stranger who isn't a Christian and I begin by introducing myself as a pastor, that conversation is normally over before it even starts. People, at least in the modern Western world, typically have a negative, media-driven view of what a Christian is. It didn't used to be that way. Fifty years ago, Christianity was more in the center of culture. But over time, it's been pushed farther and farther to the fringes of society. That means being a publicly committed Christian and following God will require sacrifice, suffering, and being misunderstood, rejected, and alone. Because that's the reality of our current situation, it's tempting to live your life in the safe confines of a very narrow Christian community. But that's not what God calls us to do. Jesus says, "You are the light of the world. A city set on a hill cannot be hidden. Nor do people light a lamp and put it under a basket, but on a stand, and it gives light to all in the house. In the same way, let your light shine before others, so that they may see your good works and give glory to your Father who is in heaven" (Matt. 5:14–16).

Imagine driving through the mountains in the middle of the night. It's pitch black, and you're about to run out of gas. But up in the distance, you can see the lights of a little community. That's what Christians are meant to be. God's plan was to send us into the world, and we're not meant to live just for our comfort and happiness. We're meant to live for something greater than ourselves. That means being willing to stand for what is right and true, even when it's hard and there are consequences. Of course, it's very helpful, when making those stands, to not make them alone. It's vital to have a solid group of supportive Christian friends. But hiding out and creating a secret order of the saints is not God's plan.

I love the two promises that Jesus makes surrounding the Great Commission: "All authority in heaven and on earth has been given to me. Go therefore and make disciples of all nations, baptizing them in the name of the Father and of the Son and of the Holy Spirit, teaching them to observe all that I have commanded you. And behold, I am with you always, to the end of the age" (Matt. 28:18–20). Jesus promises his presence. When Jesus calls you to represent him, you never represent him alone. He never sends you without first going with you. Jesus also promises his authority. He never asks you to do something without first empowering you to do it.

Will it be hard? Absolutely. Following Jesus will mean being misunderstood and rejected, just like our Savior was. "He was despised and rejected by men, a man of sorrows and acquainted with grief; and as one from whom men hide their faces he was despised, and we esteemed him not" (Isa. 53:3). That means that you should never look to the world for acceptance and confidence. The hostile, anti-Christian world will destroy your confidence. Confidence will never be found externally and horizontally (from others); confidence is only ever found internally and vertically (from God). As Christians, we have confidence because we know that what we're standing for is absolutely unshakable, irreversibly and eternally true.

I'm writing this section the week after Tim Keller died. He was a pastor who planted a church in a very secular place: New York City. He was asked the question, "What would you say to a young Christian who is nervous about the future?" I love his answer: "If Jesus Christ was actually raised from the dead, then everything is going to be alright." That's our reason for confidence in an increasingly hostile world. We don't need people to like us. We don't need culture to agree with us. We don't need our peers to think we're cool because we know that what we're standing for and who we're standing for is right. I have hundreds of thousands of followers on social media, and I've learned that I can't build my identity on what people say about me or how they react to me. I need the confidence in my heart that I'm following what the Creator has said is right and true. Would I like to be treated with respect? Sure. Would I like to be accepted and appreciated? Of course. But that's not where I get my confidence. I don't look to others for my confidence because that's not where confidence can be found.

Now, that doesn't mean that we can be hostile and disrespectful in return. In fact, the opposite is true. In the face of rejection and misunderstanding, we need to reflect love, generosity, and kindness. My wife, Luella, has been in the art gallery business for many years, and that's injected us into the cultural (and often secular) part of Philadelphia. We have had many friendships with people who are not believers. Sometimes we can see them trying to figure us out. We want to be the kind of people that these friends look at and say, "I don't believe what Paul and Luella believe, and I don't always like what they stand for, but these are two of the most loving, gracious, generous people that I know."

The secular world may be growing increasingly hostile toward the Christian faith, but the Bible still calls unbelievers lost. I think that is a beautiful, visual word picture. I live in Center City, Philadelphia, and I know Center City like the back of my hand. Often, I will be walking down the street and see a visitor who is clearly lost. Why wouldn't I want to help them find their way? Why would I ignore them in their moment of need? Why would I mock or despise them? If you saw me do that, you would think of me as a heartless person. So with your unbelieving friends or family, you have the map to help them find their way as human beings. It's the most beautiful map to the most beautiful destination that you could ever share with somebody. Don't walk by a lost secular culture, no matter how hostile it is. That's what motivates me to share my faith with people that don't believe what I believe.

Bible Reading and Prayer

I know I'm supposed to read the Bible every day and pray, but I just can't seem to be committed or disciplined. How can I get better?

I'll be honest with you: I'm not always excited about reading my Bible either. I go through periods of what I would call "spiritual boredom" when reading God's word feels burdensome, and the only reason I do is because I'm motivated by duty or guilt. Whenever I get to this point, I force myself to read Isaiah 55. I love the word picture. God invites us to a banquet table and says, "Delight yourselves in rich food" (55:2).

Whether you feel it or not, you are spiritually starving. God has placed in front of you the richest banquet of spiritual food, food that has the power to change everything about you. It is the buffet of buffets! Imagine a homeless person starving, with no food or no money to buy any food, and someone in a three-piece suit walked up to him on the street and invited him to the finest restaurant in the city. The bill was already paid for in advance, but not only that, he was given a lifetime membership to eat as much as he wanted, whenever he wanted. It would be an act of craziness for that starving homeless person to reject the invitation! That's how I approach reading the Bible. If you think of your daily devotional time as a requirement, a duty, a box you need to tick to be a good Christian or to keep God happy with you, it's going to be a struggle. But if you think of the Bible as an invitation to the best banquet you could ever consume, it changes the whole thing.

There are tools that God has provided to help. I would suggest getting a resource that can help you understand what you are reading in the Scriptures. Download a Bible reading plan and ask a friend or mentor or youth leader to follow it with you and keep you accountable. And then, on every page, look for Jesus. The Bible is not a collection of stories or a catalog of wisdom statements but rather a single story running from cover to cover. The Bible is the story of Jesus. Every passage looks forward to him, puts hope in him, points to what he alone can fix, or looks back to him with gratitude. A daily devotional time puts Jesus before you, reminding you again and again of his presence, plan, power, and promises. It will cause you to remember that Jesus is God's greatest gift to you, and the result will be a deeper love for him and a more vibrant celebration of his grace.

In the same way, prayer is an invitation. In Luke 18, Jesus tells the parable of the persistent widow, which is an invitation for us to "bother" God day and night by crying out (18:3–7). What should we cry out for? Yes, prayer includes making requests, and God encourages us to cast our cares on him because he really does care for us (1 Pet. 5:7), but prayer is profoundly more than bringing God our wish list of desires. Prayer is an invitation to be honest with your Creator and Savior.

When you pray, you should be honest that you are not as smart as you tend to think you are. When you pray, you should be honest that you cannot make it on your own and desperately need the continual help of the one who made you. When you pray, you should be honest that you don't always want to seek first the kingdom of God and would rather build your own kingdom of personal pleasure. When you pray, you should be honest that you are weak, unwise, and a failure.

Don't think about prayer as a duty to please God or a religious recitation that every Christian must do three times a day or before each meal to bless the food. If you prayed every moment of your life, you could not pray enough prayers to earn acceptance with God. Prayer is an invitation to admit who you truly are and what you truly need. How freeing is that? Run to Jesus in your weakness and honesty, knowing he is never disappointed or surprised when you do.

Going to Church

My parents make me go to church every week and I would rather sleep in or play sports. Why do I need to go to church? Is it really that big of a deal?

I can tell you for sure, Paul Tripp loves Sunday morning. I love the anticipation of the drive to worship. Am I weird? I don't think so; I'm just a person in need. I need three things on Sunday—actually, I need it every day of the week—that I get from corporate worship.

First, I need to be taught again and again and again. I need the biblical story applied to my story, so I live with a God-story mentality. I need more than just abstract teaching. What I love about the preaching in the local church is that we're taught by a pastor who is with us, who walks long-term with us, who knows us, and who can speak those truths with a specificity to people that he knows and loves. I don't think anything replaces pastoral preaching. Books don't replace that. The internet can't replace that. Conferences won't replace that.

Second, I need to hear my brothers and sisters sing the gospel into my ears. God designed and created human beings to sing—we're singing people. Through Sunday worship singing, my dull heart can be awakened by these voices. There are times in Sunday worship where tears will fill my eyes because I hear my brothers and sisters singing those truths into my life. I'm like everybody else. I have an easily distracted and forgetful heart, and these songs remind us of what is important and who we serve.

Finally, you need church because your walk with God is a community project. You and I need the body of Christ, other Christians, in our life. Why? Because we are blind, and we need other people to help us see ourselves with accuracy. It's not enough to just sing songs and listen to a sermon. In community, those gospel truths can become more personal. Other people can get to know you, get to know your heart and your struggles, and see the gaps and inconsistency of your Christian living. Discipleship is you learning how to live as a disciple of the Lord Jesus Christ.

All three—worship, preaching, and discipleship—contribute an element that is needed in the life of every believer. All are God's gifts to us. All are necessary, and together, contribute to a life of long-term spiritual health and fruitfulness. Sunday is not a duty but an invitation. That's why Paul Tripp goes to church every Sunday morning!

Obeying Parents

My parents just don't get me. They don't understand my life and their rules get in the way. Do I really need to honor my father and mother and obey what they say?

There's something very unique about the relationship between a child and a parent during the teen years. During this stage of life, you are desiring more and more control over your life. You want more independence, and this desire is not evil. In fact, these desires are part of God's plan for you because he is preparing you to go through the process where the home where you were raised will ultimately be replaced by another home—your home as a young adult.

Now, you will negotiate this weird, uncomfortable transition with your parents. And let's be real: your parents will struggle with this transition too. I know because many years ago, I was the father of four teenagers myself. At times, parents will want to turn back the clock and treat you like a three-year-old. Why? Because they're afraid. Most parents have nothing but unconditional love for you, and they're afraid of letting you go. Most parents have done their best, and even though all parents fail at times, most have given their lives and made significant sacrifices to try and protect you and keep you safe. Now that you're going off on your own, they're losing that ability to protect you and keep you safe, and that's uncomfortable for them. Most parents want what is best for their kids, and they think that their wisdom and their rules and their guidance are best.

They're not necessarily wrong. Let me say this as plain as I can: you still need parents. You're not ready to do this thing called "life" on your own yet. Every adult, myself included, still needs advice, counsel, and provision from others, so how much more do teens? Your biggest danger and threat is not the rules that your parents have for you. Your biggest danger and threat to you is you and the immaturity that you want so much to deny.

There will come a day, much faster than you think, when you are ready. Soon, you will make decisions on your own, provide for yourself, and your life will largely be in your own hands. But why rush? Why run away from the protective, wisdom-giving environment of your home? God knows that protection is still necessary. That's why he created children to live with their parents.

Your desires for independence are not wrong. God is preparing you for the next stage of life. But you can't let those desires put you at constant war with people who love you, and, although they're imperfect, want what's best for you.

Bullying and Abuse

What do I do if I'm getting bullied or abused? What should I do if I see someone else getting bullied or abused?

It's very clear if you read the Bible that you are not forced into the position of just allowing yourself to be harmed, whether that's being bullied or abused at school, on a team, at home, in the church, or elsewhere. One thing that has hit me as I've been reading through the Old Testament is how much God rages against the abuse of his people.

All through biblical history, the Lord rages against leaders who have done things to his children that should never be done. There's no indication that God would ever call his children to be tolerant of moral evil and just allow it to happen and say nothing.

Speak out. Get help. Tell the authorities or the police. Don't think that for the protection of friends or the protection of the reputation of an adult or family member that it's your responsibility to allow yourself or someone else to be harmed. God never calls you to do that.

Your God is a God of justice and mercy and he welcomes you to be honest about those experiences. I know of situations where young people have allowed abuse to take place because they are afraid of what would happen if they spoke the truth. Eventually, the truth of that abuse came out and the abusers were punished, but by then, years of damage had been done. You're never called to accept that kind of harm. Speak out. Get help. God will honor that as you do it.

NOTES

1. Adapted from Paul David Tripp, *Do You Believe?: Twelve Historic Doctrines to Change Your Everyday Life* (Wheaton, IL: Crossway, 2021), 373.
2. Adapted from Tripp, *Do You Believe?*, 84.
3. Adapted from Tripp, *Do You Believe?*, 115–16.
4. Adapted from Tripp, *Do You Believe?*, 51–52.
5. Issac Watts, "Joy to the World! The Lord Is Come," 1719.
6. Adapted from Tripp, *Do You Believe?*, 413.
7. Adapted from Paul David Tripp, *Whiter Than Snow: Meditations on Sin and Mercy* (Wheaton, IL: Crossway, 2008), 34–35.
8. Adapted from Tripp, *Do You Believe?*, 142, 148.
9. Adapted from Tripp, *Do You Believe?*, 313–16.
10. Adapted from Paul David Tripp, *Suffering: Gospel Hope When Life Doesn't Make Sense* (Wheaton, IL: Crossway, 2018), 83.
11. Eric Schumacher and David L. Ward, "Not in Me," 2012. © 2012 Hymnicity. Used with permission.
12. Adapted from Tripp, *Do You Believe?*, 78–79.
13. Adapted from Paul David Tripp, *40 Days of Grace* (Wheaton, IL: Crossway, 2020), 5.
14. Adapted from Tripp, *Do You Believe?*, 293.
15. Adapted from Paul David Tripp, *Awe: Why It Matters for Everything We Think, Say, and Do* (Wheaton, IL: Crossway, 2015), 11–12.
16. Robert Robinson, "Come Thou Fount of Every Blessing," 1758.
17. Adapted from Tripp, *Do You Believe?*, 142, 158.
18. Emily Elizabeth Steele Elliott, "Thou Didst Leave Thy Throne and Thy Kingly Crown," 1864.

SCRIPTURE INDEX

PAUL TRIPP MINISTRIES

Paul Tripp Ministries is a not-for-profit organization connecting the transforming power of Jesus Christ to everyday life. Hundreds of resources are freely available online, on social media, and on the Paul Tripp app.

PaulTripp.com

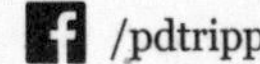 /pdtripp  @paultripp 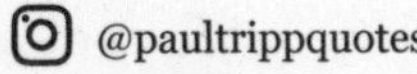 @paultrippquotes

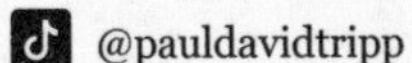 @pauldavidtripp 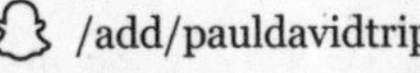 /add/pauldavidtripp 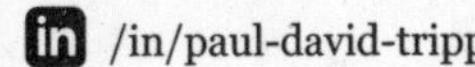 /in/paul-david-tripp/